Horace
A Life

Peter Levi

Routledge
New York

Published in the United States of America in 1998 by

Routledge
29 West 35th Street
New York, NY 10001

Originally published in Great Britain in 1997 by
Gerald Duckworth & Co. Ltd
The Old Piano Factory
48 Hoxton Square
London N1 6PB

Library of Congress Cataloging-in-Publications Data

Levi, Peter.
    Horace: a life / Peter Levi.
        p. cm
    ISBN 0-415-92008-6 (cloth : alk. paper).
    1. Horace—Biography. 2. Poets, Latin—Biography.
    3. Rome—Intellectual life I. Title.
PA6411.L49   1998
874'.01—dc21
[B]   97-35012
                                                       CIP

Contents

For Deirdre

Introduction

However hard affection for poetry pulls, I feel strongly that it is an act of temerity to publish this book on Horace. I am now sixty-five, and it must be relevant that I was taught Horace at school in the late forties by dear old Mr Mayhew, a very old Wykhamist retired from the Indian Education Service, born in the 1860s, whose amiable and as I then felt all but senile liberalism or whiggery somehow rubbed off on Cicero and on this poet. Yet there was a conventional conservatism, particularly in Horace's lyrics, like that of Sallust: it stood for severity to youth, frugality at home, magnificence in worship (*Cat.* 7-12) and the avoidance of foreign and luxurious pleasures. I think it was the Balliol don, Mackail, who wrote that Horace had projected and even invented the idea of the gentleman and man of the world, which adds a touch of complacent élitism I would then, at the age of sixteen, have accepted as normal. Today there is something farcical about the late Victorians, close to whom I class myself, yet I trust that the true flavour of Horace's poetry, which is as penetrating as garlic, has begun to attract later generations. No poet is more delicate or more sensuous, no poet is deeper or more honest, and no poet is so unlike what I once lazily imagined.

The true Horace reveals himself slowly; he is always startling. It may well be that no discipline less extreme, no music less intoxicating than the repeated stanza-forms of his lyric poems could have revealed his precision and clarity of footfall, his mastery of words in verse. Usually such a brilliance can be conveyed by translation, but in his case in English that has seldom been successful. In the Latin we know that Horace's lyrics were never or almost never successfully imitated, and in spite of all the innumerable attempts, they have never quite been transposed into equivalent stanzas in English verse. In French, Ronsard comes closer.

If we had only his hexameter poems he would have commanded our attention certainly, but we could not have imagined his flowering, his happy skill like a second nature of the Latin language. Only a handful of poems by Catullus would have startled us in the same way, as they still do. What we are told of the story of his life is a feeble but at least a genuine guide through the maze of his poems. The poetry shows his development only when it is carefully sorted through as biography. If this book offers little else, I hope it may offer a new way of reading Horace, and disclose something about him to an age that does not know Latin.

The last popular book on a large scale in English to offer a life of Horace was written by Alfred Noyes, a poet now largely forgotten, who published his

Horace in 1947: he was old by then and going blind, and intended his book as a defiant monument, since he was essentially a late Victorian romantic like Henry Newbolt, and a vehement anti-modernist. Alas the book was remaindered. Eduard Fraenkel, whose book on Horace came out ten years later, refers to Noyes without scorn. He is still curiously fresh and in a way inspiring; there is a certain breadth about him which is impressive. As a schoolboy I read him with a pleasure I have never forgotten, and the poem to Pan, *'Faune nympharum fugientium amator'*, has been one of my favourites ever since. I have discovered another somewhat alarming link between us, because I realised the other day that I am now as old as he was and my eyes, like his, are deteriorating fast.

The passion for Horace used to be commoner than it is today, so I cannot claim that as a special link, and yet I suppose it used to be a real link between all the civilised or the educated, or whatever they called themselves in those distant days when Eddy Marsh translated the *Odes*. When Captain Leigh Fermor, working with the Cretan resistance in the 1939 war, captured General Kreipe and carried him off to a cave in the Cretan mountains, the General was at first not unnaturally nervous of the villainous appearance of his captors, but the next morning was a brilliant one, and they all crowded together to the cave mouth. You could see the snow on every peak in the White Mountains blazing with sunlight, and eagles floating in the clear blue sky. Captain Leigh Fermor was entranced, and murmured to himself the first stanza of Horace's Soracte poem, *'Vides ut alta stet nive candidum ...'* The General heard him, and continued the poem in Latin to the end. The link held of course, and they became friends from that moment. There is something about this story, some resonance of the past – it could have happened after all in 1643 and not 1943 – that suggests that was the last moment of the old Europe.

The European feeling about Horace has vanished in our lifetime. There are always new and learned works in various languages about him, some ominously thin and some formidably fat; yet the poetry remains the same. I do not aspire in this book to contribute seriously to that tidal process of sifting and re-sifting by which scholarship progresses, but to write his life, since it is some time now since anyone attempted precisely that. Apart from a short account by Suetonius, Horace tells us in his poetry almost everything we know about his life; it is curiously entangled with the Italian earth, with the history of his times, and an exact moment in that brief early summer of Latin poetry which had no autumn. The reason for that withering of all the arts, or for the failure of that Roman revival of Greek arts, must be found in Roman history. These are vast themes, and I cannot pretend to resolve them with authority, but if ever I differ from received opinion either about history or about Roman poetry, I shall make it clear that I am doing so. This book is meant for readers with little or no Latin or Greek, but with some interest in poetry, and some curiosity about history.

One might almost think there was now a deliberate movement to make Horace hard work, to make him the special property of judicious professors; the same industrial movement takes over poet after poet, they survive only to wither in the serpentine manacles of theorists; as soon as you make any remark about Donne or Baudelaire or Propertius or Petrarch or even the *Carmina Burana*, you will hear the snake-hiss. Horace is apparently the most direct, the most approachable of men, and it is those who think so who have kept him alive for two thousand years. And yet it is shockingly easy to talk nonsense about him, as it is to make mistakes about history. The most liberating book about his poetry is also the most massively learned: it is Eduard Fraenkel's *Horace* (1957), final monument to that world of German scholarship which even in its tragic dispersal in the 1930s fertilised America and aroused Oxford for a few moments from her sleep.

I have adored Horace in the simplest manner since I was fifteen, and as undiscerning about poetry as anyone else, but he keeps pace with our years as he does with the ages of the world. Without being deep oneself, one can see the depth in him, and he is one of the very few poets who always leave one feeling wiser, better and more relaxed, with no diminution of energy or of appetite. Whether this has to do with his paganism, or what paganism may mean to him, is one of the avenues we shall explore, but there is no doubt that for three or four hundred years now Horace, with Plutarch, has seemed to offer an alternative to official Christianity, an alternative all the more palatable for the greatness and immediacy of his poetry. Now that I am old I find him greater than ever, yet writing about him is the most demanding and most likeable task I have ever undertaken. Is that because Bentley's formidable shadow is draped over the text of all his works? G. Pasquali's *Orazio Lyrico* (1920), E. Corbaud on the *Epistles* (1915), and Fraenkel's *Horace* had a more nourishing effect. It may be that I was less disturbed by Nisbet and Hubbard on the *Odes*, by Gordon Williams on Roman poetry, and by later writers because I had attended Fraenkel's Oxford classes on Horace, where the intellectual disturbances were seismic, so that I was less open to those later writers. But why in that case did Colin MacLeod's generous, posthumously published version of the *Epistles* and D.R. Shackleton Bailey's thin but critically severe, not to say beady-eyed, *Profile of Horace* (1982) strike me as so right and so sound? And why is it really that Horace should still be so appetising, and easier to read than any commentary or work of theory? The preference for poetry is natural no doubt, or inbred, like a taste for alcohol.

But it remains queer how difficult it is to illustrate Horace or find his equivalent in other arts. The art of the personal portrait in stone or bronze flourished in republican Rome, and for rulers as far away as Afghanistan in the same Hellenistic age, but from the time of Augustus on the artists lost confidence or lost heart outside the circles of the imperial family. On the Ara Pacis of Augustus the faces are still thrilling, but we have no convincing portrait of Horace or of Virgil. The *Aeneid* was at least illustrated in a series of strip cartoons, though only because Homeric manuscripts had a strip of pictures every few lines in the same way. Horace was not treated like that, though to judge from the Low Ham mosaic (at Taunton) Virgil was. The *Aeneid* is treated like the most passionate romance.

The Boscoreale cup has been very fully treated recently by Ann Kuttner in *Dynasty and Empire in the Age of Augustus*, but it throws little light on anything outside the ruler's magic circle in its most formal presentation. The friends have vanished, and the great tower of the palace of Maecenas on the Esquiline hill, from which Nero watched Rome burning, is irrecoverably lost. The valley of Vicovaro in the Sabine hills north of Rome still whispers a suggestion of Horace's life, but Fraenkel thought of his birthplace at Venosa as a town obliterated by earthquake in 1930. In the poems we are teased by an insouciant openness, yet Horace is not insouciant: every move in every poem is calculated; he painted precisely the partial portrait he intended, and left us a picture he controlled. We cannot expect to get behind that in this book: even the most strenuous and subtlest of biographies could not accomplish that today.

It is a problem without a solution. There are also problems about dates, because most of Horace's books can be dated, but each one is a collection and they overlap, so we do not really know the date of every poem, nor do we know when he began to write satires or lyrics. Probably he turned to verse letters only when the lyrics were not a success, but even that is only a probability. The worst problem is the date of *The Art of Poetry*, the letter to the two Pisones. We do not even have any certainty who they are. The poem is a very long and apparently ambitious letter about literary critical theory. It begins with the mad work of art and ends with the mad poet, there is some suggestion that it may be mathematically divided, but although its details are lucid and its phrases often memorable, it does not grip its subject with the hard bite of Horace's other poems. It could be a very early work, and unfinished. But the weight of Fraenkel's casually expressed opinion, and of an excellent article by D.A. Russell in the collection called *Horace* (ed. C.D.N. Costa, 1973), reinforces the impression that it might be the very latest of Horace's long letters. There are 475 lines of it, and the manuscripts separate it from the two books of his other letters, giving it the title *The Art of Poetry*. This problematic work is certainly by Horace, and not obviously unfinished. It has had a remarkable influence too, particularly in the seventeenth and eighteenth centuries, in the Middle Ages and among poets who were not quite poets, like William King in his admittedly most readable *Art of Cookery* (1709), which Russell quotes and I know John Fuller likes. In the sixteenth century *The Art of Poetry* appealed to the most ardent poets, like Sidney and du Bellay, and apparently Shakespeare, as well as to a long string of pedants: only that vainglorious ass the elder Scaliger (1561) thought himself superior. Maybe the attraction of it was that poetry was a rational activity and could be rationally discussed. Noyes translates some lines on the four ages of man to sound just like Shakespeare's seven.

Horace's lyrics were not much, virtually not at all, imitated in antiquity (the 'choral lyrics' of Seneca's plays, which were never performed or meant to be performed, are a radically different matter: whether you like them or not, they have nothing to do with Horace): that may be due to his amazing and unique metrical skill; there must have been music, at least for the Song of the Age, the *Carmen Saeculare*, which was publicly performed. We have an inscription from the banks of the Tiber recording that Horace composed the hymn for that occasion: no doubt some of the more choral lyric metres had survived in occasional use in Greek temples, which would explain how such stray curiosities as a hymn to power, which survived as a Greek hymn to Rome (the words 'Rome' and 'strength' are the same in Greek) crop up later in a literary context. Yet that was written in the Hellenistic age, when lyric poetry in stanzas had gone right out of fashion. So far as we know, the first poet to revive stanza form and use it in Latin was Catullus, a very few years before Horace. In the Middle Ages the vigorous rhythms of the *Carmina Burana* are certainly a revival of lyric form in Latin, but not of Horace's lyric forms. It is curious though that hymns went on being written, and that hymns in classical stanza form revived early in the Renaissance: I have not been able to discover the first hymn of this kind. I do not even know who wrote *Iste confessor*, but the same tenuous musical link with Horace appears to exist. This is of course the merest conjecture: one must assume that the system of scansion by long and short syllables was lost for centuries.

Because of this metrical difference between ancient and modern languages no perfect English equivalent to Latin or Greek lyrics has ever been found. Tennyson did produce a passable English alcaeic, which I have in my time used, but the nearest equivalent to Horace's lyrics on a generous scale is Marvell's ode to Cromwell. Probably wisely, it makes not attempt to use the long and short system, but adapts Horace into a stress metre; Marvell learnt this trick from translating Horace at Cambridge, or from his contemporary there, Sir Richard Fanshawe, who used it a little earlier. They were on opposite sides during the Commonwealth, and Fanshawe took over from Milton under Charles II as Foreign (or Latin) Secretary: but he died early and has never had his due as a poet. On the other hand Milton, in his undatable translation of one of Horace's lyrics (1,5), uses no rhymes, and still produces something unforgettable and unique in our language. When I went down from Oxford in 1958, I sought advice from Auden, who thought I should translate the whole of Horace, but I discovered that James Michie had already begun the same task; as I was sure I could not rival him, I never began, and indeed his full *Odes of Horace* (1963 and 1987) is by far the best modern version I have seen. In this book I have made my own bits and pieces of versions wherever I felt they would suit a particular need. For the *Epistles* I have at times used Colin MacLeod; and for commentaries on all the poems I had recourse to Kiessling-Heinze, with Klingner's text, with occasional help from Lejay and Palmer on certain poems, and of course from Fraenkel. There are a number of poems of Horace on which that great man's book is silent, but I once attended a class by him 'On those poems of Horace on which I have never lectured'.

Horace's Italy is another matter. There is a most useful pamphlet on the Sabine farm by Hallam, an article in *JRS* (1915) and an all-important official guidebook by Lugli. Lugli gives the modern history of the place. But the most informative treatment of Venosa or Venusia is in *Old Calabria* by Norman Douglas (1915, recently reprinted in Picador, Travel Classics). Douglas is dated of course, and not earnest or wholeheartedly scholarly, but he gives you a strong sense of a rustic and small town world that has now disappeared.

Mommsen has some useful things to say about Venosa, which he visited twice, once as a young man searching for the inscriptions of the Kingdom of Naples, and once as an old man with his son-in-law Wilamowitz, when he was working on a second edition. He had at that time a furious row with the Mayor, over the loss of an inscription: the Mayor had come out to meet him wearing his tricolour sash and reinforced I think by the town band, to be complimented on Venosa being the *patria del Orazio*, only to be told, 'Voi *dicete che siete la patria del Orazio, ma siete la patria dei porci.*' Pigs wallowed and snuffled then in the streets of every town in south Italy, as Norman Douglas confirms. 'It is their recreation (*eorum requies*),' remarks a Roman farmer, 'as washing is a man's.' That was about farm pigs of course, but the pig problem was equally intractable at Stratford-on-Avon in the days of Shakespeare.

The best map likely to be available to readers is one of the old ones edited by G.B. Grundy and published by John Murray, but the best absolutely speaking is Mommsen's, which is published in *Corpus of Latin Inscriptions*, where whatever Mommsen could discover about Roman Venosa is also to be found, written in Latin. The map is strangely important for Horace's poetry. Even when he sounds at his vaguest about a place he means something definite. We shall see that 'Acherontia's heavenly nest' in a lyric (3,4) has great importance, it is not only local colour. When he addresses a lyric to his friend Septimius, 'prepared to go with me to Cades', it is important that he means Spain, where Augustus was. It is instructive to keep an eye on the vineyards too. Sometimes the place-names create small puzzles, since it appears that Horace does not write poems only about places where Augustus did go, but where he intended to go, or where it was rumoured that he might go.

There is an unknown world, of course, beyond the Roman frontiers, but even here one wants to know whether Horace means something definite by 'the Dacian and the Ethiop' or not, and a map will help one to judge. The reign of Augustus was a time in the history of the world when the map was as important to the Romans as it became again to the Elizabethans, and a time when their map of the world was increasing and altering just as swiftly. Whether the extension of the known world under the Romans brought down on them disasters as great as those that fell on Spain after the great age of exploitation in Latin America, remains an imponderable question, but it may have done.

In an age of moral philosophy, Horace's philosophy was as deep as his poetry. The hardest and most enigmatic problem for his biographers is not really the difference between our shrinking planet and his expanding and intoxicating world. That difference is one that like any genuine poet of any age he is able to surmount. It is a question of tone and of realism. When Horace appears to reveal a world or his own nature, he is really closer to a writer of dialogues, that is to a philosopher and maker of myth like Plato, than he is to an autobiographer. The self he so brilliantly projects, this way or that as the argument requires, is like something mythical or fictional projected by Plato, like the personality of Socrates for example. He shows a dangerous facility, and yet we believe him every time.

This is a real problem, but let us suppose that the scenes and characters of Plato's dialogues were meant to be taken more seriously than teachers of philosophy do take them, and that Horace means what he says to be taken as literally as the dinner-party in the *Symposium*. In that case we have the fullest, the best and most compelling portrait of a poet that the world would see for a long time or had ever seen. Everything about him is interesting, his technical development, the objective and verifiable facts of his career, and that inner life of his which we surmise, as we surmise that of the Japanese poet Basho from his travel journels or that of Shakespeare from his sonnets. Yet that analogy brings us back to exactly the same problem.

I am grateful to all those who in different ways have helped with this book, both Campion Hall and St Catherine's College, Oxford, to the Quedgely branch of the Gloucestershire County Libraries, to the Greek and Roman departments of the British Museum, to the London Library for their unfailing tolerance and help, to Bodley and the Ashmolean, to Nancy Sandars and to many colleagues and friends living and dead, but above all to my wife who has made this book possible, and to Matthew who has helped in many ways.

Chapter One

We know that Horace was born at Venusia, now Venosa, a southern Italian hill town which few pilgrims visit today, and fewer still explored in the past. The older Roman town that underlay modern Venosa apparently disappeared in the disastrous earthquake of 1930, when no doubt there were massive landslides. Baedeker for 1890 tells us the town stood on the slopes of a volcanic mountain, the ancient Voltur now called Monte Vulture, *vultur* being the Latin word for a vulture. This extinct volcano rises to a height of 4365 feet, and its old crater was densely overgrown with oaks and beeches, with two small but deep lakes, one of which sustained the Capuchin monastery of San Michele, while the other was decorated with the ruins of Santo Ilarione. Beyond this extinct crater rose the peak, called the Pizzuto di Melfi. Baedeker used to offer a road of fifteen and a half miles from Melfi, a Norman stronghold to the west, or 'a bridle-path, a pleasant, sequestered route, 7½ m. only, *Venosa* (poor inn)'. In 1890 there were steamboats to go round Sicily, and at Brindisi 'The Castello … is now a *bagno* for prisoners condemned to the galleys'. The mountain still stands out against the western skyline, from the train between Foggia and Bari, and if one should wonder while observing the ruins of Paestum what lies in those threatening mountains to the east, then the answer is Venusia, the birthplace of the poet Horace. It is just north of Naples, but in Horace's lifetime most of that country was still the oak forest it had been for a thousand or ten thousand years, and the forest still sheltered packs of wolves and stray bears.

Venusia was a Roman colony, an artificial settlement of Roman citizens founded for strategic reasons, with land divided up between veteran soldiers retired from the army. In Horace's day there would have been several thousand men at Venusia, at least two thousand. The population in 1890 was about the same, seven and a half thousand persons. In 1945 there were nearly ten thousand. Horace loved the place, though he never mentions the other boys of his age without a certain asperity: to him they remained 'the huge sons of huge centurions', a centurion being a warrant officer or a Captain in our army. Roman Venusia was a frontier town, perching on a crag defended by ravines between Lucania and Apulia. Here we must be careful, because these regional names have altered with time, they are used now differently from the way they were used before the unification of Italy. Edward Lear, for example, visited Venusia when he was writing his second volume of Calabrian explorations and his Calabria was the entire south. The Romans used a quite different system, and when in doubt one must consult the map in the ninth volume of the *Corpus of Inscriptions* that Mommsen published. Horace says you could call him a Lucanian or an Apulian because farmers of both territories or races worked the land. The Lucanians were by blood or cousinship Samnites, speakers of Latin of a kind, and it was Lucanians who took over Poseidonion (Paestum) on the west coast, and generated that astonishing and most beautiful kind of painting, half Greek and wholly native Italian, which one must go to Paestum to see.

Monte Vulture dominates the coast below it from Bari to Brindisi in the south, but Venusia was not connected to those harbour towns by a direct road. It lay on the Appian Way of which it was once the southern terminus, but as soon as Tarentum fell to Rome, the road was extended southwards across the hills as far as the sea. From Tarentum the final extension of the Appian Way slid backwards round the coast a further forty-five miles to reach the garrison and harbour town of Brundisium or Brindisi, which at a stroke became the Roman port for Greece and for the East. Cicero wrote a letter to Atticus as he rested at Venusia before completing the last few stages of his journey out of Italy, on his transfer from the consulship to a military command in Asia. He was there again in the crisis before the civil war, between the murder of Caesar and that of Cicero himself. In July 44 he apparently thought of Venusia as a useful strategic point at which to halt before he took ship or retreated into one of his numerous burrows. This letter puzzles its latest and best editor, Shackleton Bailey (Vol.6 letter 410n.), who sensibly suggests that in July 44 the shifty statesman cannot really have intended to stay long at Venusia, only to enquire there about troop movements before making a dash for Hydrus, which is now Otranto on the heel of Italy, or possibly for Brindisi, returning overland to his villa in the region of Naples only if there was danger. At that time he had little more than a year to live.

Venusia is now just a hill town like many others in the south, not unlike the *Torregreca* of Ann Cornelisen (1969). By the late thirties a sixth of its territory was grazing and a tenth forest. The earthquake of 1930 is thought to have effaced its classical interest, but all the same we have an early treatment of what it once was by Keppel Craven (1821 and 1837), the friend of William Gell, with whom he went into voluntary exile as a courtier of Queen Caroline the Prince Regent's wife. The pair of them took up topography; Craven's contribution was his *Calabria*, a general word used in those days to cover a huge part of Italy, governed, misgoverned or abandoned by Naples. The Romans had called only the heel of Italy Calabria, the Byzantines used the name for the toe when the Lombards took the heel. Edward Lear explored the whole of Neapolitan Calabria from 1843 to 1848 and produced not only sketches, some of which he later worked up into oil paintings, but a travel book with a useful map and huge, picturesque lithographs. Among his most exciting oil paintings is his *Venosa*, which he finished in 1852: it shows a romantic south Italian fortified town with a castle and numerous spires, baking and dazzling in the sun, that hangs above a dark, cool ravine full of wonderful trees. This painting is a unique record of what Venosa looked like when Mommsen first saw it as well as Lear. It is in the Toledo Museum of Art, Ohio, and at least one of Lear's sketches for it is at Harvard. As I wrote in the introduction to this book, Mommsen visited Venosa twice, the second time as an old man; he arrived at the main square in a furious bad temper about a broken or lost inscription, but the Italians need not have worried. He was almost as furious in Oxford which he visited for an honorary degree, only to find the library shut. He was found battering on its doors at six in the morning. Long before Mommsen's day the twelfth-century abbey had been built from the stones of the Roman amphitheatre.

Venusia was founded as a colony in 290 BC in a strong defensive position, as we have said, on the frontier of Lucania to the west, Apulia to the east, and Samnium to the north, but Horace insists that it belonged to the same region as the ancient kingdom of Daunus. The name of that mythical king is old and Latin, like Faunus, who was an oracular forest god the Romans identified with Pan. Being mythical, Daunus is hard to trace. Philologists assert that Daunus comes from a word meaning a wolf. He was thought of as an Illyrian from the opposite coast, or else as one of the fifty sons of Lykaon of Arcadia, who was certainly turned into a wolf. Daunus in Latin myth was a brother of the mythical Iapyx and the mythical Peuketios, one of them a wind-name, the other a pine-forest name: when one comes on the name of Diomedes which is Homeric it is like coming on a character from real history. Diomedes and Achilles were remembered in an Athenian traditional song sung in the fifth century BC as living on in the Islands of the Blest, but Diomedes was also supposed to have come to Italy, where his legend was associated with the Isole Tremole near the coast below Venusia. There Diomedes was supposed to have married a daughter of Daunus.

Virgil makes a guarded use of this version, by which Diomedes is a Greek colonist as Aeneas was a Trojan colonist, and they married local princesses, in the last books of the *Aeneid*. Virgil makes Daunus the father of Turnus (of Ardea) and Iuturna, but he remains vague and legendary. Diomedes had a grave-mound on his island, haunted by shearwaters, which were much bigger than the shearwaters on the Isle of Rhum: many peculiar features of the stories told of these birds, whose nests are now to be found only on Tristan da Cunha, are to be explained by their genuine natural history, as Darcy Thompson observes. When Diomedes was buried, his sailors were trans-formed into the birds (*Aen*.XI 271f.) off Mount Garganus. Indeed the eerie and plangent voices of shearwaters were almost bound to attract a legend of that kind. The fact that they hide their young under stones and rocks and return to them on foggy nights when there is no moon makes them all the more ghostly. It is small wonder that the Duke of Urbino thought this story was preposterous, and their voices the cries of infant children of the monks on the island, but the birds were recorded in a Renaissance account of Sicily, and seen off Zakynthos as recently as 1898.

Daunia was a region according to Pliny in the northern part of Apulia between the river Aufidus and the Fertor, and its towns included Canusium, now Canosa, of which Venusia was reckoned vaguely to be a subject. Horace had no good impression of the Canusines but that is another matter: he did not like their habit of speaking half in Greek and half in Latin. There are a lot of loan-words from Greek even in the most classical Latin, and they seem often to have travelled by way of the Greek coastal settlements to the south. The Latin word for swift for instance is *celer*, which comes from the Greek *keles*, a word for a fast horse which was used for a racing ship. A surprising proportion of these loan-words have to do with the sea; the word *kontos* or *contum* for a quanting pole or a baton or wand of office gives us through Latinised Greek and through marine Latin the Byzantine official *Konto-stabularios*, and so the High Constable of France in *Henry V*, and the English village constable with his baton.

The neighbouring tribe to the Daunians were the Messapians: Virgil makes Messapus (7, 691) an ally of Turnus, a son of Neptune and a tamer of horses whom no fire and no iron could hurt, but for some reason transplants him to central Italy and makes him an Etruscan. The Messapians were certainly Illyrians, and they were close neighbours and enemies of Tarentum. The Roman poet Ennius claimed to be Messapian by blood. The Daunians and the Peucetians (both being Apulian tribes) supported Tarentum against the Messapians, although their language was Messapian. The Messapians have left two hundred inscriptions in their own tongue, using a Greek alphabet, and there is no doubt the language was Illyrian. In the late fifth century they supported Athens against Syracuse. The tribal divisions are by no means easy to disentangle: Peucetians and Daunians were collectively called Iapyges, and Messapians are hardly distinct from Calabrians, but they were all largely Hellenised before the Romans conquered them, as a visit to the Brindisi museum will reveal. The coins of Venusia showed Hermes or Castor and Pollux.

What remained was the geographic skeleton, the mountains 'roasted by the sirocco' as Horace says, the bad-tempered sea, the mooing and bellowing and groaning of the oak forest of Garganus, and the roaring winter Aufidus, the biggest river in south Italy and the least controllable. The place was 320 miles from Rome: in 851 the Saracens took it and in 1041 the Normans. Horace calls Daunus a king poor in water, reigning over a peasant people. This must refer to the watering of animals in summer. There was a population of some twenty thousand at Venusia in the early third century BC, so we are told. Even if, as seems probable, this is an exaggeration, they were enough to drink the rivers dry in summer, leaving no watering-places for the cattle. For this reason the cattle moved into the toe of Italy, as Virgil tells us, and as far north as the Sabine hills, where Horace's older contemporary Varro (on agriculture) had seen Apulian herds in the summer heat. As late as the time of Edward Lear what he calls 'Calabrians' from south Italy spent half the year with their herds in the mountains near Rome. He meant to travel home with them and plot their route, but he never did so. As late as the 1930s the herds with their shepherds would pass through the centre of Rome as if it were a village street, a week or two before Christmas. The herdsmen sold toy bagpipes to the Roman children, and Neapolitan figures of the shepherds at the birth of Christ usually include one with these pipes.

Norman Douglas complains bitterly of the lack of water when the sirocco hits him. He says the only water he could find to drink at Sipontum was mineral water from Monte Vulture which you could buy in bottles. Somewhere else he remarks that in a hot Calabrian summer wine was cheaper, as well as more abundant than water. The railway has never come closer than Rocchetta-Spinazzola, three kilometres away and on a branch line.

Horace mentions only three villages or towns around Venusia, and to one of them a mystery attaches. In the fourth ode of the third book he describes a miraculous sign in his childhood that marked him out as a future poet. He fell asleep alone in the forest, and the wood-doves covered him with fresh leaves of bay and of myrtle, and neither viper nor bear molested him. He says the story became famous, and here he names the villages: the nest of heavenly Aceruntia, the Bantine woods or glens, and the rich earth of low Forentum. The last two are easy enough to place, some ten miles from Venusia, at Abbadia di Banzi and at Forenza, both within a day's walk: Plutarch describes the death of Metellus when Hannibal's men ambushed him at Banzi. But the third name, Aceruntia, is scarcely likely to be Acerenza, a small place on a hill that is not a 'heavenly nest' or a 'nest in the sky', and not quite near enough either. There is another, more attractive solution.

The ancient town of Acherontia still exists, almost as far as you can go into the toe of Italy, on a cliff or sheer fall of a thousand feet above the river called the Acheron. It was a Greek settlement for mining and metal-working, and a chief prop of the wealthy city of Sybaris on the coast. The river is now called Mocone or Mucone, and the place Acri. Norman Douglas around 1900 found it still full of blacksmiths. It is not far from Virgil's river Silarus, where the cattle go in summer and the wild bulls fight. If this place, which was famous and is on maps, was the one Horace meant, it is hard to see how he knew it, except as a mountain town that the animals knew: there is therefore the strong suggestion that these summer migrations of the flocks and herds had been part of his life. Did he as a boy ever travel in summer with the Venusian flocks? By a law of Julius Caesar, passed because the Romans were worried about another slave-revolt, at least one of every three herdsmen had to be a free man. It is not impossible and I think it likely that he knew these tidal movements of cattle very well. In the second epode, he likes

> ... To stretch out under an antique ilex
> Where the grass springs again,
> And water slides down through the high rocks
> And the wood-birds complain ...

In the first epode of the small collection he is more specific, saying he does not want to be rich, or to have a flock

> ... That leaves Lucania and the burning star and goes
> To seek Calabrian meadows.

In the third epode he speaks of 'So great a starry mist as sits On thirsty Apulia'. All the same, Calabria to the south was where honey came from in *Odes* 3, 16.

We do not need to dwell yet on all that Horace tells us in his poems, but we must notice things his readers knew or could know, which he took for granted. In his day the big push was already on, that would transform southern Italy into enormous, slave-run estates. The law that said shepherds should give way to ploughmen, *cedant paastores aratoribus*, with two 'a's in *paastores* to emphasise an ancient and venerable law, was a despairing cry. The Roman version of a capitalist system, by which money always ruled and capital increased, had reached a climax, as Mommsen in his *History of the Republic* points out. The first great roads had been cut through virgin forest, but the vast extent of what had been public land was now diminishing, and the conditions of life from which southern Italy is even now scarcely emerging were already being laid down. As for the forest, Ennius, who was born below Venusia in the plains and died a hundred years before the birth of Horace, has left an impressive picture that Virgil imitated of the felling of the great trees.

> Through tall forest they went and axes struck,
> Felled mighty oak trees flat, cut away ilex,
> Smashed mountain ash: and the tall fir falls,
> Pines tumble down prone, and all the forest
> Rings with the shiver of the leafy woods.

Ennius is talking about that victory of Pyrrhus of Epirus over the Romans to which he raised a monument in the temple of Zeus at Tarentum: 'I conquered men until then unconquered, and by them was conquered.' So the story of the clearing of the woods was local. It is Ennius in the same book who first spoke of baaing flocks, *balantum pecudes*, which Virgil also imitated.

Enough has been said about earthquakes in the region: in the course of quite desultory study I have found memorable catastrophes in 1456, the 1780s, 1836 and 1851, 1906 and 1930. But it is the air of calamity that lies over the whole of south Italy that one should notice: the Baedeker Guide remarks sadly that Otranto 'has never got over the Turkish attack' which happened five hundred years ago, and it seems to me that the burning, waterless, pitiless dog-star and the repeated word 'thirsty' that Horace uses are for him symbols of the same condition. Admittedly Venusia had suffered real catastrophes: when the Romans took it in 292 it was probably Samnite. At Bantia ten miles away Oscan was still spoken: a bronze tablet found there carries the text of the law for prosecuting corruption, the *Lex Repetundarum* of the late Republic, in Latin on one side and in Oscan on the other. Oscan like Welsh in our own day was a terribly long time dying, and Oscan comedies were still played at Rome under Augustus. But Horace was brought up to speak Latin. Livy says Venusia was reinforced as a garrison town in 200, but in the war of the allies, that is the Italians, against Rome, Venusia defected. That business ended in the extension of citizenship to all Italy, but the underlying tension was still furious. Venusia was reconquered by another Metellus and resettled then, but under Sulla it appears that the same disaster of resettlement was re-enacted. That at least would explain what Horace says about the huge sons of huge centurions, with whom he might have had to go to his first school. Later, in 43 BC, the triumvirate confiscated and reallotted the land all over again. It is then that Horace's links with the place were cut.

How typical of the problems of winkling out Horace's autobiography from his writings all the same that he tells us briefly and categorically of the confiscation, and we know that he was lucky to get away with so light a punishment, but at the end of the second satire of the second book he puts into the mouth of Ofellius feelings that sound like his. And yet this satire is a philosophic conversation just like those of Epictetus or Telles or even Socrates himself: it is a set piece almost fit for the stage. The wise old peasant is a tough nut.

> ... Did you work any less hard
> My boys for a foreign owner to come in?
> Nature makes no man master of his own earth,
> Not me, not him, and no one else either:
> He threw me out, ill will or twists of law
> Throw him out, or no doubt his lively heir,
> Now it's Jack's field, it was Harry's field,
> It has no owner: but it can be used
> By me, by him. And therefore bravely live
> And keep your brave hearts set against bad luck.

This is moving enough, and the feeling with which the poem is charged at the end is Horace's, because Horace is the poet. But these satires are less personal than they look. Scholars long ago noticed an epigram in the *Palatine Anthology* which is in Greek but obviously from the same literary, philosophising source as our bit of Horace.

> I was Jack's field and now am Harry's, so
> On from one owner to the next I go:
> I was one man's work, now another's bother,
> But I belong to Fortune and no other.

Here as in the *Eclogues* of Virgil, who lost the swans and grass of Mantua, the feeling is a general one, which many had personally suffered and everyone had observed, twice in every generation as far as memory extended. The more personal roots of Horace's future as a poet were probably with the sheep, certainly in the forest. We know from an epode and again from an ode (3, 4) that he feared snakes and a bear 'that groans around the sheepfold at twilight'. There is something personal in that record: not everyone knows that bears prowl about moaning and groaning which I am told by Professor John North of Waterloo that in Canada they do when hungry. One would expect the wolf-pack, but Horace's wolves are mostly solitary, like the hunter who 'winters in gaiters in Lucanian snows' so that Romans may eat wild boar. It is of interest that he climbs so high for his game, because most boars are caught, at least in Greece today, when the snow falls on the mountains and

the boars are driven down to within gunshot. There is no reason to suppose
that Horace was a keen huntsman, but he had heard the bears from inside
the sheepfold it seems. He does at least know the usefulness of dogs, that is
large mastiffs, in controlling and guarding the sheep. Virgil mentions the fine
noise of hounds in the distance, but otherwise he remarks petulantly that
dogs are useful to lonely travellers in Spain, where they prevent sneak-
thieves from creeping up on you: that is the only use he can think of for dogs,
it appears in that particular Georgic.

Before Horace was born in his crowded and self-consciously Roman little
hill town, we should just sketch in the point that Roman history had reached
in its long series of crises. In 73 BC eight years before he was born the slave
rebellion named after Spartacus, a gladiator from Capua who was by birth a
Thracian, and his assistant Crixus, who was a Gaul, broke out with terrifying
force. It was not the first, which had been in Sicily in 139 and again in 104,
but it swiftly raised an army of ninety or a hundred thousand men. At this
time one powerful man might own eight hundred slaves or probably more. In
a year or two the slave army was divided, and the nucleus of it under
Spartacus was beaten in Lucania. His idea was to lead the slaves home, but
most of them preferred to live off the countryside of Italy. They were recap-
tured and all crucified side by side, stretching thirty miles from Capua to the
gates of Rome. Of all the slave wars, this was the shortest and the bloodiest.
The first lasted seven years, the second four, and this only two, but because
of the restless movement of the slaves it terrified all Italy. The Roman army
in Italy found Spartacus a difficult adversary, and the last of the rebellious
slaves were slaughtered by Pompey, who brought home a colonial Roman
army from Spain for the purpose. It was on the edges and in the furthest
corners of the Roman world that armies flourished and grew huge: so that
Augustus as Emperor ruled as a perpetual general, with the military authority called *imperium*. His authority in Rome itself was a subtle and complex
novelty: constitutionally it was ramshackle, but the Romans like the English
never really had a constitution (though Mommsen spent years trying to show
what it was). The city of Rome was ruled by great families and alliances of
blood and of political advantage.

Most of Horace's mature poetry suggests that he was intimate with all
these formidable cousins of one another and grand mutual friends, but he
began as an outsider. His father had once been a slave, we do not know whose
but their name was Flaccus. An ex-slave usually took the name of his
ex-owner, the person who set him free. That was generally a reward but it
could be for service or loyalty of any kind. There were two noble families, that
is families who had once been consuls and might be again, both of them called
Flaccus, both at Rome. On the other hand Cicero was on good terms with a
Flaccus who owned large gardens outside Brundisium, and that might as
easily be the man. A certain Statilius Flaccus, probably an ex-slave, was a
Greek poet at the same period.

How Horace's father ever became a slave no one knows, but I hazard the
conjecture that he was sold off as a prisoner of war at twenty years old
somewhere in Italy in the 'social war' in 89 BC and lucky in his master who

let him free after twenty years. In the fourth ode of the third book, Horace most curiously names a lady called Pullia as his nurse in Apulia, and if this information is right, then she was another ex-slave, because Pullia is a noble family name recorded in inscriptions. This is an argument of Mommsen's; he was a republican himself who lost his chair as a Berlin professor in 1846, so he must not be accused of snobbery. The oldest and most reliable manuscripts also support 'Pullia' but the resulting bit of Latin verse causes me anguish.

> *Me fabulosae Volture in Apulo*
> *nutricis extra limina Pulliae*
> *ludo fatigatumque somno*
> *fronde nova puerum palumbes …*

It would mean 'Me in Apulian Voltur, outside the doorstep of my fabling(?) nurse Pullia, tired out with playing and sleeping, as a boy the doves with fresh leaves (covered).' What is all this nonsense about a nurse? This line causes such panic in scholars that they try to take *fabulosae* with *palumbes*. Surely the correct reading is *extra limen Apuliae* which would yield 'in Apulian Voltur outside the threshold of my fabled nurse Apulia', the word nurse only being a metaphor for the place? It was the kind of way Romans often spoke of their native country: Cicero in verse speaks of 'my father's mountains, my cradle'. But the argument that defends *Pulliae* and opposes *Apuliae* is the very strong one that the first 'a' in Apulia and Apulian is always long in Latin. In an unusual outburst of fury, the Thesaurus Linguae Latinae couples those who defend *extra limen Apuliae* with those who want *mare Apulicum* at *Odes* 3, 24, 4 as 'followers of bad manuscripts'. Whichever way it goes, this is not the happiest line that Horace ever wrote. If *Apulo* is all right, then *Pulliae* must be a slip of the pen? Some ingenious scholars have altered *Volture in Apulo* to *Vulture in avio*, Apulian Voltur to trackless Vultur. But there was a river Volturnus and surely a Voltur dividing Campania from Lucania, anyway Apulian Vultur was not trackless. But Puglia is its name now, so the 'a' must have shortened in the course of time: the lady Pullia with her doorstep seems to me like something in a German folk-tale. She is absurd and should be obelised, which is as near as scholars get to guillotining. Whether or not this was really his nurse's name, his mother is not mentioned at all, and was evidently dead before he grew up. I see that Mommsen thought as I do that Apulia was Horace's nurse.

The name Horace comes from the Roman tribe of the Horatii and carried with it the right to vote as a Roman citizen. We are assured by the expert in this subject that when the Venusians became citizens this name was distributed as their voting ticket. Few of them would ever undertake that long journey over the mountains and up the Appian Way, which took twice as long as the week it took Lucilius a century before to get to Sicily, mostly by ship. If they did attend an election then they would use the special enclosure built for each of the tribes in the Campus Martius near the bend of the river Tiber. Horace's only personal name was Quintus. It occurs at least as an initial on his only surviving inscription, which was for the great Roman games and ceremonies of the gods that Augustus held in 17 BC. CARMEN COMPOSUIT Q. HORATIUS FLACCUS. Maecenas on his death-bed wrote to Augustus only '*Horati Flacci ut mei esto memor*': remember him as you would me'.

There is at least no doubt about when the poet was born, on 8th December 65 BC. The poet himself gives the year and the month, and Suetonius who wrote under Hadrian gives the day. In ode twenty-one of book three Horace addresses a wine-bottle of the same vintage, sealed under L. Manlius Torquatus and L. Aurelius Cotta. In the thirteenth epode the wine was pressed 'when my Torquatus was consul', but that is an early poem when the wine must have been less venerable, perhaps not quite twenty years old. It is pleasing to know Horace could still find the odd bottle as old as he was at the time of his hymn to the wine-bottle. Messalla Corvinus for whom he opened it was an old friend, as we shall see.

There is really more doubt than scholars like to admit about Horace's father's career and talents as a *praeco*: he was certainly some kind of wheeler and dealer or small businessman. He was not a political or financial official because it is unlikely that Venusia had a *praeco* in that sense. He used the power of his voice. There was a businessman at Pompeii who took down on waxed tablets affairs of a hair-raising complexity, and wherever his pen scratched the wooden tablet through its wax coating, the transaction has been immortalised by the volcano that engulfed the city in fire. This man's affairs have been to some degree disentangled, but we do not really know what analogy they offer for those of the ex-slave. There were specialist auctioneers of wine, for example, but here again, probably not at Venusia. There is a dialect poem about a cattle auction at Hawes above the Yorkshire dales which conveys the bright eyes, the leisurely atmosphere and the tension under the surface of country auctions. We know only that the family had a little land. We know that Horace's father who placed all his hopes in his bright son took him to Rome and perhaps saw him off to Greece for his education: that was an expensive item, and it was ambitious beyond the means of a small town. When Martial says, 'If your boy is thick, make him an auctioneer', he is not being serious. Horace's father must have had a sharp eye for business, but a sharper one for morals, because when Horace went to school at Rome it was his father who acted as his chief attendant, a little like the slaves called *paidagogoi* in Plato but in a city with deadlier dangers.

The family land in the south was lost in the end after Caesar's death by confiscation and the resettlement of a new generation of military veterans: the usual fate of a small landholder in Horace's and Virgil's generation. Horace as we shall see constantly harks back to Venusia and the country around it, to 'the moan of Garganus and the Tuscan sea' and 'Garganian oak woods labouring in north winds'. He says the same of Venusia, but there is a certain affectionate pride in his voice when he talks about home. He wanted to settle later as Virgil thought of doing near the old, decayed port of Tarentum, a Spartan colony now basking through a weak but happy old age. We do not know when he first went there, but it was not far to the south. The poet of those Greek cities, some of which were now only ruins in the fields, was Theocritus, and to him and his technical lessons Horace like Virgil was attentive.

What kind of literature was available to them, in Greek or in Latin? The chronicle of Latin writers before Horace's generation is terribly brief. In the second half of the fourth century BC Latin poetry was unrecorded, and Menander, subtlest of Greeks, can hardly have foreseen his successors. In the third century when Theocritus (d. 260?) and Callimachus (d. 240) wrote their poetry in Alexandria, the Romans had barely begun. Livius Andronicus came to Rome as a Tarentine captive, that is as a slave: his Latin poetry has a moving and archaic quality, and his translations of Homer's *Odyssey* were vitally important in their day. How long they went on being read is a matter of dispute: we have no manuscript and rather few quotations of this great milestone. The Muses become Camenae, who were once the nymphs of springs, and the Greek Fate, Moira, becomes the Roman death-goddess Morta. But it is probable that his handful of adapted tragedies, produced at Rome in Latin from 240 BC onwards, made a deeper impression. In that century the uproarious Greek farces of southern Italy were still flourishing; of those we have many illustrations and some fragments, but of the tragedies of Livius Andronicus only a few seductive lines; the Romans were not yet up to any art like the boisterous vase paintings of the civilised south. At the end of the third century, all the same, a choral song for young girls in the ancient Greek style was commissioned from Livius, and in his honour a temple of Minerva on the Aventine hill was consecrated as a kind of poets' guild-house or club.

His narrative verse was written in the old Saturnian metre. No one has ever perfectly understood its scansion, so criticism of it is highly unreliable: yet the ear can hear its rhythm, and it has a pleasurable drumbeat, though it is less supple than the Homeric hexameter. The sound of it is not unlike that of Anglo-Saxon alliterative verse of which it is perhaps a remote cousin. The stiffness of it and the thumps survive in the triumphant and mocking chants of the legions, which were always in a stressed or marching metre quite undiluted by literature. In the acclamations of Emperors in the circus the rhythm of those chants survived Rome and invaded Greek. '*I Ánna mas eyérasen, ma sú tin ananéosas*: Our Anny grew old but you gave her a new constitution.' That was sung when the Emperor took a bride out of a convent, and married a nun. The Saturnian metre had in Horace's day been defeated by the tidal rush of Greek sensibility, but Horace was not unconscious of the old sound values, nor did he despise them. The first great influence on the Roman hexameter was Ennius, born near Venusia at Rudiae (239-169), and the graves of the Scipios were inscribed in his lifetime in finer lapidary verse than anything then being composed in Greek. It is among the graves of the Scipios that elegiac couplets suddenly oust the old Saturnians, in about 139 BC.

The best surviving archaic poet in Latin was surely Naevius (*c*.260-201). He went to prison at the end of his life and died in exile in Africa, but he came from near Capua and he had been a soldier against Hannibal. He wrote tragedies that were his own conceptions on purely Roman themes, as well as a splendid epic on the Punic wars which it looks to me as if Horace plundered for his Regulus ode. Eduard Fraenkel admired him very greatly, and it was the ability which he demonstrated to pick out the genius in a fragment of a few lines that ignited my own enthusiasm for this obscure writer, and to peer closely at Horace's judgement about him. Naevius probably wrote his own epitaph, which was preserved in literary sources; it is hard to know who else could have written it.

> If it were right for the immortals to weep for men
> Divine Muses would weep for Naevius the poet,
> When he was handed in to the treasury of Death
> People at Rome forgot how to speak Latin.

He wrote nearly thirty comedies as well as an epic and his six highly original tragedies: with him Latin literature may seriously be said to have begun. A quarrel with the powerful family of the Metelli was the cause of his downfall, but its origin remains utterly obscure. His power is immensely great, whether he speaks of the Titans, the double-bodied Giants and great Atlantes, 'and Rhuncus and Porpureus, sons of Earth', or the 'clear thunder-blast of the lightning of Jupiter'. Naevius was deeply influenced by the Greeks, but his archaic force is a coincidence of period with the much earlier archaic Greeks, and for that reason he was little imitated.

Caecilius (245-168) and Plautus (240-184) present a Roman theatre these writers had prepared, and the work of Plautus survives in bulk. It is admirable, and although the basis of the comedy is Greek, it shows innumerable signs of transplantation to Rome, where it flourished in the fertile ground of small town life, which was indeed comic. The laughable world of the Plautine stage is never wholly absent from the satiric poetry of Horace. It was in their lifetimes (239-169) that the great if slightly absurd figure of Ennius adapted the hexameter to Latin. At first it was like iron hammered by hand, its ornamental touches were absurd, and its whole effect as 'epic' far removed from what was to come, but through the work of Ennius classical Latin literature as we know it became a possibility. Ennius and his nephew or cousin Pacuvius came from Horace's south, one from Rudiae and the other from Brindisi, and both wrote for the stage, though Ennius in his hexameter epic poetry, 'old daddy Ennius' as Horace calls him, who 'never leapt forward to tell of arms without a drink', was a crucial influence on Virgil. Caecilius the comic poet came from Milan, which in his day was still in Gaul. The development of Roman poetry, like the expansion of Italy, had not yet become headlong. The Greek Euphorion (250-c.180), a contemporary of Plautus, was still writing the most sophisticated poetry in the world. I do not rate it highly, but he was the gilded or the silvery star that dazzled young writers in the Rome of Cicero. Euphorion was librarian to Antiochus of Syria; he was a Greek by birth though he died in the East. He was famous for narrative poems with exquisite settings, though we have few fragments of his verse.

Throughout the second century BC the adaptation of Greek models into Latin gathered speed: Terence (c.190-159) started writing as a slave; he was born in Africa, and became an expert in the works of Menander. It used to be thought the speed of his dramatic action and the fine knotting of his plots were his personal contribution, but it now appears from papyrus texts that Menander taught him all these tricks. There is something wonderfully supple and controlled about his Latin which even Plautus had not attained. He is a polished writer and appeals to ages of the world that pride themselves on polish, so at present he is out of fashion. Horace quotes him (*Sat.*1, 2, 20) and must have admired him; he speaks of 'Caecilian gravity, Terentian skill', or Terentian art. When Terence was set free by his master at about the age of thirty, he went at once to Greece, and there, hidden somewhere in the mountainous convolutions of that place, he died or disappeared, which may be all that he ever wanted. He had studied and fallen in love with Greece, and Greece swallowed him up.

His contemporary Accius, another dramatist, was an Umbrian like Plautus but an interesting link, because Accius was a friend of old Pacuvius who was Ennius's kinsman, and Accius (170-90 BC) was known to Cicero. It is therefore reasonable to say that Roman literature was no more than three generations old. Accius's tragedies were admired by rhetoricians, but he was as various and as fertile as any Hellenistic scholar; he even wrote an inscription in Saturnians, surely the last ever written, to be inscribed on a temple. His language is inflated, 'lascivious swift dolphins foam about The beaks of ships', or 'you would believe Two Marses came together in their arms'. All the same, Accius was imitated by Virgil and Horace had studied his use of the iambic as he had studied Ennius's dramatic verse 'sent out upon the stage, loaded with weight' (*ad Pisones* 258-9). Both poets favoured heavy syllables, and it is typical that Cicero quotes quite a long bit of Accius about a storm to end all storms and Triton flinging rocks about.

Lucilius is another matter (*c.*180-102). He was a noble Roman citizen from a small town in Campania south of Rome. His brother and father were senators, his niece was Pompey's mother, and he was rich. To Horace he was a model as a satirist, and as a self-portrait painter. He has all the swiftness and bite of the comic stage, but he is close to reality. 'Satire,' as Quintilian says comparing Greek and Latin achievements, 'belongs entirely to us.' He neglects the contributory stream of philosophic verse which we shall have cause to mention later, and he ignores the more distant but still shining example of fifth-century Athenian comedy, and yet Lucilius is a writer of marvellous originality. He began in trochaic metre, went on in mixed metres and ended up in hexameters, in which Horace was to follow him. He is a fully Hellenised and philosophised poet without any diminution of his native and gleeful wit. His powerful invective overshadowed other aspects of his work because it is so immediately enjoyable: it is possible that it blinded Horace in his youth. We have a great number of scattered fragments of his thirty satiric books, luckily excellently edited by the German scholar Friederich Marx (1904), so that in spite of the fragmentary text he is the most interesting and pleasurable of all these early writers, and the one who did most to make Horace's own astonishing life-work possible. Naevius who still awaits his Marx must be content with his greatness. Virgil was born in 70 BC and

Horace in 65 BC, Maecenas about 70 and Augustus in 63 BC: those dates are important.

About the same length of time as had passed at the birth of Horace since Roman literature began has passed now since Lord Byron was born. Rome about 300 BC was a free port for Greek trading with Italy, and little more: she was allied with Carthage against that extraordinary freebooter Pyrrhus the King of Epirus. In the third century BC the first and second Carthaginian wars followed. Before the third Carthaginian war (149-6) Terence had died or disappeared, and Accius was twenty-one. In the thirties of that century Lucilius was serving as a Roman Knight with the army in Spain and turning to verse. The great slave rebellions were in 139 and 104 BC and 73-71 BC, and the final convulsion of Italian tribes against Rome was from 91 to 87. The explosion of intellectual energy that began with Lucilius reached a climax with Virgil and Horace. Virgil was born in 70 BC and his *Georgics* are the first Roman poetry to belong to all Italy. He was a Mantuan and he studied first at Cremona, then Milan, neither of them far from Verona, where Catullus lived (c.84-54), whose friends, including Cinna and Pollio, he inherited. Lucretius was another northerner, who shared a patron Memmius with Catullus, and heavily influenced Virgil. Of the writers I have mentioned several from the early years to Terence had been slaves; from the time of Catullus they were all Roman citizens, but none of them was born in Rome.

Valerius Cato, born about 90 BC, was a northern poet and teacher who taught the generation of Catullus and perhaps that of Virgil, and more minor poets like Cinna and Furius Bibaculus of whom we know alarmingly little. 'Latin Siren' they called him, Grammarian, and 'only critic, only poet-maker'. It is easy to exaggerate his influence, but there is no doubt that Catullus at least drank deep from the same springs on Helicon that refreshed the young Virgil. Catullus did not live (d. 54?), and his life might not have lasted beyond Philippi anyway, or indeed as long. Lucretius (c.94-55) died nearly as late, but the interest of Cicero, who had read him in 54, would not have saved him in the dangerous years that followed. It can be said in favour of Valerius Cato that he showed interest in Lucilius, but as for Furius the things we know about him are so contradictory that Fraenkel used to be content to divide him into two, one turgid writer of bad epics and one delicate composer of sweet nothings: I do not think his case was conclusive though I believed him at the time, but Alexandrian poetry I fear has room for two such poets inside a single skin. The question is not of much moment; if there were two, then Horace disliked and mocked them both. There is no doubt all the same that the new wave Latin poets at whom Cicero sneers as 'the claque of Euphorion' did accomplish the final move that made Latin equal to Greek as a literary language, and Roman poets equal or more to Greek ones. Of some of these writers we know curiously little, and the new fragments of Gallus for example were terribly disappointing, but classical Latin poetry begins with Virgil and Horace; even Lucretius, dazzling as his attempt is, was not yet fully master of his tools as his metrical lapses show. Those I mean include Tibullus (d.19) a Roman Knight in the circle of Messalla Corvinus; to one or other of that circle the poems in his third book must be attributed. There remain

Propertius (*c.*50-*c.*3 BC) and Ovid (43 BC-AD 17). Ovid is more than twenty years younger than Horace and already a lesser poet, despite his abundance as a source for later writers, and his undoubted genius, which is not in every line or phrase of the diamond mine of his writings. With him or at the very latest with Juvenal (*c.*AD 60-124) classical Roman literature was over: rhetoric and the rhetorical schools killed it, but that is not my subject. Neither Virgil nor Horace attended those places, but Ovid did and his performances there were noted not without irony by the elder Seneca.

For Horace there was no Verona, there was no circle of friends of Lucretius or Catullus. His father, who had gained the inestimable gift of freedom and had risen from the position of *coactor*, a collector up of money and of goods working for a small town auctioneer, to be himself the auctioneer, determined to avoid the local school, which was run by a certain Flavius, and brought Horace north to Rome, a journey of a fortnight. There were no boarding schools, so he stayed with the boy himself and took him to the school of Orbilius, a famous whipper like Keate of Eton or Busby of Westminster. This move was important, since it appears to mark Horace's father's retirement from work: he could not have set up as an auctioneer in Rome, where he must have lived on the money he had saved. How many years had he pursued his percentages? Perhaps for fifteen, since two years before Horace was born. Horace couples his father's job with 'the pursuit of small business', so the words *praeco* and *coactor* cannot be confined to the meaning 'tax collector', as Suetonius suggests. Since he was now a wealthy man, able to provide Horace with the same retinue as a nobleman, so the poet tells us, his financial success in the south must have been startling by our standards, but we hear a good deal about self-made men in the second and first centuries; the Roman nobility engaged in commerce with the same vigour as the lesser people, as we can see from their banking centre and their statues on Delos for example; the Trimalchio of Petronius was a comic exaggeration of course, but he was the climax and the logical outcome of the movement to which Horace's father belonged, the wave which he was riding. Orbilius the schoolmaster came from Beneventum on the Appian Way. We know that among other things he taught some Ennius, and Livius Andronicus's Latin version of the *Odyssey*. Like other teachers of grammar, he bitterly criticised living persons, and also the conditions of Roman life. He had opened his school at Rome at the age of fifty two, years after Horace was born, but the poet is quite clear that he gave an education as good as any Knight's or nobleman's.

Grammar was not as old as Roman literature: it was invented in order to teach the Romans and other barbarous people to speak Greek correctly. Orbilius was a *grammaticus*: even the word is Greek, though he appears to have applied the rules of his severe subject to Latin. Whether Horace learnt Greek from him, or at home at Venusia from some stray Tarentine, or from a private tutor, or when he went to Greece, is curiously hard to determine. It is not important: we would rather know what books he read and at what age. To judge from the habits of cultivated Roman society, Greek came like second nature to him, but Latin was pounded into him at school. Julius Caesar was taught Greek and Latin and rhetoric by a single tutor, M. Antonius Gnipho who was a Gaul from North Italy. To judge by results he could quote Pacuvius as readily as he quoted Greek. The other languages of Italy, such as Oscan, were rapidly obliterated, and since the Greek-speaking world extended beyond the Roman empire, there appeared no reason for a Roman to speak anything more than Latin and Greek. Varro (116-27 BC) on the Latin language indicates the preoccupation with correctness, though his was only the second generation of these Roman studies. The pioneer had been his master L. Aelius Stilo, a Stoic who had investigated the authenticity of the plays attributed to Plautus, and commented on the gnarled text of the most ancient Roman laws; another of Stilo's pupils was Cicero.

No doubt Homer is massive enough to teach his own lessons, but it is a strange thought that Horace received him in a moralised form. One was taught, because this was the current Greek fashion, how Ulysses defied the Sirens as the soul should defy the senses, and the image was to be seen on tomb-stones, or one was taught what damage the anger and the sulks of Achilles did to his own side, how perjury undid Troy, and even how Homer himself might be criticised. There is a pedantic air about all of this which suggests it must derive from the philosophers. Their quarrel with Homer goes back to Plato's *Republic* but when it gets into the discourse of the classroom the argument has reached a lower level. Epictetus says (bk 3, ch.24) that Odysseus was wrong to weep for his wife far away. 'Odysseus, if he did weep and lament, was not a good man.' The Stoics sought on the whole to make Homer acceptable by allegorising him, and this cloudy habit invaded the ancient commentaries and Eustathius, but Horace was taught Homer moralised, as Ovid was moralised in the Middle Ages, and not allegorised. It may be that the Stoic Crates of Mallos, who visited Rome as a diplomat in 168 BC and luckily broke his leg so that he stayed on lecturing, was the source of Roman investigations into such matters, but the mature Horace emerges as an Aristotelian, and there is a distinction to be drawn between his memories of school and his own judgement about what after all was a central literary concern of his life. He deals with Homer as a moralist in the first thirty lines of the second letter of his first book, in a letter to Maximus Lollius.

> While you declaim the writer of Troy's war
> At Rome, I have reread him at Praeneste;
> He says clearer than Crantor and Chrysippus
> What is or is not beautiful, disgusting,
> Useful or not. This is why I think so,
> So listen Maximus if you are free ...
> ... the rage of kings and peoples who were fools:
> Antenor sought to cut the cause of war,
> But Paris? To reign safely and live happy;
> He would not be compelled. Old Nestor hurries
> Between Achilles and Agamemnon,
> To make up their quarrel, but one of them love bites,
> In both of them the same anger burns.

The kings are crazy and the Greeks suffer,
Sedition, trickery, crime, anger, lust,
Committed inside and outside Troy's walls.
As for what virtue and wisdom can do
Odysseus gives a useful example,
Tamer of Troy who viewed many cities,
And manners among men, and the wide seas ...

This may all be written tongue in cheek; it is certainly not very different from what he says he learnt at school. When he has got to Circe and her swine and the Sirens, he goes on:

We are a number, no more, we consume,
Penelope's suitors, or the youth
Around Alcinous who care too much
For their own pretty skins, they sleep till noon,
While thieves get up at night-time to cut throats,
Then will you not get up to save yourself? ...

It appears that the lesson was well learnt and long remembered, and the weight of popular philosophy was behind it. This letter of seventy-one lines is an invitation to virtue, and that undertone was terribly strong in Horace's education, where it took much of the place we have given in the last two hundred years to religion. Horace has a religion, which is another matter, but it was less moralised than Homer as he learnt Homer. At the same time his father, who taught him by the examples Rome provided what he should do and not do, sounds very close to a philosopher, not one of many words, but a wise observer and a maker of pithy comments. 'One should be ashamed of behaving like such a man, pleased to follow such another course.' It impressed Horace all his life that his father was perfectly willing for him to pursue small gains as a collector or an auctioneer, providing he was at least decently brought up and educated. That is an attitude that still exists in our day, or has done in our lifetimes, but I have the impression it is rare now and was rare in Roman times. It is hard of course to separate Horace the moralist from his self-portrait, and even more so to separate his father from the voice of a philosopher, that is a satirising observer and moral philosopher, which he is given. At least there is no doubt about Horace's strong affection and gratitude for him, and it is noticeable that their relationship contains no element of guilt. In the matter of sex, Horace as a boy found his personal modesty well defended, and later he is pleased with whatever sexual favours are freely offered, and that is that. He does not think all sins or all faults are of equal weight, as the Stoics did: he believes we should forgive one another and exhaust our lifetimes in becoming better people. We shall have to recur to the subject, but his morals are like a suit made of good, durable tweed that will last a lifetime: or so they appear to me at the beginning of his life. He gleefully reports a remark once made by Cato, that young men should use

brothels rather than 'screw other people's wives' (*Sat*.1, 2, 31-5). He depre-
cates the drama that attends on secret adultery, when the lover must flee

> Unbelted, barefoot, in the agitation
> Of fear for money, arse, or reputation ...

His father's advice (*Sat*.1, 4, 113) was to avoid adultresses, but in the second
satire Horace is not, as Fraenkel points out in a sensitive and balanced
analysis of the poem, arguing from personal experience; he is just composing
a well-finished and racy piece of satiric verse on an old and well-worn theme.
One should avoid extremes: married women on the one hand and whores on
the other, just as one should avoid spending all that one inherits.

> I have some middling vices and a few
> Faults in my nature that may come to view,
> Only like blemishes on a fine body:
> I am not avaricious, you will see
> Nothing sordid, but pure and innocent
> (Or so I boast), and dear to every friend.
> My father is the cause, poor man whose whole
> Wealth was a little field, but the local school
> Where the huge sons of huge centurions
> Went with their slates and money once a month
> Was not enough, but I was brought to Rome,
> Taught arts like any Knight's or noble's son ... (*Sat*.1, 6, 65-77)

Horace tells us that he once tried writing poetry in Greek: that sounds like
an early attempt which he says Apollo stopped. It may well have been at
school, and one can understand the temptation to a young man first luxuri-
ating in the Greek language, who is too young to realise he is carrying coals
to Newcastle or owls to Athens. No doubt the whole episode was a bit like
Donne writing Spanish verse or Milton in Latin or Italian, or like Thomas
Gray in Latin. There were of course Latin poets who wrote in Greek, and later
Claudian wrote in both, but in Horace's time such people were mostly writers
of epigrams, so it is probable enough that Horace began as a boy in that way.
The whole generation of his upper class contemporaries dabbled in verse, as
Cicero had done. Pollio addressed obscene insults in verse to Augustus, 'but
I was silent,' remarked the Emperor; Augustus himself started composing a
tragedy about Ajax, in his bath, but 'his suicide was by the sponge,' the
Emperor said. Horace did not yet know these great men, yet in the late forties
BC he was young, decent and enormously promising: his father had been right
to believe in him.

Chapter Two

There is no doubt that at this stage of Horace's life, one thing led to another. His father disappears from the story, with a warning to live frugally, and be content with what money he has inherited. That suggests he did not see his son as a successful man of business. If he died when his son was twenty-one, say in 44 BC, about the time when Caesar was appointed dictator for life, refused the title of a King and was murdered anyway, then Horace had probably gone to Athens. He writes to his friend Julius Florus in a late letter (*Epist*.2, 2, 41f.).

> I was brought up at Rome and there I learned
> What Achilles did to the Greeks while his wrath burned,
> Kind Athens taught me something more of art
> Planting goodwill and conscience in my heart
> To seek truth in the Academic forest,
> But hard times moved me from that pleasantest
> Of places, to the storms of civil war
> Untried in arms and too untried by far
> To face Augustus Caesar in his might:
> Philippi finished me, and cut my flight
> To the low ground, without estate or home:
> Only bold poverty to spur me on
> To writing verses ...

This translation is not exact, the Academic forest is the Grove or Sacred Wood of some forgotten demigod called Hakademos, whose boundary stone survives, but seeking for truth in the forest is a joke of Horace's. He says clearly that he was left without 'paternal hearth or land', and this must refer to confiscation of his small estate at Venusia. It seems to emerge from this that his father had already died, and that might be how Horace could afford to go to what was the equivalent of a university city. While he was there he was recruited by Brutus to serve on his staff as a 'military tribune'. These small groups of officers were supposed to make themselves useful in battles, but although they might go on to become professional officers of high rank, Julius Caesar had found them a mixed blessing. In the critical moments of a battle in Gaul he came across his tribunes weeping in their tent. But the scrawny fellow was full of energy, he seized a sword, led a charge, and saved the day. The tribunes could be anything from aristocratic youths getting experience to agreeable companions chosen for their conversational or literary talents.

Brutus was driven into armed opposition slowly and step by step: he was a reluctant assassin and a most reluctant warrior. He was or had been a very rich man, and he and Cassius raised an army which was gloriously fitted out. He was twenty years older than Horace and an aristocrat, whose ancestor L.J. Brutus was the founder of the Republic and consul about 500 BC. Another ancestor had done well in a campaign in Spain, been consul in 138, and was once a patron of Accius; two more of his kinsmen had died under Sulla and under Pompey. In Athens, where Brutus arrived when he was forced to abandon first Rome, then all Italy to the avenging force of Mark Antony, republican or libertarian sentiment was traditionally strong: Harmodios and Aristogeiton were still worshipped as heroes for an assassination four or five hundred years ago. There he must have gathered up the youthful and promising Horace on his way east. In Asia he met his unlovable associate Cassius, and raised money from the quaestors of Asia and of Syria: Brutus had been a quaestor himself and knew the ropes. As for military affairs, he had fought under Pompey, only to be pardoned by Caesar after the battle of Pharsalus. At Philippi he turned out to be an excellent and dashing junior officer, but a useless general. The Senate put their hope in him, voting him first only the province of Crete and organisation of corn supplies, then command of all the troops in Greece, Macedonia, and on the Yugoslav coast, where the good-natured but somewhat infirm ex-consul Vatinius surrendered to him in 43 BC. Vatinius was attacked once by Calvus, the friend of Catullus, and that speech was well known and considered to be a classic, but it does not seem to have done Vatinius much harm, since he rose to his height in the shadow of Julius Caesar. In the summer of 42 BC after some skirmishes against Thracian tribesmen and a successful siege to extract money from the Lydians of Xanthos, Brutus and Cassius were ready to move back into Europe. The battle of Philippi was fought in late October 42, at a place that was once called the Springs, on the Via Egnatia, where colonists from Thasos had settled and Philip of Macedon had founded a grander town as his centre for the Thracian gold mines.

Mark Antony had not given perfect satisfaction to his master, Julius Caesar, but he had shared the consulship with him in 44, and after some manipulation of Caesar's papers, and some politic and conciliatory behaviour to the assassins, he began to recruit men at arms, and passed an (illegal) law giving himself control of Gaul for five years. By early 43 he had to take refuge there, because he suffered military reverses at Modena in 43, where Decimus Brutus had defied him, and because a new figure had stepped on to the stage, Caesar's heir Octavian. He and Hirtius, one of the two consuls for 43 who were both Caesarians, defeated Antony in April, but there his luck turned. Decimus Brutus wanted to join the assassin Brutus, but his troops deserted him, and Antony had him murdered. The other consul Pansa was dying and Hirtius was dead, so the Senate put the assassin Brutus, who had an extraordinary reputation for rectitude, in command of any troops loyal to them. The governors of the western provinces, Lepidus, Pollio and Plancus, allied themselves with Mark Antony, and Octavian was reconciled with him. In November 43, Lepidus, Antony and Octavian were recognised by the Senate as a triumvirate to rule for five years. A list of their personal enemies was drawn up; among many other names, some later pardoned by Octavian, Cicero's was on it, and he was murdered and dismembered for public display in Rome.

Cicero's letters from Caesar's murder onwards give a fascinating insight into Roman life. He says more than once that 'these people fear peace as we fear war', he wishes more fire in Brutus's speech, he wills to reconcile all opposites, he is at the centre of machinations but not of power. Hirtius will be guided by him. He is worried by Octavian's signs of founding a power-base, he mistrusts the names of his agents, and 'You can count on Hirtius; I hope to see Antony in worse trouble than he is at present ... I want to help Brutus in every way I can ... I am glad he has been staying at my house ... The tree has been felled but not uprooted, so you see how it is putting out shoots.' By May 44 he sees that the assassination of Caesar was fruitless, and Varro has warned him of the danger he will be in if he goes to Rome. It is this time, when events were moving so swiftly, yet ruled only (so it seemed) by Chaos and old Night, that I can conceive of the young Horace writing that epode of his (16) which is so hard to date. Its extreme fears do not seem to fit any later crisis, because once Horace has come into the circle of Maecenas the despair it expresses would be inappropriate and offensive. The Jewish prophecy in it would not be relished by Augustus, who called in two thousand such books and had them burnt.

The influence of Virgil which has been seen in it may easily be an influence the other way. There have been some signs of a movement among scholars to push its date backwards, but Professor David Mankin of Cornell in his edition (1995) still leans towards a date later than Actium, if only because of the position of the poem in the book of *Epodes*. That is a frail support, and we do at least know by 44 or 45 BC Horace had already started to write: the trivial anecdote that he sets at Brutus's headquarters in Asia (*Sat.*1,7) was clearly written before Philippi, so Horace had written that at least before 'poverty spurred him' to write. As for the connection of this epode with Virgil's fourth eclogue it is indeed curious. Both poems deal with prophecy but while Horace is writing in despair Virgil is so radiant with optimism the eclogue has been taken to be literally Messianic. But Pollio, Virgil's early patron, was consul in 40 BC, and the consulate is mentioned; Colin Hardie thinks the child who is to rule and restore the toppling world must probably be the expected child of Antony and Octavia, whose marriage sealed the treaty that renewed the triumvirate in 37 BC. We do not need to decide that slippery question, nor the question of whether it was Pollio's child or Octavian's or Antony's.

If one has once grasped the nettle of the early date of Horace's sixteenth epode, say late 44 BC about the time of Horace's twenty-first birthday, other things about it fall into place and confirm the dating. The poem imagines a disaster that fits the fears of those years immediately after the death of Caesar, it does not foresee the role of Octavian, it claims the role of sacred prophet and poet in an amazing manner that fits a poem written far from

Rome, and the liberties it takes with Roman institutions and assemblies, including the Right to Deal Directly with the People, also suggest a young man far from home. The story of the Phocaeans and the foundation of Marseilles is taken from Herodotus, of whom there was a cult in Greece that spread to Rome in the next generation. There is also an overtone of Solon's fiery political speeches in iambic verse. But above all the depth of Horace's fantastical despair fits that moment and no other moment. The poem is an important landmark in his life. The pun on Rome and force exists only in Greek and comes from a Jewish apocryphal prophecy.

> Another age ground down by civil war:
> Rome falls by its own force,
> The Marsian neighbours could not finish her,
> Nor all Porsenna's horse.
> Not jealous Capua nor sharp Spartacus
> Nor faithless Allobrox
> Nor wild blue Germans nor our fathers' curse
> Hannibal in his rocks:
> Because our blood is cursed and we shall crash,
> Wild things come thronging round,
> The barbarous conqueror will tread Rome's ash
> And hoofbeats lash the ground,
> The airless sunless bones of Romulus
> Will be scattered and mocked.
> What's to be done? Best of our populace,
> For what relief you looked
> Seek the Phokaian solution,
> City accursed, leave shore,
> Field and hearthgods, your road lies over ocean,
> Leave all to wolf and boar,
> Go where your feet carry you to the wind's landfall
> And the wild Afric air:
> Will you go? any better thought at all?
> The omens are set fair.
> But swear to this, that no one shall turn back
> Till rock swims in the west,
> No one shall turn back home till mountains crack
> And rivers wash their crest ...
> ... you have courage, then leave women to wail,
> Fly past the Etruscan sands,
> The wandering Ocean waits for us, set sail
> For the rich happy islands.
> There earth unploughed yields wheat in her season,
> Vines flower unpruned, greenly
> The olive buds and grows fruits on and on,
> And figs hang from the tree,
> Honey in hollow oaks, streams running free

Leap lightly from the mountain:
Nanny goats come unbidden to milking
Their friendly udder swells,
No bear circles them groaning at evening
No earth with vipers fills ...
... no illness hurts the flock no star shall smoke
Heat down on to the sheep,
Jupiter kept this shore for his good folk,
Still gold, when ages weep
To bronze and so to iron hard as rock:
Which you by me escape in poetry.

The translation is a little free, but it gives some idea of most of the mixed elements of the original: I left out only one of those long lists of impossible things, miscegenations and so on, for which the ancient world had an affection that never ceases to surprise me, and a few lines about the climate of the happy islands. They are of course the landscape of the poet's youth, transformed into a golden age. As for the allusions early in the poem, Romulus had a grave in the Forum, Porsenna was a legendary Etruscan king (I gave him horsemen, as I gave Hannibal his rocks, for a rhyme). The faithless Allobrox lived in the mountains from Nantes to Geneva, and Horace says they rebelled in time of trouble, but historians are shocked by this accusation. The wild blue Germans present a graver problem, because the *caerula pubes* can indeed mean 'blue youth' but it also means 'blue pubic hair' or 'blue balls'. David Mankin preserves the decencies and assures us the Gauls went into battle naked but the Germans never, and further he says that the Germans were known for ferocious blue eyes, and only the British for bodies painted blue with woad. I do not myself trust any part of this elaborate explanation, but the reader may picture the savage Germans as he or she will, I have veiled them in decency but against my better judgement.

There is a certain strain of frivolity in this poem, though not in this part of it. It becomes wilder and more frivolous when the Phocaeans take ship. To abandon Rome was not a serious idea, and Horace was much more shocked than I was by the bones of Romulus scattered under the hoofbeats. The resonant cavalry noise by the way is found in Virgil too, but they both get it from Ennius and from Homer before him. The other golden age kind of poem that Horace wrote in his epodes was the second, which also has a streak of the unserious. It seems to be a lovely and cloudless panegyric of country life, until we are told at the end that the whole poem was said by a miserly stockbroker who did not mean a word of it. That is a simple mixture of iambic hexameter lines alternating with tetrameters, very chaste and effective.

How good to see the sheep come hastening home
Out of their grazing grounds
And weary oxen bear the upturned plough
On their tired necks, hear sounds
Of peasant slaves that bee-swarm of the house

Around the gleaming gods.
So spoke the moneylender Alfius
Soon to be squire for good?
But on the Ides he took his money in
To lay it out again.

The sixteenth epode alternates iambic with dactylic hexameters. The whole book of these seventeen poems, which Horace called 'iambics', are called epodes because the metres, which are varied, nearly always alternate two different metres to form a couplet. The originals of all these couplets can almost always be found among the fragments of the archaic Greek poet Archilochus, and they have been named by grammarians 'Second Pythiambic' or 'third Archilochian' and so on: these names are no use at all except for passing examinations, poets never remember them and I shall ignore them. But they really do make up a special section of Horace's work. The odes are mostly more elaborate. They cannot be proved to have begun before Philippi or perhaps before Actium, which was another battle eleven years later, in which Horace cheered on the winning sidelines. But that was celebrated in an ode as well as in an epode, and one form of epode got used for an ode (1, 7) as well, so the kinds of poem overlap. A few forms occur in Hellenistic Greek or even in Latin writers, but substantially in their Latin form they are Horace's invention. We do know all the same that with the exception I have mentioned (1, 7), Horace got tired of writing his 'iambics' before he tired of lyric verse, and his odes revived late in life but his iambics did not. This has something to do with subject-matter: the iambics can be savage, the odes much more infrequently so, and the late poetry never.

At the same time or soon after, when the republican atmosphere of Athens and the philosophic teaching of that city had carried him away like the Pied Piper and he was with Brutus in Asia, he was writing satiric poetry. The earliest poem we can date is the seventh, and its first word is '*Proscripti*', the person was real, and he was on the list to be murdered compiled by the triumvirate. He was called Rupilius Rex and a most unsuccessful man. He fought Caesar, fought under Attius Varus in Africa in 47, and was first exiled probably by Caesar, and then under sentence of death from Mark Antony served on Brutus's staff in Asia. Cicero knew him as a Bithynian tax officer, so he had useful experience. He had risen to the height of praetor at Rome between catastrophes, which meant a kind of deputy-consul with the responsibilities of law; there were eight of them at the time, and he might have gone on to govern a small province. Someone of his name, possibly a grandfather, had been a consul a century before this incident. We know nothing about his fate, it is improbable that he survived to see Horace's seventh satire, which is fierce. It is no more than an anecdote written to amuse friends, but it begins with 'The pus and poison of Rupilius Rex, The man on the list, and how that hybrid Persius Had his own back on him ...' and ends with '... so why not cut this King's Head off? That's your family business.' The two of them are 'like Bithus and Bacchius', two gladiators, and their case is heard by Brutus as praetor of Asia. Horace takes his tone, and even the word 'pus', from Lucilius.

Lejay, who was a sensible and learned professor of 1911, and the first detailed student of Horace in French to publish since Madame Dacier in 1681, thought this satire was written at Rome in 41 BC, but there are problems whatever the date was, though it appears to be written at the time of the scene it describes, before the death of Brutus, and I accept as Fraenkel did that it was. It is astonishing that it was never suppressed, but that fact is all of a piece with Horace's lifelong refusal to deny his past, a refusal that Maecenas and Octavian accepted. The world must have seemed an amazing place to Horace, suddenly in command of troops in Asia in 42 BC, and his loyalty to the friends he made at that time was long continued. Messalla Corvinus was just a year or less younger than he was, though he was an important commander under Brutus: he transferred his loyalty first to Antony, then to Octavian, and fought Sextus Pompey, son of the great Pompey, in 36 BC, the Illyrians and an Alpine tribe: in 31 BC he was consul and fought at Actium, and had a triumph for a victory in Aquitaine in 27 BC. He disliked power in civil life and preferred his privacy: he survived Horace by sixteen years. He died covered in honours, and a patron of writers and Horace's friend. Pompey was another even closer friend of Horace who seems to have gone on fighting long after Philippi, but where and in what army, and who he was or who his kinsmen were remain unknown. We know only that an ode of Horace welcomes him home at last.

Horace was proud to have served as a 'tribune' and to have commanded legions; he was conscious of being criticised later by Roman gossips as the son of an ex-slave for holding so high a rank. In fact in the years that followed not only would he mix as a friend with the great men of Rome, but his job as treasury clerk in an office that furnished true copies of legal documents was one that usually went to a Knight: so however he managed his transformation, he had stepped up in rank or class to a higher level than his father's. No doubt his father had stepped down to become a slave: he sounds like a provincial Italian enslaved perhaps in the 'social war', say in 89 BC twenty-four years before Horace was born. The centre of Athens was a university town, but those Romans who went there were of the rank to which Horace had already moved. The Academy, where he met Brutus as a fellow-pupil, was a few miles outside the walls, a pleasant enough walk as Cicero describes it in *De Finibus*. It was that short walk no doubt that raised Horace in Roman upper class eyes to the level of an equal. There were other, less reputable schools of philosophy. Epictetus the Stoic was once a slave, and there were slaves among the Epicureans: the Cynics were beggars. Horace's status remained honorary, because rank in Roman society depended on descent by blood, and on a sufficient income – the Knights like Athenian Knights, the Riders of the Parthenon frieze, had to provide their own horses for example, like British militia officers down to 1914 – and above all on public and political services, a ladder which ended in the consulate and the 'nobility' of senators and governors overseas. To that ladder Horace did not aspire.

His position, favourable as it sounds, has an important consequence in Roman law, because under laws repeated and reinforced by Octavian (Augustus), a plebeian could not marry into a noble house, and if he did so his

marriage would be invalid. This fact casts a light on the flirting tone he takes
with young women in his odes. The women he knew well socially and mixed
with belonged to the nobility and if ever he mentions one then he gives her
by convention a Greek name. In his lyrics, Horace can be heterosexual or
homosexual at the drop of a hat; in this he follows the tradition of Greek
songs, and no doubt of life. But it has some importance that he is set free to
write as he chooses about real women, whores young or old, or Greek boys
like Ligurinus, who is named after the place where he was born, Liguria, and
about other figures of fantasy, because Roman society could not tolerate his
marriage, if he had any mind to marry into a class above his own. As for what
his real feelings were there is one lady called Cynara for whom he appears to
have felt strong affection, but her name is a disguise, and there is a whore
called Canidia who seems to me a figure of fantasy, whom he attacks with a
peculiar virulence. His lyric poetry follows rules of propriety, so that the
Soracte ode is addressed to a Greek name of obvious hollowness, Thaliarchus
which means the celebrator, for the simple reason that the poem ends in what
would be bad behaviour for a young Roman nobleman.

He had thought out all these matters: in particular he was careful at first
to criticise individuals whom he took from the pages of Lucilius, and only
gradually did he desert that great satirist, as we shall see. It is a pity his
passage through Athens left no trace in the writings of Cicero's friend
Atticus, who was living there in some grandeur as an Epicurean, which
Horace also claimed to be at least once. The truth about that is that he liked
scoring off the Stoics who were severe fellows, and he greatly enjoyed
youthful pleasures; he had no taste at all for metaphysics, and probably he
thought Epicurean atheism was metaphysical. He was not so to speak an
earnest follower of Lucretius. As for Atticus, he owned all the grazing
grounds of Epirus, and lent money to politicians in need from Marius to
Octavian. His estate outside Athens contained a fine classical temple of the
Graces, naked no doubt. When Cicero was murdered in December 43, Atticus
edited the volumes of letters they had exchanged; he lived for twelve more
years, and Agrippa the best friend of Octavian married his daughter. He died
by suicide at the age of very nearly eighty. It is highly likely that he knew
Horace, but he was a very rich man indeed and a shrewd old political
buzzard.

Cassius was the manipulator of Brutus. He had fought in a number of
wars, and survived the disastrous battle with the Parthians that Crassus lost
when Horace was a boy, and the war that Pompey lost at Pharsalus when
Horace was seventeen. Caesar pardoned him, but Cassius forgave less easily.
He became the praetor in charge of foreign lawsuits. After the murder of
Caesar he sailed to Asia at the end of summer, took over armies from
Bithynia and Syria, then one from Egypt marching to relieve Dolabella, and
then in Syria Dolabella's army too. Dolabella had contrived to have Trebonius
the governor of Asia assassinated for dealing with Cassius, but too late;
Brutus and Cassius extracted six times the entire (colossal) annual revenue
of Asia (and Antony after Philippi took nine times that sum). By then
Dolabella had died by suicide, but Cassius had taken Laodicea and went on

to sack and pillage Rhodes. So when Brutus and Cassius set off for Europe they must have had the highest hopes. One must remember that it was not until Philippi that Antony proved himself as a general: a betting man might have put his money on Cassius. Unfortunately on the first day of the battle his camp was captured, Cassius was convinced that the battle was lost and killed himself as Dolabella had done. The next day the battle was really lost and Brutus in his turn killed himself. It is curious that Dolabella had happily and vigorously joined the conspirators when Caesar had died. He certainly repressed the religious cult of Caesar, and he was happy to take the consul-ship and then the governorship of Syria for five years. It was when he had Trebonius assassinated that he was declared a public enemy. He was a dissolute character we are told, and a son-in-law of Cicero, who worried about him. As for Trebonius, he had been an important member of the conspiracy, whose task was to detain Mark Antony while Caesar was assassinated.

We do not know how much Horace knew about all these events, even about the battle. It is not in the least clear when he ran away at Philippi: we assume he was on the staff of Brutus not of Cassius: certainly that is what the seventh satire suggests. All that Horace will tell us is that he threw away his shield and took to his heels. In the poem to his old friend Pompey, he says Mercury saved him in a cloud: but these are traditional Greek myths about escaping from a battle, the lost shield occurs in Archilochus first and the divine cloud in Homer.

> ... Pompeius you were first of all my friends,
> With you we saw the slow days to their ends,
> And crowned our shining hair,
> Scenting the Syrian air.
> With you I felt Philippi, the swift flight,
> The shield I flung away in the lost fight,
> Smashed valour, brave mouths found
> Biting the dirty ground.
> Swift Mercury had wrapped me in dark air
> And bore me through the enemy full of fear:
> But the wave sucked you in
> To the storms of war again
> So offer God the dinner still owing,
> And lay yourself worn out with soldiering
> Down under my laurel,
> Don't spare the doomed barrel ... (2, 7)

The reference to Syrian scent in the first stanza I have translated is really to something called Syrian *malabathrum*, with which the young men crowned their glittering black hair. It seems to be the oil of the cinnamon leaf, but it could be acquired all over the Levant I suppose, and even in Rome. Or does 'Syrian' refer to the Syrian campaign under Cassius? Surely not, be-cause Syrian or even 'Assyrian' scent (2, 11) is among the Syrian trading goods Horace often mentions. Syrian products did not really have a Syrian origin: they were mostly from India, as the etymology of the word *mala-bathrum* suggests: rather as the wine of the Levant was all called Malmsey (from Monemvasia) in the Middle Ages.

Still, there remains a question about Horace in the East. Did he stick close to Brutus or had he reason to wander? In the eleventh letter of the first book, some twenty years or more after Philippi he addresses a certain Bullatius about travel, and Horace seems to know many interesting places.

> How were Chios and famous Lesbos?
> And lovely Samos and royal Sardis?
> Smyrna and Colophon or did you like
> Some city like Pergamon, or did it strike
> You that you could settle in Lebedos?

These places were all notoriously beautiful except Lebedos, which was ancient and not uninhabited. Pausanias says it had wonderful hot natural springs which were therapeutic. In fact it must have been an antiquated spa. It lies near Clazomenai unexcavated to this day. There is no way of knowing what happy memories Horace may have had of it. The letter says it was a more deserted spot than Gabii or Fidenae, which were melancholic enough. The Greeks at this time wrote epigrams about deserted Troy and Mycenae. Latin literature does have a few references to the pleasures of seeing the herdsmen pause among ruins: Propertius has a lovely line or two about Veii. Horace does not linger long at Lebedos, he is anxious to point a moral. Rhodes and Mytelene make it plain that any example of a Greek site in the Levant would do. His last shot is Ulubrae, a place in the Roman marshes remarkable for the number and noise of its frogs. You can be happy anywhere, he means to say. Alas I do not really believe that the unconfirmed evidence of this moralising poem indicates that Horace has been to all these places. He was surely not at Cassius's siege of Rhodes or with him at Smyrna? I am certain he knew Gabii, and Fidenae, and Ulubrae, and it looks as if he had been to Lebedos.

> Do you know what Lebedos is like, really?
> More abandoned than Fidenae or Gabii:
> I would like to live at Lebedos all the same
> Forget my friends and be forgotten by them …

Was it a landmark on his escape from Philippi? How did he escape, anyway? If he had been captured he would have been sold as a slave, that is certain, and could count himself lucky not to be executed. But there was a marsh on the edge of the battlefield, and probably a way through it. (Readers may want to know more about Philippi, so I offer in the Appendix Plutarch's account of that battle from his life of Brutus.) Horace's friend was or later became Messalla, but after the fighting was over the poet's best course would be to find a boat to Thasos, the nearest island, which was shaggy with forest and big enough to hide him until Antony went away. From Thasos he could reach

Athens, and in Athens of course he could go to Atticus or to any other friend. But he would make for Italy as fast as he could, because Antony was staying in the East. Greek Asia was therefore particularly unsafe.

Meanwhile Antony's brother Lucius began another civil war against Octavian; he was consul in 41 BC and opposed Octavian's wholesale redistribution of land in Italy to his legionaries. We have the gravestone of at least one of these men who had served seventeen years: the problem was urgent and it was politically essential to settle the old citizens down. Early in 42 BC Brutus had been forced to execute another of the brothers of Mark Antony whom he had captured at Apollonia a year after Caesar's assassination, but who by 42 was trying to get Brutus's armies to mutiny. They were an active band of brothers. Lucius was besieged by Octavian at Perugia, the Italian hill town which is close to Assisi and was then called Perusia. Octavian took it early in 40 BC, forgave Lucius, and sent him off to a command in Spain where he died, but Octavian's soldiers were permitted to pillage the town, which he then refounded and settled with his veterans. It is a curious fact that Mark Antony had two sons by Fulvia, ex-wife of Clodius and Octavian's former mother-in-law, one of whom Octavian executed at Alexandria, while the other was brought to Rome by Octavia and was married by her to her daughter by Marcellus, called Marcella. He felt himself to be a poet, he wrote an epic to rival the *Aeneid* about Diomedes, and sought to inherit the empire. Horace (4, 2) reproved him for imitating Pindar, but the Emperor reproved him more violently for adultery with his daughter Julia and for his ambitions: he was permitted in the end to commit suicide in 2 BC.

It is hard to imagine with what eyes Horace looked again at Rome. He was twelve when Milo murdered Clodius in a gang war, and Clodius's gang burnt down the Senate House for his funeral pyre. Milo went smiling into exile at Marseilles to eat red mullets, but when Horace was seventeen Milo and Caelius, two of Cicero's most infamous friends, brought out their gangs again, and he was executed in 48 BC. These men had gangs of gladiators, there was no question of a revolutionary rabble. The Rome where Horace had grown up had been a nasty and dangerous place. To trace this fever to its source would lead us back several generations before Horace was born, to Marius and Sulla and other mafiosi. Physically the city was in poor condition, the temples crumbling, monuments often damaged, and Octavian, whom let us now begin to call by his title Augustus, had a right to boast that he found a brick city and left one of marble. Both Virgil and Horace approached him guardedly, but in the end they supported him and played as much part as the architects did in his construction of a new Rome.

One must remember that although the poets Gallus and Pollio and Maecenas held high positions under Augustus by the time of Philippi, and Messalla Corvinus having changed sides probably soon afterwards, each of them was in some sense a patron of other and socially less well established writers. Among those they patronised I particularly like the idea of Varius, who wrote an Epicurean epic on Death, with special reference to that of Caesar. What can it have been like? Like Lucretius? He also wrote a Latin play on the disgusting story of Thyestes which Augustus rewarded with a large sum of money. Augustus had come to light in a Spanish campaign of Caesar's when he was eighteen in 45 BC; he was brought up by his mother who was Caesar's niece, and it was only when Caesar's will was opened that the young man discovered (in Apollonia on the Albanian coast where he and Agrippa were supposed to be studying) that Caesar had adopted him and made him heir. His behaviour from that moment on was smart and swift and quite ruthless, as if life were just a game of chess played against the clock. In October of 40 BC he and his close friends Agrippa, Maecenas, and Salvidienus Rufus had made a new pact with Mark Antony at Brindisi, confirmed at Tarentum in 37 BC, to rule the world. Salvidienus alas had to be executed, Pompey's son was defeated and died, and Lepidus was got rid of: from 31 to 25 BC, Augustus was consul every year, and with Antony and Cleopatra silenced at last, he was everything we mean by a victorious Roman emperor. If Virgil's fourth eclogue really was (among other things) an answer to Horace's despairing sixteenth epode, then it was written for the treaty of Brindisi.

No doubt modern readers will ask how much did Horace understand of all this? It appears that he understood more than he said, but there are some matters he never questioned that do seem extraordinary. The empire was a system of world exploitation and it was surely bound to fail, was it not? He does not seem to have been sure of that, and the empire in his day was an astonishing success. Augustus won so often and over such an area of the world that only the remotest regions defied him, and in most cases their day would come. When he lost some legions in the forests of Germany he wept and cried out: he could not bear it. Tacitus puts into a dead man's mouth the sentence about the Romans that they have created a desert and called it peace. That sour note is not quite heard in Horace. Indeed there is a biting moral edge to him, but it is not turned towards politics. I think after Philippi he swiftly realised his mistake. It was not against Augustus the unknown that he had fought, it was against disorder and civil war and the impeding of due process in the state, it was against Mark Antony. Because Augustus won in the end, we imagine Philippi as his revenge on Brutus and Cassius, but he was not even present, he was ill. His ultimate victory was not pre-ordained. For people like Horace and Virgil and Propertius and Tibullus that victory just seemed the only hope for Italy and for civilised life. It is hard for us by hindsight to see what other hope there was, at that time.

So Horace swiftly found himself a safe position in the civil service as *scriba quaestorius*: it was a position not a job, but it did involve him in work among the records and in all the business that records can generate. He seems to have kept this position for a long time, and it explains what he was living on when Maecenas discovered him, and before his success began. That was swift but not immediate, and no doubt it depended, precisely as Horace says, on his friendship with Virgil and their intense admiration for one another. But meanwhile, what was he doing for books? After a triumphant Illyrian campaign in 29 BC, Pollio is supposed to have used the spoils to build the first great public library at Rome. But the question remains; what kind of books would or could a private gentleman in the thirties own at Rome? There were learned men like Varro who clearly had a vast number and one might borrow or have them copied, and ancient commentaries on Horace tell us that the brothers Sosius were famous booksellers and publishers. We have even recovered examples of the sort of little scroll, which Wilamowitz described as 'just the right shape for keeping in a Roman lady's *corsage*', corresponding to the slim volumes which poets still write today. Krinagoras of Mytilene, who was Lesbian ambassador to Julius Caesar in 48 BC and lived on long into the next century, used to give presents of books to his Roman friends, what looks like a case of Anacreon in five volumes to a girl called Antonia for example, or it might have been Alkman, or the *Hekale* of Kallimachos to a nobleman. He was a poet himself, though he confined himself to epigrams, and there is something exquisite about his taste in books that recalls the circle of Catullus and Furius Bibaculus the 'Latin Siren'.

Fraenkel used to entertain his pupils with a fantasy of Horace in Athens spending time in antiquarian booksellers and so discovering, for himself and alone, archaic Greek poetry. Horace certainly knew it more deeply than anyone else, and used it more effectively: we have already observed his interest in Solon and in Herodotos and Archilochos. But had he bought books in Athens or in Asia he would have lost them at Philippi. There is an immediate Greek influence on his very earliest poems, but it is contemporary: it is the influence of the epigram, particularly the anecdotal epigram, often a story with an elegant verbal point which one may call an acquired taste. The odes, particularly the later, greater odes use the Lesbian archaic poets Alcaeus and Sappho, whom Krinagoras might well have supplied, but also Pindar; yet in general the 'nine lyric poets' who were classical, are not present as influences in his earliest poetry. He had read a lot as a boy, and of course in Athens, but like any young poet he went on reading and plundering. His excitement about adaptations and the kind of metres he played with go back to the generation of Catullus, before the long-lived Krinagoras was born. His other Greek contemporaries who have left us a few poems in the *Palatine Anthology* are characters like the idiotic court poet Diodoros of Sardis or Antipater who was Piso's friend and gave him astronomic hemispheres, and Statilius Flaccus who sounds like an ex-slave like Horace's father and perhaps from the same household. He is not a deep or a very good poet, but his occasional similarity of subject-matter to Horace is worth keeping an eye on.

Before we turn to the less datable epodes, there is another anecdotal satire, the eighth, which is one of a number of early poems that concentrate on stories about magic, and on the horrible Canidia. Lejay discusses the subject with a mixture of precision and glee that I find admirable, in his introduction to this poem (*Sat.*1, 8), and the Greek magical papyri that tell you how to perform the magic rituals have since his day been published. I once attended a learned congress of papyrologists in Oxford, since one or two of them were my friends, and since I had to speak about something chose to make my contribution on the Prose Style of the Magical Papyri, which luckily was not a subject that had attracted more serious students, but these ritual instructions turn out to follow a convention much like that for cooking

instructions and that followed by the witches in *Macbeth*. Lejay quotes what
is still called the Great Paris Papyrus: 'Take thirteen needles, and plant one
in the head, saying, I pierce her through the head, and two in the ears and
two in the eyes, and one in the mouth and two under the breast, and one in
the hands and two in the private parts and two in the soles of the feet, saying
each time ...' and so on. Lejay also gives a valuable account of the area of the
Esquiline outside the walls of Rome, between the Viminal and the Esquiline
Gates, which Horace knew well before Maecenas had transformed it. It was
where bodies of the executed, of slaves and the very poor, were flung into pits
to rot. The pits were open, so there were animals as well as practitioners of
magic, who can be traced archaeologically all over the ancient world, even in
Athens in the fourth century, and confirmed and illustrated by anthropology:
the figure of wool, for example, which would swell with blood and (it was
hoped) take on weird powers. These places were full of disease, and it is
fascinating that they were never wholly suppressed. They represented the
lowest of low life as Horace knew it. He treated Canidia in different ways in
different forms, as if she were a cartoon character, but this satire is the most
circumstantial and makes one's blood run coldest.

> I was a fig-tree trunk, no use at all:
> I might have made Priapus or a stool
> But the carpenter somehow preferred a god
> So here I stand, a god made of fig-wood
> Terror to birds and burglars without words:
> The reed stuck in my head frightens off birds
> From the new gardens where they shit and play,
> And my red cock frightens the thieves away.
>   This is where dead bodies of wretched slaves
> Were carried out and left by fellow slaves,
> The common grave of the extremely poor,
> Pantolabus, Nomentanus, therefore
> A thousand foot this way, three hundred there
> The monument not to belong to the heir. (*Sat*.8, 1f)

So far he is merely setting the scene and his own tone, which is more amusing
and less decorous than I have made it. The whole poem is a mere fifty lines.

> Now you can live on the healthy Esquiline
> And stroll along the bank when it is fine
> Where the whole field was a horror of white bones,
> But thieves and beasts are not the only ones
> Who trouble me, but the women vexing
> The souls of men with poisons and chanting ...

The resettlement and cleaning up of the Esquiline was carried out by
Maecenas, under the prompting of Augustus, as his other friends like
Agrippa and Pollio undertook other parts of Rome. Horace is scrupulous to

treat his low life characters as nasty left-overs from the past, even though we know from archaeology that past was never wholly buried, or rather not the whole of it. The palace of Maecenas stood there all the same, and when their day came Maecenas and Horace were both buried there. It appears to me that when he wrote this satire Horace was probably not on intimate terms with Maecenas. Priapus the garden god from Lampsacus was essentially a fertility symbol; he spread through the whole Roman world, and one notices that the first few lines of this satire could be trimmed to an epigram about him, of which there were many. Some have survived, attributed to Virgil.

> I can't get rid of them, when the lovely moon
> Shows bright, they look for poisoned weeds and bones.
> I have seen Canidia black-aproned
> Bare footed with her hair loose, and beyond
> Sagana howling with her, deathly white,
> Tearing a lamb to pieces with their teeth,
> Their nails like claws scratching the earth beneath.
> The blood ran in the pit to raise a spirit
> So they could get some answer out of it,
> They had a woollen image and a wax one,
> The woollen big to beat the little one;
> The one of wax beseeching, and it knows
> That it will go the way that a slave goes.
> One calls Hecate, one Tisiphone,
> The moon above blushed red and you could see
> Snakes and the hounds of hell sniffing for scents
> While the moon hid behind the monuments.
> If I'm lying let crows shit on my head
> And let me be pissed on and be beshitted
> By Julius, Pediata, Voranus.
> So while Sagana and the ghost chorus
> Resounded there so shrilly and so sad,
> And a wolf's beard and the eye tooth of a mad
> And spotted snake were buried in the ground:
> The wax doll burnt up with a crackling sound,
> And vengeance came to me on those Furies,
> My wood split in a fart to foul the skies:
> They ran, their magic herbs their strings, their teeth
> Their wigs dropped in confusion underneath.
> Well, you'd have laughed yourself almost to death.

The anecdote is nothing much, it is so heavily framed or distanced that it ends in laughter as it began in the grotesque world that is after all a kind of humorous picturesque. In the *Epodes* Horace treats Canidia more sharply. There are witches and corpses and love-magic in the fifth epode where the same nasty couple murder a boy. I quote John Penman's excellent translation (1980).

> ... And thus, dissected out, his dried
> Liver and marrow shall provide
> The magic essence of
> The draught that rouses love ...
> ... The Ariminian Folia must
> Have been there, with her manly lust
> And her Thessalian rune
> That draws down sun and moon
> From heaven – or so the neighbourhood
> Of idle Naples understood.
> Gnawing a long-nailed thumb
> With blue teeth, overcome
> By anger, stood Canidia ...

The boy, at the end of this poem (which by the way is a hundred and two lines long) turns to a Fury and prophesies his vengeance on the wicked old women:

> And wolves with carrion-crows combine
> At large over the Esquiline
> To strew your limbs, that shall
> Receive no burial ... (*Epod.*5)

This epode is not framed in unseriousness though the most horrible parts of it are very funny, in English as in Latin. It begins with a speech of the terrified boy, as it ends with his parents. It is on the whole more sad and more horrible than the amiable satire we have been looking at. The last epode of all, the seventeenth, names the old witch, who behaves and sounds like the awful Canidia of the Esquiline, though there are difficulties. Horace (if it is Horace) addresses her for fifty-two lines with a storm of reproaches, and she replies with thirty-one. Are these two long speeches meant for a mime? We know little about such dramatic performances, and less about their experimental stages. This is not a burlesque, and it is either the most realistic of all these poems, or the flightiest: why is Canidia given a son called Pactumeius? Why does she call her adversary 'High-priest of Esquiline enchanters'? I do not think these final words (from John Penman again) can be meant for Horace.

> ... What was your hope? That I, at whose behest
> Wax images move on their own (as you,
> You meddler, know), and who can snatch the moon
> From heaven with songs, raise the cremated dead
> And mix love potions – did you hope that I
> Might have to weep because, employed on you,
> My skill had come to nothing in the end?

Although I have treated the satire first, it is at least as likely that it is the easier, slightly maturer Horace's work, written when he began to feel at ease in his own skin. The Esquiline in the *Epodes* is a pit of disease, teeming with low life and poison, but in the satire the influence of Maecenas and 'the new gardens' just touches it. The epodes are more experimental in form, and in all these poems Horace shows what appears to us a wonderful originality. I would judge that the murdered boy and his vengeance came before the even more perfectly balanced dialogue of the wizard and the witch. None of them is at all like Theocritus or Virgil on love-magic, though they both handled the theme. Indeed the end of the murder poem is like the end of the sort of treatment in elegiac couplets we might expect from Tibullus or Propertius. Maybe Horace had a source in low life and its literature that has not survived. Certainly Canidia is mentioned in one short epode (3) addressed to Maecenas by name. It is about some food that was a gift to Horace but had too much garlic in it and nearly poisoned Horace: he wonders if Canidia had a hand in the cooking. It is as if she were a well-known character about whom there were stories, and Horace is ringing the changes on them. Virgil's reapers tranquilly consume garlic and thyme 'the smelly herbs' for lunch, crushed up by Thestylis in the second eclogue: Horace says 'O the tough guts of reapers', so there could be a connection. To pursue this joke into the poem *Moretum*, which is not by Virgil, would be to take it too far. Garlic was peasant food, as potent as the magic charms of Marsians and Sabines in the last epode, that is all. Horace said it tasted worse than raw hemlock, which I have never tried.

There are other epodes that may be as early as these, but it is time that we considered the book as a whole.

Chapter Three

Suetonius in his Life of Horace puts it neatly: When his side was beaten and he had asked for and obtained pardon, he obtained by purchase a treasury clerkship, *scriptum quaestorium*. These clerks were assistants to the magistrates, and Mommsen showed that they could hold their office for life: a clerkship could be bought, as Horace for example bought it. His poverty therefore was not so dire that it cut him off from this middle class kind of career. L. Pomponius Niger who left us his gravestone in Pisidian Antioch (in Greek Asia) was a veteran of the fifth Gaulish legion, and a *scriba quaestorius* at a period when he must have been Horace's colleague: there were thirty of them. It is much more interesting to ask how Horace entered the circle of Maecenas, to whom his *Epodes* are dedicated. The answer is that Virgil introduced them in about 39, the year of the amnesty for civil war offences, and of the publication of Virgil's *Eclogues*, a success on an astounding and unusual scale, as they deserved to be. One must stress that although the friendship was personal and became intimate, it was also literary, as Horace makes plain in the tenth satire of book one.

> ... Pollio's foot treads out the deeds of kings,
> Varius stands supreme in epic song,
> But to Virgil the country bred Muses
> Gave all softness all smiling graciousness ...
> ... Let Plotius, Varius, Maecenas, Virgil
> And kind Octavius Valgius lend me still
> His praise, and Fuscus and the two Visci
> (I speak sincerely of them all) and whether
> Pollio or Messalla or his brother
> Bibulus, Servus, Furnus – let me end
> Without the list of scholars and my friends ...

We will hear many of these names again; it is enough to note here that there is a break of a tactful kind which is probably also a break in intimacy after the two Visci. He tells us how he met Maecenas through Virgil and his friends in the sixth satire, which Suetonius rather neglects.

> I return to myself, an ex-slave's son,
> Whom they sneer at being an ex-slave's son:
> Being now your friend Maecenas, being then

In command of a Roman legion as tribune ...
... Kind Virgil and then Varius told you of me,
Then we spoke a few words but I seemed
Tongue-tied from shyness or I was ashamed,
I did not say my father was famous
or that I rode round on a Tarentine horse:
I said who I was, you briefly replied
As your way is; I went and came back when
Some nine months later you asked me again,
And you invited me to be your friend ...

Horace expresses his pleasure that the basis of their friendship is not family alliance but a certain shared moral philosophy, which is a principal theme not only of their friendship but of this book of *Satires*. For that reason I want to stress it here, before we dive into the somewhat muddy waters of the *Epodes*, because it is the guiding star of all Horace's poetry, and the key to his development as a poet and as a man. 'In this I am content: You know the infamous from the decent ...' As a theme it is strongest in the *Satires*, but it spreads into every kind of poem. He has based his *Satires* on it, that is on his moral philosophy, within the limits of that kind of poem as Lucilius had defined it, within his bizarre but severe limits. It enters also into Horace's *Epodes*, tumultuous and experimental as they are.

The collection as he published it, as he sent it to be copied and sold to the public, contained seventeen poems, the first of which was a dedication to Maecenas. Seventeen is a ragged number, as if in the end he had tired of these queer couplets, defined only by their metre and their tone, which is caustic or despairing or in which the ink seems to burn the paper. He is proud of adapting into Latin the work of Archilochus and his tone of voice, but enough is enough, and he does not really want to imitate the powerful invective which drove the ancient poet's father-in-law to hang himself. Greek lyric is in many ways in closer touch with reality than the poetry of Horace can aspire to be. The reason for just seventeen epodes all the same is hard to find. Probably it was Virgil in his ten *Eclogues* who set the fashion for a decimal system of poems. Horace wrote ten satires in his first book, then thirty-nine and twenty and thirty odes: eleven more would make a hundred, but his intention is probably to offer the first nine as examples of nine metres he can use for lyric poetry, which makes thirty, twenty and thirty odes as the contents, properly speaking. With the epodes he stopped when he was exhausted, or wherever that particular stage of experiment came to an end. The word 'epode' is a title fixed to this book by grammarians centuries later: Horace called it his 'iambics' as Catullus had also called his insults. The epodes are not all earlier than all the satires or all the lyrical poems, since they go on to Actium (31 BC).

You will go in galleys among the tall
Battle-towers of the fleet
In dangers like Caesar's, sharing them all

Maecenas at drumbeat
My friend, while we who shall live in happiness
If you live, or despair,
Shall on your orders pursue idleness
Sweet only if you're there ...

That is how he begins: the war might be Actium or some earlier naval action
against Sextus Pompey, son of Julius Caesar's great enemy. The point is that
it does not matter: Horace and Virgil are left behind on land. We are willing
to go, he says, if you want us, across the Alps or into the Caucasus or the last
bay of the west. What good would I be? I shall be less frightened in your
company than left alone: I will undergo this or any war, not for the sake of
many oxen to plough my acres, or a flock moving between Lucanian and
Calabrian grazing grounds before the dog-star rises, not for a villa shining
on the heights, your kindness is enough for me, I shall not collect riches to
dig into earth like Chremes the miser, nor to waste them like an heir.

The moral line of this little poem is clear enough to us already: Horace
wants no more than enough. Chremes is a character from Greek comedy, and
from Plautus, and so is the heir: they are material from what Plutarch (as
well as Horace in the *Satires*) calls 'Aristophanes and Plato', meaning Plato
the comic poet, not the philosopher. Only the metre makes this little poem an
epode, it could as easily be material for a satire, only it is too brief. The metre
is brilliantly ominous at the beginning, with the small fast galley flitting
under the menacing battle-machines of the great ships. Both Caesar and
apparently Maecenas preferred the galleys for their speed, rather as command in a tank battle could be exercised from a jeep. John Penman calls these
sailing galleys with oarsmen 'skiffs', which is really too light altogether.

There is little more to be learnt except from the details of the Latin. The
famous word 'idleness', *otium*, had a distinguished career in Catullus –
'Idleness, Catullus, is the matter with you, Idleness has destroyed Kings and
great Cities.' It could be used of study or any literary pursuit, as Virgil uses
it at the end of the fourth georgic (459-566). 'At that time while Caesar ... the
sweet Siren was nourishing Virgil In flowers of ignoble idleness ...' The Siren
is Naples and the idleness is literature of course. I find these lines so
intoxicating that it is hard here not to indulge in long paragraphs about
idleness. For the Romans any life without business is ignoble idleness.
Horace implies that he has been told, You were no good at Philippi, you were
terrified; stay at home and write a poem, so this is his protest. War of course
meant loot and money, but he does not want that, he just wants what is
enough. It will turn out quite soon to be what we would call a lot: a country
house, nine slaves and a long river valley and some woods, not to mention a
little town house and a few slaves there. But at this stage his idea of wealth
is as imaginary as the villa shining on the heights at Tusculum where Cicero
had one. Virgil had the powerful instinct to pick his form and stick to it, and
he spent the thirties finishing the *Eclogues* and then writing the *Georgics*,
which he read to Augustus in 29 BC. Horace was working as hard but with a
less clear sense of direction, and of course he was five years younger:

twenty-three soon after Philippi when Virgil was twenty-eight and it appears already a bewitching poet. It is strange for a man who claims to be so frightened that Horace seems to have hated every aspect of war except the danger, which as a philosopher and as a friend he accepted.

Let me here introduce Sir Richard Fanshawe's complete version of the second epode. He was Milton's contemporary and successor as Foreign Secretary to Charles II but he did not live long, so he is neglected as a poet.

> Happy is he, that far from mental toil,
> Like the old Mortals, ploughs his Native soil
> With his own Oxen; out of debt: Nor leads
> A souldiers life, still in alarms; nor dreads
> Th' enraged sea: and flies at any rate
> From Law-suits, and the proud porch of the Great.
> What does he then? He, lofty poplars joyns
> Unto adult and marriageable Vines;
> And the wild branches with his Sickle lopt,
> Doth better children in their rooms adopt;
> Or in a hollow valley, from above,
> Beholds his lowing herds securely rove;
> Or, his best Honey, which he means to keep,
> Puts in clean pots: or shears his tender sheep.
> Or when plump Autumn shews his bending head
> With mellow Apples beautifully red,
> With what a gust his grafted Pears he pulls;
> And Grapes, the poor mans purple! whence he culls
> The fairest, for thee Priap; and for thee
> Sylvanus, Guardian of his husbandry.
> Under an aged Oak he loves to pass
> The heates; or lolling on the matted grass.
> Between deep bankes a river rowls the while;
> The birds they prattle to the trees that smile;
> A purling brook runs chiding all the way,
> Which gentle slumbers to his eyes convey.
> But when rough Winter thundring comes, to throw
> The treasures open of the rain and snow;
> Either with dogs, behind him and before
> He drives into his toils the tusked Boar;
> Or spreads his thinner Nets beside some bush,
> An ambuscado for the greedie Thrush,
> And (dear delights) inveigles in his snare
> The Travailer-Wood cock, and the Coward-Hare,
> Who at these sports, evades not all those darts,
> With which loose love assaults our vacant hearts.
> But if a vertuous Wife, that bears sweet fruit
> Yearly to one, and guides the house to boot:
> (Such as the Sabine, or the Sun-burnt froe

Of him, that was chose Consul from the plough)
Build of old logs, 'gainst her good man comes home
Weary, a fire as high as half the room;
And shutting in knit hurdles the glad beasts,
With her own hand unlade their swagging breasts,
And drawing this years Wine from the sweet Butt,
Dainties unbought upon the Table put;
Your Lucrine Oysters cannot please me more,
Nor a fresh Sturgion frighted to our shore,
Nor any rarer fish. No Pheasant Hen,
Or Quayl, go down my throat more savoury; then
An Olive, gather'd from the fattest bough;
Cool Endive, wholsome Mallows; or allow
A Lamb upon some mighty Festival;
Or Kid from the Wolfs jaws; that's worth them all!
Amid these feasts, how sweet 'tis to behold
The well-fed sheep run wadling to their fold?
To see the wearied Oxe come trayling back
Th' inverted Plough upon his drooping neck;
And the Plough-boyes (the swarm that makes us thrive)
Surround the shining Hearth, content and blith!
All this the Us'rer Alpheus having sed,
Resolv'd (what else?) a Country life to lead;
At Michaelmas calls all his Moneys in,
But at Our Lady puts them out agin.

The second epode is one we have already looked at: the praise of country life, about the lucky man working inherited acres with his own oxen and free of debt: he is not disturbed by the soldier's snarling trumpet or horrified by the angry sea, he avoids the forum and the proud house-fronts of the powerful: he spends his time training his growing vines up poplar trees or watching his lowing cattle in a sheltered valley, cutting useless branches and grafting better ones, or putting his pure honey in tall pots, shaving sick sheep or when Autumn's head rises in the fields, beautiful with mild apples, etc. ... and so it goes on for seventy lines. It is a poem that the English have always particularly liked and imitated. The last four lines, where the whole poem turns out to have been spoken by the usurer, are a very small twist in the tail of the poem. Neither the first epode nor the second shows any of the savagery we expected, they are mild and rather beautiful, with a tendency to memorable landscape, and this memorability, which of course is a matter of words used frugally in the right places, is their only sharpness. The wife imagined is very down to earth, 'a Sabine woman or the sunburnt wife Of a Swift moving Apulian'. The birds complaining in the woods and the leaves rustling above the running water sound as if Horace had been reading the *Georgics*, but who knows. His honey is pure and in the amphora, Virgil's is dripping down a hollow oak tree.

The third epode is an outburst to Maecenas (who is named) over the taste of garlic.

> Whoever broke his father's aged neck
> With wicked hand or worse,
> Let him eat garlic worse than raw hemlock
> – Tough guts of harvesters! –
> What is this poison raging in my belly,
> Was it the blood of snake
> In which the herb was boiled that deceived me
> Or was Canidia cook? ...
> ... And never such a swarm of stars could turn
> Apulia mad with thirst
> Or Herakles with shirt of Nessus burn
> Till he was fit to burst.
> Was it your idea of a joke Maecenas, this?
> If so my prayer is said,
> That your girl's hand may push away your kiss,
> She'll cringe at the edge of the bed.

I have left out a few lines in the middle about Jason and Medea, which are splendid, but the fireworks of allusion in Horace's poems do not work for us as well as they once worked. This little poem is a slight thing, it has no very serious point, and it is not as savage or quite as convincing as the equivalent piece of invective by Catullus would be. The allusions are second nature to Horace, yet all the same they do not fit him like his own skin. The skill he offers is very like that of an epigram, and the realism and the classicism combine in the same way. If this epode had strayed somehow like the *Moretum* into the pseudo-Virgilian works, we would like it I suppose, we would be pleased with it and think it curious, that is all maybe. The curse against Maecenas means only, May you too stink of garlic.

The fourth epode is solider invective, but against whom? There were Roman scholars who wrote about 'the persons named by Horace', but alas they are highly unreliable, and when we are told in a note that this was a freed slave called Menas who became an admiral under Pompey we must remain sceptical. We are also told it was really a certain Vedius Rufus, but the same applies. It is doubtless true as Kiessling and Heinze say that he intended someone in particular, but we do not know who. The rank of tribune was one Horace himself had attained too of course, but this man sounds like the scum of the earth, with which Rome was well supplied. I had suspected that Horace might have been adapting Lucilius the satirist, who had this sort of temper and had served in Spain, but that is unlikely, as Otho's law, about seats in the theatre and how many rows were to be reserved and who qualified, was passed only in Horace's childhood, when Lucilius was long dead. This epode is a piece of pure fury, a white-hot blaze. As a poem it is admirable.

Like wolf and lamb my quarrel with you is
At the same heat:
O hide scarred and burnt from Spanish lashes
And shackle-toughened feet
Now you may walk in all the pride of money:
Luck can't change yobs.
Wandering up the Sacred Road do you see
Wrapped round in robes
Written on the faces of the passers-by
The freest indignation?
This man was flogged by the Night-watch: they let fly
At the herald's invitation,
Now he ploughs a thousand acres of Falernian ground
And trots the Appian Way.
It's in the front seats this great knight's to be found,
And Otho's had his day.
What good are the great faces of the ships' beaks
That loom in their places
Against these bandits while the orator speaks,
With this for a tribune, this?

Professor Mankin is uneasy about this piece of rhetoric, yet it seems as
effective as all but the best of the fragments of the Roman orators that have
come down to us; admittedly we are not given the man's name or really his
precise offence. Professor Mankin thinks it snobbish; he wonders whether a
woman may be speaking. Perhaps it belongs to the bad days of Horace's
earliest attempts at verse, when a number of bandits had entered politics and
combined their new and their old vocations. Horace's attitude seems to me
both allowable and perfectly proper under the circumstances.

The fifth epode is the brilliant and in a way evil poem about Canidia
murdering the boy. It is redeemed from the extreme of nastiness by our
comfortable self-assurance that such things do not happen, or if they did it
was long ago and in another country. I do not think such armour of the
reader's can really justify the poem, which is meant to be, and is horrifying.
The reader must suspend disbelief. Who were Canidia or Varus her unfaith-
ful lover or Veia the slave or Folia who could draw down the moon? They are
mere stage scenery, like some of those figures in Theokritos who are inter-
changeable or who blend with the landscape. Virgil wrote a sinister eclogue
about love-magic, but this goes far beyond it. Dio the historian is not as
reliable as we would wish, but he maintains that Maecenas was putting
pressure on Augustus in 29 BC, the year of the amnesty, to put down
witchcraft. It appears to me that Horace knew a lot about it, surely at first
hand, but this poem is of course a fiction. In the first ten lines the boy speaks,
Horace sets the scene in all its disgusting detail in another forty lines, then
Canidia makes her crazy speech for thirty-two lines or so, and after four lines
of explanation by Horace the boy says his last words, fifteen lines. It is of
course Horace's idea to highlight the unhappy boy and his final curse, but the

main spotlight is on Canidia. The woman called Folia of Rimini is a professional witch. Professor Mankin discovers that at Rimini years before Horace was born a cock crowed in Latin. It was the kind of place where that might be believed in 78 BC, that is the point, and scarcely a broomstick ride from Thessaly. Its isolated, gloomy and misgoverned atmosphere in the centuries before the reunion of Italy are hard to describe or imagine. In classical terms it was half Greek, and in the Renaissance it was the stronghold of the Sforza family, whose disastrous blood ran in Charles II and the British monarchy through Henrietta Maria.

> 'Whatever god in heaven governs
> Earth and the human race,
> What is this riot? What crowd turns
> On me its terrible face?
> By your own children if Lucina may
> Attend deliveries
> And by this empty purple cloth I pray
> And God who will punish this,
> Why do your eyes stare like a stepmother's
> At an animal for slaughter?'
> He spoke with trembling mouth and his honours
> Were ripped away after.
> That ungrown body, that might move the wicked
> Heart of a Thracian,
> Canidia with the hair wild on her head
> That adders fasten
> Commands the wild fig ripped up from the dead
> And cypress death will char,
> The eggs of filthy toads smeared with their blood
> And the night-owl's feather
> All the weeds of Iolcos and of Spain
> Or whatever's deadlier:
> Old Sagana moves through the whole house then
> To sprinkle hell's water ...

So far he is writing with simple realism as if he were M.R. James, who knew this epode of course, but he is doing so in a rhythm mounting towards a climax; in this the metre he is using is as useful as ever, so that whatever retards the climax heightens the tension. Old Sagana goes round with a bucket of Avernus water (from a sulphurous lake south of Rome that no bird dared to fly across, hence in Greek A-ornis, in Latin Avernus) just like a devout old person with Lourdes water, only here its meaning is reversed. Her hair stands up on her head with horror like a sea-urchin's spines. Iolcos is an allusion to Medea, a famous witch and child-murderess. The boy's 'honours' are his amulet which he wears as a Roman citizen and the purple-bordered toga he wears as a child. Both were intended to keep away evil, and the same kind of toga was worn by magistrates for the same reason. Canidia needs bones, presumably human from the Esquiline, stolen from a starving bitch, to keep her fire up. The cypress is not a mere grave-marker as it is today, but charred wood from a funeral pyre.

Sagana's task leads on to Veia's, which is worse, her status being lower as her name (from a place) implies. She digs the pit where, as Penman puts its,

> ... like a floating body in
> Water that comes up to the chin
> All buried but his face
> Day-long the boy shall gaze
> At often varied feasts, with eyes
> From which the lustre slowly dies ...
> ... And thus, dissected out, his dried
> Liver and marrow shall provide
> The magic essence of
> The draught that rouses love.

Folia must have been there too, with her manly lust and her charm to draw down the moon; so all Naples believes. Canidia was there raving and calling on Night and Diana ruler of secrets. 'Now, now be present, turn your anger and divinity against enemy houses, while the wild animals lie up in the fearful forests sleepy with sweet slumber. Let the bitches of Subura [a road in Rome] bark at the old adulterer and let everyone laugh to hear them ...' He is smeared with a scent which is Canidia's masterpiece. But her spells are not working, even though Medea used the same formula.

> The bed that he lies in
> Exudes oblivion
> Of each and every concubine ...

Maybe he knows a better witch than Canidia is? Marsian sorcery will be no use against her, so Canidia will mix poisons still more potent. Varus's desire must burn

> With all the ardour which
> Flares from dark-smoking pitch ...

The boy begins his seriously worded and impressive curse, because he knows now that no prayer can soften the women, as Canidia sees her magic is useless. 'Magic poison right and wrong has no force to alter human fate. I curse you with dire detestation that no victim can turn away. When I die at your command I shall come to you as a fury in the night, I shall sit on your troubled heart and drive away sleep with fear. You will be smashed with stones in the alleyways from every direction, obscene old women. Your unburied bodies will be torn by wolves and the birds of the Esquiline. This sight my parents who alas outlive me shall see.' It is powerfully written and passionate, it is no piece of playing with words; in fact I find it too horrifying to attempt a full translation: it is repellent as well, but most deeply horrifying. Can Virgil have challenged him to deal so fully with this theme? It is more than a ghost-story or a fiction or a piece of grotesquery, is it not? Canidia's career in Horace's verse is only beginning: she will appear in odes as well as satires. This epode all the same is as realistic in its own way as a modern short story, and we must suppose that such things happened, and that Horace had known such women. Is there some degree of unwarranted passion against women in the poetry? If so, we shall come across it again; it is Horace's dark side. Or is he simply following (as I believe) a vein of darkness that ran through Roman life?

The next epode is a furious reply to some attack on the poet, maybe in verse. Bupalos and Lycambes refer back to Hipponax and Archilochos, almost mythical characters from early Greek poetry whom Horace alone has led us to admire. As the number of their fragments increases we turn out to have been right to trust him, and we have come to envy the supply of their poems that he had. They are the key to the epodes, they are where he found nearly all his metres, and their aggressive energy is splendid, even as Horace is able to reflect it, a little less full-bloodedly at times no doubt.

The sixth epode is a short exercise in this type of material. Against whom was it intended? The discretion of Horace in not telling us does weaken his poem a little, or more than a little. If one is permitted to conjecture, then two minor literary characters called Bavius and Mevius had incurred the fury of Virgil in the third eclogue as well as of Horace (*Epod.*10) and one of them may be intended. Suetonius wrote about them in his *Poets' Lives* (Rostagni's edition 1956, p.124 ff.) and it is surprising what a lot is known. Domitius Marsus, an epigrammatist of the time who liked Maecenas and on whose work Suetonius drew, wrote a venomous epigram against Bavius in a book called *Hemlock*.

> Bavius and his brother shared together:
> Like-minded brothers on the whole,
> They shared lands, house and money, even the weather,
> Two bodies and one soul.
> But when one's wife had learnt to lie with the other
> The other gave friendship up
> And all was anger and fraud, brother and brother,
> Divided rule, divided sleep.

One had been the other's guardian it appears. We have a few other epigrams from *Hemlock*, which must have been a formidable collection. One was on Orbilius the flogging schoolmaster and one on Tibullus which is neither here nor there. 'Death sent you off Tibullus with Virgil' etc. Marsus was not a good poet alas.

As for Bavius, he went off to Cappadocia, and there he died. Rostagni calls the idea, which had crossed my mind too, that Mevius was the brother whose property Bavius embezzled(?) 'seductive but insufficiently founded', and I

fear that is true. Of Mevius we are told by Suetonius only that he stank of
he-goat and of garlic.

> Why annoy innocent bypassers you dog,
> Coward to the wolf-pack,
> If you turn your empty threat this way you dog,
> I'll bite you back:
> Like a Molossian or a tawny Spartan
> The shepherd's friend
> Through the deep snow prick-eared I follow on
> Any beast we find.
> You fill the forest with your fearful voice
> Then snuffle bread,
> I warn you, I warn you, I've a threatening poise
> With a sharp-horned head.
> Like your scorned son Lycambes you will see
> Or Bupalo's enemy:
> If some black tooth beast has once gone for me
> Will I weep like a small boy?

It is not much of a poem after all, and the moment when Horace grows
stag's or bull's or buffalo's horns having started dog to dog is even laughable.
He is too good-tempered by nature for his chosen medium. This epode adds
to the impression we already have that the whole book is a sort of ragbag of
all kinds of minor pieces: yet that is a dangerous opinion if it leads us to slide
over the seventh, in which the only negative mark is the lack of a date. But
after hesitation I am disinclined to make it a companion piece to the epode
we discussed first in the last chapter. It seems like that poem tidied or
trimmed down, certainly shortened, and less despairing, therefore less an
offence against Augustus. It is anti-senatorial that is all, as Augustus had
often had reason to be. The blame is on the curse of Romulus, and the poem
is very strong. The threat of civil war fits the wars with Antony well enough,
since he controlled some senators at the war for Perugia, and later. But the
poem could be earlier than one thinks. What I am sure of is that between this
seventh and the sixteenth epode lies Horace's full maturity and technical
mastery.

> Where are you rushing, where, you criminals
> With sword bare in your hand?
> God knows by now enough Latin blood falls
> On the sea and on the land.
> It is not the Romans now raging to burn
> Proud envious Carthage,
> Or teach the innocent British till they learn
> To wear chains on Rome's stage
> But as the Parthian prayers to heaven go
> Till Rome by its own hand falls

– The wolf's, the lion's manners were not so
They sought other animals –
Is it blind madness or sharp force or guilt?
I wait: you haven't replied.
Silent and white as if all blood were spilt
They stand there stupefied.
So it is; a hard fate rings the Romans round,
A brother murdered then
When innocent Remus' blood ran on this ground,
And a curse on his children.

There is no doubt that Horace is deadly serious. He does not by the way speak of Rome's stage (it is Virgil who has them woven on his baroque stage curtains in the second georgic); Horace says it is not that they will learn to wear chains on the Sacred Way (walking as prisoners in a Roman triumph: he calls them not innocent but 'untouched'). The sense is the same really, and of course it all came true within a hundred years. Horace will never again express himself quite so bitterly about the Roman capacity for empire, for greed and for self-deception. It was of course (as he pointed out) self-destructive. The only sympathy one has with anyone in this poem is with the poor 'untouched Britisher', yet also at least the shadow of sympathy for the Romans under their curse, in which incidentally he makes one fully believe. This poem is a masterpiece with no word wasted or out of place. As Robert Lowell put it in our own age, at the end of 'Waking Early Sunday Morning',

> ... peace to our children when they fall
> in small war on the heels of small
> war – until the end of time
> to police the earth, a ghost
> orbiting for ever lost
> in our monotonous sublime.

The eighth epode is an astonishing and repellent outburst of a sexual nature against a woman. She is old and rich and apparently has Stoic pamphlets between her pillows. Horace has been unable to oblige her as a partner and sends the most appalling message. There are unfortunately a considerable number of these nasty poems by Philodemos in Greek as well as one or two later Romans, and the tradition of thinking them funny, which is probably not continuous, goes back through Catullus and derives from Archilochos. The lady is not named in Horace's verses, even with a pseudonym, but she is both literate and very grand: she wears huge pearls and has 'triumphal images' to be carried in her funeral, images of her distinguished and noble ancestors who triumphed in their day. In aristocratic houses the wax models or death-masks of the ancestors accumulated with time. Horace is particularly vengeful about the squalor of this lady's sexual appetite, let alone the nastiness of her parts. Her breasts flop like a mare's udders, her place is like a cow's hole, and she has rotted for a long age of the world. The whole disgusting piece is just twenty lines long, and the lady, let alone her characteristics, may be imaginary (let us hope).

The ninth is nearly twice as long: it looks forward to celebrating a victory of Caesar's at sea, against a woman under whom Romans serve 'ah will posterity believe it!' and the sun observes her disgraceful mosquito-net among the banners. This cannot but be Cleopatra, and the battle Actium, the epode is insulting to her and by implication degrading to all women: why should it be such a disgrace for Romans to serve the Queen of Egypt, what is wrong with the useful mosquito-net, and who are the 'wrinkled eunuchs' the Romans serve under? Has Horace discovered in himself a store of venom against Mark Antony? He has not discovered his quite different and moving view of Cleopatra, his tribute to her will be an ode (1, 37) which is a tribute after her death. In this poem we must suppose she is still alive. At Actium in the battle between land-forces the Gaulish cavalry deserted to Caesar's side, and so it does here, so although the Egyptian fleet has fled, the consequences at Alexandria have not yet taken place. The enemy has been beaten both by land and by sea, and Horace is already crying out, 'Io, Triumphe!' Antony has wandered away to Crete in disorder or to the Syrtes, the sands north of Tunisia, or wherever the wind carries him. Horace calls for bigger cups and stronger wine, which is a cure for nausea whether that comes of drinking too much or from the imagination of seasickness. 'Dissolve our anxious fears for Caesar in The god of wine.'

As a poem the epode is not perfect, and it seems disjointed or episodic: Horace will manage this sort of thing far better in his odes. But both for better and worse, it is written at a precise point in history, which as things turned out was the critical point of Caesar's and therefore also Horace's career. Indeed the history of Rome and of the whole world hung on it, and the Roman victory marked the end of civil war for a long time to come. Had Antony won, Horace would not have survived, nor Maecenas. From this day on there will be an alteration of tone in their relationship. Horace was not in the ships any more than he was in the cavalry. He jeers at the enemy, but perhaps no worse than the Romans often jeered: military humour was ribald, and no doubt worse things were said. Horace had almost certainly seen Cleopatra, who lived in a grand manner at Rome when she was Caesar's mistress, but I wish I knew where Horace got the sensible mosquito-net from. Is it a popular joke from years earlier? After Actium Plutarch tells us that Agrippa wrote to Augustus several times warning him he must come at once to Rome. 'This put off the war for some time', and it was not until the next spring that he moved against Egypt. Antony's cavalry and his fleet deserted and the final scenes followed, more or less as Shakespeare has them.

As for the poem, the two lines beginning 'Io Triumphe' and the shorter lines that follow them being all iambic are reminiscent of the marching rhythm of Roman soldiers, which we shall hear again but more clearly in the odes at the very end of Horace's life.

> 'Io Triumphe, why delay about the gold
> Chariots and the white oxen?

Io Triumphe, did you bring a man so bold
Home from Iugurtha's war or when?'

I offer this feeble version only in order to stress the metre, which in Latin of course is meticulously Greek. Why does Horace say the beaten enemy have put off purple for dull grey? That must be what a defeated land army does in order to escape: it must in fact be what Horace did at Philippi. Then what about the wind 'not his own' that carries Antony off to Crete? Or the south wind to the Syrtes? Learned men tell us that the Syrtes mean Cyrenaica where Antony had four legions, but I think matters are more confused. No one at Rome knows yet where he has gone: he may as Horace says be carried 'by the uncertain sea'. Horace did not trust the sea. He nearly died at some time in a ship off Cape Palinurus south of Paestum, and it is possible (though we do not know it) that his adventure was in a fleet action against Sextus Pompey: I feel this theory is too imaginative, as Horace refers to whatever happened as an accident among others like nearly being hit by a falling tree. Still, most death at sea was by accident and by the forces of nature until the nineteenth century, and Horace's distrust of the sea was sensible. In this poem it merges into the 'flowing sickness' that wine will cure, or so he hopes.

The tenth epode to the awful Mevius of Virgil (*Ec.*3, 90) is a finely contrived piece of twenty-four lines modelled on the Greek of Archilochos, or possibly Hipponax as Professor West maintains. We have by a stroke of fortune a piece of the right poem on a Strasbourg papyrus but the attribution is missing. I hope it is not from mere wooden-headed loyalty that I follow Reitzenstein and Leo and Fraenkel in thinking the Greek really is by Archilochos. The discovery of the fragment which was first published by Reitzenstein in an article in 1899 and discussed in a pamphlet by Leo in 1900 when Fraenkel was still a young student must have thrilled him; there was a special charge of electricity in his discussion of it even in old age, and his written treatment in his *Horace* (pp. 24-36) is a remarkable display of his critical talent. He fears that having studied the Greek we may dislike Horace by comparison, but that is a hurdle we must take. His summary is that 'Horace did not attempt to reproduce the true nature of the old Greek *iambus* which had partly suggested to him the theme of his epode. His borrowing was confined to the most general outlines of the subject. As if to make up for the resulting loss, he embroidered his own poem with many elaborate devices, most of them derived from Hellenistic poetry. Consequently what had been a weapon in a serious struggle became in his hands a dexterous display ...' It is true not only of Archilochos but also of Alcaeus and Lucilius that Horace's own poetry widens its scope gradually, from his early apprenticeship to the original Greek models.

Ill-omened that ship swoops and dives
That carries stinking Mevius,
Take care east wind to whip it on both sides
With the worst wave there is,
May the black east wind fling rope and oar broken

Into upended seas
As the south wind attacking high mountains
Snaps shivering oak trees:
No friendly star be seen in the black night
Where grim Orion falls,
As when the Greeks rowed homeward from their fight
So shall this storm appal.
When Pallas turned her fury from burnt Troy
To Ajax's doomed ship,
O how your sailors drip sweat suddenly
While muddy pale you weep,
And that unmanly howling and praying
Against the Almighty's will
As the wet south wind and the rebellowing
Sea smashes your vessel.
Now on the curved shore may the gulls enjoy
Rich spoils, meat of the best,
I'll slaughter a sex-mad billy goat by and by
And a lamb to the Tempest.

There is a note of gleeful laughter in this poem it seems to me, that says Horace knows it will not come true, but all the same he is a hearty ill-wisher. Pallas Athene's attack on the ship that bore Ajax is a famous quasi-epic incident. The employment of curses with this oddly literary character is a Hellenistic convention: Fraenkel quotes from the Curses poem (Dirae) in the *Appendix Vergiliana*, which comes from a minor writer of this period.

May the Thracian wind blast with a mighty force
And the east wind spew cloud and tawny dark,
And the African wind menace his heavy rain …

Probably this and Horace's epode draw from the same Hellenistic source, which was Greek and is lost to us. Archilochos is more savage and by no means literary: he means and believes in every word he says. 'May he gnash his teeth like a dog face down and helpless at the edge of the surf. So I would like to see him suffer who trod oaths underfoot, who was once my companion.' The tension is physical and even where Horace exaggerates he is not able to imitate that. It would be too dangerous, and the world has altered. Archilochos was all but a bandit, to whom loyalty was a vivid reality and his enemies also vividly real. He is a wonderful poet of a kind our civilised world will not see again. Horace is a cultivated poet of a different kind. The epode was translated in the American War of Independence by Philip Freneau and turned against Arnold; Freneau is better than Tom Paine, but the result is flaccid and too polite.

With evil omens from the harbour sails
The ill-fated barque that worthless Arnold bears –

God of the southern winds call up the gales,
And whistle in rude fury round his ears ...

The centre-pieces of this book are now past, and we come to a love poem more in the mood of the *Odes* though it is more personal. Its pattern will be taken up in the last *Odes* (4, 1), it is about sex rather than love, and it assumes or reveals an unashamed bisexuality. It is addressed to Pettius of whom we never hear again; an ancient annotator says he was a fellow soldier, but there is no special reason to believe that. His name was Oscan, and occurs only in the country, never in Rome, so he might be a friend from home: we have no idea at all. The twelfth epode is about a similar girl, Inachia, named after the mythical Greek father of Io. In both these poems Horace comes close to the elegiac couplet, though he avoids it; his metrical dances are trickier.

'It is no pleasure now to write my little verses as I used to do,' he tells Pettius, 'stricken as I am with serious love; love seeks me out to burn for soft boys or for girls. This is the third December since I stopped raving about Inachia that shakes down the glory from the woods.' That phrase comes from a poet of Catullus's generation, and Virgil also uses it. December is the month of his birthday, so no doubt melancholy is in order for that reason. He is ashamed of what an object of gossip he has become, since his deep sighs and his silence prove he is in love. He has complained of his poverty, and strong drink has revealed all his secrets. So he staggered off home but found himself outside the old door. Now he is in love with Lyciscus, a Greek boy with a streak of wolf in his name and good with girls. He needs another flame:

For some girl white and fair
Or some sleek boy tying back his long hair.

There the poem ends: he is *mal-aimé*, he confesses not without irony, and although this poem is slight, it is able.

The other poem is less cool and more passionate but still humorous. It is frank and insulting to the girl: but again by implication the poet is blaming himself, this time for some degree of impotence and over-sensitivity to smells. The girl reproaches him for nearly half the poem, but the details are conventional. The poem is dramatic and one wonders how on earth it will end, but Horace seems to tire of it. There are other characters, Inachia the rival and Lesbia the friend (stolen from Catullus?). Professor Mankin thinks the word Lesbia may have a naughty sense here, but that does not seem called for. The boy who is a better lover than Horace, Amyntas of Cos appears to be stolen from Virgil: if so he is a simple joke, and may have been a traditional one. He is a peasant out of Theocritus: so 'in his groin it stands firmer than A young tree clinging to a mountain-side' (John Penman's version) would fit. Who knows? The only other extraordinary lines in this epode are about the poor girl's powder and crocodile-dung face stuff which comes off in her heat. Scholars assure us that the compound was used at Rome, and that the words for it are dignified, which I find surprising. The dung is supposed to have removed blemishes from the skin: the mind boggles.

Horace is pleased with his trick of introducing a character and then leaving the closing verses to that person to speak in the first person. That is what he did in the twelfth of the epodes and he does it again with wonderful effect in the thirteenth, and there was something like it in the fourth. There is a serenity about the thirteenth which is a relief, and the story is an unmixed classical legend: Chiron lived in a cave on Mount Pelion and though he was a centaur was also a sage. The hexameters flow beautifully and powerfully and the other half of the couplet runs well enough. And yet the whole story is a persuasion to heroic death which is not to be alleviated except by wine and conversation. If we knew its context in life this epode might strike us with the deadliest despair. Its message conveys effortlessly and in a pure form a strong and important part of the morality Horace drew from lyric sources and distils for us into Latin poetry.

> Terrible tempest has narrowed the sky,
> It falls in rain and snow, now woods and sea
> Hiss with storm-wind. My friends let us take then
> The luck the day offers: our knee-joints are green,
> It's decent, wipe old age from our forehead,
> Pour wine made under my Torquatus, a good red,
> Silence about the rest: the kind god may consent
> To reverse out chances: so now pour the scent
> And with the strings of Cyllenean Hermes
> Set free our minds from old anxieties.
> The noble centaur to Achilles sang this:
> 'Unconquerable, born mortal, son of Thetis,
> The ground of Troy awaits you, small Scamander hides
> His freezing streams for you, and smoothly Simois slides,
> There is no return, the Fates have broken the thread,
> Nor can your blue mother carry you home dead:
> Then shrug away all sadness your life long
> With wine and conversation and with song.'

The procedures of this poem are subtler than may appear at first reading. It is an old soldier's poem, and its meaning comes at the end, but first who are Chiron's or Horace's friends? We do not know and it does not matter, because they are Horace's imagined friends in terrible bad weather and some prospect of death. It is not made clear that they are with the sage in his cave on Pelion or that the centaur's song is just a myth like others. The poet's wisdom is not as pure nor as deadly as he makes Chiron's. The confusion is eerie and the wine, as old as Horace was, makes it eerier. Thetis the mother of Achilles was a sea-goddess. Zeus wanted her but learned she was fated to bear a son greater than his father, so she was left to Peleus who was mortal. In the *Iliad* Achilles has a choice of dying young and being famous or surviving, and chooses to die, which he does later at a god's hand. But there were doubtless other versions and when Archilochos wrote Homer's ink as it were was still wet on the page. It appears to me that this powerfully melancholy poem could derive from Archilochos.

The next epode is an apology to Maecenas for not writing an epode. It is worth noticing because the theme will recur, and if Horace has filled up the end of the poem with twaddle then at least it is tactful twaddle. Horace feels as if he had drunk Lethe, or as if a god had put an end to his unfinished iambics, and it pains him to be reminded. Anacreon of Teos had the same problem, when he was in love with Bathyllos of Samos. This is both problematic and interesting to anyone who attempts to chart Horace's career. Does he refer to lyrics or should we remember that Anacreon did in fact write some iambics as well? What does it mean to say that Anacreon often wept his love 'without elaborate metre'? The name of the boy or the young man Bathyllos is interesting because ten years later or so Maecenas owned a slave with that name, who was a genius at what the Romans called pantomime: he was a dancer who danced all the roles in the plot in silence while someone else told the story to music. Maecenas and Horace we may note are intimate about their amours. 'So you are on fire too, poor fellow,' says Horace, 'and if no lovelier fire burnt besieged Troy, be happy in your luck. I am tortured by the ex-slave Phryne who is not happy with just one man.' How much of all this is real? Probably only the skeleton or not even that. Maecenas wanted some love-intrigue verses and so Horace shows himself in the usual shaming light. In real life we know that Augustus is said to have quarrelled with Maecenas after an indiscretion with a girl, but not a shadow of that incident, which was later I think, ever crosses Horace's page.

The last poem we have to discuss is longer, but as light in weight. Both the fourteenth and this fifteenth epode continue to alternate a dactylic hexameter, the heroic metre of Homer, with shorter lines; so does the despairing sixteenth; the seventeenth is pure iambics like a Latin play.

> Night, and the moon shone in the quiet sky
> Among the lesser stars
> When you before the great goddess faithlessly
> To my words fitted yours.
> Like ivy round an oak tree you clung on
> Your arms clinging to me,
> Wolf to the flock, to sailors Orion
> Disturbs the winter sea
> While the breeze shakes Apollo's uncut hair
> For so long we shall love ...

Here the storm breaks; the poem is lovely in its words and reminiscent of Catullus, but it is not quite psychologically convincing. 'O Neaera you shall suffer if there is any manhood in Flaccus, he will not give you up to a better man night after night ...' and so on as if this were one of Ovid's endless elegies. Ovid's facility was involuntary, but Horace does not suffer from that fault, and of course Ovid does not always. Here I think Horace has simply made a mistake of tone. 'Rich in herds as you may be, with all the gold in

Pactolus, the beauty of Nireus and the secret wisdom of Pythagoras reborn, you in turn will lose her, she will roam. And I will laugh.' It is terribly conventional, every metaphor and phrase has been rubbed smooth. Yet even so, Horace is a great poet, and even the ghost, or the mere sketch and outline of his affair is a little moving I must admit.

And what a collection this is. The details and even the rhythms of certain poems stick in one's memory like burrs. The range of experiment is quite great, and one has no idea if one has read only the *Epodes* in what direction he will take off next. We would not have foreseen the poet of philosophy. His object seems almost to be to stuff the most, and most explosive variety into a narrow space: into a book that today would be too short, and here and there too slight, to publish. There are twenty-two or in other editions twenty-four pages. They are a separate book, and those that do not add to Horace's reputation as a poet or else as a moralist do cast unexpected light on him in his late youth, that is until he was thirty-five. But they leave the most personal questions unanswered. Had he settled down to live peacefully with small love affairs, or is the handful of ashes which is all they have left really a kind of graveyard of the affections? We shall see when we pass on to the first book of *Satires* that sometimes he writes about real things that were close to him: at least as much so as Catullus had ever done. The most surprising thing about him is his happiness, but perhaps happiness is always surprising.

The most memorable and haunting of the episodes is surely Altera iam teritus bellis civilibus aetas – Another age is crushed with civil wars, with its beautiful, despairing solution and its vision of the fall of Rome. Here for the first time, we have the work of an unquestionably great poet, so it appears to me.

Chapter Four

The publication of the *Epodes* and his association with Maecenas and with Virgil certainly made Horace a subject of gossip and of knowing remarks, but the *Satires* made him famous. In them he kept the position he had begun to outline in his iambics: a public critic and private friend of the Romans, to neither of which Catullus's ambitions had extended. Horace's position was like that of Lucilius in many ways, though he was not rich or noble or in any way grand. He would have liked to have undertaken a one man revival of the comic theatre of the fifth century BC, though of course that was impossible, because the popular political theatre never survives for long, whether it is Brecht or Aristophanes or even the heavy Roman peppering of satire in the comedies of Plautus. Why that should be would involve us in another book different from this. Catullus was an arrogant and fastidious private aristocrat, who had written that he did not care twopence for Julius Caesar, or to know whether he was a black man or a white man. That position was no longer tenable at Rome: Ovid was a Knight, but he did not write like one. Juvenal was terrified of attacking live targets, and he was exiled like Ovid although he was a Knight. It was essential to Horace's position as a poet that he was a genuine personal friend of the great men of Rome, and also that the public mood of reform in the last twenty years of his own life strongly appealed to him.

By the time he wrote his last epodes he was capable of writing personal lyrics, that is his odes, in a style and with a confidence only Catullus had touched. Greek lyric poetry had not entirely died out: we know of an ode to Power, which is by chance the same word 'Rome' in Greek as the name of the city. The Greeks of Horace's lifetime showed some interest in their own ancient lyric poets, and this is how Horace got hold of the texts. Krinagoras even sends Antonia a present of Anacreon with the dedication of a kind of Greek epode: one elegiac couplet, then two lines of iambics then a concluding elegiac couplet (*Epig.*7 = *Anth.Pal.*9, 239). Is it possible that Anacreon himself wrote such queerly mixed metres, and does that explain Horace's epode (14, 12)? The music when it was written down must have survived, and certain lyrics were used apparently in temple worship. We have at least one early ode (1, 4), which earns its place as an ode because it is one of the variations of metre Horace promises, though in fact he never repeats that metre, and later (4, 7) rewrites the whole poem to make a masterpiece: the metre of Ode 1, 4 occurs almost though not quite exactly in an epode (16). Plancus, who wrote history when he retired, noticed that this ode in couplets was dedicated to L. Sestius, a former consul: we know he was an ally of Brutus down to Philippi, and that he fought there (*Dio*.53, 32). He was not a consul until 23 BC though, and there is no sign in the poem of such a dignity, so Plancus is not exact, he was a future consul. His father was once defended by Cicero who thought him a morose old boy: the speech *Pro Sestio* has survived. The son also had survived, and Horace remembered his friends.

The other two odes in which Fraenkel (on 4, 7) has observed 'epodic structure' might also seem candidates for the title of 'early', though we shall not conclude that they are: 1, 7 strongly recalls the Chiron poem (*Epod*.13) and the other is about the grave of Archytas (1, 28) which was near Tarentum. The structure or architecture of Horace's poetry is a fascinating subject of study from the *Epodes* on, but 'structure' is not an argument for date. Klingner divides up 1, 4 into stanzas of four lines, but he cannot avoid a sentence running over from the fourth stanza to the last, as they often do between one couplet and the next. Andrew Marvell's poem on the Bermudas on the other hand is often printed without stanza breaks which it demands. Ode 1, 4 should be printed continuously, like an epode.

> Sharp winter drains away: west wind and spring
> Dry ships move seaward trundling,
> No beast in stables or ploughman by his fire,
> In meadows now no frost-glitter.
> Now the moon watches while Venus from Cythera dances,
> Nymphs hand in hand with the nice Graces,
> Light foot-beats, while sad burning Vulcan oversees
> The Cyclops in their factories.
> Now tie green myrtle round your gleaming head
> Or flowers the free earth bears instead
> And sacrifice to Faunus in the wood-shadows
> Ewe-lamb or billy-goat he may propose.
> Pale death kicks with the same foot at the poor man's door
> Dear Sestius, and the King's tower:
> Life's brief sum forbids us any long hope from it,
> Night will press in and the fabulous Spirits,
> And Pluto's narrow house: once you get in
> You will not dice who's to be lord of wine
> Nor be entranced by Lycidas for whom the swarm
> Of boys is hot now, and the girls will warm.

The poem is sad as well as light-hearted, a mixture that the entire Hellenistic world understood and craved. The Romans had toy skeletons to dance at their drinking parties, but I do not know whether they feared death more or less than our world. The stir of the coming of spring was a theme well known to the Greeks, but Sestius was at Philippi, this is more gruff comfort for a fellow soldier. The feast of Faunus is in December, so here he stands for Pan: the beasts of the open field are slaughtered for the god of the wild forest. The poem is a simple, lucid piece of writing, all its ironies are obvious, only the metre Horace chose for it limps a little. The dry ships dragged down to the sea are moved by winches, I suppose, out of their sheds.

The surrounding poems are to Maecenas, to Caesar Augustus, to a girl, and then to Agrippa with a mention of Horace's new friend Varius. The seventh ode in the first book is the very beautiful poem to Plancus. Horace is distinguishing between the cities and islands people love; I will give the interesting version in the Penguin *Horace* by W.G. Shepherd. The poem at first seems to need no comment beyond saying that Tibur was the court's country place, their Windsor, near Rome, and Teucer was Ajax's brother, whom his father exiled from Salamis for letting Ajax die; so Teucer went to Cyprus and founded a new Salamis. This is a curious and perhaps a pregnant tale to choose to recall for Plancus, who was close to Antony and had his own brother killed (or did he only permit his name to be listed?) under the triumvirate. Plancus came over to Octavian's side at the last moment, in 32 BC, so the poem cannot be earlier than that. Augustus thought well of him and as censor he proposed the title Father of the Country, Pater Patriae. He was buried in a tomb of excessive grandeur at Caieta. That is not Horace's concern: he begins with a list of lovely places, in the form of 'Some speak of Alexander and some of Hercules ...' which is old as any verbal form known to the Greeks. He is welcoming Plancus home to Tibur, and to 'apple-orchards wet with running streams', but then in line 15 he starts a transition, cheering up Plancus with wine after his 'sadness and laborious life', and this leads suddenly to Teucer of Salamis. We must assume that the quasi-fratricidal undertone was unconscious, I suppose.

> ... With mellow wine, whether the camp refulgent with
> Standards or your Tibur's dense shade
>
> Now holds or shall hold you. Teucer fleeing from Salamis
> And his father, is said to have twined
> Around his wine-steeped head a poplar crown,
> Addressing thus his grieving friends:
>
> Wheresoever Fortune (my father's better) shall bear us,
> There we shall go, my comrades and peers.
> Under Teucer's fate and command, I never abandon hope.
> Absolute Apollo has promised to Teucer
>
> An unforeseeable Salamis in another country.
> O valiant men who with me have often
> Suffered worse things now drive out care with wine:
> Tomorrow we take to the mighty sea.

It is harsh comfort, and 'take to' in the last line is really 'replough'. What is much more exciting is that the last three lines gave Virgil his inimitable sentence '*O passi graviora, dabit deus his quoque finem*, You that have suffered worse, the god will end this.' There is no doubt about Horace's

priority, as Virgil did not begin work on the *Aeneid* until some years after
Actium. I cannot leave this poem without airing a conjecture that it may be
earlier than we have said. Plancus was Antony's governor of Asia, so it is
possible that Horace met him at Tarentum or at Brindisi in the negotiations
with Antony. It is possible that his changing sides was already in the air: we
do know he abandoned Antony because he disapproved of Cleopatra in the
end. This scenario would fit the poem, yet I know no evidence for it.

The Archytas poem (1, 28) follows the convention that the grave or the
dead man may have a conversation with a passer-by. For twenty lines
someone is talking to one of the ancient sages of Tarentum, who died about
340 BC. He was a mathematician and the 'founder' of mechanics, but he was
also a Pythagorean, hence the references to reincarnation. Now he is buried
on the sea-coast; Matinum was a region of Apulia, maybe in the area of
modern Mattinata on Mount Garganos. Ancient scholars guessed it was a
'Calabrian mountain or peninsula', but Lucan (9, 182) talks of the Apulian
renewing his winter grass by burning, and 'Garganus and the fields of Voltur
and the shining cattle-fields [*buceta*] of Matinum' so it may lie south of
Brindisi towards Otranto on the low-lying heel of Italy. It is certainly
somewhere in Horace's remembered, childhood world, because 'the woods of
Venusium' feel the storm-blast (26). It is only after the first twenty-two lines
that we realise the ironic and hostile address to Archytas is spoken by the
dead body of a drowned sailor, who at the end of the poem menaces and
beseeches the passer-by for the three handfuls of earth that will cover him.
The ghost turning nasty suggests the epode, but real tombstones provide
plenty of evidence for this among other lines as the one a writer of epitaphs
may take. It is a world of popular poetry and belief that is as wild and
amazing as that in which Horace's classic calm prevails, and Horace is
always conscious of it. All the same, I do think this is more like an epode than
the mature poem that Fraenkel discerns in the trick of not telling us who is
talking. The ancient Greek commentary on the *Antigone* of Sophocles makes
it clear that those who passed by and left the dead unburied could traditionally be cursed. Here he is a sailor (23), but what the whole diatribe has to do
with Archytas is a conundrum. He is linked to Tantalos father of Pelops,
Tithonos and Minos, all privileged though all dead in the end, but the bizarre
and Greek flow of thought does recall popular verse.

It was necessary to deal with these three odes if only symbolically, so that
the reader realises Horace's development into the mature poet that he swiftly
became was not specialised to one type of poem, but overflowed into other
kinds. We have seen that the poem under Brutus in Asia and the lively one
about the fig-tree stump are epigrams overgrown into something else. Yet
among the *Satires* where their metre fixes them they are noticeably brief.
There are two books of *Satires* by Horace, the second of them showing an
astonishing technical ease and sophistication as opposed to the first, but
there is no clear criterion for dating the first book. If it is to be connected with
the farm in the Sabine hills that Maecenas gave him, then it could have been
finished by 31 BC before Caesar had resettled his veteran soldiers: and there
is some reason to suppose this. Fraenkel thinks the first epode hints at this

resettlement, and surely the sixth satire of the second book does so. One of the enigmas of Horace's life is his relationship with Maecenas; it was to Maecenas he dedicated the *Satires* as well as the *Epodes*, and the timing could be first book one of the *Satires*, then the present of a farm, and then Actium, the *Epodes* and the early *Odes*. That would make Horace terribly active in his early thirties, but there is nothing against that. The *Epodes* are a much stranger, more heterogeneous book than the *Satires* and there were not many of them; in some ways they are more intimate than the *Satires*, so it would be prudent to publish the *Satires* first and to hold back the *Epodes*. I suspect that is what happened, but readers are left to make up their own minds.

When we enquire what relationships were usual between poets and Roman magnates, we find the Epicurean Greek poet Philodemos settling at Rome under the protection of the Pisos, one of whom bought him a very grand house at Herculaneum, and a little later we find him influential over young Roman poets, even in politics, in which he was republican. He died about 35 BC. He was an eminence to Siron, head of the school of philosophers among whom Virgil flourished, and scholars discern his influence on Varius and others, yet he never seems to have moved from the shadow of the Pisos at Herculaneum. Gallus was a Knight with a political career, which ended in his suicide in 26 BC after he over-reached himself in Egypt. Parthenius was a prisoner of war sold as a slave but then let free. It is not clear who looked after him in Italy, but he is said to have taught Virgil. Virgil himself was a client of Pollio and of Gallus then a member of the intimate circle of Maecenas, so was Varius, who was extravagantly rewarded by Augustus after Actium for his tragedy *Thyestes*; Virgil and Varius were taken over by Augustus, and there was an attempt to take over Horace made by the Emperor, which failed. Suetonius who wrote most about poets was an imperial secretary familiar with the archives of the Caesars, but he has no high view of poetry. He tells us Vespasian was very generous: he paid a hundred thousand a year to teachers of rhetoric, Latin or Greek, and poets and actors he would buy. He sneers that Horace insinuated himself into the friendship first of Maecenas, then of Augustus. We know that is not quite right. But Horace did live for a time in Maecenas's close friendship almost like a member of his household. We shall be able to trace many aspects of their relationship.

Maecenas was a Roman Knight and Etruscan nobleman; he was by profession an agent of Augustus from the siege of Perugia onwards, and a diplomat by temperament pacific. He came from Arrezzo, was or became enormously rich, and married Terentia the sister of Varro Murena. Augustus had an affair with her, and she is thought to have heard from her husband and told her brother that his treasonable conspiracy had been uncovered, so Varro Murena and Fannius Caepio came to a sticky end around 23 BC. Maecenas is supposed to have experienced a coldness from Augustus after that, but nothing confirms it and we shall see that Horace's behaviour is an argument against it. Maecenas was a poet of a kind in the Catullan school, but not by serious standards any good. He was sleepless, nightingales and music and running water could not sometimes bring him sleep. The best description of him occurs casually in Tacitus, who is dealing with Crispus, the nephew and adopted son of Sallust the historian (*Ann.*3, 30). 'He although he had an easy way to honours, imitated Maecenas, so that without the dignity of the Senate he outdid in power many who had triumphed and many who had been consuls, differing from old traditions of neatness and attentive care with an abundance and affluence that came close to luxury. Yet there was an underlying energy to his mind that was equal to great affairs, and all the keener the more show he made of sleep and lethargy. Therefore while Maecenas was alive he was the second man, but he soon became the chief repository of imperial secrets, and he knew all about the killing of Postumus Agrippa, and as age advanced held on more to the appearance of the Emperor's friendship than to real force.' One must understand that the transition was from Augustus to Tiberius: Postumus was the son of the great Agrippa born after his father's death in 12 BC, but Augustus first adopted and then disinherited him for wildness, the Senate exiled him, and he was put to death as soon as Augustus had died.

With Maecenas Horace remained on excellent terms. While his friend whizzed here and there on Caesar's business, Horace followed when invited, beaming amiably. Maecenas was a highly complicated man, but Horace was quite content to observe and explore him, and to offer a friendship as genuine as if they had been on equal terms. For whatever reason, and however amicably they were to exchange letters, he never chose to come so close to Augustus. The seasick man they say should never visit the engine-room of the ship he is sailing in. There is at least a shadow of Epicurean philosophy in the *Satires*, which he appears to offer his friend as a kind of therapy, a remedy for anxieties. Octavian himself after all had wanted to take over where Cicero had left off in a full exchange of letters with that old lizard of a man Atticus.

The first satire of the first book is a kind of manifesto piece or almost a contents page; it is addressed to Maecenas.

> How is it Maecenas that no one,
> Whatever fortune offers or reason
> Has given, lives with that fate contented,
> But everyone praises someone else's trade?
> O happy merchants! the old soldier cries
> With all his bones broken with victories,
> Yet the merchant when the gale drowns the boat
> Dies with O happy soldier! in his throat,
> One moment death or victory, then rest!
> The lawyer thinks the farmer's life is best ...

It is the most innocent exercise in moral philosophy. A god offers them all the role they crave in life, and of course they all want to change back to the one they had before. It is all written in a charming, lively verse of some polish but not too much, recalling the way Plato tells us stories when he is in the mood.

Teachers give boys a biscuit and they learn.
But we mean something serious. Well then, turn
Back to these ploughmen, sailors and so on;
They bear their work in and out of season
In order to be idle in old age ...
... No heat is hot enough to bar you from gain,
Not winter nor fire nor the sea nor iron
As long as someone's pile's more than your own.
Then why that gold, that silver pound by pound
Dug up then buried in the secret ground?

Grain by grain, point by point, he insists, he sticks his philosophic knife in deeper: and yet this does not really cover the contents of his first book of satires, indeed it fits better with the second book, as is no doubt to be expected since dedication pieces like this are generally written last. The argument moves from one example to another yet it remains the same. 'You prefer a big pile of grain, a big source of water? Then Aufidus will carry you away.' Tantalus is an example, and we know that this at least comes from Lucilius, who was the first to philosophise his verse in this way: scholars have classed the little story as Stoic, but Teles uses it too and it belongs to the general store of Hellenistic moral philosophy.

When Tantalus opens his lips to drink
Rivers run past him yet he cannot drink:
You laugh at him? Only alter the name,
The story is about you, and the same ...

His examples are abundant, his story-telling varied. We hear of the miser Ummidius whose ex-slave woman split him down the middle, of Naevius the miser from Lucilius, and Nomentanus the spendthrift whose cook Sallust the historian bought for a fortune. Horace believes in what Aristotle called 'the mean', the path that avoids extremes.

The man who has lived happy and with zest
Departs from life like a full dinner guest:
It is curiously hard to find that man ...

One more quick couplet and the show is over, in a hundred and twenty-one lines of amicable discourse that he could have directed at anyone: he offers it to Maecenas not as a sermon, but as entertainment. When we get a little deeper into his book, the unusual variety and energy of which this form is capable will strike us more forcibly.

Fraenkel gives a full analysis of the second satire, which after an opening that misleads, begins again (5) with a diatribe of some twenty-five lines against lack of balance. Horace uses parody of Ennius (37f.) as he began with one of Homer. The subject of the mass of the satire, the next hundred lines, is to be sex. 'Colleges of flute-women, medicine-sellers, Beggars, ballet-men,

wallowers, all that kind ...' he begins. There is an allusion to the Self-re-
venger, a play by Terence, then the transition to sex is like this:

> ... Rufillus stinks of scent, Gargonius goat.
> No middle road. Some will not touch a lady
> Unless her ankles under skirts are shady.
> Another wants a smelly brothel whore:
> When someone he knew came out of that door,
> Well done old boy, were Cato's words divine.
> When filthy lust comes flooding through the vein
> This is the place where young men ought to come,
> Not screw other men's wives ...

Jokes about Cato and his sayings were numerous, and his 'words divine',
sententia dia Catonis, are a grand archaism. Horace has a number of rather
strong-smelling jokes to make once he is embarked on the subject, Galba the
lawyer who speaking as an adulterer said he opposed the penalty of castra-
tion, Sallust the historian's nephew who had a craze for ex-slave women,
Marsaeus who was Origenes's lover (who gave house and home away to an
actor) but swore he never touched a married woman, and so on.

> Don't mess your father or the family name:
> Aren't married women and decent girls the same?

His examples creep close to home: Sulla's son-in-law Villius and his rival
Longarenus must have been a famous tale. Horace proceeds in this poem by
worldly wisdom, it is not extremes he is attacking, he just says at the end as
at the beginning that adultery is mighty dangerous. As Fraenkel points out
he is not drawing on fresh experience, but pursuing an artificially chosen,
well-worn theme. Lejay quotes a long passage from a Greek comedy by
Philemon which is relevant. It is probable enough that Horace is trying to
match Lucilius in openness of speech, as in a way he does, and also in relating
his poetry to real life which he hardly does, because the realities he treats are
never quite what happened yesterday or to him. Still the climax of the poem
gets better marks from Fraenkel, if only for its *brio*, and he likes the insult
to Cerinthos.

> ... Nor between snow pearls and greenstones has more
> (Though you may have, Cerinthos) than a whore
> In shaped young leg or thigh you could adore ... (80-2)
> ... So while I fuck I do not have to fear
> Her man come home to take me in the rear,
> And the dog barks as he breaks the door in
> And the entire house echoes with the din,
> His wife leaps from the bed turning quite white,
> Cries Oh, fears being beaten on the feet:
> Me torn tunic, no belt, barefoot, sensation,

Fear for my arse, and money, and reputation.

It cannot be denied that Horace either stuck in the beginning to show he was worried about 'the mean', or else started out with the best intentions and the subject took over. He had said (24),

> Whenever these fools find a vice they fly
> And run at once into its contrary.

But it is a tricky matter to follow or even to define 'the mean' in sexual behaviour and Horace has used material he could scarcely have conscripted into poetry in any other way. Philemon in his play brought in Solon the great lawgiver of Athens rather as Horace brought in Cato, but Horace is more dashing and racier. Can Lucilius have been very much better?

The third satire is moral in the same way, and it takes some musing to reach its true subject, which is tolerance between friends.

> All singers have one vice: upon request
> They will not sing: unasked they won't desist.
> Tigellius the old Sardinian
> Had that fault: Caesar could command the man
> Yet begged for his father's friendship and his own
> And got nowhere. If he chose he went on
> From egg mayonnaise to apples, *Io Bacche!*
> From the top note to the bottom all the way.
> There was no balance about that man,
> Often like one pursued he ran and ran
> Then other times he could proceed as slow
> As a priest in the procession of Juno,
> And now two hundred slaves, now he had ten,
> Now Kings and Tetrarchs and grand words, now halt,
> A three-legged table and a shell of salt,
> And a coarse toga that keeps out the cold.
> All night long till the dawn broke he pored
> Over a book, and then all day he snored.
> No man was ever so inconsistent.
> 'What about you then? No vices? Content
> With different vices, and maybe lesser.'
> Maenius attacked Novius who wasn't there,
> So someone said 'And you? Don't you really know
> Yourself, or do you speak as Ignoto?'
> 'Oh, I forgive myself,' Maenius said.
> Foolish self-love, blameworthy and wicked. (1-24)

We have reached the heart of the matter: we observe every vice in a friend with the eyes of an eagle or the diagnostic snake of Asklepios. When the holy ship brought the god to Rome in the fourth century to set up his hospital he arrived in the form of this clever snake, but alas that is all we shall hear about him; Horace was not devout to snakes. When he has thoroughly ventilated the need for mutual tolerance (72), he moves on to insist against the Stoics that there is a crucial difference between small faults and seriously offensive ones. Once again, the structure of the poem is the thing to watch, because that of the argument follows it. The last section of the poem, which I think of as 120-142, is written with gaiety and glee, but the argument against the view that all sins are equal is vigorous and convincing, and one has only to compare it with such writers as Augustine and the rest of later moralists, to see what a pleasure it is to be reading this decent, sensible and funny poet (99-120). Horace is at his best on the origins of law and society, of which he takes a Darwinian view and explodes the Stoic idea of 'nature'.

> When the first brutes crept on the first ground,
> Disgraceful herd without one meaning sound,
> They fought with nail and fist for nut and bed,
> Then clubs and then with armaments instead.
> They then invented word and sound and sense,
> The town and law: so much for innocence.
> No more thieving and no adultery:
> Cunts had caused wars before Helen you see,
> But in those days they perished unrecorded
> In herds the big bull wholly overlorded,
> And Law came from the fear of lawlessness:
> The ages of the world evolved like this,
> Nature knows not the just from the unfair
> Or how to deal out good, what to acquire
> Or what to flee, and reason is no use,
> With the same sin to steal young cabbages
> Or desecrate the gods of mysteries ...

The poem ends with much jeering at the wisest and best of men who is supposed to be the happiest and the King; Horace says the Stoics thought this man, greatest of philosophers, was a cobbler, and I must report that there is evidence in Greek for this curious view. Horace makes a lot of jokes about this Rex, here as in the seventh satire. There was a Roman version of the children's rhyme 'I'm the King of the Castle, Get down you dirty rascal', which is at the back of his mind. The people in this poem existed though Maenius was already lampooned by Lucilius. The bad philosopher mocked at the end, Crispinus, was an even worse poet, in the fourth satire.

The fourth satire is about satire: that is, this is the first poem we have seen (apart from some lyrical boasting) that begins to establish the huge proportion of his work that he devoted to the art of poetry and to criticism. His self-defence or self-description is more about the moral position of a satiric poet than about his literary position. This seems to me admirable, and I imitated his emphasis on the morality of satire in a poem I wrote many years ago for the television series *That was the week, that was*. I say this not as a

boast nor to compare small things with great, but to emphasise that one will
do well to take Horace perfectly seriously. His poem begins with the splendid
line 'Aristophanes, Cratinus, Eupolis ...' and it would be fair to admit that at
this point in the book I first feel completely at home. Admittedly the poem
has a hidden programme: Horace begins with the resounding names of
Athenian fifth-century comedians and to them he swiftly attaches Lucilius;
it seems to the reader a proper but a slightly academic treatment, but it is
suddenly transformed by Horace's confession that personally he picked up
his satiric habit from his father's criticisms of the Roman world, which of
course were a way of educating the young man. In fact it is surely usual that
one learns what to think of people and their behaviour from one's father, is
it not?

> Cratinus, Aristophanes, Eupolis,
> All those writers of early comedies
> If a man was blameworthy, bad or a thief
> Adulterer, knifer, or in their belief
> Infamous, they described them in writing:
> On this depends Lucilius, following
> His own rhythms and metres and joking,
> Nobody's fool, robust at making verse,
> And there his fault lies, two hundred or worse
> Composed in one hour standing on one leg:
> A muddy river needs embanking, but big,
> Prunable, talkative, lazy at writing
> At least at writing well: that he wrote a lot
> I admit, but here comes Crispinus, the sot
> And challenges, 'Choose paper, place and hour
> And umpires, and we'll see who writes the more ...'

I have a tiny mind, says Horace, and few words, but you are a bellows to heat
iron: do as you like. I fear recitations because a lot of people dislike my kind
of writing: most of them are avaricious or ambitious, so they fear verses, they
hate poets.

> There's something of another side to this,
> A poet doesn't just finish verses
> Or write as I do much as he would speak:
> Think a man is a poet if you like
> Who has some genius, and some godlike mind,
> Who has the mouth to utter a great sound:
> Give him the honour of a poet's name.
> Comedy and poetry may not be the same,
> The bite and force not in the word or thing,
> So without rhythm it would be mere talking ...

This is not the most stringent part of the satire, but it is often quoted, and no doubt it is interesting to see that Horace quite deliberately comes close to 'mere talking'. Lucilius had already used the word *sermones*, conversations, for his verse (which I translate here as talking), and Horace calls his book 'conversations' or 'talks' though it soars and swoops to high as well as low levels, and in this he chiefly differs from writers like Pope, and perhaps every other translator. He does not write with that hammer-blow force, line by line, which would allow his *Satires* to work in English blank verse; that dubious triumph was reserved for Juvenal in a more decadent age, and is wonderfully repeated in English by Robert Lowell. Once you have the trick of a single line of Juvenal you can go on to do the whole poem, because there is only that trick. Horace slides, meanders, muses, roars like Niagara, he is full of subtle twists and English writers have seldom made much of the *Satires*; that does not mean that they are less than the greatest of Latin literature and the most enjoyable.

Pure Latin is not enough, he says (54). If you change the order of words in these *Satires* or in Lucilius you will not discover once the metre is dissolved 'the torn limbs of a poet dismembered' (63), as you would with 'Discord most foul broke ope War's iron gate' (which is Ennius, and which Virgil imitated). Horace will now go on to consider whether one is right to suspect this kind of poetry. He does not seek vulgar publicity for his works, but why should any decent man fear them? It is secret slander we should all fear: Horace has not attacked any fellow-guest.

> If I speak freely and maybe laugh a bit
> You must forgive me on one ground for it,
> My dearest father taught me the habit ... (105)

This gives the satire a second wind for its last forty lines. Horace is like a racehorse romping home, since he has won the argument. Later, as we shall see in the last satire of this book, Horace will come to realise that 'naming the guilty men' is not the be-all and end-all of the art of satire even for Lucilius. Fraenkel used to think that the letter to Augustus, which was among his last works, was the masterpiece of his hexameters, and I would not disagree, yet while I am reading earlier poems I am extremely fond of this, seduced perhaps by Horace's reading of ancient comedy, and the poets he prefers, not all of whose works have come down to us, but whose fragments convert all students with any sense to his preference for 'early' comedy; seduced also maybe by the subtle, rippling procedure of his verse in this poem.

> 'The wise man says what to avoid or seek
> And why, for me it is enough to keep
> The manners of an antique world young man
> And your life, your fame, as your guardian:
> When you are strong you'll swim without a cork,'
> I was educated with this kind of talk ...
> ... Young minds grow strong

Out of observing other people's vice;
My middling pardonable sort of vice
Has grown to second nature ...
... I muse, and in an hour of idleness
I play on paper. Middling vice, no less!
And if you do not like it I'm afraid
I can call crowds of poets to my aid,
We are like Jews, a Jew you shall be made.

Horace's view of Roman Jews is of no great consequence: they occur a number of times in his *Satires*, and in this case Cicero (*Pro Flac.*66) confirms that they were thought to be a sinister force like a secret society. Here they are only a joke to conclude the poem.

The fifth satire is apparently the most famous, and it has certainly seemed to me the most re-readable for nearly fifty years: but that no doubt is just a habit. It is full of incident, it has no moral content that stands out from it, it is just the description of a journey, an Epicurean view of dear friends, a snapshot for posterity. It is certainly modelled on book three of Lucilius, who was going to Sicily and took the western route 'What you longed to see, the Straits, Messana, The walls of Reggio, and Lipari ...' (102-4). Part of Lucilius's route was by sea 'All play, all up and down, all down and up, A game, a joke: the other way's hard work – Goat mountains, Etnas, awful Athoses'. But Horace went at first by the Appian Way then by a curious route to Brindisi, and in the south Maecenas made a treaty (40 BC) between Augustus, whose first marriage he had just arranged, and Mark Antony. In 37 BC he made a second treaty with Antony at Tarentum, after a diplomatic mission to him in 38 BC, and a number of scholars, who I suspect have been misled, believe that the journey in this poem happened on that occasion. It will be better to settle this matter at the end of the chapter. As usual, readers may choose for themselves. It is interesting on what intimate terms Horace shows himself to be with the great man, and yet how little really this affects his daily routine, and how remote the great man's business seems to be from the poem, which reads like a modern diary. He takes fifteen days to get to the walled city of Brundisium, by a route that diverges from the Appian Way from Beneventum; the longest distances in a day are the last two days, from Bari to Brindisi with a halt at Gnatia, thirty-seven miles one day and thirty-nine the next. That is done with horses, but the jump across the mountain from Beneventum to Canusium (Canosa) seems to have been accomplished by being carried, in four-wheeled carriages (86) not in 'litters' as Cowper imagines, over unpaved mule-tracks. Lucilius had slid past the Cape of Palinurus past Paestum and its marshes by sea, and arrived in half the time. Had Lucilius gone by land, as Cato did to his Lucanian estate, he would have travelled by the Via Popilia, which would not have been so easy. The point of Horace's route, which left the Appian Way and struck across the mountains well north-west of Venusia, was to get as soon as possible to the coastal plain where such a party could make better speed. There is a Roman

road that has been traced from Beneventum making straight across, called
the Via Traiana, but that had not yet been built.

> We reached Aricia out from great Rome
> And a middling inn; I had set out from home
> With Heliodorus whose skill was to speak,
> Of all alive by far the most scholarly Greek:
> Then Appius's Forum, full up then
> With sailors and malignant merchantmen.
> We did this journey in two days, lazily,
> Athletes take one, but the Appian's best gently
> Addressed; though here the water was filthy
> My stomach goes to war with me and sends
> No peaceful news, we dine waiting for friends.
> Night shadows earth and spreads stars in the sky
> Slave boys and sailors curse and time goes by.
> 'Pull in.' 'Three hundred eh?' 'That's enough now.'
> Money collected, the mule tied up, and so
> An entire hour goes, marsh frog and mosquito
> Drive away sleep, far gone in drink sailor
> Sings of his love somewhere, then traveller
> Protests and then he sleeps, the mule grazes
> Rope loose, the sailor ties it to a stone
> And lies down on his back to snore alone.
> Day came, we felt the barge was not moving,
> Some angry man arose, started beating
> Mule and sailor with a strong willow wand:
> About four hours Feronia, in your pond
> We wash our hands and faces, lunch, three miles
> And then the glittering rocks and dark defiles
> Of Anxur ...

The poem feels as if it could go on for ever, with occasional verses of real
poetry about the stars or the rocks and the slow narrative. Lucilius is livelier
but this is unique in its feeling for slowness and in such images as the frogs
and the mosquitoes, and the poor mule. There were plenty of mocking or
jokey verses about mosquitoes or even frogs, but this scene has a needling
realism. Every place has its anecdote: at Anxur they met Maecenas with
Cocceius and Fonteius Capito; Cocceius was consul in 39 BC and at present a
diplomat: their mission was 'to bring friends together', that is Antony and
Caesar; the year was now 40 BC. Capito, 'perfect gentleman' as Horace calls
him, was Antony's viceroy in Asia. The party is now grander, and at Formiae
they stay at the house of Varro Murena, a kinsman of Maecenas by adoption.
But it was the next day that was 'by far the best' because at Sinuessa they
met Plotius and Varius and Virgil.

... Souls more sincere and free
Earth never bore, nor closer tied to me.
What embraces and what pleasures happened!
There's nothing I'd compare to a smiling friend.

At Bridge of Campania Maecenas went off to play ball, but Virgil and Horace, with weak stomach and bad eyes, went quietly to sleep.

An anecdote of nearly twenty lines (50-70) records a rustic entertainment by a pair of buffoons treated in a mock-heroic style which is beyond my powers to translate. Cowper made a dashing attack on this whole poem, but he calls his version an imitation, and it is not quite complete. Horace has more variation of tone, he is not always light-hearted. They took 'the straight road' (71) to Beneventum, where the kitchen went on fire as thrushes were being roasted for their dinner. It may be worth pointing out that diplomatic dinners took a lot of organising: Plutarch's grandfather saw twelve wild boar turning on spits for Antony at Alexandria, but when he remarked what a huge party he was told it was just for eight, but Antony required his boar done to a turn, and since he never knew in advance when he would wish to dine, this was the cook's way of playing safe.

From here Apulia revealed my good
Hills the sirocco burns, we never would
Have got across but a country house nearby
Invited us: fire-smoke and weeping eye
Came next from wet wood boughs and burning leaf,
And here I waited up, what crass folly,
Till midnight for a girl who lied to me.
Sleepless, intent on love, and then lay down
And slept: a dirty dream stained my night-gown.

It is sometimes said that this frank and unusual anecdote exists here in imitation of something similar in Lucilius, but that is not at all clear, and depends on the difficult and meticulous sorting of fragments of that author into the right order. What Lucilius said may come from a different context altogether. I think we must accept that in this account of his journey Horace has a right to be entertaining and to embroider, but that on the whole things happened as he says. The lonely house with the smoky fire where no guests were expected certainly rings true. Of course it is interesting to us so long afterwards to get a glimpse of what it felt like to be a Roman, and to live through all these things, so it is the fact that Horace is ordinary, not the fact that he is extraordinary, that we value in the *Satires*. And it suits him also to emphasise this aspect, because the self, the portrait he presents, is the basis of his *persona* as a moral philosopher. At times it is fascinating to us to observe some simple fact of Roman life. Earlier they have probably been in coaches, and now they clearly are, and flying. How can this be before Trajan built the road across the hills? To me this is a real puzzle, and I must suppose that an earlier road existed which was negotiable by a horse-drawn carriage, an Italian, non-military, pre-Roman mercantile road. They must have existed before the Romans in Italy as they did in Britain. Unfortunately Horace is coy about place-names because they will not fit his metre, and we have no way of knowing what exact route he took at this point.

They stayed in a little town where water was abundant, and bread so delicious that sensible travellers carried it with them to Canosa, where eating the bread was like gnawing gravel, and the water was not wonderful. 'Here Varius must leave his weeping friends.' They arrived tired at 'Rubi', which is now called Ruvo, but he does not say Ennius was born there, and maybe he does not know. The journey was long and rain made it worse. As the weather cleared, the road deteriorated, until 'fishy Bari's battlement'. Horace says the road then led them to Gnatia, built when the nymphs were angry: that is to Egnatia in Apulia (at last) where the water (*lymphae* = *nymphae* as an inscription from Vicenza shows) was poor. This is to modern observation untrue of Torre d'Agnazzo, but when one is tired old jokes like familiar friends or even bad jokes are best, and this is both. There one is supposed to believe that the incense melts and smells without fire in the temple, but Horace thinks that is a Jewish superstition. If anything queer happens in nature, he says, it is not the gods who bring it about. Brindisi is 'the end of this long journey this paper'. It will be seen that ever since the mountains around Venusia came into view, he has been galloping, and the last few days have gone by at a furious pace. I do not think the entire poem is much more than a sketchy portrait of poets in a landscape, but it is mysteriously gripping. Some of its meaning is supplied by the next poem.

The sixth satire is one of gratitude to Maecenas, 'The fact that no Lydian who colonised the Etruscan country was ever more noble or generous than you, Maecenas, and that your grandparents on both sides commanded great legions, do not make you look down on unknowns like me, as many people do, son of an ex-slave as I am. Snobbery is nonsense: how should we behave, far, far removed as we are from the mob? People prefer to vote for an aristocrat, and if my father is not freeborn, Appius the Censor would throw me out of office, if I had it: and rightly so, for not sitting quiet in my own skin.' Lucilius has something to do with the examples, but scarcely with the precise arguments. Horace goes on to discuss distinctions of dress and the bad feeling they may attract, and the honour of magistracy and special seats in the theatre. It goes without saying that the world he is discussing is not our world: it is small enough and crowded enough to be venomously envious, and to avoid popular envy in it you must be circumspect.

> I return to myself, son of an ex-slave
> Who is sneered at as son of an ex-slave
> Now Maecenas because I share your life
> And in the past because the drum and fife
> Of a Roman legion played me their own tune
> Whom I commanded then as their tribune

It is not right: it is not just an honour to have Maecenas for a friend, since he is particularly careful about who he takes on (51). 'I cannot say it was good luck won me your friendship or chance of any kind. It was my dear Virgil ...' He tells the story as I have already translated it. 'I count it a great matter that I pleased you who discern the decent from the nasty, not by the illustrious father but the pure heart and life. If my nature has a few middling faults but is good otherwise, if I am dear to my friends, the cause was my father, and the education he gave me. He brought me to Rome and he himself was my unbribable guardian with all the teachers. I suffered no disgrace and no shadow of it. He was not frightened anyone would blame us if I became an auctioneer or an auctioneer's collector, as he had been. Nor would I have complained, all the more praise to him and thanks from me.' No doubt the verse does add to this, but it is written in letters of fire, and would have the same effect in prose. 'I do not regret having had such a father. If we had to live our lives over again, I would choose him and not nobility, crazy as I would be thought. Who wants the burden of getting more, making more acquaintances, getting companions, feeding horses, buying carriages? As it is I can go on a gelded mule to Tarentum if I choose with a bag making sores on his side and a rider sores on his back. I do better than you great senator and a thousand others. I go where I want, I walk alone, I ask the price of flour and produce, in the tricky circus or the forum at evening, I attend service, and go home to leeks and peas and pastry for dinner: three boys to serve it and a marble slab, two glasses and a jug, a cheap flask, a dripper, Campanian ware. Then I go and sleep, and I don't care about getting up tomorrow. I lie until ten in the morning, then I wander about, I read or write in silence, I anoint with oil, and when the sharpening sun bids me I go to bathe, not the Campus or the ball-game. I have a little lunch, just enough not to fast all day, I idle at home. This is the life of the unambitious. I console myself that like this I shall live happier than if my grandfather and my great-uncles had all been state officers.'

The poem is not very long, but it turns very smoothly in its hundred and twenty-one lines from the thanks to Maecenas to the gratitude to his father, and from that to the self-portrait of twenty-one lines, which are most endearing, and perhaps the best-written piece of the kind the world had ever seen. One can spot Lucilius here and there behind a word or a phrase, but the personality is purely Horace. Of course if it was written so soon after Philippi as 40 BC it comes early among the satires. Horace's view of himself is young, and his father has not long been dead. There is something almost religious, or as he would say philosophic about his contentment. Even his food sounds enviable, and the reading and writing that he says he silently enjoys are the same now as then. The oil before bathing or before exercise is a queer custom to us, but it was surely sweet-smelling. Of the whole first book it may be this satire or the fourth is the very best, but the journey to Brindisi is a pleasure, and we have not yet exhausted Horace's variety; for better or for worse he gives the impression that he has set himself boundaries in his satires which he will now try to break.

The seventh satire is the earliest of all, and the eighth must I believe be nearly as early. One is about the argument in Asia under Brutus, and the

other about Canidia: we have mentioned them already, and there is no more
to say except that by being mere anecdotes they alter the balance of the book
towards a lighter and less formal kind of poetry. The ninth satire is the most
trivial story of all: it is about how to get rid of a bore. What interests us about
it is simply the antiquarian information it contains, and the play of characters. It is admittedly written with great charm. No one can know who the bore
is, though the Italian scholar Volpi (1755) convinced himself it was Propertius, who was only between four and fourteen years old at the time. Lucilius
is not thought to have any hand in it, and it remains a mild, satiric, social
observation, though the philosopher Zeno gets sharply attacked in passing in
a parody of an oracle (31-4). It is impossible not to quote the seductive
opening lines.

> Wandering the Sacred Way as I often do,
> Quite wrapped up in – I do not really know –
> Some nonsense ...

The bore is someone Horace knows by name, who wants, as Suetonius would
put it, to insinuate himself into the circle in which he knows the poet moves.
'Did you want something?' 'You know us scholars.' By line 10 Horace is
suffering torture and trying hard to escape. 'I have to visit someone you don't
know, He lives over the Tiber far away By Caesar's gardens.' 'Just as you say;
I have nothing to do, I'll come your way ...' The gardens were the ones Caesar
left to the Roman people, now therefore a public landmark. We know a good
deal about gardens around Rome, not only from Plutarch but from Cicero who
was negotiating to buy one for his wife's monument, though close to Rome
they were becoming harder to acquire. Augustus kept mammoth bones and
such natural wonders in a temple in these gardens and Pausanias went there
to see them. In Horace's poem of course it is the most casual reference, like
saying 'beyond Regent's Park'. He turned down his ears, he says, like a
donkey intent on wickedness. 'No one can write verses as many or as quickly
as me. You will esteem me like Varius. No one can dance as softly, and
Hermogenes may envy my singing ...'

> 'Have you a mother or a family
> Who need you alive?' 'I have nobody,
> I buried them all.' 'Lucky them. Now I'm left.
> Knife me! I feel that fate hovers aloft.
> The Sabine woman sang to me when young:
> Not poison nor the sword shall sort him out
> Not coughing nor hurt ribs nor the slow gout
> But someone talkative shall do for him,
> Beware such men during all your lifetime.'

The old woman drew lots to tell his fortune which she shook up in an urn.
One could have it done at Praeneste in a temple of truly baroque grandeur,
or one could have it from any old Sabine woman in a hut. They now pass the

temple of Vesta (35), where the bore has a case coming on, but he prefers to neglect it and cling to Horace's company. 'How do you get on with Maecenas? (43) I could be an ally there.' They meet Fuscus Aristius, a friend of Horace to whom both an ode (1, 22) and the tenth letter were dedicated, but he refuses help, this being the Sabbath (69-70); at last someone serves a summons on the bore and Horace is free. 'So Apollo saved me.' There is no sense in belabouring this trivial piece, particularly in view of what follows it. The subject must have been conventional and may come from comedy. Plutarch discusses how to deal with them. 'Am I boring you, Aristotle?' 'Sorry not at all, I wasn't listening.' 'How do you like your hair cut, Sir?' 'In silence.'

The opening of the tenth satire and the last of this book refers in clear terms to the discussion of Lucilius in the fourth. The opinions he lays out now are sternly classical, and Lucilius gets only limited praise. In this satire for the first time he begins to show his powers as a critic.

> Yes I did say Lucilius's verse
> Can stumble. Who so loves Lucilius
> As not to admit that? It was a fault
> And yet he rubbed the city down with salt
> And I praise him for that on the same page.
> That doesn't mean I grant every passage,
> Which means agreeing Laberius's mimes
> Must be the loveliest poems of our times ...

Laberius sticks in one's throat, because the only substantial fragment of him that we have is one of the most thrilling bits of Latin I have ever read. Admittedly it was exceptional: he was a Knight and a member of the old nobility who wrote mimes (of which really we know nothing); Julius Caesar compelled him in old age to appear himself on the Roman stage in a production of one of his own works. Why? Was it a whim or was there a reason? Laberius did of course appear but he made a 'curtain speech' as we would say, of extraordinary and eloquent ferocity. It is a very moving speech, and one must simply suppose that Horace had never heard of it. Aulus Gellius the antiquarian quotes it, but our business is only with Horace.

> It is not enough to make them laugh at you,
> Though even that I admit is a virtue:
> You must be brief and never overburdened
> With words that leave ears weary in the end.
> You need sad conversation and some jest
> Taking their turn as the elocutionist
> And the poet, at times urbanity:
> Spare yourself, thin your flow deliberately.
> A joke cuts better than sharpness like a knife
> Through serious matters, I have found in life.
> Those men who wrote the early comedies
> Took a stand and are worth copying in this.

> Pretty Hermogenes and his monkey-face
> Who only crows 'Calvus and Catullus'
> Have never read the men of whom I speak.
> 'But what an achievement to mix Latin and Greek.'
> O slow to learn ...

As Fraenkel used to point out, and as he writes in his *Horace*, the point is that the poet hated the fashionable habit of poetry that drew only on Hellenistic views: he wanted to go back for his model to fifth-century Athenian comedy. On what evidence we have, Horace was perfectly right, but of course the enterprise is difficult; between Rome and the fifth century stood Plato, and Horace was as inclined to draw what he could from philosophy as he was to write really as Aristophanes wrote. Or let us say that at Plato's *Symposium* he would have been seduced by Socrates even more than he would have been drawn to Aristophanes. At least that is my own feeling in the matter. I am not certain though that Horace's severe rules for conversation in this satire so far apply to ordinary social talk. He seems to be talking only about poetry, even if he means *sermones*, conversations, and yet for a moment he discusses rhetoric or grand discourse. When he talks about humour he has just mentioned Laberius and the stage, and he has the poets of early comedy in mind as examples, but for whom? The furious line about those who know only to chant the names of Calvus and Catullus is not a rejection of Catullus, who has after all led Horace to ancient lyric. He rejects only an insufferable clique, as one might have spoken in the 1950s of young English poets starry-eyed about Lorca.

In this poem Horace has an eye from the beginning on definite targets; so far these are only sighting shots. Laberius and Catullus and Calvus belonged it seems to the same generation, which I suspect, or the cult of which, irritated Horace and his friends and allies. The next few lines are complicated by a confusion of the text: the case of Petillius, the late Pedius who died as consul in 43 BC and was one of Caesar's heirs, being a nephew, and Poplicola Messalla Corvinus, a friend of Horace since his Athens days. Messalla had written Greek bucolic poetry but his Latin was stringently pure. The point of this sentence, however one works out its details, is Horace's strong opposition to mixtures of Greek and Latin 'like a two-tonguer from Canosa'.

> When I wrote Greek verse born this side of the sea
> Romulus in a vision spoke to me
> After midnight, that hour when ghosts talk true:
> 'Coals to Newcastle is the trouble with you.'
> So the Alpinist is cutting Memnon's throat
> Or shakes the yellow head of Rhine, my note
> Twitters, not meant for Tarpa or the stage
> Repeated as example for our age ...

The Alpinist is a turgid epic poet with Homeric ambitions, who Horace says

Let

elsewhere 'beslobbers the Alps with snow', a phrase used by the poet (named Furius) of Jupiter. Tarpa was a powerful critic under Pompey, in the age of Laberius.

Horace goes on to admit Fundanius, who was a friend of Maecenas (*Sat.*2, 8), is the best comedian. This Fundanius may well be a Roman Knight of that name who went over to Caesar in Spain in 45. Then comes

> Pollio who sings
> In hexametral rhythm the deeds of kings;
> Courageous sharp epic no man can write
> Like Varius, the Muses who delight
> In country things have granted to Virgil
> All softness, charm, and sparkling overspill.
> This is what Varro of Atax tried in vain
> And others too, I am one in the chain
> But less than our great founder: I don't dare
> Attempt that crown that's settled on his hair.

A nice compliment to Lucilius certainly, and a manifesto for the poetry of Horace's own new generation. Yet of all of them Fundanius has perished, Varius is no more than a question mark, and we are relieved not to have the poetry of Pollio, for fear we would not like it as much as Horace and the Virgil of the *Eclogues* say they do. Varro of Atax wrote a line both Horace and Virgil imitated about how winter 'has shaken down the honours from the grove'.

Horace now returns to self-defence over his criticisms of Lucilius. 'I said he ran like a muddy river, and do you find nothing to blame in Homer? Does pleasant Lucilius not alter Accius the tragedian? Does he not laugh at Ennius? He was like Cassius the Etruscan who wrote enough books for his own funeral pyre.' Lucilius may have been pleasant and urbane, but muddy and unpolished, he wrote poetry the Greeks never handled, but if he were alive today he would cross out a good deal, and scratch his head over his verse and bite his finger-nails.

> Turn your pen back to write and to rewrite,
> Do not seek for the mob to admire it.
> Be happy with few readers, only a fool
> Longs to be dictated in some low school.
> I do not ...

He defies that flea Pantilius, or the backbiting Demetrius or the fool Fannius, guest of Hermogenes Tigellius. No doubt these people existed once and would have recognised themselves in his verses. Horace wants approval only from Plotius and Varius, who would edit the *Aeneid* one day when Virgil was dead, Maecenas and Virgil, Valgius to whom Ode 2, 9 was offered, dear Octavius (a Mantuan we are told who can be found as poet in the pseudo-Virgilian *Catalepton*) and Fuscus and the two Visci. Fuscus and the Visci have been mentioned in the last satire.

> Without self-seeking I may speak of you
> Pollio, Messalla and your brother too
> Bibulus, Servius, Furnius the fine
> And many others, learned friends of mine ...

The list has now turned to politicians. Pollio and Messalla we know well, but Bibulus was a son of the wife of Brutus by an earlier marriage, who fought at Philippi and was an officer of Antony's and a diplomat for him at Rome in 35 BC; he died in Syria in 32. Servius may be the man married to Valeria Messalla, whose daughter was the Sulpicia of Tibullus. The brother of Messalla Corvinus, or rather his half-brother, was captured by Brutus and taken on by him, and later commanded Antony's right wing at Actium. Furnius also lasted with Antony until Actium. The third line I quote (85) therefore contains three names even more offensive to the regime than Horace's other friends. This must be a gesture that has political meaning. I think it must mean reconciliation, and the poem must be written soon after Brindisi or Tarentum, and must in some way celebrate the treaty. The war with Brutus was forgotten and forgiven. When Augustus saw a bronze statue of Brutus in Milan, we are told by Plutarch, he teased the Milanese about it, but respected it, and them for their loyalty, in all seriousness. The lines about 'other friends and learned men whom in prudence I pass over' underline that he had, as probably most Romans of his circle had, friends it would not be safe to mention even now.

> And on these poems I hope they may smile,
> I would be sad if they succeed less well.
> Go quickly boy and write this in my book.

Here the first book of *Satires* ends. This last poem was a lively performance, strongly stated from a literary point of view but bearing a closer reading I suspect. I do not think it can be more than a year after the Brindisi poem. The second book of *Satires* remained unfinished: there are eight satires in it, and they diverge both from the rules he had set himself and from those he later followed. It seems probable that moral philosophy was the guiding star that led him in a new direction. The one thing we know is that the *Epistles* or as I call them Letters followed, so that either he wrote the later satires with the odes, which on the whole I doubt, or when the odes (1-3) were in the last stages of being finished. There are a number of interesting political and dating problems which arise with the odes; the world was not placid either before or immediately after Actium. In the early twenties Augustus established himself solidly as Emperor, and it was at that stage that Horace began to be drawn into his political plans. So I will put off the second book of satires as if they were a single poem, with the exception of 2, 6, because that concerns Maecenas personally and Horace most personally: it celebrates the gift of the Sabine farm where Horace lived for the rest of his life.

It was not just a farm in our sense of the word, it was a river valley that extended a number of miles. There is no doubt about its identification either.

It is north of Rome, and not far from Mount Soracte which the Tiber isolates from the other Sabine hills. We will discover the full details of Horace's farm in a later poem: it was not just a farm but a modest country house like an Old Rectory, which because of the estate that went with it represented both a place of refuge for writing and an adequate income for the writer. From now on the Sabine farm as it is usually called will be a continuous theme interwoven with Horace's poems in book after book. It was thrilling to him and has been attractive to many generations of visitors ever since it was found by Lucas Holstein, Milton's friend and guide. The local villagers believed in the late nineteenth century that Horace had been an Englishman, because so many of them came on pilgrimage to his house. The fact of its being an easy distance from Rome may have had something to do with that. Here what is important to us is the date of the poem, which is luckily the one datable record in the second book: in 31 BC Augustus was summoned home to Italy to deal with a mutiny of veterans dissatisfied with their resettlement, and as he boasts on his monument (Ancyranum) he resettled them all, and even paid for the land on which he did so. Since it is a question in this poem where he will put them, we must date it soon after Actium, and that therefore must be the date of the gift of the Sabine estate in the hills north of Rome, from Maecenas to Horace.

The whole satire turns on this gift and on Horace's preference for the country life over town life. Its climax is the story of the town mouse and the country mouse: one of the best of all Horace's stories and the most brilliantly told. I was unable to resist giving it in a version by Cowley, the poem from whose manner in translating Horace Pope learnt his trade. He seems to me incomparably funny and readable. But the satire is a longish one, there are seventy-six lines to go before he begins the thirty-one line story, and they had best be treated here. For several reasons, I thought I should translate the text as well as I can while I comment on it.

> This I was praying for, a grazing ground,
> Room for a garden, lasting water found
> Near to the house, a bit of hanging wood:
> The gods gave me more of it and more good,
> This is enough, I do not ask for more,
> Mercury, make it mine, this and no more.
> If I have not increased it wickedly
> Nor will waste it or lose it culpably,
> And if I am not given to foolish praying
> Nor am I a fool who wastes his time praying
> 'Oh give me that lost corner of my grazing!'
> O for a pot of silver ...

It will be seen that the motto and meaning of this poem is the one unspoken word, Enough. What he says is *'Bene est*, That's fine,' which I translated as 'This is enough,' over-pedantically perhaps.

Horace is now well advanced on his moral or secular sermon. When he has dealt with treasure-hunters, as common in real life surely as they were on the comic stage, he makes his own prayer, adapted from Callimachus.

> 'Fatten the flock and all things that are here,
> Except my wits. Be guardian, as you are.'

The constant interjection of these little prayers and bits of wish much enlivens the syntax, towards the manner of the other poems of the second book, which I take it have yet to be written.

> Now I am in the mountains in my fort
> What else have my Satires to talk about?
> Ambition is no plague nor leaden breath
> Of wind, nor heavy autumn, nor sharp death.
> Dawn god or Janus if you should prefer
> From whom men take business and life labour,
> Begin my song …

After twenty lines he has turned on a new tack. First the rather shocking intrusion of sirocco, thundery weather and death (Libitina) in her Roman form knocks us off balance, then Janus, very much a city god, takes over the poem. Horace is called to Rome on business (23-4) and hates it. He blames the god, but who knows whether Maecenas may not be to blame, directly or indirectly? He must struggle through a busy Italian crowd. They blame him for pushing in his hurry to get to Maecenas (31), 'But when I get to the black Esquiline, A swarm of town business that is not mine Assails me. Roscius wants you at the Wellhead early tomorrow. Tell Maecenas to sign this carefully.'

> Seven years now or nearly eight have gone
> Since Maecenas took me up as his own … (39-40)

We must therefore assume that they have been close friends since 37 BC, but that they knew each other a little earlier. In that case the journey to Brindisi must have been either when they first met or else later than the treaty in 40 BC. The group included Cocceius all the same, and he had to do with the treaty, which anyway is hinted at in Maecenas's talent for bringing friends together. A careful reading of the poem with this question in mind shows that Maecenas and Horace did not exchange a word (nor does Virgil say a word). Maecenas is only complimented as *optimus* on his arrival, but the hugs and embraces and 'best of dawns' are reserved for the other writers. The journey to Brindisi may even have been the first time they ever met, and Horace might have been Virgil's guest on it? Historians, who are influenced by Sir Ronald Syme's view, tend to put the journey to Brindisi in 37 BC to fit the peace in that year. That dissolves our problem only to create two others: it makes the friendship begin later than I would put it, which I suppose is acceptable, but it also makes Maecenas go a long way out of his way, to

Brindisi, when by keeping to the Appian Way he could have gone directly and much more easily straight to Tarentum. One answer is that Antony was expected at Brindisi but went on to Tarentum (Appian 5, 93, etc. and Plut.*Ant.*) so the diplomatic dance ended there. Yet a mystery does remain, because Antony arrived at Brindisi with three hundred ships and was turned away by the town. Had this already happened when Maecenas and his poets arrived? Horace does make it clear in his next line that he is thinking of travel in 37 BC, but the conversation he suggests would not last as far as Brindisi.

> I mean to be in his coach on journeys,
> And to confide in me trifles like these,
> 'What's the time?' 'Do you think Gallina the Thracian
> Will be a good match for the Syrian?'
> 'If you're not careful morning frost can bite ...'

Everyone sees them together, everyone asks Horace, whose ear has holes in it on these matters (46), about the Dacians, about whom by the way Augustus lies in bronze on his monument, and about whether the troops are to be resettled in Sicily or elsewhere.

> So the day's wasted while I pray in vain
> O country, when will I see you again?
> And spend my time on old books or indeed
> On sleep and lazy hours, when shall I lead
> A happy life forgetful of business?
> O when the beans you knew Pythagoras
> Little and green in plenty of bacon fat?
> Nights, dinners of the gods I have been at
> Eaten at my own hearth with my house boys
> What food and drink! and everybody drinks
> His own measure ...

The house boys are in principle his slaves, but they were born on this farm and they are tied to it like Russian or medieval English serfs. Horace is delighted with them and their conversation. They talk, or so he claims, of 'what belongs to us, where it is wrong To be ignorant, whether man lives in happiness By virtue or lives better with riches, Whether friends come by right and wrong or habit, And what is good what's the supreme of it?' It may be thought unlikely that the Sabine house boys are really so metaphysical. So suddenly, 'old Cervius the neighbour babbled his tale', and in thirty more lines the satire will be finished. I will leave the climax as Cowley translated it to the discussion of the second book of *Satires* in its proper place, in Chapter Eight.

Chapter Five

Epic poetry is in some sense natural to mankind, and it will emerge from any preliterate culture if you leave them alone for long enough: Maurice Bowra used to believe it came only from heroic peoples in heroic or sub-heroic ages, but it may be natural for pastoral, cattle-raiding peoples to consider themselves heroic. Only the Irish have an epic, the *Tain*, in which the hero is the bull. But lyric poetry is a more delicate matter. For that you must have the right music, the almost courtly way of life with its manners and its relationships, and poetry that is performed as song, or to put it the other way songs written by poets. In England following the Italians and the French we did once enjoy an age of lyric poetry, but Surrey and Wyatt scarcely began it and the Civil War ended it when it had lasted just one generation, from about 1590 to 1630. The Romans had no such thing, they had only Horace, on his own, reviving the antique art of Greek lyric verse, only in Latin and with little attention so far as one can see to any original music. What is more, when the first three books of his *Odes* were published, they were not a success. His friends and the Emperor were thrilled with them, but they were above the head of the wider public. Music takes a long time to die out, and some sense of the right music seems to have persisted: there was also popular music for the superficially similar stanzas of popular song, just as we have 'pop' music that superficially resembles poetry. Sometimes the modern folk movement has indeed produced songs that are like simple, memorable poems, but Horace was attempting something deeper.

It is true as Fraenkel said of that age that the deeper a Roman was, the more deeply the ancient Greeks had entered into him. It is still debatable for example whether ordinary Romans could actually hear the rhythm of quantities, an imposed Greek system after all, in the way they spoke Latin. In the last generation they had used queer, supposedly archaic spellings to emphasise long syllables, as in the law phrase *paastores cedant aratoribus*. In verse they were prepared for Greek sound values, but in lyric verse, where the values are far more complex, one is less certain. The metrical systems of Greek and Latin lyrics take time to learn, and in the 1950s many of us found them as difficult as Alice's first step through the looking-glass. But Horace produced Roman lyrics in a wonderful variety and what appears at first to be effortless abundance. They seem today like the central task of his life, and like a lifework; yet in the first three books there are only eighty-eight poems, and in the later fourth book only fifteen more: just over a hundred, many fewer than the sonnets of Shakespeare, though they are often much longer than fourteen lines: in fact they make a book of about the same size.

No analysis has ever yielded an exact order in which they were written: to pick out here and there what we see by gossamer arguments as early or late leaves a confused impression. We will therefore deal with them mostly in the order in which they now appear, which after all was deliberately contrived by the poet. The first poem of the three books is to Maecenas and apart from the poet's claim to immortality (3, 30) so is the last (3, 29). The first nine poems of book one are deliberately chosen to show nine metres (there were nine Muses) even if he may never use one of them again, or he may introduce a brand new variety later on. The last of the nine is from the sixth-century Greek Alcaeus, the alcaic, Tennyson's favourite and mine. These stanza forms have an undertow that works deeply in us as we read stanza after stanza in the Soracte ode (1, 9), it takes us over and we cannot forget it: at least

> While we are green and while morose white hair
> Keeps away, and the meadow and shadowed square
> Brief whispers intercept,
> And rendez-vous are kept.

I am far from suggesting that my stanza form is equivalent to Horace's; for that you must learn Latin or consult Tennyson's poem to F.D. Maurice. What I use is the English adaptation of Sir Richard Fanshawe which Marvell used for his ode to Cromwell: it comes from the great age of English lyrics and it remains a curiosity of history that in our Commonwealth period these two poets were on opposite sides. Only one ode of Horace was translated by John Milton, no one knows when, and it is inimitable.

We must begin by exception with the second last ode of book one (1, 37), because it has the earliest clear date in all the *Odes*. It commemorates Caesar's naval victory at Actium and ends with a vignette of Cleopatra

> Fiercer than wilful death and in no dread
> But scorn of the fast ships and to be led
> In proud triumph unqueened
> Being of no humble mind.

One must not exaggerate; this is not an ode in honour of the Queen of Egypt, although it does greatly honour her. Its hero is Caesar, and Cleopatra comes in only as his honoured victim, at the end of a sentence twenty lines or (as I believe) twenty-eight lines long, with Caesar exactly at the centre of the poem, in line 16. The first stanza is a prelude that stands on its own, full of Roman ritual with a Greek sub-structure about the time being ripe for a drink because the tyrant Myrsilos was dead, which Alcaeus had laid down. The Queen is then insulted for some eight lines for planning a funeral pyre of the empire (8)

With her contaminated flocks
Of men disgusting with the pox,
Quite drunken with good luck,
Who suffered fortune's shock ...

The long sentence begins with a 'But' where I have written Who, and I see
that Kiessling and Heinze mark the transition with a mere colon, and the end
of the first stanza with another, giving the sentence a clear run for thirty-two
lines, and making this a one-sentence poem, something I was hardly daring
to suggest, though I had felt it was right. Horace bequeathed the habit of such
long sentences to Tennyson who planned his *In Memoriam* in twenty-line
sentences, a few of which survive. Horace turns to praise her in line 21.

... Fated monster: who nobly sought to die
Unterrified being more than womanly
Of swords, the quick fleet bore
Her to no hidden shore,

She saw her palace in ruins and gave
No sign, she handled serpents and her brave
Body nursed them and drank
Their venom black as ink ...

It is perhaps worth pointing out that Roman protocol had demanded that
since Antony had laid all his provinces at her feet war was declared against
the Queen, and was not a civil war. There were other considerations also:
Julius Caesar had several children by her and the old man had been Augustus's uncle and adopted father, so she was a kinswoman. Anyway he was
always merciful to the defeated, or so he boasted on his monument, so
Horace's attitude was not out of order. Livy, according to a wildly unreliable
writer, said the Queen often told people she would never walk in a triumph,
and it was said of another Cleopatra that she was more than womanly.
Horace says that only Caesar terrified her, which is the central phrase of the
poem. It was with Maecenas, who was left in Italy with Horace, that he
intended to drink, not without admiration of Cleopatra. The snakes may be
a myth though it was widespread: Propertius claimed he had 'seen the
snake-bites on her arms' and Virgil believed in them, but only mysterious
snake-tracks were seen in the sand, and Cleopatra's ladies did not survive.
Was it murder then? It is some comfort I suppose that A.S.F. Gow, a very old
boyfriend of A.E. Housman who survived at Trinity, Cambridge into my day,
maintained that the Egyptian cobra's bite is painless. A fuller and more
bloodcurdling account of this poem may be found in the *Commentary* by
Nisbet and Hubbard (1970). They prefer the treatment of Actium in the
baroque manner in Virgil's *Aeneid* (83, 697 etc.). This poem of Horace's is so
carefully written it is all but over-written, but personally I agree with every
word of Fraenkel's high estimate of it (158-61).
    There is one other ode that may possibly belong to the same epoch as this,

because just as the Cleopatra poem is tied by extreme contrast to the Actium epode, we come at the end of this poem to a reference to Horace's change of mood since his epodes. The poem (1, 16) to a girl whose name is not given is not what grammarians used to call a palinode, a poem withdrawing the offensive allegations of an earlier poem, it is a simple dissuasion of a pretty girl from writing offensive epigrams or epodes, particularly against Horace. I too, he says, used to write these things in my youth but now I try to be mild not grave, as long as you take back your insults and remain my friend, and restore my peace of mind. She has been teasing the famous poet with little fire-crackers as it were, so in order to be nice he replies with a charming and polite poem asking her to stop it.

> O·lovelier daughter of lovely mama
> Do put an end to iambics, send them far
> Out in the Adriatic sea,
> (Into the fire would do for me) ...

Nothing shakes the mind as badly as grave anger, not even the most tumultuous gods: nothing deters anger not sword or shipwreck or thunderstorm. Prometheus made man with bits from everything, the lion's rage included. Look what anger did to Thyestes, it ruined cities and brought walls down and under the plough (21). Control your mind: I too in my sweet youth was tempted by madness and rushed raging into swift iambics. That is really all there is to this charming piece, but its lightness and the fact it is untranslatable should not blind one to Horace's tact, his skilfulness, and his new mood. He has turned over a new leaf, though it may have been late in the day: for all we know to the contrary, this ode may be ten years later than the mass of the *Epodes*. To whom was it written? Horace suggests familiarity, so it must be to the daughter of a family he knew, probably noble. I could guess at a daughter of Octavia and Antony, but that is such a flimsy guess it has not the weight even of a conjecture. The only thing that could support it is the fact that her brother was a poet.

Book one begins with thirty-six continuous lines of choriambics, as in English 'You are Older than I, snowier haired My dear', with the first two and the last two syllables free, though Horace ends with an iambic and begins with a spondee. The habit of using lyric metres in continuous series dates from the early Hellenistic age, and it may well have been started by Callimachus in Alexandria, who transformed even Pindaric themes into elegiac couplets. It was that fact that set Horace free to cast about in lyric metres to do what he could with the mighty Pindaric structures. His relationship with Pindar lasted all his life and it was never easy. It is not the subject of this book, but it has been seriously studied since 1810 in Germany, and sometimes in English. Pindar was to Horace at first a glistening but a distant star and Horace himself never employed a stanza that was longer than four lines, he had determinedly put down roots in Lesbian music and Lesbian poetry, particularly in that of Alcaeus, earlier than Pindar's time.

The first ode of the first book had to be special, and its metre which sounds like a trumpet call is the same as that of the last poem in the third book (3, 30) in which Horace still more insistently claims his immortality by right of his lyric poetry. This first poem is mostly in the form of Some talk of Alexander, etc., which we have noticed before.

> Maecenas, offspring of ancestral kings
> O my defender and my sweet glory:
> Some men like to collect the Olympic dust
> On chariot wheels ...

Some are crazy about elections to state office, some like to gather grain, some farm, some sail, the merchant fears leisure and profit spurs him overseas. Another man drinks away daylight sprawled under a bush or with 'his head at gentle holy water-springs'. Soldiers like the trumpet braying against the horn, the winter huntsman neglects his tender wife.

> For me the ivy on a poet's brow
> Is entry to the gods in heaven, the cold grove
> Where lightly Nymphs and shaggy Satyrs dance
> Set me apart from men, if Euterpe
> And Polyhymnia do not refuse
> The long pipes and the Lesbian lute-note.
> Make me a priest of lyric poetry
> And my high head will strike the glittering stars.

The last words are a sort of frozen apocalyptic vision in which the poet is a kind of god. Does he believe it? Scarcely, but the ornament is traditionally his, and a metaphor that was alive. Euterpe and Polyhymnia are names of Muses, chosen for their sound which is musical: elsewhere he takes Melpomene, it does not signify because although the Muses were soon to divide up their special functions, Clio for history and so on, that had not happened yet, and so Horace naturally offers nine examples of lyric verse to the nine. This poem is not as pedantic as it looks; one should notice how its themes interweave coldness and greenness as it nears its climax. Each one is innocently introduced, the arbutus and the spring, the snow and the freezing grove: and the grove is suddenly a little eerie, and we are ready for the climax, which in Greek is proverbial. Virgil has the Cyclops (*Aen*.3, 619) 'rear to his height and beat at the high stars'. The word Horace uses for priest is also 'bard', and he would have prophetic powers.

Maecenas came from near Arrezzo and Tacitus says his family name was Cilnius; he claimed to have Lydian blood and to be royal. However that may be, the Romans were used to family religion that touched the gods through public or private legend. Julius Caesar had made the splendid boast in a graveside speech for his grandmother when he was twelve, 'On my father's side I have my blood from the immortal gods, on my mother's from many kings.' Horace's second ode is to Caesar Augustus: he is the winged Mercury new-lighted on some heaven-kissing hill to avenge Julius Caesar. He will go back to dwell with gods, but meanwhile long may he linger among us, father of his people, and their chief or leader (*princeps, dux*). These are not official titles maybe, though 'Father of the Country' attained official status in Augustus's old age, when Horace was dead. I do not think the title of Mercury was ever taken up, except maybe in Asia, but it fits the poem very well.

This ode is fifty-two lines long, thirteen sapphic stanzas, the only one of all these metres that seems to have survived in continuous use, or was it revived perhaps, for the oriental cult of Roma which the Romans encouraged. She had her pretty, round temple even on the akropolis of Athens. The poem winds its way brilliantly from natural disasters, hail and flashing lightning striking the temples of the gods, floods of the infuriated Tiber and civil war, to expiation (29). There is a fine drawing of the Forum under flood water by Claude Lorraine which is in the Ashmolean Museum at Oxford. The lightning flashes blood-red, as it does in Greek in a word used by Pindar: *phoinikosteropas*, crimson-flashing, referring to the red-hot look of a meteorite or thunderbolt. The person to execute the vengeance of God for civil war may be Apollo, his shoulders cloaked in glistening white cloud, or laughing Venus or Mars,

> Or in disguise of human youth on earth
> Wing-sandalled and as Maia's son draw breath,
> And formed like man take on
> Vengeance as Caesar's son.

That is echoed in one of the proudest sentences on the monument of Augustus. 'Those who murdered my father I drove into exile by legitimate judgement of the courts and avenged that crime and deed, and afterwards when they made war on the Republic I overcame them twice in battle.' This is of course a special way of manipulating reality, and to us perhaps a strange attempt. From the point of view of the poem the important word is 'I avenged'. Then when are we to imagine the poem was written? It begs him to stay long on earth and not be wafted away to heaven by our vices, and Brutus and Cassius are not mentioned, he is asked only not to let the Persian cavalry ride unavenged (51). Horace had spoken earlier of steel that should have been turned on the Persians (22) and not on one another; there he says Persians but here 'Medes', an antique and vaguer equivalent. Whether he really meant the Parthians becomes uncertain; the Parthians were more of a real threat, and the Romans were still furious about the defeat and death of Crassus, and the ignominious retreat of Antony. They 'rode unavenged' over most of what had been Persia, but unluckily Roman resentment of them is undatable. There is one doubtful piece of evidence in a bit of stucco ceiling that may be Augustus with Hermes's wand, in the National Museum at Rome, which could just as well be the reflection of our poem. But there is also a coin type, a denarius minted in the East showing Mercury sitting naked on a rock, inscribed *Caesar divi f.(ilius)*, Caesar son of the divine (Caesar). That has to be early, and before 29 BC. Any further deduction leads only further into uncertainty. The poem from its position looks like a later composition, although it may easily have been faked to a 'dramatic date' of say 30 BC. At this time Horace's relationship with the Emperor appears to be formal and not close.

All these dedications early in the first book hang together. The third, which is in its musical metre and its sound very beautiful (where the poem to Caesar as Mercury is more harshly dramatic) is dedicated to Virgil on his way to Greece. Horace wishes him calm seas and prosperous voyage.

> So may the Cyprian goddess show
> And Helen's brothers, shining stars
> And Aeolus stop the winds' wars,
> None but Iapyx be let blow:
>
> O ship, set Virgil safe ashore
> On Athenian earth to roam
> And then bring him safely home
> Half my soul and my heart's core ...

Horace then goes on for forty lines about the perils of the deep, and highly convincing they are too. One believes that he really mistrusts ships and the sea, which men are mistaken to attempt,

> And Daedalus the empty wind
> With wings not given to mankind,
> Hercules broke through Acheron:
>
> Nothing for men's too hard to test,
> Who through our crimes on earth below
> Fools that we are will not allow
> The angry lightning flash to rest.

Hercules breaking through the Acheron like a man breaking his chains to escape from hell and death is a little obscure. It is as if Horace runs two of the hero's labours into one, as Acheron itself broke out of the rocks under Acherontium: or there may have been a local version of the story by which Hercules broke his way out of the underworld and Acheron at once. This is a gloomy but a lovely set of verses to write to his friend. Helen's brothers Castor and Pollux the heavenly twins are also St Elmo's fire, the running light that appears in the rigging of ships: the same 'dull blue glare' once observed by Sir J. Thomson on the pinnacles of King's Chapel, Cambridge. Nisbet and Hubbard offer a pleasing variety of references to this phenomenon.

The fourth ode is to blessed (or rich) Sestius, and we have already dealt with it; all that remains is its position in the book, which is curious: Maecenas, Augustus, Virgil, Sestius. He was a soldier with Horace at Philippi. Historians say that he was an intransigent republican and that Augustus respected him for it, and made him consul in 23 BC for that very reason. Under Brutus he was an official in charge of supplies in Macedonia. The consulship has been taken to be evidence that Horace wrote him a poem as consul of the year, but there is no overwhelming reason to believe that, or to accept that the ode was addressed to him in 23. He is a friend never otherwise mentioned by Horace, perhaps not a member of Maecenas's circle, probably very rich and possibly not literary. But his place here is not an 'official' part of the dedication of Horace's book. The next ode will have no dedication at all, and if Sestius was placed fourth because of his consulate he should have been third, before a mere private friend. So I think it is an early poem, like an epode, and placed here only for its metrical interest.

The fifth poem is scarcely more than an epigram, just as an epigram by Leonidas of Tarentum stands behind the fourth (*Palatine Anthology* 10, 1, much quoted by Cicero), but in the fifth the convention of a dedicatory epigram is perfectly followed through. That is a formal exercise performed with marvellous precision. If it is no more, yet it is so excellent as a performance that it has always been popular in modern times, for its coolness, its jokes and little ironies, and because our attention has been drawn to it by John Milton who translated it better than any other poem by Horace has been translated into English.

> What slender youth bedew'd with liquid odours
> Courts thee on roses in some pleasant Cave,
> Pyrrha for whom bind'st thou
> In wreaths thy golden Hair.
>
> Plain in thy neatness? O how oft shall he
> On Faith and changed Gods complain: and Seas
> Rough with black winds and storms
> Unwanted shall admire:
>
> Who now enjoys thee credulous, all Gold,
> Who always vacant, always amiable
> Hopes thee: of flattering gales
> Unmindful. Hapless they
>
> To whom thou untried seem'st fair. Me in my vow'd
> Picture the sacred wall declares t'have hung
> My dank and dropping weeds
> To the stern God of Sea.

The sixth ode differs metrically from the fifth only in the length of the third line, but it would be a master with more than Milton's powers who could convey that small difference in as good a translation. In the dedication we have the great Agrippa with a mention of Varius thrown in. Agrippa was the most practical friend Augustus had, he was a right arm to him, much more so than Maecenas, and there are buildings that commemorate him in France (the famous Maison Carrée) as well as in Rome.

> Varius will write of you as a strong
> Winner, that winged bird of Homeric song,
> Fierce in ships and horses wherever
> Our soldiers have made war.
>
> I cannot deal with that Agrippa, the fine
> Fury of Achilles unable to give in
> Or with Ulysses doubling round seas
> Or Pelops' house of savages:
>
> I am too small for great themes, Modesty
> And my unwarlike Muse forbid for me
> To attempt the genuine praise that yet abides
> Yours and great Caesar's deeds.

One more stanza full of antique examples, and one quiet concluding stanza that promises to write about love or a party, and he has finished. I take it Horace has honourably performed a task as quite a young man. He is not deeply engaged in refusing to write an encomium on a military hero. I only repeat that one should not underestimate Agrippa, who was a true friend to Augustus from first youth. I am glad all the same that this reproof was not addressed to me, in spite of its enjoyable ironies.

The seventh poem is to Plancus, and maybe the two have been deliberately placed together, because it is mostly about the beauties of the Levant and as if war had never existed, until it turns with the name Plancus (19) as an earlier poem had with Sestius (4, 14) to a darker and deadly serious tone. We have dealt with the seventh ode already, but it is useful to notice again at this point that Horace seems to be most serious in poetry when he is apparently artificial, and vice versa maybe. Teucer's advice to his friends lingers in the mind in a way that many poems do not. What one remembers even of the ode to Augustus may well be the bad weather and not the sad metaphysics of sin and vengeance or the Medish horsemen unavenged.

The eighth poem almost sings itself, it is one of those works of art that in its aspiration to the condition of music has gone slightly too far and somehow achieves musicality so that one hums it and forgets it. It is a lovely piece written for a girl who does not exist, Horace reproves her for distracting a boy with the charming name Sybaris (who does not exist either) from the proper activities of adolescence. The whole thing is only sixteen lines long, and it is so good that maybe I should treat it more seriously, but I cannot. Horace's passion is the ghost of a candle-flame in a mirror, it is too beautiful to detain our attention. The ninth ode is quite another matter.

This has been placed in its position as a climax of the nine metres, and its metre is the grandest, the most fluent and cello-like of all, the alcaeic. It has no dedication because you cannot dedicate to a noble Roman a poem ending in bad behaviour in the street. The person called Thaliarchus, Master of the Celebrations, has a Greek name which survived only in romances like *Apollonius King of Tyre* (ch.6), the source of Shakespeare's *Pericles*, and there is something Shakespearean about the name. The poem is very vivid, but also subtle. It begins with the stiff white snowy peak of Soracte, a limestone mountain isolated from the Sabine hills by the Tiber, and visible in the northern skyline from Rome in Horace's day and even in the 1930s. Snow on Soracte would be an ordinary observation. The forests labour under the weight and the rivers are iced over. So more wood on the fire and open a *diota*, a 'two-ear', what the Greeks call an amphora, of decently old Sabine wine. The gods can improve the weather, do not worry about tomorrow, enjoy today, evening on the Campus and in the squares, the girl laughing at the corner, the bracelet snatched from her arm or the ring from a not unbending finger. Everything has altered from the word 'dissolve' in line 5: the weather is springlike, life is open air, the cypress and mountain ash are still and stiff but the young (16) are dancing, there are whispers and laughs, and the girl's finger not quite resisting transforms the mountain. White snow gives way to dark green and then light and supple green (11 and 17). This poem has been thoroughly and studiedly composed in a way that recalls Virgil's *Ecologues* or Baudelaire perhaps but is seldom associated with ancient poetry.

> Look where the gleaming snow has come to rest
> On high Soracte, the laborious forest
> Can hardly bear the weight,
> Ice grips the rivers tight:
>
> Dissolve the cold, and lay a load of wood
> On to the fire, and then unseal some good
> Four year old Sabine wine
> Dark from the jar and fine:
>
> Leave the rest to the gods, as soon as they
> Put down the winds that fight on the boiling sea
> The cypress and the bent
> Ashes stand silent.
>
> Whatever's coming don't fret about it
> Just count the day's good fortune as credit
> Don't despise sweet loving
> My dear boy, or dancing,
>
> While youth is green and melancholy white
> Is absent, and from field and squares the light
> Whispers rise this evening
> Where lovers are meeting.
>
> And now from the most hidden corner
> The girl's betrayed by her laughter
> Where her bracelet takes wings
> Or ring to finger clings.

I have attempted a version of this many times, none of them satisfactory, so that what I offer now is the mere sketch of a translation meant to underline the points I want to make. It is a remarkable poem in spite of its contradictions, and it could very well be Horace's first attempt at the alcaeic, a strong horse that pulls in directions of its own. The 'my dear boy' character is the house slave or young serf 'Thaliarchus'. Horace is not in Rome I think, but he imagines himself there, only the trees and rivers are really those of the Sabine hills, the sea where the winds are fighting it out, a queer enough conception but Homeric for a storm, is surely off Canosa, and there is something about the girls and the dances and the thieving lovers that suggests somewhere far to the south, Naples or Tarentum. It does not matter in the least. The original of this poem by Alcaeus in Greek has been preserved, but only a very few lines of it, and then something about cushions which suggests an erotic ending.

The book properly begins with a hymn to Hermes, to Mercury that is, in sapphics, adapted from Alcaeus. It is a brief, strongly felt and simply worded ancient hymn. Mercury is 'eloquent son of Atlas' because as Euripides says in his *Ion*, Atlas begot Maia and Maia begot Hermes: Maia like her sister Taygete was one of the Pleiades, localised on Mount Kyllene, as Taygete was in southern Greece. This ode is very clear; the first thing it says about the god is that he was the civiliser of mankind in words and songs and gymnastics. The stanzas also are clearly divided, the second calls him messenger of the gods, father of the lute, and joking thief. Apollo was threatening him for stealing his cattle when he found his arrows had been taken too and laughed. The story comes from Alcaeus as of all people Pausanias records, not when he was wandering around Kyllene on his way to Nonakris, in a particularly good temper (7, 20) but à propos of a statue of Apollo, naked with one foot on an ox-head, that he came across in Augustan Patras. The only reason to record this is that Horace's hymn might cause the antiquaries of Patras to point to Alcaeus in explaining the statue: Pausanias does not sound as if he believes them and nor do I. Alcaeus seems to have invented the story in the second hymn of his second book. Fraenkel regarded this as a sufficiently prominent position to explain whatever needs explaining about Horace's choice of the hymn: but he was furious at the time with the idiocies of other scholars, and this bulwark was not really necessary to his attack on them, which was both sharp and funny, and not a bad example of Fraenkel in a rage with Lutheran Christianity (161-6). The fourth stanza is Hermes guiding Priam to beg back the dead body of Hector:

> ... Who guided rich Priam out of the grieved
> City of Troy, and with your wand deceived
> The proud Atridae, the Thessalian fire,
> Patroclus' pyre.
> You lead all holy souls to their glad seat,
> Command those airy throngs with wand of light:
> The gods who are above delight in you,
> And those below.

The eleventh ode is a brief eight lines of choriambics against fortune-telling addressed to Leuconoe, a Greek name that has no particular meaning, and the poem itself has no great weight; it is only another metrical experiment, the sketch for a poem rather than the thing itself. But the twelfth is a definite assault on the Pindaric lyric: it begins with the line from Pindar made famous in modern times by Ezra Pound's *Mauberley*, 'Tin' andra, tin' heroa, tina theon, What god man or hero Shall I place a tin wreath upon?' In English as in Greek, without the Poundian irony of 'a tin wreath upon' this is the grandest of openings, bold, simple and surprising: it is what used to be called sublime, or high, and characteristic of Pindar. The ode is a compliment to Caesar, much like the second ode of this book, and it conveys some sense of the 'triadic' structure or stanza form of Pindaric poetry, a structure more visible to the eye in modern editions than it was in antiquity. It is a structure in a special sense of the word: the poem follows Pindar's second Olympic quite closely in its own stricter metre, in all its five sections, each of which is twelve lines long, three Latin sapphic stanzas. Pindar puts gods first, then heroes and then man; Pound altered the order for the sake of his admittedly amusing rhyme. Pindar answers his own question with Theron, who as a human winner glorifies Zeus and Herakles founder of the games, but Horace answers with three separate groups, each one symbolising Augustus, who appears at the end as you would expect, like someone in a pantomime: *deus ex machina*. He maintains his grandeur by a reminiscence of the Agamemnon of Aeschylus on Zeus: I have nothing to compare to him, weighing all in the balance, but Zeus ... Later (4, 2, 37) Horace has the effrontery to apply this mighty formula to Augustus. I wish I knew where he got it if not from Aeschylus. As for the symbolism, Apollo is the saviour of Actium, the Romans among the heroes (Romulus, Pompilius, Tarquin and Cato) are a queer bundle, but they lead us into history and towards Julius Caesar, and 'the Julian star' (46) shines among men. Caesar enters the poem with a crash of drums only at 51-2. Technically this is an amazing performance, something grander than a state ode, a real mingling of religion, heroism and ancient history with the reign of Augustus.

We are considering Horace's life as bits and chips of it emerge from his works. The question therefore at once arises, how could he possibly lavish such compliments on Caesar Augustus, whom we may never have quite learned to like, and to whom Horace was close enough to know that he did not by any means dwell on such a pinnacle? The question is better faced than swept past. The very extravagance of grandeur and of Pindaric Hellenism kept Augustus at a distance. What we shall find later is that Augustus did not complain of not being exalted in Horace's lyrics, but of not being treated as a familiar friend. Queer as it is to us, the entire stage-play of the great gods in their temples was perfectly well known to be a charade, an elegant and traditional way of talking. It is also very odd indeed for us that hindsight makes it virtually impossible for us to focus on Augustus, on the elaborate and successful conjuring trick by which he pulled the Roman state out of the ruins of the wicked republic, and with the powers of tribune and war-lord made himself look permanent. How he did that in detail is in the new edition

of the Cambridge Ancient History, just published as I write (1996). Horace
was not the principal propagandist, he was both mesmerised and one of the
mesmerists. I note that he insisted on putting 'Cato's noble death', which was
by suicide in the face of Julius Caesar's victory over Pompey, into the climax
of his list of heroes.

> And shall I tell of Romulus or the cloud
> Kingdom of Pompilius or the proud
> Rods of Tarquin, or else the heavy breath
> Of Cato's noble death? ...
> ... And as a tree grown in a hidden age entwines
> Your fame Marcellus, and among others shines
> The star of Julius like a blazing moon
> When stars are stone.

It is all on too high a plane to be translated today. One should notice that
when Augustus commissioned a hymn from Horace years later to be sung at
the Roman 'Games of the Age', the *ludi saeculares*, it was in the same sapphic
metre and its imitation of Pindar's construction was the same. There is
another and a last observation to make, for which I will quote Fraenkel. 'In
the early ode (1, 2) Horace had ventured towards a compromise with certain
religious conceptions of the Hellenistic East. In (1, 12) he does nothing of the
kind. Not only is there in this ode not the faintest hint of a possible deification
of the ruler, but all that is said about him is kept within the bounds of
strictest Roman propriety.' This paradox is quite true: his role is to triumph
over the Parthians 'who threaten Latium' (!) or the Chinese or the Indians,
peoples far away.

The thirteenth ode is about an imaginary affair. The poem owes something
to Sappho, by way of Catullus maybe. It is an extremely physical poem, where
the excluded lover attacks Lydia for her appetite for a boy's waxen arms and
rosy neck, for the damage she does to them when drunk and the bite-marks
the boy leaves on her lips. Let her not hope for those sweet kisses in which
Venus distils her quintessence for ever. Happy are those whose bond is
unbroken, whom quarrels will not separate. That is all, except for the second
stanza:

> Neither my colour nor my mind
> Will stay in place, a liquid flows
> Secretly to my knees and shows
> How I am burnt with fires refined.

It is deliberate policy on Horace's part I am certain to position this next to
the climax of his Pindaric poem.

The fourteenth which immediately follows it is about a ship in danger,
'Though of Pontic pine she stood, Daughter of a noble wood' (Catullus again).
The ode is an allegory about the state,

Once my weariness and my heart's fire,
Now my care and my desire,
May she avoid those flowing seas
Between the glittering Cyclades.

It must have its origin in Alcaeus, but it has wandered away on its own and one cannot date the crisis. There may well have been good reason to obscure Horace's true and surely republican feeling in the ship allegory, but the obscurity envelops it like a sea-mist.

The fifteenth ode is an antique Greek story retold from a new point of view, a prophecy Nereus sang to Paris as he sailed home with Helen. You will run away from Diomedes (28-32) like a stag that sees a wolf on the far side of his valley, you will forget the grass and run panting 'And after certain winters Greek fires will burn Troy's houses down'. The role of Diomedes is perhaps a homely touch, but otherwise the ode is purely neo-classic: it has nothing to do with Horace's feelings, Nereus speaks nearly the whole poem and the poet might as well be writing in the nineteenth century in Paris or in Livorno or in provincial Athens. The fact is that he is following Bacchylides, a poem without a strong enough flavour to penetrate the Latin text. There is no obvious reason why it lacks even the pretence of a dedication. Scholars have made subtle criticisms of the metre and noticed echoes of an epode (10) at the beginning and of the *Satires* in stray words, so they agree to call it early. So it may be, but it is as impersonal as a jigsaw puzzle, it is competent, and I have no idea of its date.

The next ode in order, the sixteenth, we have already handled, and placed early, not without hesitation. The seventeenth raises the nagging question of where Lucretilis is. English fans used to talk about it as familiarly as if it were Eton or Box Hill, but no one knows where it lay, nor do they know where Ustica was or what shape. Still, this is a lovely composition, very like one or more of those Greek epigrams, which are always Hellenistic, never early or austere, that Horace often did imitate. In this case Nicaenetus of Samos (Gow 146) is quoted, and 'Underneath this myrtle shade On flow'ry beds supinely laid, With od'rous oils my head o'erflowing ...' which is Cowley but merely pretty. Tyndaris is invited to a goat-infested life; her queer name makes one assume she is no great lady, and in the last two stanzas the poet suggests she is used to bad behaviour. But it is the enigmatic country setting that gives the poem its charm; only the whereabouts are enigmatic. The countryside of Horace's Sabine house is well known, it was first identified by Milton's Oxford friend Lucas Holstein who was his guide in Rome in the seventeenth century: he had worked in the Bodleian library and may well have taken Milton to see this landmark. The local patriotism of the Italians has attached the names of places in this poem to that landscape, but the truth is they could as easily belong to Tarentum or to Naples or anywhere in Italy. The girl's name Tyndaris has a southern ring to it. Elsewhere he uses the same famous name for Clytemnestra, the wife of Agamemnon.

Now swiftly Faunus from Lycaeon's rock
Comes to Lucretilis and my goat-flock,
Guards them from summer day,
Keeps rain and wind away.

In the safe woods they seek out arbutus
And lurking thyme, young wives of an odorous
Husband that need not fear
The serpents hidden there,

The shegoats need not fear the wolf of Mars
Wherever your sweet pipe's re-echo jars
Ustica's smooth stones
And fills the valley's tones;

The gods protect me Tyndaris, their art
And their religion living in my heart,
Here honours country-born
Are yours from a full horn.

Here in the hidden valley, here most far
From the tempestuous heat of the dog-star
Sing Penelope and sing
Glass Circe on the Teian string …

Already Horace by introducing Teos and the lute (meaning the ancient Greek Anacreon) has gone too far, if this poem was meant to end as it began, as a shepherd's lovesong to a shepherdess. Of course he expresses a nostalgia that many felt for the pastoral world of Virgil and Theocritus. The wolf might be Sabine, but the shepherd's outburst about religion and music in his heart suggests that he is not Horace. The last two stanzas of the poem speak of innocent Lesbian wine, Bacchus battling with Mars, and a certain Cyrus tearing 'the crown in your hair and your innocent dress'. It sounds as if she is a Lesbian character, like Daphnis and Chloe: Horace must have known the first Greek romances after all. Lesbian wine is too expensive for goatherds in the Sabines. On the other hand Lucretilis and Ustica could be Italian place-names; Pan is transformed to Faunus, and Lycaion to Lucretilis; Ustica sounds a hot, burnt place like the town where Cato died, not like the valley of the Digenza. Perhaps we are in wonderland.

The eighteenth ode is to Varus and it is written in pure, flowing choriambics. Horace tells his friend Varus to plant vines at Tibur, some five or six miles from Horace's farm; we can have no certainty which of many Romans with the same name he was complimenting, but Nisbet and Hubbard think it was P. Alfenus Varus, a man about twenty years older than Horace, who was born at Cremona, and whom Catullus addressed in the same metre. Horace takes his first line from Alcaeus in just the same metre: it is a kind of motto borrowed from old Greek poetry and a pointer to those interested, but in this case the motto is all we have from Alcaeus's poem. Alfenus Varus was a patron of writers as well as a highly distinguished lawyer, and if few people took the allusion to the Greek, that fact would be part of the compliment. The poem is sixteen lines long. Horace discusses the dark side of alcohol as well as the bright side: it is a most rational poem and has a number of those sudden striking phrases so much admired a hundred years ago. The nineteenth ode is about an onset of Venus, the girl Glycera is purer than the marble of Paros, which was translucent, Venus has descended on Horace and he cannot talk about Scythians and Parthians, he must worship at once. It is another poem of sixteen short lines, and fine though one does not believe a word of it. But the opening 'Savage mother of cupids' recurs in a later poem (4, 1); Pindar has already called her 'Mother of stormfooted desires'.

The twentieth ode is to Maecenas, written who knows when, after a time when the great man had been seriously ill, and was publicly applauded in the theatre when he reappeared. This poem warns Maecenas that the drink will be humble, but the vintage is from when he was applauded, and the famous Knight has wonderful wine every day. There is no undertone, it is a poem calculated to give pleasure. In the theatre Maecenas would sit in the special rows reserved for Knights, and there is a story about those seats that illustrates Horace's position, and the degree of fame it was possible to have at Rome, a city small enough for everyone to know one another, as used to be true of Dublin. Pliny sat next to a Knight from Spain, who asked him in the way enquiring people often do open a conversation with a stranger, Are you from around here? You know me in a way, was the answer, you almost certainly have my books at home. Oh, said the stranger, Pliny or Tacitus? Pliny tells the story just a generation after Horace's time, but anecdotes about Virgil and Horace confirm that they too were recognised and gossiped about. This poem is in a sense private, but not too private to be published. The Epicurean Philodemus wrote several invitations in the form of epigrams in verse, one of them to Piso (Gow and Page 21-24), but Horace's poem is subtler and more consoling. What Philodemus offered Piso is not specified, but other meals of his sound disgusting.

> You will drink tankards of cheap Sabine wine
> Which I myself in earthenware laid down
> Dating from the vintage when the theatre roared
> And stood to applaud,
>
> Maecenas famous Knight, and the river banks
> And the Vatican hill resounded with their thanks:
> The river you were born by, whose image
> Floated homage.
>
> You may drink Caecuban or what the wine-press
> Of Cales offers but I must confess
> My wine-cups never see Falernian
> Or Formian.

The river is the Tiber because Maecenas was born near the source of that great river at Arrezzo; then at Rome it reflected (as its bank re-echoed) the applauding theatre and the ancient Mons Vaticanus. Maecenas was applauded in the Theatre of Pompey, where that statue of Pompey at which Caesar was murdered and 'which all the time ran blood' had been resituated; it was on Mars's Meadow, the Campus Martius, in the bend of the Tiber. This theatre stood south of S. Andrea della Valle, where the streets still follow its lines, and the echo came from the Gianicolo, not the modern Vatican, but all that area across the Tiber was part of the Augustan Vaticanus, which after all was the remnant of a district that had stretched as far as Veii. The names of the wines in this poem have led to much learned discussion of the *appellations*, but they were not *controlées*, and we have not tasted any of them. Cales is the modern Calvi, and to be pedantically accurate (which is often advisable in Horace's odes) the poet speaks of Caecuban wine, the press at Calvi, Falernian grapes and the Formian hills.

The twenty-first ode is the sketch of a formal hymn for boys and girls to Apollo and Diana, in or rather 'after' the manner of Catullus (34). It does not sound like a real hymn, since it is unclear who is saying which words, but it does establish Horace's real interest in the trickle of tradition of sacred music that survived. Callimachus had already written imaginary hymns; the real Hellenistic Greek ones that we have tend to be lamentable, like the paean in Greek to Titus Flamininus who proclaimed the 'freedom' of Greece in 196 BC, which ends 'Great Zeus and Rome / and Titos and Roman / Faith: *ie ie Paian, / Ō Tĭtĕ sōter*. (O Titus saviour.)' We have inscribed evidence of a school outing at Magnesia in 129 BC when a hymn was sung to Artemis, and no doubt a jolly time was had. But it had never occurred to Horace that one day he might really write a real hymn. Even his place-names are a surprising mixture: Algidus may be a tall point in the Alban hills, or why not above Rocca Pia above Sulmona where the Italians ski on the Gran Sasso d'Italia? The black forests of Erymanthus are in Arcadia, but green Gragus is in Asia, in Lycia: all these are for Artemis, and Apollo has Tempe and Delos, which are more conventional. They are to save Caesar when he moves against the Persians or the British. The poem by Catullus is much better.

The next ode to Horace's friend Fuscus used to be sung by the whole school when a pupil died in a German grammar school before 1914; Eduard Fraenkel in old age could still do a stirring rendering of it, though as a small boy he said he could never understand what Fuscus had to do with it. In fact the poem is a piece of fantasy, and one might as well ask what Lalage has to do with it. We are told by a highly unreliable commentary on Horace that Aristius Fuscus was a teacher who wrote comedies, but all that we really know of him is his admiration for Horace as a poet. The ode speaks for itself: Lalage is a Greek name, not usual because it means Chatterbox.

> A decent life and free of crime will show
> He does not need his Moorish spears or bow
> Nor poisoned arrows Fuscus that still shiver
> In heavy quiver,

Whether he goes by the glaring Syrtes
Or the unfriendly Caucasus, or sees
What countries fabulous Hydaspes licks
Where her wave breaks.

A wolf fled from me wandering unarmed
Singing of Lalage and left me unharmed
In the Sabine forest in the green walks
Where the wolf stalks.

Not even Apulian Daunus nourishes or hides such a monster in his oak
forests, the poem goes on, nor does the land of Juba, dry nurse of lions. Put
me down in the coldest spot on the planet or the hottest where no one lives,
'I shall still love Lalage's sweet laughing, Her sweet talking.' If the poem is
true, which you can believe if you choose, then the last two lines are all that
is left of what he was composing in the green walks. What does it matter?

In the very next poem, too delicate and too fragile to translate, Chloe is
like a calf running for her mother in trackless mountains in fear of every leaf
that stirs. But here is a puzzle set by Bentley that exercised A.E. Housman,
the most brilliant English Latinist since that great man: one has to choose
veris (spring) or *vepris* (thorn-bush). The stanza goes 'For whether spring has
come in a shivering of leaves or the green lizards push through the bracken,
heart and knees tremble', or is it as Bentley suggested 'For whether the
thorn-bush in a shivering of leaves ...'? Housman denounces the nineteenth-
century taste for the rustle of spring and prefers the thorn-bush. Klingner
records the bramble as a conjecture of Gogavius, a scholar so obscure that
this sounds like an insult; in fact Gogau and Salmasius, Milton's enemy, both
liked thorn-bush, and Bentley was eloquent for it. Housman declared his
view in 1911 in *The Confines of Criticism* which was published only in 1969.
If *vipera* (a viper) could be substituted I would like it better, but the gram-
matical arguments are delicate and nicely poised, so I must be content with
the text that is traditional I suppose. All the same viper and lizard go well
together, and both appear in the woods.

Housman justly remarks (p. 35) that 'Communion with the ancients is
purchasable at no cheaper rate than the kingdom of heaven; we must be born
again. But to be born again is a process exceedingly repugnant to all right-
minded Englishmen. I believe they think it is improper, and they have a
strong and well-grounded suspicion that it is arduous. They would much
rather retain the prevalent opinion that the secret of the classical spirit is
open to anyone who has a fervent admiration for the second-best parts of
Tennyson.' There are fewer of those today than there used to be, so I am not
ashamed of my lingering affection for *vipera*. Housman's swipe at the cult of
second-best bits of Tennyson does worry me about the bits of translation that
I offer, but they are not poetry, they are only an attempt to explain what I
am talking about. Whichever way you take the second stanza of the twenty-
third ode, it is a beautiful poem. It ends, I am no African lion or tiger: but
stop following your mother now you are old enough for a man. Fraenkel felt

that *veris* and the shiver of leaves suggested the advent of a god, and by this time the seasons were gods of a kind; I had the same thought independently.

> Whether spring comes shivering through shaken green
> Or lizards pushing through brambles suddenly seen,
> The trembling fit will seize
> Upon her heart and knees.

My own preference would be Whether a snake ... Bentley's is Whether the thorns come in a shiver of shaken green, but let the lovely little poem rest. It is so simple it might be a real love-poem, a serious fantasy.

The twenty-fourth ode is to Virgil, to lament the death of Quintilius, but the ancient commentaries have made a dog's breakfast of the poor man: born at Cremona like Alfenus Varus, who is spelt Varus not Varius but called a poet by confusion with Varius: and Varus and Varius were both students of Epicureanism under Siron. In the *Art of Poetry* at the end of his life Horace praises Quintilius as a critic: that is all we know about Quintilius Varus and it is praise enough. Scholars shiver at the formality of this ode and mutter at its mixture of consolation and lament, but for no good reason. The metre is that of the loud-singing muse, Melpomene. My translation is looser than usual, and even so I fell over my feet at the simple ending.

> What shame or moderation in longing
> For my dear friend? Then teach me how to sing
> Songs of grief Melpomene, and inspire
> The flowing voice and lyre.
>
> Now that Quintilius' slumber is
> Perpetual and Modesty and Justice
> Her sister, naked Truth pure Faith
> Have suffered the same death.
>
> Many good men's eyes wept at his end,
> None more than yours Virgil, no better friend
> In vain protesting how familiar roads
> Stole him to the harsh gods.
>
> Yet what if you more beautifully sing
> Than Orpheus to the trees played out his string,
> Will blood to empty images return
> When with dread wand the stern
>
> Mercury drives him into his black flocks
> Who is to prayers harder than the rocks?
> Terrible: yet patience makes more light
> What altering's not right.

The next ode is a mean but effective poem to 'Lydia', like so many Greek poems, that is to nobody, a whore abandoned in old age: there are twenty lines of it. A lot of poems of the same kind exist in Latin and Greek but so far as I remember they are all repellent. The shut windows rattle less, the door loves its threshold though once easy on the hinge, and so on. The twenty-sixth poem is a mere twelve lines to Pimpleis, an obscure word for a Muse, asking her to help him celebrate Lamia; the family was distinguished and from now on Horace often mentions them. The earliest of these Lamiae was a friend of Cicero, the next generation a soldier and governor of Nearer Spain in 24 BC (and he is probably the one), and his son was consul in the next century. The fact remains that we do not know what this soaring compliment is about.

The twenty-seventh ode is twice as long and very moral. It is a little drama about a boy. Thracians took their alcohol neat, and this party is drunk.

> There is enjoyment to be found in cups,
> Only Thracians fight. So please give up
> This barbarism inviting
> The god to restrain from fighting.
>
> Persian daggers don't fit wine and the lights
> So let there be an end to all these shouts
> And to all these disgraces,
> Friends, remain in your places.
>
> Shall I take the powerful wine's part as well?
> Then let Opuntian Megilla's brother tell
> From whose happy wound he sighs
> From what arrow he dies.
>
> I will not drink for any less reward,
> Whatever Venus is gripping you so hard
> Nothing to blush about
> But innocent love found out.
>
> Whatever's the matter drop it in my safe ears:
> O, a Charybdis worse than all my fears!
> O my poor lad, the shame.
> You're worth a better flame.
>
> What witch can help you? What Thessalian
> Poison, what god? Not even on
> Pegasus will you get free
> Of the monstrous one and three.

The last phrase means Chimaera. Horace is showing again his tendency towards dramatic form, which never came to anything except in his criticism, and that much later in life. The speaker here is not the Master of the evening because he can be ordered to drink, he is just an older man determined to stop the quarrelling: Horace for example, though the Greek names suggest we are not in Rome and the whole scene is imaginary. No doubt he had seen such evenings. Nisbet and Hubbard took the surprising view that this ode was 'the cleverest poem that Horace ever wrote in his life'; they thought it was like Browning. I am extremely doubtful, I think it is one of those poems which most poets write, in which technique outruns love, and there is nothing left but technique. One could argue that happened even to Shakespeare at times.

We have already dealt with the Archytas ode, the twenty-eighth, in which Archytas turns out to be addressed by the bones of a dead sailor: which, being long dead himself, Archytas would not mind. The general lament for the antique dead (7-16) is fine all the same. Iccius to whom Horace addresses sixteen lines of reproachful compliment is the person to whom he also wrote his twelfth letter. He seems to have acted as Agrippa's agent in Sicily in 20 BC, but this is earlier in his life. He seems to have joined the army, no doubt as a tribune, for Gallus's expedition into Arabia. Horace does not think much of the motives of this move, which were mostly mercenary. The reports sent home were mostly lies, losses were horrifying, the entire profits were a remedy for snake-bite, but Augustus recorded on his monument that his men had conquered the Sabaeans. The spice trade which they controlled was notoriously mysterious, and the Three Kings of Christmas must have come across the desert, whether from Petra or from Ma'rib or Mariba in the Yemen. 'Iccius, do you envy the rich treasures of the Arabs and prepare hard soldiering and knit chains for the unconquered kings of Sabaea and the nasty Persians? What girl what boy will you enslave? Rivers can climb mountains and the Tiber run backward if you exchange your books of Panaetius and Socratic house for Spanish leather, you who promised better things.' The only detail to arouse our interest is the books of the philosopher Panaetius 'collected from everywhere' that the young man was abandoning. Sicily must have been his reward, and more remotely the family he engendered, which climbed the highest crests of nobility until Domitian cut off their heads.

The thirtieth ode is two stanzas to Venus from 'Glycera', imaginary as a prayer, pretty as a list, the heated boy (Cupid), the Graces with loosened belts, the Nymphs, and Youth unfriendly without you, and Mercury. The thirty-first wants to know what the poet should demand of a newly dedicated Apollo. What should he pray for? Not the riches of Sardinia nor the pleasant cattle of hot Calabria, not gold nor Indian ivory, nor land on the Liris between Latium and Campania. Let those to whom fortune allows it prune the vines of Cales or go to the Atlantic three or four times a year,

> While I on olives graze
> On mallow and on peas.
>
> To enjoy what lies before me, to be strong,
> Apollo grant me, that is all my song,

> Decent age, sound mind, see
> My lute for company.

This is a charming poem, and its quiet closure is the most impressive thing about it. It is pure philosophy, including the diet, and strongly suggests the morals of the second book of *Satires*. Apollo on the Palatine was dedicated on 9th October 28 BC, and two days later came a vintage feast called the Meditrinalia, so he includes a good deal about drink. Propertius wrote two poems for the dedication of Apollo; it is typical of Horace to be two days late and so herbivorous on the occasion. Admittedly about Actium which excited Propertius Horace had long ago said his say.

The thirty-second ode is to his lute.

> If in the shadows we played like idlers
> Grant me what lasts for this and many years,
> Help me my lute to sing a Latin song
> That will last long.
>
> First played upon by the old Lesbian
> Ferocious fighting man, infantryman,
> Who tied his ship up on the soaking shore
> Battered before,
>
> Who sang Bacchus the Muses and Venus
> And the boy who clings to them and sang for us
> Young Lycus, lovely dark-eyed, how he'd wear
> His glossy hair.
>
> Glory of Phoebus, lute-shell, and to Jove
> Delight of the feasting there is above,
> Sweet refreshment to me, if I know how
> To call on you.

The compliment to Alcaeus is most generous, but also it suggests a special reason for Horace's sense of closeness to the older poet: it is an element I noticed in Maurice Bowra's relationship with certain ancient poets, I mean the simple fact of being an old soldier. Poems have been addressed to the lute-shell, the tortoise from whose death the art began, they may be found in the Homeric hymn to Hermes, in Sappho and in Pindar, but this gentle and charming ode goes its own way.

Next comes an ode to Tibullus, full of jokes, though the bad-tempered ex-slave woman who Horace says he has fallen for does ring all too true. The theme 'X loves Y who loves Z' is of course as old as folk-song. Horace tells Tibullus to cheer up about Glycera: we know he was rich, handsome, and a Roman Knight. Tibullus was in his twenties or thirties being ten or twenty years younger than Horace, though he was dead by 19 BC. It appears to me that Horace tries to imitate the sparkling simplicity of his manner as an elegist, but after the first stanza he hardly succeeds. He refers to home for some reason, Apulian wolves and the Adriatic foaming in the curved Calabrian bays. This poem might have cast, and in someone else's hand than mine might still cast, light on the relationship of these two poets, which did not end here; it is evident enough that they were good friends, but 'miserable elegies' does not add much to criticism.

The thirty-fourth ode is an unexpected and apparently serious claim to return to religion. Fraenkel deeply disliked this thought, and rightly remarked that if it was a conversion it was not permanent. Still, he was impressed by a certain touch of religious dignity and depth about the poem. It appears to me a fine bit of verse with a psalm-like genuineness: Horace was never a dogmatic Epicurean so he may believe in Zeus if he chooses, and in the shadow of the tremendous hymn to Fortune that follows it, this looks only like a first stuttering. It is not about any real event surely? But we shall see.

> I am a mean infrequent worshipper,
> In crazy wisdom a long wanderer:
> But now I must turn back
> Reversing my old track.
>
> Because Jupiter breaking aside cloud
> Often with flashing lightning or with loud
> Thunder above has brought
> Horses and chariot,
>
> Over brute earth and wandering streams to pass,
> The Styx and Taenarus's atrocious
> Cave and the Atlantic
> Shake, he is strong to take
>
> The highest from its height and to promote
> What was obscurest to the crest of light:
> Fortune with whizzing wing
> Loves to change everything.

The poem has a strong ending yet it looks unfinished. It is not really all about a thunderstorm, or Horace's overdramatic idea of a conversion, but it could be an approach to some secret subject: if for example Maecenas was in some disgrace. Augustus is supposed to have mated with Varro Murena's sister, Maecenas's wife, and quarrelled with Maecenas over it. In 23 Varro Murena was executed for conspiracy. Yet I do not think any moment in those events could have provoked this poem, and there is no evidence that the Etruscan Knight was ever really disgraced. Is the poem just about earthquakes? That is more possible though it sounds more like rumours and rumbles and echoes of earthquake in the mountains. Why mention the Styx? Jupiter is not in the underworld but in Greece: Taenarus is the tip of the Mani where the wild rocks expire into the sea. Styx is very close to Kalavryta, a Roman colony not far from Augustan Patras. These places really are in earthquake country, and Horace takes a similar view of the Spanish mountains. After his great triumph in 29 BC Augustus reorganised the state in 27 and received remarkable honours, but in 27-5 he supervised the annexation and 'pacification' of Spain. Has Horace got his doubts about that process? I greatly doubt it, and in despair of every conjecture I can dream up, I must abandon the mysterious and powerful little poem.

The thirty-fifth ode is formal and very grand. *Fortuna* is better translated as Providence than Luck: every great city worshipped a Providence of its own, but Providence's special shrine, an entire hillside of baroque elaborations with a temple on the top, was at Praeneste, the greatest shrine in all Italy. Horace calls her goddess of Antium (Anzio) which was a more accessible place and one he knew better; it was as ancient as Praeneste. This ode used to be thought late in time: but Caesar is off to Britain (30), there is groaning over the scars of civil war, so why do we not go off and persecute the Arabs? These aspirations are not at all easy to date, they are like scraps of antique newspapers torn to rags and out of context, blowing about the street. I must confess that I disliked this long poem as a schoolboy, and have never recovered an appetite for it. It could be as early as 35 BC, as J.D.P. Bolton suggested in 1967 (*Class.Quart.*, 451f.). It is forty lines long and in the alcaic metre that Horace favoured in the thirties, and which is mostly in this first book. All three books were published at once and Horace has deliberately mingled early with late, but it is possible by close peering to discern at least the ruins of an original book that might have appeared earlier, as even the austere Nisbet and Hubbard (p. xxix) admit. There is an iron quality, a formal coldness about this ode that reminds me of the attempts at rococo ornament in cast iron still to be seen on the outer wall of the Demidoff house, near the Tretyakov Museum in Moscow. The behaviour of Faith and Hope and Necessity is hard to grasp, particularly as it all ends in Providence looking after Caesar (29). Horace is better at personal and familiar gods than at these abstract figures.

In the next ode Numida is back from a Spanish adventure, and young Lamia is delighted: they were boys together. Numida can kiss Damalis. None the less Numida defies identification and his name may be disguised because of the bad behaviour of Damalis. Or is he an ex-slave who has been to Spain on business? He could have been there as a secretary or aide to Lamia's father in 24 BC. The position of the ode here is to match the cheerful opening of the Cleopatra ode, Now it is time to drink.

> Bring incense and stringed instrument,
> Let the calf bleed as it was meant,
> For Numida's Guardians
> Who brought him safe from Spain.
>
> Dear to many friends he is,
> None of them gives him more kisses

Than sweet Lamia in mind
Of all boyhood with his friend.

Together they put togas on,
Mark the day with a white stone,
And the winejar standing ready
And the dancing feet are steady.

Damalis must not design
To challenge Bacchus in strong wine,
Let there be roses at the feast
And the lily that lives least.

Everybody's eyes languish
For the love of Damalis,
Now the new couple combines
And like lascivious ivy twines.

In this brief and extremely animated poem, one may feel that here if anywhere we are offered entrance into a real event, and a real song maybe that was sung. But it is not so: the poem is an affectionate and lively dramatic representation of the different stages of the entire party, that is all, and it manipulates the characters who play a part as if they were in a comedy. It represents Horace at his most brilliant and dramatic, where lightness of touch is all. After it comes the magnificent Cleopatra poem in which hilarity turns to relief, to taunts, and at last to her monumental elegy. Horace had great respect for suicide, as in Cato's case, and as we shall see later in the thought of his own.

This first book of *Odes* closes with a tiny poem of two stanzas, in sapphics, as the thirtieth ode is. I suspect that once the thirtieth was the last ode of the book, but that adding nine in various metres at the beginning displaced the original ending. It might have ended with a little prayer to Venus 'And Youth unfriendly without thee, And Mercury'. Now it ends with a simple-looking pair of stanzas which marvellously combine the philosopher's Enough with the convivial tones of Horace's poetry, and some shadow perhaps of the erotic.

My boy I hate these Persian contraptions,
And these wreaths all tied up in ribbons:
Do not seek out where the rose lingers last
When it is past.

Simple myrtle does not need you to add
Elaboration, it will not look bad
On you serving me under the straggle of vine
As I drink wine.

The poems all make different demands on a writer about Horace, and they offer many contrasting pleasures. In this book there is not much said about Augustus, and wars are largely more distant than thunderstorms. We have dipped deeply into Hellenistic epigrams and much more deeply into the brave Alcaeus and the convivial Anacreon. The friends are from the Augustan upper class, or they are poets, and only in the young Lamia can we discern the beginning of one of Horace's avuncular relationships with the sprigs of nobility that will flower at the end of his life. At present his eye for young women is expressed mostly in a series of feints, and the ones for whom he expresses a robust and lustful feeling are no better than they should be. He seems to be confined to that world, and his erotic urge for boys is at least equally unreal.

Chapter Six

I had been tempted to put the second book of *Satires* after the first of *Odes*, but the chronological mix-up of the *Odes* is inextricable and the later *Satires* are not easy to date, so it will be better to treat all the *Odes* as Horace intended, as a single publication. On the rickety basis of what we know (not as much as we imagine) of ancient history, scholars generally put that moment in 23 BC. That would explain the ode to Sestius and its position, as he became consul in June of that year. The reference (1, 12) to Marcellus and his glory, though he was just an ancestor with the same name, is surely before the late summer or autumn of that year, when Augustus's heir Marcellus died? This is a doubtful argument, but it is nothing to the quagmire of the decline and fall of Varro Murena or Licinius Murena the brother of Terentia wife of Maecenas. His indiscretion was at the trial of Primus in 22 BC (we are told) and he was executed for conspiracy with Caepio, soon afterwards. Horace's publication does look earlier than this enormous scandal, which apparently was in 22. No date for any of the odes is later: so we may doubtfully accept that they were published in 23 BC. It was important to get these questions cleared up before embarking on the second book, which will involve us in some smart arguments about Licinius. Of all the arguments for 23 BC I am personally most drawn to the argument from Marcellus, whose fame 'grows like a tree for a secret age', in the same line as the glitter of the star of Julius Caesar (1, 12, 45-7).

The second book begins with a poem to Pollio about the civil war, ending with a reproach to the Muse for the dreadful subject. Horace was not one to whom the civil wars had been a mere interruption: he speaks openly and very seriously, the more so in this poem because it is not to Augustus. His reference (12) to the Athenian buskin, the high-heeled shoe worn by actors in tragedy, is an echo of Virgil, who uses a similar phrase in his dedication of the eighth eclogue (10) to Pollio. When I was still a student I published a wrong-headed article about Virgil's dedication in the German periodical *Hermes*, though I repented of its shortcomings long ago. This line of Horace guarantees the genuineness of the lines of Virgil I was attacking. It is much more interesting that Horace dates the civil war period from Metellus, Q. Metellus Celer the husband of Clodia, and consul in 60 BC when Horace was four or five years old. That is when the triumvirate began of Caesar, Pompey and Crassus, which ended in such waterfalls of tears. Pollio was a sober and influential historian and Horace himself writes like one in this ode.

What in Metellus's consulship began,
Civil war's causes, vices and treason,
The play of Fortune, all the alarms,
    Friendships of princes and the arms
Oiled with unexpiated blood,
The dangerous gambles: these you understood
And understanding walk where the fires flash
    Beneath the dangerous ash ...

Horace invites him to step aside from this formidable role and from the tragic theatre, from his distinguished advocacy, his work in the Senate (he was consul in 40 BC) and his Dalmatian triumph as a general – the compliments thunder on for line after line; Pollio really was an illustrious figure, and his grandfather as a good provincial Italian had fought against Rome in the 'social wars'. All the same no one can make complete sense of his 'Dalmatian triumph', and I am glad in a way to record that Virgil's eighth eclogue which welcomes him home, and on which I had ignominiously failed to cast light, continues to puzzle historians to this day.

    ... Now with the horn's dark muttering threat
And with the crash of the trumpet,
And flash of arms you frighten those who run
    And horse and rider tumble down.
I seem to hear the great warmasters thrust
Down into not ignoble dust
And all the earth, all things resigned
    But Cato's terrible mind.

Horace has seen or heard something of Pollio's history apparently, and perhaps long before it was public, and he is also conscious of Sallust and Jugurtha.

    What field is not made rich with Latin blood
Where have the impious battle-graves not stood,
Down to this day; even the Medes attest
    The rumoured ruin of the west.

As he reaches his climax he speaks not only of Latin blood, but of 'Daunian slaughter': he is an Italian not a Roman, and so is Pollio, and that surely is an important link. Rome is not in fact mentioned once in this poem. As a glance at Horace's view of history, it is all-important. Pollio was ten years older than Horace, from Chieti, a veteran since his twenties, a staff officer of Caesar's invasion of Italy in 49 BC and many later campaigns against Cato, Pompey and others; yet as a historian he was even-handed, and Catullus and Calvus had been his friends when Horace was a boy.

    The next ode is to Crispus Sallust, the great-nephew and adopted son of the historian Sallust: old Sallust was ten years older than Pollio and twenty

older than Horace, and he died in 35 at about fifty: like Pollio he had belonged
to the provincial aristocracy. For a time he had been in public life, but he
despaired and withdrew to mature swiftly into an admirably bitter historian
of recent Roman history: Tacitus owes him a lot. It may be that much of our
disenchantment with the nastiness of Roman life is due to these wonderfully
bitter and personally thwarted historians. Crispus, whom Tacitus as we have
seen compared to Maecenas in his grey eminence, remained a Knight, but
was extremely rich, from copper mines in the Alps. His son (adopted again)
was more flamboyant when his time came, was twice consul and married first
Nero's aunt, and then his mother. Crispus owned wonderful gardens between
the Pincio and the Quirinale, no doubt inherited from the historian, who was
prosecuted for peculation in North Africa.

> Silver has no colour Crispus when it is found
> Or when it comes like loot out of the ground,
> It is the temperate using that refines
>   Until it shines.
> Proculeius will live for a long age
> Who loves his brothers with fame for his wage
> Whose ranging wings shall never droop
>   Or downward swoop ...

This brother Proculeius lived in favour with Augustus, but his brothers
included Varro Murena and quite possibly Caepio: the ancient Commentary
that tells us this does not make much sense. After a long and meritorious life
Proculeius committed a gentle suicide due to illness of the stomach, let us
hope in extreme old age as Horace prophesied. You will reign more widely,
Horace warns Crispus, by taming your greedy spirit than if you join Libya
and Cadiz and all the Carthaginians serve you on both sides: hydroptic thirst
is incurable, and Phraates is acclaimed as King of Persia but Virtue dissents:
her kingdom and safe crown and personal laurel go to whoever doesn't swivel
an eye to inspect enormous piles of treasure. This banal philosophic reproach
might look better in a satire. Scholars sniff Stoicism, but to me it just sounds
like the usual popular 'moral philosophy'. This poem is not much fun in itself,
because Horace appears to prefer Proculeius. Maybe he was made to write
the poem by Maecenas? Phraates (who can be spelt Prahates according to our
manuscripts) dates the poem somewhat insecurely about 25 BC.
  The third ode of the book is to Dellius, a slippery and nasty character, the
Somersaulter or circus rider of the civil wars as Messalla called him, meaning
one who jumps from horse to horse at high speed. He was a pimp for Antony,
who fancied a kinsman of Herod, an intriguer and a drinker, who had written
lascivious letters in the course of manipulating Cleopatra. Horace is less
severe than he was to Crispus, but quite as gloomy in his prophecies: this ode
is resonant with death, and death hums like a swarm of bees, more loudly
towards the end. All in all, this book is turning out to be full of guilt-inducing
severities; the change of mood is deliberate: we are to be shown the lyric poet
at forty. The old Greeks had discussed white hair and the loss of teeth with

an appalled sincerity, and Horace, who was forty in 25 BC, was evidently
determined to bring the subject back into fashion. Dellius had deserted
Antony at the last second of the last minute, after Actium, and Augustus had
accepted him, though he did not employ him. Dellius wrote an account of
Antony's Parthian war but otherwise we hear no more of him. How did
Horace know him unless from the Philippi campaign, when he served under
Cassius? His next ten years had been spent under Antony, but let us suppose
that Dellius and Horace had been friends. When this mountebank committed
his first act of treachery, by deserting to Cassius and offering to murder his
former commander, Dolabella the proconsul of Syria (43 BC), Horace may
have heard of it, but only as a distant rumour. It is of course possible that in
his busy diplomacy in the thirties Maecenas had noticed and been amused
by him.

> In hard times remember, keep a balanced mind
> And in good times do not be insolent
>   Because spirits are high:
>   Dellius, you will die,
> Whether you live all days melancholy,
> Or bless yourself in a private field-holiday
>   Which you may choose to pass
>   In drinking on the grass,
> Where the white poplar and the enormous pine
> Their hospitable shadows intertwine,
>   And water quivers and bounds
>   To shiver through the grounds.
> Bring wine there and the unguent and the brief
> Rose that will flower for so short a life,
>   While time and business slow
>   And the three sisters allow.
> You will lose your house and lose your glens
> And the villa where the yellow Tiber runs,
>   Your heir have the mastery
>   Where you build out to sea.
> Rich and wellborn, and blood of the noblest
> Or a poor man and blood of the lowest
>   Death is hard, you will die
>   Unpitied under the sky:
> We are all compelled to go the same way,
> Sooner or later your day and my day
>   Jump from the urn, our note
>   Of exile, the poor boat.

Horace ends more strongly with 'eternal exile' and his expression for ancient
blood is 'from Inachos' a legendary king of Argos, grandfather of the human
race and ancestor of the first colonists of Italy: Falerii and Caere for example.
I have altered the punctuation of the third stanza, and regret my failure to

convey the 'black thread of the three sisters' which jumps out at the reader
at the end of the fourth like a jack-in-the-box. The whole poem is really like
a fire-cracker under Q. Dellius's chair, and even the picnic in the middle of
this ode is not an invitation. It appears that Dellius reappeared after his
thirteen years of service abroad very rich, but it is not so obvious that Horace
felt affection for him.

The fourth ode deals with Greek names but the people are in love: the girl
is a slave, though Horace assures the boy she is 'bound to be' of royal blood
(15), a convention so common in comedies that it was accepted at least in
poetry as a received truth. The last stanza is of some interest to us.

> Her arms and face, her smoothness in position
> I praise in honesty – have no suspicion –
> Because time shows me shaken it appears
>   By forty years.

It would be more accurate no doubt to have written 'the smoothness of her
thighs (Have no suspicion) honestly I praise', but the limbs may be the calf,
with which the only rhyme would be 'do not laugh', and I balked at that.
Horace at forty in 25 BC thought himself very old.

The fifth ode of the second book has Greek names again: it is not one of the
most famous, but the advice it offers is surprisingly free. That might be an
effect of age as it often is with poets. It is about a heifer not broken in to bear
the yoke on her neck or up to the weight of a bull rushing to make love. Today
that must to most people seem an imaginary and somewhat lewd scene, yet
in Horace's day it was not. When it is observed in the open air it can seem
terrifying and godlike; the weight of the bull can be a ton or two. Horace does
not go on to bring examples from Homer to bear as he did in the fourth ode,
but stays with his metaphor: Your heifer's mind is still in the green meadows:
rivers console her for the heavy heat, she likes to play with the calves in the
wet tidal meadows. Surely the poet is back among the Calabrian cattle of his
early days? Do not long for the unripe grape, autumn will soon mark out the
bluish clusters (purple is one of his colours). She will come for you: swift-run-
ning age will give her the years it takes from you. Lalage will look for a
husband, and be more loved than fleeing Pholoe, or Chloe with the shining
white shoulder pure as the moon at night on the sea, or Gyges of Cnidos who
if you put him in a dance of girls he would confuse visitors with his long hair
and ambiguous face. There is no more than a hint of the Lesbian about this,
but the sexes are pleasantly confused, so that Horace seems to be saying
Leave her alone, she'll grow out of it, as any old dowager would say. I am not
able to reproduce precisely in English every delicacy in this surely most
beautiful poem.

The cattle are freer of course than most English cattle, but it is a relief to
see that the Romans like the French understood the delicious taste of animals
from the *prés salés*: Romney Marsh for instance. There had been poems about
animal as well as human eros, and poems about waiting for a girl to mature,
as early as Anacreon and as recently as Catullus (8), who turns on the poor

girl with sneers and reproaches. Horace is wiser as well as more controlled, somewhere around his fortieth birthday. The ode has been accused of beginning brutally, but I do not accept that view, and do not think it could arise except in a society as oddly ignorant of the facts of life as ours. The image is extremely vivid certainly, but it makes one feel a gentleness about the girl which is just the mood Horace means to engender. The only criticism one would make of this ode is that the need to preserve ambiguity leads the poet into some difficult syntax where he introduces the other girls: Lalage will be more loved (*dilecta*) than fleeing Pholoe or Chloe trailing the moonlight (surely out of Sappho?) or (quite suddenly) Gyges of Cnidos, to whom the whole of the last stanza is devoted. The hinge is *quantum non*, which at once recalls Catullus, 'loved like no other', *amata quantum amabitur nulla*. It is the shadow of a criticism that the third stanza about the colour of autumn grapes is in itself wonderful, but as an image for the girl I feel more at home among the cattle.

The sixth ode is either a tease, which would make it unique and essentially a private poem, or six stanzas to Septimius refusing an invitation to come to Spain. There was a campaign there in 29 BC, but there was no possible reason for Horace to go then. The most important invitation of his life was from Augustus, to join his household as the private secretary. We are lucky in having an exchange from those negotiations which I am sure were after 27 BC when Augustus had settled the Roman constitution, more or less. They must also probably have been before Varro Murena's conspiracy, and so within the few years in which the three books of *Odes* were being finished. Now it happens that Augustus was in Spain as general in 26 BC. Later he fell ill there, and nearly died; the war had to be finished by his deputies in 25. That visit had been an attempt to subdue the 'Cantabres', and it is quite on the cards that Augustus would have attempted to lure Horace to follow him. The Romans did in the end subdue Spain, but Augustus was not the only general in history to have found that an extremely difficult task. I think he attempted it for two reasons, firstly because that was where he was picked out as a lad to be Caesar's heir, and secondly I conjecture because it was important for him to show some success as a general, in order to justify his control of the army. He would see how Rome got on without him and he would give his legions something to do. So I accept the suggestion that Caesar being in Spain invited Horace, and the further suggestion, which I do not know who first made unless it was Rostagni (1934), that this ode should be treated as a supplement to what we know of the negotiation.

Suetonius in his Life of Horace says, 'Augustus also offered Horace responsibility for his letters, which is what he means when he writes this to Maecenas: "In the past I was capable of writing my own letters to friends: now that I am terribly busy and unwell I want to capture our friend Horace from you; so he will leave that dependent table of yours to come to my royal one, and help me to write my letters." He did not mind when he was refused, and he did not leave off offering Horace his friendship. There are letters which in order to prove my point I shall cite. "Consider that you have some rights over me, just as if you were living with me: you will be right and not

presumptuous in doing so, because that is the relationship I wanted with you,
if your health would have allowed it." And again: "You can hear from our
mutual friend Septimius how I have you in my thoughts, because it happened
that he was there when I mentioned you. Just because you are so proud as to
spurn my friendship, that does not mean I am going to look down my nose at
you in return." Besides this among other jokes he calls him "purest penis"
and "funniest of little men", and he enriched him in this way and that. He so
much approved of his writings and so much took the view they would last for
ever ...' As an imperial secretary a hundred and fifty years after the odes,
Suetonius knew the archives and quoted liberally. 'He was,' he says, 'a short
and fat man, as he describes himself in the *Satires*, and as this letter from
Augustus describes him. "Onysius brought me your little book which I think
well of, however little. You seem to me to be afraid your books should be any
bigger than you are, but though you lack height you do not lack body, so you
will be able to write on a tankard and the circumference of your book will be
vast, as is that of your belly." In sexual matters he is said to have been
intemperate: he is supposed to have had a room full of mirrors so that
whichever way he looked he would see the act going on. He lived mostly in
the remote country, on his Sabine land or at Tibur, and they show you his
house near Tiburnus's grove.'

The room with the mirrors has shocked scholars, but Nell Gwynn had one
just like it, and I doubt whether she got the idea from Suetonius. No doubt
the room was pointed out by the guides to Horace's house: but we are not
certain whether Horace had a house of his own at Tibur, or called his house
Sabine or at Tibur indifferently. Tivoli is some thirty miles from Rome, and
Horace's Sabine farm some five or ten further on. The important scrap of
letter for us is the one that mentions Septimius. At the time of our ode he
must have been a young man; the antique Horace commentaries say he was
a Knight, which is possible and likely, and an ex-soldier friend of Horace,
which is less so. He cannot have been middle-aged in 21 BC when the poet
recommended him to Tiberius (*Epist.* 1,9). At any rate he seems to be ten
years younger than Horace, who mentions his age again in this ode and at
the end his death. If Augustus really gave him the house Suetonius mentions
at Tivoli, then by this time he has been given it. Behind the poem stands one
by Catullus to Furius and Aurelius in the sapphic metre, handled with an
astonishing delicacy and equal indelicacy.

> Septimius to Cadiz and the Cantabrian rocks
> My friend, where they have not learnt to bear our yokes,
> To the barbarous Syrtes where the Moorish waves
>   Thunder and rave:
> Still may the seat of my old age remain
> Tibur foundation of the Argive countryman,
> I am tired out with the sea and travelling
>   And soldiering.
> But if the unfair Fates will not allow
> I shall seek Galaesus with my flock and go

To where Laconian Phalanthus was ruling
  A country King.

Phalanthus founded Tarentum, the sheep would seek the river Galaesus down there in the south, as Virgil's shepherds might. The fantasy is charming but the exotic names are an attempt to outdo Catullus. 'That bit of land most laughs for me' (Catullus on Sirmio) 'where the honey is as good as Hymettus and the olives as good as green Venafrum.' Venafrum is in Campania and its olive trees and their oil were renowned. Everyone said so except Virgil who appears to have a blind spot about olives.

There Jupiter gives a long spring, autumn heat
And Aulon loves Bacchus, there's no defeat
To suffer from the old Falernian vine
  Or from its wine.

There is a continuous impulse of warmth in these eight lines and more about Tarentum, which is where Aulon 'the Valley' is. This enthusiasm at least Virgil shares: it is where he finds his old man with the market garden. Its obvious advantage was that short of taking to the water Tarentum was as far south as you could get. I have dared to mistranslate 'warm mist' as autumn heat because Tarentum was not a foggy place, and the season of mists and mellow fruitfulness was meant. 'That place and those blessed hill towns demand us both: there you will sprinkle the warm ashes of your friend the poet with the tears you owe.' So the poem ends in a sad little scene: has Horace really been very ill, and is that why he has been longing to take his flocks back to the scenes of his childhood? It is possible, because Augustus, whose health was as rotten as his, was genuinely ill at just this time, at just the same time of life, the onset of age in the ancient world. If Horace's poem were a mere excuse it would be too contrived.

The seventh poem of this book is to Horace's early friend Pompey; they had served in Asia together before Philippi as young men, but Pompey was sucked back into the fighting and it looks likeliest that he was amnestied after Actium in 30 BC. He may have been a kinsman of Sextus Pompey, who was successful against Rome and ruled Sicily until 36 BC when he fled and was executed. At one stage Sextus controlled Corsica, Sardinia and Achaea, as well as his Sicilian base, so Horace's friend if he was really a kinsman could have served with him for a few years. All Horace mentions is Brutus and great relief that this friend is back under Italian skies. Who knows where he might have been? We have dealt with this poem at an earlier stage, but looking at the poem in the position Horace gave it one should notice that the early severity of this book is now forgotten, and if old scars are still being licked then the process has become enjoyable: nature has been restored. Yet the very next poem treats the worst behaviour. It is to a bad girl called Barine, that is a slave's or a tart's name, because she comes from Bari. Does Horace laugh at her wickedness as he comforts his friend Pompey? The nasty

Dellius seems a world away. 'How smooth the cups wine and oblivion fills: Pour the sweet unguent out of the big shells ...' (21-3).

The eighth ode is to Barine: this girl is not only no better than she ought to be, but her name is as I have just said a giveaway about her social origins; good behaviour is not really to be expected from her. Horace is gleefully tolerant:

> If any penalty for perjury
> Had ever done you harm, Barine,
> If you were the worse by just one black tooth
>   Or gave one nail to truth
> I would believe: but the moment you bow your fool
> Head with broken oaths you shine more beautiful
> Than ever in your sin, public anxiety
>   For youth and gallantry:
> It is all right to deceive your mother's ashes then
> And all the silent signals of the entire heaven,
> And all the gods who never lose their breath
>   In the bleak ice of death.
> Venus herself laughs at all this I say,
> The simple Nymphs laugh and Cupid in his wild way,
> Always sharpening red-hot arrows one by one
>   On the bloody stone ...

Everyone is terrified of her, the younger generation of her new slaves, and the older ones who refuse to leave her though she has betrayed them, and 'mothers fear you for their sons, and mean old men and virgins newly wed fear you, in case a breath from you might delay their husbands.' This poem is not in Horace's usual vein, it is almost complacently wicked, with certain touches of Catullus perhaps. It is as light as it could be, as airy as Byron, and yet something underlies it: Venus may laugh, but do we? If we do not, then that also has been delicately contrived by Horace. The manuscripts call the girl Julia or Julla Barina, which is an extremely unlikely guess, but she may of course have been an ex-slave if she ever existed at all, which I reckon she did not.

The ninth poem is to Valgius, and suggests he should sing about Caesar's eastern conquests rather than the soft lamentations for a Greek slave-boy which Valgius has been pouring out night and day: the ode is wonderfully phrased but it is rough consolation, rather a rebuke. C. Valgius Rufus (*Sat*.1, 10, 82) was an *homme de lettres* and an old friend of Horace. He dedicated a *materia medica*, a book on the uses of herbs, to Augustus with a prayer that 'this great Prince's majesty might cure every ill that afflicted humans'. Unfortunately he never finished this compendious work on plants, but the grand eloquence of the preface (he wrote a treatise on eloquence as well) might explain that look of sweet concern and bewilderment which is the expression of Augustus in his official portraits, assuming that he had just read Valgius. Still, he made Valgius a consul in 12 BC. We have a reference to the Homeric grandeur of his verse, and a fragment about drinking rough wine and warm milk outside a cottage, bits about a journey, an epigram, and a poem about Etna. He greatly admired the older poet Cinna, whom he celebrated in elegiac verse, weighed down with classical allusions, to deadly effect. Cinna himself had been torn to pieces by the mob at Caesar's funeral, and is remembered by Shakespeare, 'Tear him for his bad verses.' If Valgius really admired him so much it is a link that they both entered politics, and both had great facility in verse.

It has been suggested that Mystes, the dead slave-boy, never really existed, or else this ode would be far too heartless, but I do not myself think Horace incapable of a barb or two. Some modern scholars have gone so far as to say the boy had abandoned Valgius for another lover. In that case he would be an ex-slave, but Horace has already made it plain one should be discreet about such matters. Still, it is quite clear that Horace is talking about lamentation over a death. Scholars believe that Horace is copying one of the few fragments of Cinna that we have, in his few words about the evening star, which is a curious thought and would I suppose make his attitude to Valgius softer than it seems to me. We are also told that Horace was parodying Virgil, but that is surely stuff and nonsense. This entire cobweb of scholarly fantasies arose after Fraenkel's death, and makes one grateful for the vigorous manner in which he defended Horace from every scholarly fantasy and exaggeration in his lifetime: Horace did not write riddles.

> Clouds do not ooze down rain without end
> On to the shaggy fields Valgius my friend
>> Nor do the storm winds roar
>> On to the Caspian shore
> Nor does Armenian ice lock the land motionless
> Month after month, nor the oakwoods of Garganus
>> Labour as the wind grieves
>> And ash trees lose their leaves,
> Your weeping verse insists over Mystes
> Taken away, and when evening rises
>> Love stays and will not run
>> From the swift returning sun ...

'Lovable Antilochus was not mourned for months on end by his old father, nor did his parents and Phrygian sisters mourn Troilus for ever. Leave off these soft laments, let us both sing new trophies of Caesar Augustus, rigid Mount Niphates, Euphrates conquered and the Scythians riding within narrow limits.' The ode seems to be written about 29 BC, and a certain imprecision about the geography arises from an element of fantasy (not parody I am sure) about Caesar's triumphs. They do not ring in the least true, nor is Horace's heart in the sad death of the late Mystes, who may indeed never have existed at all. Maybe this is just a gentle tease, a familiar gesture to a friend about his insisting (9: *urges*) style of elegiac.

The tenth ode is to Licinius Varro Murena, whom we have met before, whose sister was Maecenas's wife, who quarrelled with Augustus over his prosecution of Primus for unauthorised use of troops in Thrace and was accused of being in Caepio's conspiracy, tried to escape with a Greek Aristotelian philosopher he employed, was captured and executed. The Greek was let off, so escaping was not the crime in question. This ode about the middle way being best must be before Murena's decline and fall. His great fault is said to have been violence of language. It is worth underlining the fact that Horace liked the family and let the poem stand, and no one objected even after Murena's execution. It was a world in which power was God, and at times one shivers at how easily those who sought power could have a fatal fall. 'Do not forever press on into deep water Licinius, nor, since as a prudent man you are horrified by storms, push too close to shore. The golden middle ... Jupiter brings back ugly winters, and removes them.'

> If it is bad now yet it will not be
> For ever, Apollo makes the silent lute to be
> Musical once more, not always does Apollo
>   Stretch out his bow.

The poem is twenty-four lines long, not written with great intensity but with a magisterial calmness. I greatly wish that we knew how old Murena was, but I imagine not very.

The eleventh ode is to Quinctius Hirpinus to whom Horace wrote his sixteenth letter, with a warm and charming description of his Sabine farm. The Hirpini were an old Italian people, and this friend of Horace may well be a kinsman of an old man, long dead, who made himself extremely rich rather nastily under Sulla, by buying up the estates of those 'on the list'. Our Quinctius might even (by a wild flight of conjecture) be Pollio's brother-in-law, which would explain why he and Varro Murena occupy the centre of this book. 'Do not fret,' Horace tells him, about the Spaniards and Scythians (the Adriatic cuts them off),

> Light youthfulness and beauty run on air
> Backwards and snowy white in the dry hair
>   Drives prankish love away
>   And easy sleepy day.
> Flowers are not so glorious and one
> Turns to two faces in the blushing moon,
>   Eternal schemes wear out the mind
>   And human powers have an end.
> Why not lie down under some mighty plane
> Or why not here, below the giant pine
>   With roses in white hair
>   And Syrian scented air?
> Bacchus scatters gnawing anxiety,
> I ask only which of the boys will be
>   First to weaken the wine

> In the passing stream?
> Who'll fetch wandering Lyde out of the house?
> Bring that whore and her lute of ivory close,
>> With her hair done up tight
>> In a Laconian knot.

I do not know why the whore has her hair in a bun, in Spartan style (Laconian). It is interesting to know there were a number of slave-boys at the picnic, and the wine we are told was Falernian. This is a charming invitation to the feast, selective in description as usual. But now they both have white hair, so this cannot be an early ode. Horace waves his hand like a magician to banish this man's troubles. They sound remote and last only for one stanza. I must confess that I had not intended to translate so much of the poem until I felt its wind lifting or skimming it along. It is a relief that Horace calls Lyde 'that wandering whore', because we know where we are, and because he does not pretend to have complete control over her.

Now the odes begin to get a little longer. The twelfth is some pointed advice to Maecenas himself. 'Do not try to match the lute with the Spanish war [won by Scipio in 133 BC] or Hannibal or the Sicilian sea red with Phoenician blood, or the wild Lapiths: you tell Caesar's battles in prose Maecenas.' Can he really have considered all these themes? The queerest of all is the first, the Numantian war which Lucilius fought in but abjured as a subject. It is rare in the *Odes* to find his traces, yet Horace imitated that abjuration in another poem. It may be relevant that the ruins of Numantia were only a hundred miles from where Augustus was fighting in Spain. He says Maecenas is to tell of 'Kings led by the neck'. He goes on to explain: 'The Muse wanted me to sing of my sweet lady Licymnia', and mutual love and her flashing eyes. If you believe as some people have done since late antiquity that this is code for Terentia, wife of Maecenas, mistress of Augustus and sister of Licinius Varro Murena then it is up to you to sort out the happy family, but I do not. She is admittedly treated rather grandly in a metre like that for the dead Infanta. When she dances and goes to Diana's festival, when Maecenas (23, *tu*) would give all Arabia for a lock of her hair, Horace might almost mean Terentia; but not in the last stanza when she twists her neck for burning kisses or with easy ferocity refuses and delights when they are stolen, or steals them herself. This is not the way the Roman nobility talked of their wives: so once again, Horace did not write riddles. What is more positive is that the poem looks quite early, though I do not insist.

The thirteenth ode berates a tree and whoever planted it, because it fell on Horace's head: he then muses on the other world which he so nearly entered. The tree stood on his land (*agro meo*) in the valley. This curious and to us pleasing little accident is not untypical of the tendency of Hellenistic art to take tiny subjects, not just in poetry where Martial has a swineherd killed by a tree, but even in sculpture, where the flower-garlands on the Ara Pacis Augusti have bees crawling on them. This accident really happened, apparently on 1st March, after the late winter gales. In another ode the poet's misadventure coincides with the recovery of Maecenas from illness, and the

wine he opens (3, 8) is from the vintage of 33 BC or possibly 66 BC; the early
or middle twenties are the likely date for drinking the 33, but the 66 would
be an antique, possibly from the year Maecenas was born, and is much less
likely. Scholars have confused this matter with elaborately rickety arguments. Alcaeus in the underworld is thought to echo Virgil's Orpheus, but the
link is trivial and likely enough to derive from a common source: besides, we
do not know whether Virgil foreshadowed Horace or, as I think likelier,
echoed him: Virgil read his finished *Georgics* to Augustus in 29 BC. This
scratching and scrabbling for an exact date therefore gets us nowhere. Still,
the curse on the tree is a ripe example of curses on the inventors of things:
and it is set at the Sabine farm.

> On a black day you were planted on my land
> And settled there by an unholy hand
>   For his grandchildren's ruin
>   And the peasantry's cursing,
> The man who did it broke his father's neck
> And spattered blood round inside the shack
>   Where his host lay at night,
>   He used the poisoned bite
> Of Colchian venom and all things forbidden
> Unhappy wood, and left you ruinous, hidden
>   In my fields to fall down
>   On your master's innocent crown ...

'You can never be too careful, the sailor may be terrified of the Bosporus but
he never fears death from somewhere else. The soldier fears Parthian arrows,
the Parthian fears Italian power, but it's the death you don't imagine that
carries you off. I very nearly saw the underworld and Aeacus the judge, the
seats of the blessed set apart.'

> And Sappho still whose Lesbian strings complain
> For girls of her country, your golden strain
>   Alcaeus and re-echoing far
>   The ills of ships and flight and war.

Sappho laments for girls gone abroad: she does so in poems we have of
hers. Alcaeus also laments this subject-matter in poetry that we know. But
is it the underworld that makes their poetry so sad, or was that really the
quality Horace sought out in their metres? On the whole I think it is the
underworld, because although Alcaeus in Horace has an undertone of sadness, the more obvious thing about him is courage as one faces the
world-wandering sea. Recent scholars have made the astonishing suggestion
that Sappho was not lamenting the absence of friends but groaning over
'street-girls': the insouciant vulgarity of the suggestion defies comment.
There were paintings of Alcaeus and Sappho on Greek vases, and their
solemn beauty centuries after their death demands a decency in this poem,

which the usual meaning of *popularibus*, 'girls of her own country', confirms.
In the next stanza I have faked the last line.

> In holy silence stand the wondering shades
> And yet the mob crowds to hear violent deeds
>   And tyrants put to death
>   Ride on their heavy breath.
> What wonder if the hundred heads drip tears
> And the monster mastiff lowers his dark ears
>   While the snakes enmeshed
>   In the Furies are refreshed
> Prometheus now and Tantalus are deep
> In the deceiving trances of a sleep,
>   Orion's hunger sinks
>   For lion and swift lynx.

The underworld is a dream world, but its strange unreal beauty is easier
to carry off in two or three brief stanzas than in the form of a distended epic,
so Horace has an easier task than Virgil in the *Aeneid*, who must introduce
philosophy, and the real dead of the Roman world, and even a kind of
topography which is not convincing, and a prophecy of the future which is
still more regrettable, or seems so to us. For Horace the entire darkness is
the trembling of a lute-string. The saddest of his poems about death follows
this one at once. It is the fourteenth and used in the last generation to be the
most famous. Sadly, we cannot be certain about its dedication; Postumus is
a real Roman name but this Postumus could be any of a number of people:
even the likeliest of them is not very likely, being a very young man to whom
Propertius wrote verse later, a kinsman who lived later still to be wealthy
enough to own the expensive Caecuban wine that Horace mentions. I think
he was an elder kinsman of this person and of Propertius too. Propertius's
Postumus (3, 12) was married to Aela Gallia, daughter or sister of Aelus
Gallicus, governor of Egypt, whose close friend Seius was a nephew of
Maecenas and patron to the geographer Strabo: but this rather closely
knitted circle is too late in the reign to include Horace's Postumus: he was
their cousin or great-uncle no doubt. Propertius was only in his twenties,
probably his early twenties, when the *Odes* came out, Maecenas late in life
showed interest in him, but Horace growls about him (*Epist*.2, 2) in a late
letter. Yet there is a touch of genius about him, to our eyes.

> Oh Postumus, Postumus, the years run
> Away like water, nor does religion
>   Delay wrinkles, or the same
>   Death that nothing will shame.
> Three hundred bulls felled every day
> Do not placate Pluto: his tears are dry,
>   He crushes Geryon
>   And the sad Tityon

With triple rivers: and one day all men
Whom the earth nourished sail away again:
All kings tomorrow,
All poor farmers go.

'Avoiding the sea is no use, we must visit dark Cocytos and his languid
wandering river You must leave earth and home and your nice wife and none
of your trees but the hated cypresses will go with their brief master.' The
hated cypress, as we have seen, was used for funeral fires, not for windbreaks
in cemeteries as it is now; Postumus may have hated it because it was the
wild cypress encroaching on his orchards, but the more conventional view
that the Romans liked it for its obvious gloom is well attested too. There were
in those days entire forests of wild cypress. 'Your heir will drink the Caecuban, and spill on the pavement of the rooms what you keep under lock and
key, a wine grander than priests' dinners.' The only sin of Postumus appears
to be his wealth and his wine.

The fifteenth ode is more purely moral and addressed to nobody in particular. Horace disapproves of lavish fish-ponds bigger than the lake Lucrinus
(hence the hillside Lucretilis?) near Puteoli and Naples, which is smaller
today than it was. Agrippa had joined it to Avernus to make a vast and safe
harbour for his fleet. Now the planes carry no vines and the olive grove
nourishes only sweet-smelling flowers, no vegetables. That was not what
Romulus decreed and long-haired Cato and the ancients: they liked small
private expense, more public expense, no north-facing cool colonnades. No
turf was neglected, and towns and temples were decorated at public expense
with fresh stone. The ode is strange in its details and oddly stern, but it is
curiously sympathetic, and the fresh stone at the end is lovely. '... but
decorate the town And temples with fresh stone', which must date from
around 27 BC.

The sixteenth ode is to Pompeius Grosphus, who farmed a large estate of
fertile land in Sicily, probably near Agrigento, but his ode has signs of a
gentle Epicurean cult of the quiet, secluded life. It is written in five blocks of
two stanzas each. The second of the middle two has been much attacked: it
is not of great value, but Fraenkel defended it and I accept that he is probably
right; some of the greatest experts have admired this ode greatly: let us see
what it reveals. The first and most obvious point to make is that the repeated
word 'idleness' comes from Catullus (51) and is used by Virgil at the end of
his *Georgics* in a particularly subtle way: the Siren of Naples or Capri has
nourished him in idleness as a poet. At the end of his treatment of the ode in
his *Horace* (211-4), Fraenkel remarks that 'Horace's personal creed has its
centre in the mellow wisdom, the resignation without bitterness, of which the
whole ode is a perfect expression ...'

The sailor when dark cloud covers the moon
Caught out in the open Aegean
When no sure star shines down for anyone
Wants idle peace.

Idle peace Thracians in furious war
Idle peace the Persian with his fine quiver
Pray for Grosphus, gems will not buy them or
    Purple or gold.

Neither treasures nor the consul's men can still tumults of mind or anxieties
that flit around the stuccoed ceiling: you live well on little when your father's
salt cellar glitters on your little table and fear and sordid desire do not take
away your light sleep. Why are we so brave at spearing so much in our brief
time? (Care breaks the bronze-covered warships and does not leave the
cavalry; it is swifter than the deer or the wind.) A mind glad with what is
present hates worrying about the beyond, and tempers the bitter with a
gentle laugh: nothing is blessed from every aspect.

    Swift death took famous Achilles,
    Long age withered Tithonus with ease,
    What the hour has denied you, I may see
        Given to me.

'A hundred flocks and mooing cows may wander over Sicily for you, your
chariot horses may be whinnying, and double-dyed African wool may cover
you: to me a truthful Fate has given small lands and the thin breath of the
Greek Muse, and to despise the mob.' This is indeed the mellowest and most
peaceful poetry, as Fraenkel promised: the moral philosophy might come
from any dialogue, except that here Horace is curiously benign about the vast
wealth of Grosphus, which we know was inherited from a long past. Tithonus
shrank to the size of a grasshopper: he did not die young like Achilles, but he
lived to wish he had. There is a mild, mildly increasing melancholy about the
early stanzas, but the beginning recalls the first satire, though 'idle peace'
softens it. I read somewhere recently that Grosphus had mining interests,
and we are told he traded abroad: no doubt, since the grandest Romans did
so. But it makes no difference. The flocks and the cattle may occupy a large
area, but they make only a rustic noise in this poem. The double-dyed purple
wool does admittedly sound excessive, and poets agree it is a pleasure to have
a few fields and the thin breath of the Greek Camena, as Horace says: but
Grosphus does not sound an unhappy man, and we may hope that he attained
otium, idle peace or happy idleness.

The book is drawing to a close. The seventeenth ode bids Maecenas to stop
complaining. Within the long but scarcely knowable story of their relationship, it marks a moving episode. The sixteenth ode has sweetened the mood
at last, so that this falls perfectly into place.

    Why do you frighten me with your lament?
    The gods are not, and nor am I, content
    That you die before me,
    My pillar and glory.

'If some swifter violence tears you away Maecenas, part of my soul, then why would I live on? That day ruins us both; I have sworn a loyalty that I will not go back on: we shall go, we shall go, if ever you lead the way as friends ready for the last journey. Neither the breath of fiery Chimaera nor hundred-handed Gyges if he rises up again shall ever tear me from you: Justice and Fate have decided that. Whether the Scales or Scorpion stands against my birth-hour, or Capricorn over the western sea, our stars are incredibly conjoined: Jove's protection shining snatched you from Saturn, and slowed Fate's wings when the people crowding the theatre roared three times for happiness: a tree-trunk on the head would have ended me, if Faunus had not stopped it, the protector of men under Mercury. So give victims, build a shrine: and I will sacrifice a humble lamb.'

The twining of fates explains the beginning of the poem I suppose, and Maecenas is said to have believed the astrological nonsense, but Horace did not and nor do I: he is just consoling his worried friend. We have met the applause in the theatre before, and the tree which fell and did not fall: one assumes it got caught up in another tree. The last journey is not suicide, only the last of many. It is a beautiful poem and one hopes Maecenas was pleased with it. I cannot think of him without remembering the thunder of waterfalls and the loud noise of nightingales; they were heard until 1820 from the Truglia at Tivoli, once the Sibyl's cave, if one slept at Sant' Antonia: people used to say that was Horace's villa at Tibur, but I doubt if he ever had one there. What it could more easily be is a villa of Maecenas where Horace stayed. Maecenas was recommended the sound of waterfalls by his doctor, Antonius Musa. Now the Truglia is dry, as the Pope diverted the water, and I have no recent news of the nightingales, though they were heard there in living memory.

Ode eighteen is against an unnamed wealthy man again: it is not person-ally intended, it is a social poem that cut a wide swathe, and he was neither the first nor the last to make hay of that meadow. The metre which is old is trochaic, like Peter Piper picked a peck of pickles, eh? More so admittedly if you read the four line stanzas as long couplets: but the orthodox view is that the trochaics alternate with iambics. Piper pickled Peter's nose In competi-tion for a bowl of roses. He does not have gold or ivory in his ceilings, or 'Hymettian beams pressing down on columns cut in furthest Africa'. Hymet-tos marble is bluish grey, and L. Crassus in 90 BC and Brutus a little later were proud of a very little. Horace is just suggesting luxuriance, but Roman luxury grew so fast in his time that his examples seem banal: Spartan purple means sea-purple from shells in the water around Kythera. I am, he says, happy (or rich) with just my Sabine estate. One day treads on another and new moons rush to die: but you … Here the moralising takes a nastier tone, which often begins when he mentions building out into the sea. Everyone dies, he says. The poem is not of very strong construction, and might be extremely early for all I can see to the contrary: it is thought to have some connection with Virgil's second georgic (466) and Lucretius (2, 20) but the Horace is too weak to bear such a strain of kinship.

The ode to Bacchus is quite different (19). It begins with the clear assertion that Horace has seen the god sitting on the rocks and teaching. Fraenkel says 'he had only to shut his eyes', but that is not a full explanation, and the stanza gets more improbable as it goes on:

> I saw Bacchus on rocks teaching his songs
> (Mankind believe me) saw the listening
> Nymphs and goatfoot group
> Of Satyrs, ears pricked up.

It is hard to keep up Horace's intoxicated tone, which was not easy for him to sustain either. 'I am terrified,' he says, interjecting a few Bacchic whoops strictly in alcaic metre, 'and my mind shakes with fear, my breast is full of joy, spare me O Free god, spare me for I fear your heavy thyrsus,' which is a pine-cone with magic power on a wand. 'It is right for me to sing the Bacchae, and the wine-spring, the rich streams of milk, and the honey dripping from hollow tree-trunks: right to sing your blessed partner a star in the sky, and the house of Pentheus terribly broken down, and how the Thracians killed Lycurgus.' Pentheus confirms one's feeling that all this derives mainly from the *Bacchae* of Euripides; Lycurgus had attacked the vine. It is interesting that Ariadne the new partner figures in the Villa of the Mysteries at Herculaneum, and that Lycurgus figures on a cup of glass strangely coloured from about the same period in the British Museum. Horace quotes verbally from the *Bacchae* in a later poem. Now the nineteenth ode becomes a more normal hymn. Before we follow it the question remains of Horace's conjuring trick: are we really supposed to believe he saw these things? I think we are meant to suspend our doubts; and the shock of the opening of this poem almost makes us do so. And yes, of course it is just a conjuring trick. To Horace its unreality surely lay in its antiquity and its being Greek.

'You turn streams, and the sea, and wet on your remote peaks govern the hair of the Bistonides with a knot of vipers.' The reader can be reassured that no one has ever made much sense of this: the Bistonides were Thracians, and the marine episode is thought to have some connection with Lycurgus, no one knows just what. The clue must be in a lost tragedy. 'In the war of the giants you drove back Rhoetus with a lion's claws and terrible jaw'; the claws and jaw are thought to be the giant's though I prefer to think that the lion and all its attributes belong to the god. One could argue out this knotty muddle, but it is not part of the vision and we must abandon it, since it tells us nothing we did not know about the vividness of Horace's visual imagination. There is a lion at Delphi in a frieze I had in mind. 'You were always reputed better at dancing and at jokes, and not a natural fighter, yet you were the same in peace and in war. Cerberus saw you glorious with your golden horn, gently rubbing his tail (on you) and harmless, and as you left his triple tongue licked your feet and legs.' It will be seen that Horace's box of tricks in this poem is inexhaustible, and that its baroque extravagance is deliberate. What he achieves in it, that is in us, is a state of wonder, that is all, and quite enough too.

The twentieth and last poem of the book is a kind of rehearsal for the last of the third book. His sign is the wild swan's flight. I am lucky enough to have

lived by swan-infested rivers and pieces of water most of my life, and there
is no bird more eerily beautiful in flight nor so amazing and star-like on dark
water at evening. Swans do make ungainly noises but we should forget those
and remember the powerful whizz of their wings, which appears to be the
origin of their legendary song. The legend was rife among the ancient Greeks,
and that is where Horace got it. Virgil was even keener than Horace on these
white birds in the green meadows around Mantua. In the Hellenistic period
there were many queer tales of people turning into birds, and Horace
gleefully transforms himself, but for him the swan is a symbol of his wide
recognition and his immortality as a poet. No doubt he felt that after what
he had just claimed for Bacchus, his own cycnification was a pardonable way
to bow out.

> No ordinary no light wing
> Carries me through the liquid air singing:
>   I stay on earth no more
>   But above envy soar.
> I'll leave cities, no poor man's blood,
> Not him Maecenas that you understood,
>   I shall take flight from here
>   Quite free of death's water.
> Now, now over my legs creeps rougher skin
> And I become a white bird of heaven,
>   Now I can sense feathers
>   Cover back and fingers,
> And now more famous than old Icarus
> I'll cross the groaning coast of Bosphorus
>   A singing bird that goes
>   To the northern meadows.

I left out some of the places he intends to visit: the Syrtes and North Africa
singing as he goes, and then the Hyperborean fields, where Apollo is worshipped in the north and griffins guard hoards of gold, as Herodotus tells us:
nor had Tacitus anything likelier to propose.

> No dirges then at my empty funeral
> No grief or gloom and no lament at all,
>   There is no honour to add,
>   No reason to be sad.

The second book has a spiny unity all of its own. It does I think read like
a separate work, and perhaps at some stage it, or something like it, was
intended to be one. But as we shall now see, we had by no means exhausted
Horace's originality or his variety in these two books, these fifty-eight poems.
The material of the *Satires* has found more than a toehold in them. This last
book has been scanty and formal in its praises of Augustus, but we shall see
that change with time.

Chapter Seven

In the first six poems of the third book of *Odes*, the poet 'somewhat loudly sweeps the string'. They are the grandest poetry that Horace has ever written, they represent the height and intensity he can best achieve in lyric poetry. They are not precisely state poetry, because that can hardly exist, yet they are something very like it. As the second book ended at a high point of grandeur close to the hysterical unless one is carried away by it, so the third begins in a solemnity one can scarcely credit until it envelops the mind. The convincing thing about Horace is his atavistic power of language: all Latin prose and poetry reads somehow as if its cold head-spring were the tombs of the Scipios, and Horace's perfect matching of words and rhythms is part of that effect, as if the rhythms, which are Greek and which he explores gradually, came naturally to him or like a second nature. In his attacks on the sublime he is as laconic as an inscribed stone of two or three hundred years before his birth.

We have spoken of the key word *otium*, idleness: so for an example of how Horace expresses himself we might consider a brief poem of Housman, scarcely more than an epigram, the skeleton of a dead leaf. It has no obvious origin in Horace.

> Soldier from the wars returning,
> Spoiler of the taken town,
> Here is ease that asks not earning,
>   Turn you in and sit you down. ...
> ... Rest you, charger, rust you, bridle,
> Kings and Kaisers keep your pay,
> Soldier, sit you down and idle
>   At the inn of night, for aye.

This stuck in my head forty or rather fifty years ago when I was a boy: it had a dreamy quality that seduced me, and it has a dark side, as Horace has. Now I like it for its perfect procedure, its level and yet varied tone, and because it is unanswerable, it is all that needs to be said. Although I believed I knew the poem by heart, when I came to check it I found that I had remembered only the first and last stanzas of a four-stanza poem (VII, *Last Poems*), reducing it to something much more like a Greek epigram, and I still cannot help preferring it in the stronger form. The last line of the first stanza betrays the perfectionism of composers of elegiac couplets, to which neither Shakespeare nor Horace is a prey, but the end of it, the sentiment of *otium*, and the address to the soldier, are in their way Horatian. The British Museum have a gravestone from Rhodes in the antique manner, made in the first century BC. It is a relief carving of a sad soldier mourning himself, naked, leaning on a spear with a snake twined around it. He is wearing a fifth-century helmet pushed back from his face, like Pericles, and he stands at present in shadow, in a corner near the entrance to the Elgin marbles. He might for all I know to the contrary be one of those who died when Cassius besieged and looted Rhodes; he is certainly the kind of man to whom Horace dedicated many of his odes.

The first six poems of the third book are written from the heights of the Roman state, from the battlements as it were, though they are not addressed to any political assembly. Horace cannot quite give up his first ambition to be a bard all the same.

> I hate and spurn the mob: let them stand far,
> And be silent: songs never heard before:
>   Priest of Muses my voice
>   Chants them for girls and boys.

He is a priest who hates the mob because it is profane, uninitiated, and he calls for silence as Romans did before a sacrifice, he is a priest of the Muses, who at least at Athens had a real cult, and at Rome a temple of 'Hercules of the Muses': he is represented on coins of the consul Q. Pomponius Musa a year after Horace was born. The girls and boys are not schoolchildren but two choirs to sing Horace's hymns. That temple was repaired under Augustus, it had an altar that Plutarch mentions and a colonnade called Philip's, after the restorer. It was near the modern Piazza Mattei; a statue stood close by recording the capture of Ambracia, which by then was the capital city of King Pyrrhus of Epirus, by M. Fulvius Nobilior in 189 BC. He brought home some terracotta Muses painted by the famous Zeuxis, and this venerable loot was in the temple Horace knew in the Piazza Mattei, where there was also a wig-shop for women. But that famous consul had 785 bronze statues and 230 marble ones carried in his triumphant procession: they must have altered and diluted Roman taste. 'Priest of the Muses' has become a Roman title one could adopt if one chose: it was not a real title as Priest of the Camenae would perhaps still have been. Nobilior was a personal friend of Ennius; his idea had been to have 'the peace of the Muses' defended by Hercules (*Musarum quies*), an aspiration not foreign to Horace.

> Kings to their own flocks are terrifying
> And it is Jupiter terrifies Kings:
>   He can lay Giants low
>   With the flick of an eyebrow.

The Latin says he did triumph over Giants and rules all with an eyebrow. A certain unreality has invaded the poem: who are the Kings and the flocks?

'Kings' was a word with more meaning to it for the Romans than one would expect, and it may be we are in the Bronze Age, when Jupiter's famous triumph over the Giants is fresh? But we recur at once to the pattern of the first ode of the first book, and the first satire too: the various ambitions of men. In this landslide of heavy stones it is no surprise that they come to no good. Sicilian feasts such as Grosphus might provide, and the birdsong and lutesong that might lull Maecenas to sleep, are no good here.

> The gentle sleep of country labouring men
> Does not despise low houses nor the shadowing
> Banks nor the whispering sound
> Of wood-waving west wind.
> If all you want is what is just enough
> The billowing sea doesn't worry you nor the tough
> Fall of Arcturus in the least
> Nor the Goat rising in the east.

The rich man has bad companions, Fear and Threat who climb where he climbs, cling to the bronze-plated warship, and behind the horseman sits black Anxiety: '*aber immer fuhlbar sitzt hinter ihm die Cura*'. It is one of Horace's deadliest images, and one of those ironies beloved of M.R. James in his ghost stories. The black-muffled rider clings to the galloping man from behind as he tries to escape. Nothing is any use, so why exchange my Sabine farm for more troublesome riches? If we rescue the shreds of this poem from its lengthy stuffing of moral philosophy, it is surely addressed to Maecenas, though he is not named, and its theme is the dregs of that accustomed theme in which the farm is Enough, and the poet lives in the country with his Muses. But the poetry has taken on a granite sound.

The second ode appears to be about education and consequences, and it praises virtue in the noblest terms, yet it tails off in some peculiar mutterings. Once again, Horace is some kind of herald angel, addressing nobody: and that may be the trouble with his poetry here. Maybe he is better when he has to give and take and make allowances for the friend he addresses: maybe he is a better Epicurean than he is a Stoic poet.

> Let the boy learn confining poverty,
> Grow up robust, fit for keen soldiery:
> Hurt the Parthians, make them fear
> His riding, and his probing spear ...

Plenty of literary evidence exists that this kind of sentiment was constantly reiterated by the Romans: if Horace got it from anywhere, no doubt it was from Sallust (*Cat.*7), yet the cavalry did not consist of Knights, but of 'allies', that is of mercenary levies from wild country: the cavalry who disappeared in North Yorkshire and were never seen again were Thracians for example. So who are the Roman boys to be brought up in this robust manner? There was an aristocratic equestrian game called the Troy Game which was tradi-

tional, so there was some bite to the patriotic ideal, even if it was immediately
diluted by training in 'rhetoric'. Horace says they should 'live in the open and
know fear'. Like the Boy Scouts, does he mean? At once he is off on a diversion
about Queens and Princesses sighing from their battlements as the Roman
comes chasing their sons and brothers. He slaughters them as a lion would.

> How sweet and fine to die for your country:
> Death just as much pursues him who would flee ...

The transition is abrupt, but wrenched from its context, in which the domi-
nant theme is that Death will get you whether you are brave or not, *Dulce et
decorum* supplied war memorials for two generations of the British. 'Virtue
gleams with honours untarnished and does not take up or lay down the axes
of power at the people's breath: virtue opens heaven to those who do not
deserve to die, and spurns the wet earth with his flying wing.' Here Horace
has suddenly meshed with reality, though these lines might seem the most
unreal of all. *Dulce et decorum* was awarded to both sides, the ambiguity was
deliberate. Virtue is Augustus, who is not going to be voted out of office, and
Horace is linked to him. That seems to me at least the structure of thoughts
that underlies this passage (13-24). Horace then turns to muttering about
confidentiality. Faithful silence is the thing, and there are people one would
not go sailing with, because Jupiter might hit innocence and guilt together.
It is quite impossible not to summon up such figures as Varro Murena. I do
not therefore believe that this poem is about nothing discernible: I think it is
about something unknown. The Greek parallels for Horace's advice do not
affect the issue, he is not just repeating ancient wisdom, but reviving it in a
situation we cannot quite recapture or date. In the third ode Augustus will
be revealed, and it could be that the second is meant only to serve as a kind
of antechapel.

> The just man moves deliberate to his ends
> And all the wrongly clamorous citizens,
> > No tyrant who threatens
> > Will shake his solid mind
> Nor the wind swelling the unquiet sea
> Nor Jove's great hand and lightning flashing free
> > Crack him if the world breaks in,
> > Found fearless in the ruin.
> By that art Pollux and wandering Hercules
> Came to the fire-castles and sit at ease
> > With Augustus who sips
> > Nectar with his bright lips.

The relationship of men and the gods had always been a delicate matter
in the ancient world, from the time when humans (for a little) stopped
grovelling. The sight of little Phoenician figures of men kissing the earth with
bottoms in the air is really shocking when one comes on it suddenly in a

Greek Museum in Sicily. On the Parthenon frieze the gods are taller but between them and the procession there intervene some specially tall old men, the heroes I suppose. These half-human demigods included the inventors of things and by the Roman period monarchs. In Greek practice they used to include great athletes, whose statues could do miracles. That was in Pindar's time, and Pausanias later than Horace still records the stories. Then there were divine heroes of tribes, and of places, who held an entire social system in place in the Athenian countryside, and were successfully manipulated by the fifth-century democracy. Julius Caesar was a hero in heaven, if only because his death was marked by his comet, a 'hairy star' as an English version of Suetonius by Phillimore Holland calls it. But Augustus was still alive: we saw in the first book at the end of the second ode that he was a god 'in disguise' who had to be begged to stay on earth, but now here he is sipping away on a sunset cloud. The starkness of the image is at once allayed by another example.

> And by this art, Bacchus Father, all heaven
> Welcomed you as your tigers pulled you in,
>   And Quirinus on Mars's team
>   Fled Acheron and things that seem ...

So far the poem makes sense of a kind, but here (17) suddenly Juno enters the scene complaining about Troy, cursed and destroyed for well-known legendary reasons by herself and Minerva or Athene. She feels tender towards 'the child of the Trojan priestess' (Ilia) all the same, though her sons are Romulus and Remus, provided that Rome does not revive Troy. There are seventy-two lines of this ode, and the last fifty are full of the same crazy theological speculation about the Roman future. Juno guarantees the future and warns the Romans against greed. Her lines contain much magnificence but it is like the pieces recovered from an ancient temple whose architecture is lost. Yet we sense an optimism, a sense of universality in this poem (53-6).

> Whatever world's end to this world is set
> His arms shall touch and he shall visit it,
>   Zones of fire rioting
>   And clouds and dews raining.

Sallust speaks of the desire 'to explore the unknown, in the habitual manner of human cupidity', and no doubt that is the other side of Horace's noble coin: both I suppose are to be seen in Walter Raleigh. Fraenkel used to feel that this passage bears out how the Roman 'shall, in this as in every other respect, be also the heir and preserver of what is noblest in the Greek tradition', which seems to me to be truer of Horace than it is of any normal Roman soldier. And yet, and yet ... I cannot forget that the source of the Nile was discovered in the next generation by a couple of Roman centurions in a canoe. Horace ends this overtoppling poem with a diminuendo. 'Muse, what has this to do with your amusing lute?'

Yet he is intending to give full play to the lyric treatment of epic themes, which does after all go back to Alcaeus, and the next poem, the fourth, is eighty lines long.

> Descend from heaven Calliope, begin
> A long drawn out tune on the flute my Queen,
>   If you prefer clear voice,
>   Or the lute, Phoebus's noise.

This long poem is the one about Apulia and Mount Vultur that we have had occasion to examine already because of Horace's childhood adventures in the woods: but all that is only an introduction to his vocation as a poet. Wherever he goes he belongs to the Muses, that is the Camenae (21), and it is only at line 37 that he gets to Caesar and his theme.

> High Caesar tired of soldiering all day,
> When all his regiments are put away
>   Seeking his weary labour's end
>   Your grotto entertains as friend ...

The entertainment of Caesar in a mountain cave by the Muses themselves is a lovely fantasy; it goes back to the *Musarum quies* that Hercules protects. 'You give your gentle wisdom and are pleased with it; we know how Jove defeated the Titans ...' There is not any room for doubt therefore that Jove attacking the Titans is a metaphor for the mission of Caesar, or part of that mission, because the Muses in their cave are an even better metaphor for the civilised life, of which Augustus against whatever expectation really was the protecting Hercules.

> ... But when their wild
> Arms Pelion on Olympus piled
> What help did Typhoeus or strong Mimas bring
> Or Porphyrion's great height threatening
>   Enceladus, Rhoetus: these
>   Speared heaven with whole trees,
> Against Athene's sounding shield they fell ...

The whole splendid battle-line passes before us, Vulcan, Juno, and the archer who washes his loose hair in the pure Castalian dew, who holds the Asian thickets and his native woods, Delian and Patarean (Lycian) Apollo. Force without wisdom falls by its own weight, but temperate force the gods promote. 'Hundred-handed Gyges is my witness and Orion who attempted pure Diana and was tamed by her virgin arrow. Earth moans for her monsters sent with a lightning flash to lurid death, nor can the swift fire eat away Aetna which holds them down. The vulture does not leave the liver of Tityos, he is the jailer, and three hundred fetters hold the lover Pirithous.' The only allusion too important to be left to guesswork is to Pirithous, the friend

Theseus had to abandon in the underworld when by magic they were trapped there by the Queen of Hell, and the story like that of Gyas belongs to popular folklore. Pirithous was a Lapith whose wedding Theseus was at but did he love the Queen of Hell or just Theseus? We shall meet Pirithous again. It is an act of gratitude and respect to acknowledge the inspiring influence of Pindar in this ode, and in particular of Pindar's first Pythian: to Horace the most formidable of influences and the most inspiring for the rest of his life.

Set aside this fourth ode for a moment and you see that the third and the fifth are closely related, long stories. Where exactly do these tales come from? The third ode must have a Latin origin because of the nature of Juno's strange and lengthy interruption. It has nothing so far as I can discover to do with the Council of the gods in Lucilius, though Juno had an argument with Venus there (see Servius on *Aen*.10, 104f.), and it is not absolutely excluded. The solemnity of the language indicates a more deadly serious source; should we not look for a clue in the fifth ode, where the story of Regulus takes up most of the poem? Here I believe that the source is Naevius, a poet whose fragments are pitifully few and short, but the greatest of all the early Romans, and well known to Horace. He had written Latin tragedies on Roman themes and comedies but also an epic on the Punic wars. Regulus must have figured in that; a propaganda quarrel had arisen as to which side had tortured the other, and this was the background motive of part of his poem. He dealt also with the wanderings of Aeneas and with Dido. Those scholars who have understood his importance have usually missed his genius, but in this case behind the powerful ending of Horace's poem and behind whatever lies behind Horace's ode, there is the scene in the *Iliad* in which Hector says goodbye to his wife and goes into battle. There are many cases in literary history in which a great poem derives from some jejune or minor piece, but here is one in which Naevius seems to have given two remarkable though uncharacteristic poems to Horace: yet even here he begins with Pindar (*Pyth*.6, 23-7).

> We have believed that thunderous Jove reigns
> In heaven, and Augustus now shall reign
>   When our empire extends
>   Over Britons and Persians.

They are the ultimate people, that is all, and the Romans know little of what lies beyond them, as Tacitus makes obvious in his work on Germany. Livy tells us in a fragment (55) that Augustus on his return from Britain assured the Romans that by war or treaty of friendship (it was the latter and he had not landed on the island), the whole world was now bound closely to Rome. But this stanza is the merest formality. He turns at once for two more infuriated stanzas about the soldiers of Crassus who had settled down happily and married in Parthia: 'Marsians and Apulians under a Medish king!' This is intended to lead up to the main business of the ode (13-56), which is the story of Regulus. He was a prisoner on parole to put the Carthaginian case to the Senate, but he begged them not to accept terms, and

then returned to Carthage. He was tortured to death by having his eyelids
cut off and being chained in the sun. Whether this story is true or not, it was
believed at Rome: he was captured in 255 BC and the mission to Rome was
about six years later. Of his death we are told by Horace only that 'He knew
what the barbarian torturer had waiting, but just the same he pushed aside
his family and the people blocking his return, just as if he was leaving the
long affairs of his clients with a law case decided, and going into the country,
to Venafrum or to Spartan Tarentum'.

There is a peace and a distance about Venafrum, which Horace mentions
for the oil and olive trees there; it lay high up on the slopes of the mountains,
on the edge of Campania. Later in time it was a shooting-box of the Kings of
Naples where they slaughtered wolves, foxes, wild boar, deer, and other
game. At the time of Regulus Venafrum still spoke Oscan, and at the time of
the 'social war' the Venafrans murdered all the Romans they could catch.
Tarentum fell under Roman protection in 272, and was not violently handled
until Hannibal had occupied it and Rome took and plundered the place at the
end of the century. But Horace is not concerned with these historical details:
he is telling a story that is folklore, and in his story-telling Tarentum is its
ancient Spartan self, since in the eighth century BC it had been founded by a
Spartan. Its success as a city dated from the decline of Croton in the later
fifth century. To Horace it was an image of peace and pleasure as it was to
Virgil; in his letters it is leafy and unwarlike. But in the end of this ode it
stands up as starkly as a stone monument: the word 'Lacedaemonian' has a
sense of danger and of courage however submerged in peace it may be.

> They say he pushed away her kiss with a breath
> And his small sons like a man sentenced to death,
>   And bowed his head and frowned
>   More grimly at the ground. (41-4)

His speech to the Senate, which is given, echoes in a bigger mirror what
Horace has already said about Roman prisoners in Parthia. He has bent the
two cases a little to make them more exactly like each other, but that is
subject to the overriding sense of climax in this poem, which from the
ominous 'They say ...' to the end continues to mount, until the terrible
quietness of the final stanza.

The sixth of these towering statements begins with a warning to the
Romans to repair their temples and to fear the gods. He speaks as if to one
man, to one Roman, as Virgil's Anchises does in a fit of prophecy in the
underworld (*Aen*.6, 851) and as oracles did (Ovid *Fasti* 4, 259).

> Roman you will pay for your forefathers' sins
> Till you rebuild gods' temples from ruins,
>   Roofs of worm-eaten oak,
>   Statues filthy with smoke.
> To be below the gods your rule defends,
> To this fix all beginnings and all ends

Gods take a heavy fee:
From wailing Italy ...

Enough of this you may feel is quite enough: Horace is about to plunge into the social reforms that Augustus and many others must have favoured. He grumbles again about the impertinent Parthians. 'The Dacian and the Ethiopian came near to taking the city in the grip of seditions, one feared for their fleet the other better with arrows.' Is this not nonsense? I fear that it is: these peoples had no such intention or organisation, Horace is talking like the lowest of nationalists. The Dacian fleet was on the Danube, and as for the Ethiopians, Horace is a little like Pope Pius XII begging the Americans not to let hordes of black men loose on Rome in the 1940s. 'Ages fertile in sin first stained marriage and race and homes, and hence the disaster flowed to people and fatherland. Girls learn Ionic dances, and from early childhood meditate incest. Soon she wants younger adulterers.' (25) Horace is in the grip of his own story, the girl acts on command of her husband, and couples with the master of a Spanish ship (31). 'The youth was not from parents like those which stained the sea with Punic blood, and felled Pyrrhus and mighty Antiochus and fearful Hannibal.' They were country-bred and good with the hoe (37-8) and carried logs for their mothers.

When the sun altered shadows on the hill
And oxen left their yokes and drank their fill;
    Pleasant times the sun brought
    With his departing chariot.

Horace has suddenly changed his mind about the severity of the poem, and tells us instead what a cheerful life it was in the Sabine cottages. He ends with a stanza of blistering damnations, as if he is imitating the village elders, and perhaps that may really be the secret of this ode; then the poem ends.

What has time's damnation not ruined?
Our own fathers worse than their fathers had sinned,
    Worse in our generation
    We breed a wickeder nation.

And yet by the position of this ode Horace will immediately begin to mock all its forty-eight lines of twaddle. The seventh ode is to Asterie, a girl whose husband is trading abroad, faithful and weeping, while intrigues entrap her like those in any Roman comedy, and she is keen on her neighbour Enipeus. There are a bewildering number of characters in the poem, including the antique example of Proetus who is tricked into plotting Bellerophon's murder by his deceitful wife: she was called Stheneboia (ox-strong) so Horace does not name her. No one can ride like Enipeus on the Campus Martius or swim the Tiber as well as Enipeus, though Horace I think mocks his upper class gyrations.

> No other boy can manoeuvre his horse
> So well on the Campus Martius course by course,
>   Or plunge without a shiver
>   Into the Tuscan river.
> At nightfall shut your house, do not look down
> At querulous flute-songs sounding from the town,
>   Although he calls you hard
>   Be stony, keep the door barred.

In the world that Horace has already created in the *Odes* it is all but inconceivable that she is really going to resist him all night or night after night, and Horace does not mind, he is not offering serious advice to stern Romans, she is a light Greek. He does not have a real prejudice against 'Ionic', that is Athenian dances either. I liked this poem beyond reason when I was a boy, and chose it when we were told to pick a poem and learn it by heart. I got some funny looks for choosing it, but I did not really know what it was about and had not seen the connection with the sixth ode and the Spanish ship; it reminded me of Shylock's advice to Jessica in *The Merchant of Venice*, and I loved the way it imitates flute music. Now it seems slighter and more of a joke, but it is a joke I am glad the poet bothered to make. The tempter in the third stanza is what reduces it to farce.

> But the messenger of his unhappy host
> Is sighing for Chloe and burns like toast
>   With your fires he must blaze
>   And tempts a thousand ways ...

What is actually happening in this verse remains a little obscure, but the fifth stanza piles one thing on another in the same way, when the 'messenger' has already told us about Proetus and Bellerophon,

> He tells how Peleus came near death as he
> Ran away chastely from Hippolyte,
>   And tries a hundred tales
>   That have sin in their tails.

The whole poem is a mockery, and these parodies of classical and tragic events fall naturally into place. It is noticeable that on this ode Fraenkel has not a word to say, but he feels that the sixth ode is very early, which is as near as he will go to criticising it. He sees the likeness of the ship's captain to an epode (17, 20) and the deeper similarity of the political attitudes of those days. He finds the breakdown of morality ruining the state in the philosopher Posidonius and in Sallust: within the governing class it is of course an observable truth. He finds civil war and self-destruction as punishment that the gods inflict for an ancient crime in Cicero (*Marcell*.18) and persuades us that the attitudes of ode six are normal: he is certainly persuasive, yet I am not persuaded, and he does not defend the Dacian and Ethiopian threat, or the long passage (17-32) about sexual mores in Italy and their catastrophic effect on politics.

With the seventh ode Horace has evened the score, and the eighth is written for Maecenas, whose name is in the central stanza. The kalends are the first of the month.

> What am I doing on the March kalends?
> Why the flowers, why the pile of incense,
> Why is the coal placed on the living grass?
>   Well you may ask.
> O learned in the speech of Latin and Greek
> I vowed a sweet feast which Bacchus would like
> And a white goat, being near killed by malignity
>   Of a falling tree.
> This is the feast day in the returning year
> To remove cork and pitch from the amphora
> That has been drinking smoke and kept quite full
>   Since Tullus was consul.
> Maecenas, take a hundred cups, your friend's all right,
> And bring the watching lamps out into the light,
> Far away from us be all anger and noise
>   And grief and sighs.

Let go your civil worries about the city (he was governor) because Dacian Cotiso's army has melted, the Parthians are fighting each other, the Cantabrians are chained in Spain at last, the Scythians are thinking of withdrawal. Don't worry about the people's burdens, you're a private citizen, don't be so anxious, take the gifts of this hour, and abandon severity. The Romans do not seem to have been sure of what people Cotiso was King, but it was on the lower Danube. We are perhaps in 28 BC, and Augustus is home. The invitation is not as casual as it looks, and nor is the poem. It celebrates the peace of Augustus at its most triumphant moment so far, and the peoples that are disposed of are a crescendo.

> And now with bow unstrung from the empty fields
>   The Scythian yields.

Of the first six poems in the book the first and sixth speak of social morality in general terms, the second is beautiful but mysterious, in the third Augustus has an apotheosis, the fourth is about Horace's vocation, about the court (at Praeneste, Tibur and Baiae) and Caesar Augustus refreshed in his cave with an epic tale of theomachy. Here for the first time we have a serious parade of political achievements, and it is addressed not to the Emperor personally, but to his friend Maecenas.

The ninth ode has a lovely metre and a dialogue structure in which every stanza answers the last; this is the simplest of dramatic love poems and all the characters are Greek. I do not think Lydia and Chloe are meant to be always the same person. 'While you liked me best I was happy.' 'While you preferred me to Chloe, Lydia was supremely happy.' 'Chloe rules me now, she can sing and dance and I'd die for her.' 'I would die twice over for Calais of Thurii, son of Ornytus.' 'What if old love came back and Chloe is shaken off?' 'He's prettier than a star, you're lighter than a cork and angrier than the Adriatic, but I'd love to live and die with you.' The simplicity and pathetic ordinariness of the poem make it work wonderfully.

The tenth ode is a monologue of five stanzas which is more heavily or rhetorically musical and therefore succeeds less well. The lover is insulting which makes the poem less palatable: it is a terrible night and he is tired of his vigil, she is no Penelope, no kinder than snakes, no softer than an oak, he is not going to stand the rain and the hard pavement for ever. One is not surprised but one is not touched either: this ode is mere fantasy.

The eleventh ode has another dramatic plot. At first it seems to be a hymn to Mercury, but after the introduction he is asked for a song to enchant Lyde (the last ode was a monologue to Lyce).

> Mercury – Amphion learnt from you to sing
> And knew your art to move the stones by song,
> From you the clever tortoise learnt the sounding string
>   Re-echoing,
> Once neither nice-mannered nor talkative
> Now rich men's tables and the temples love
> Your voice, tell me a tune and Lyde dear
>   Will lend an ear.
> Like a three year old mare she plays in the meadows
> Still fearing to be touched, still starting at shadows,
> Not coupled yet, still immature that head
>   To be mated.
> You can lead tigers and the forests will
> Follow and the swift rivers will stand still,
> The dreadful doorkeeper of the world below
>   Will smile for you,
> Cerberus, in spite of the hundred
> Snakes hissing on his frightful head,
> His black breath and the spit that dribbles forth
>   From triple mouth.

So the pains of the underworld are lightened; we have of course heard all this before, but the two versions are each good enough to stand, and Horace was right to reject neither. One may all the same feel that this ode has gone off course and the poet has forgotten Lyde, who is only a weak excuse. She returns at once (25) as if he had remembered her suddenly. 'Let her hear about the punishment of girls in the underworld.' This is pure folklore from south Italy, as we know from painted pottery: possibly it began as an oriental tale; the same punishment occurred in the Knidian painted room at Delphi, which was full of folklore and which Pausanias described under Hadrian, before it was destroyed by an earthquake. We are then given at full length and for no reason the story (33-52) of the good girl who refuses to let her lover die, and is content if he carves her story on a stone. This final ridiculous embellishment is supposed to show how we know the story is true: it arises without question from the prose romances that were written at this time. One can see why Horace left this ode in his collection, its components are charming and without the irrelevant girl there would be no way of holding it together, no excuse for it.

Ode twelve has a metre so simple and a rhythm so intoxicating that one hardly notices what if anything it says. The metre is two shorts and two longs, as in 'Put a small worm in an eel-pie or a cow-pat'. The girl is Neobule, and she is distracted from her household work, weaving wool like a Roman lady, by Hebrus of Lipari, swimming in the Tiber, unbeatable boxer and runner and a horseman better than Bellerophon: he is a good boar-hunter too. Most of the poem is a single sentence: we have met the swimmer before, in ode seven of this book, in the same river. These boys with a father's name or at least a native place (ode nine) are all Greeks, and they are a resource for Horace: they all come from his south, Lipari is an island off northern Sicily, but the boys are all a little like noble Romans on their horses and with their boar-hunts and amateur athletics from the Greek gymnasium, just as the girls are a little Roman too. One wonders whether Horace is in love with either sex or both, or is it only an image? In the eighteenth century what roads there were in Apulia were 'paved' with the crumbs of Greek pottery, and in Horace's lifetime there must have been painted vases that survived, not all of them in tombs. Bellerophon as an ideal athlete might come from some such source. 'Unhappy are the girls who give no play to love, nor wash away evils with sweet wine.' Is there not something Greek, something southern about that opening?

The thirteenth ode of the third book is addressed only to a spring of water. The sentimentality of Italianised English and Germans has set up a traditional view that this lovely water-spring must be in Horace's valley where his farm was, not thirty miles from Rome, and easy enough therefore for tourists to visit. But the earliest evidence we have, which is in a Latin charter of land-rights from the twelfth century (1103), tells us the Fons Bandusiae was one of the springs at Bantia, it speaks of a *fons Bandusinus* and a *Castellum Bandusii*. The water on the hill was the bait Hannibal left for the Roman army he ambushed and annihilated there, according to Plutarch. Since his day and since Horace's, the springs have dried up in one place and burst out in another: Norman Douglas explains what happened in *Old Calabria*. Bantia was about ten miles from Venusia, just about the far end of a walk for any active boy, and certainly within grazing distance for a flock. Horace spoke of the Bantine hollows or glens, *saltus Bantini*, and the question would have seemed closed were it not that in his sixteenth letter he refers to a stream in the Sabine hills that is fit to give a name to a place, 'the Hebrus is no more cold or pure as it runs through Thrace'. There he surely means the Digentia or Licenza. Scholars are obstinate in their shambling way, and suggest that Horace named his Sabine spring after one he remembered. With

such wrongheaded obstinacy one cannot argue. It is highly probable that the
little waterfall and the ilex are partly imaginary and merely literary, he is a
poet after all, not a camera nor a maker of postcards, even though this poem
is so famous. The spring 'of Bandusia' might refer to some goddess or nymph,
or it may be a local 'of', as in the Bay of Naples. The little piece is like a
epigram.

> O Bandusian spring, clearer than glass
> You are worth flowers and wine, tomorrow will not pass
> > Without a he-goat dead:
> > Horns swelling his forehead
> For love and battle promise to unfold,
> But in vain, his red blood will stain your cold
> > Water, your banks and rocks,
> > Infant of lecherous flocks.
> The dreadful hour of the blazing dog-star is
> Unable to touch your delicious freeze
> > Calling oxen from ploughing
> > And goats from wandering.
> You too shall be among the noble springs
> Your hollow boulders shall have one who sings
> > Your ilex tree, your sound
> > Leaping down to the ground.

This is by general admission one of Horace's loveliest poems: it is pure
landscape, in pure dream country. It is visually as sharp as it could be, it
flows from stanza to stanza, it is musical and undisturbed even by a god,
except that the sacrifice implies one and perhaps Bandusia was a nymph or
an old Sabine Camena, since they were associated with water-sources. This
waterfall does sound like Bantia as Norman Douglas describes it: Ovid uses
the same word 'leap down' (*desilit*) for the place where Proserpine was
gathering flowers in the damp grass, and Tennyson thought it the only
valuable thing he learnt at school (*Fasti* 4, 428). The ploughing beasts are not
really bulls as Horace calls them, so I translate oxen; and the wandering
goats could be sheep, but who knows and what does it matter? This is a lovely
little bit of verse, quite untranslatable within the conditions I have chosen,
and curiously memorable when one has forgotten more important things. It
is like the perfect Latin version of a Greek epigram, only the epigram does
not exist.

Ode fourteen is an attempt to accommodate two themes in one poem,
Caesar in the central position coming home from Spain and the Pillars of
Hercules, and Horace celebrating in stanzas that will flower and reflower
later in his life, and then the feast, a pretty girl, and the sadness of age and
white hair; he was not so meek when Plancus was consul. We can see from
the implicit self-criticisms of Horace in his later versions of this sort of poem
that the party needs to be muted. Plancus in the seventh ode of the first book
was already an elderly man; indeed Horace must have thought him old when

he was consul in 42 BC. This ode deliberately recalls him and he was certainly alive and active, even if he was perhaps born as early as 90 BC. As late as 22 he was censor, and it was then he proposed that the name Augustus should be given official status. 42 was the year of Philippi, but my feeling is that here '*consule Planco*' is a compliment and almost a dedication of the ode. There are very few personal dedications in this book, and only to the grandest of old gentlemen, apart from Maecenas and Augustus. The procession to meet Caesar sounds like the queue of grandees who figure on the Ara Pacis, who like Italian processions to this day are having trouble keeping quiet and looking solemn. They are led by the woman married once only (5), Augustus's sister, and the mothers of the choir of boys and girls, whom Horace (10) calls on to keep silence. He is like one of the marshals of the Parthenon frieze, though he does not have to deal with the problems created by cattle and horses.

> This day for me is a true festival
> Banishing worry: I shall not fear at all
>   Riot or violent death
>   While Caesar rules the earth.

This comparison with the Rome of his youth is an important plank as it were of his new platform, and it is surely justified. He widens the contrast by speaking (19) of a cask that remembers the Marsian war, before he was born, 'if any jar escaped for us From wandering Spartacus' (19-20). The end of the poem recalls his own riotousness, 'when in hot youth I played the fool When Plancus was consul'. It is a charming diminuendo of the serious theme on which the whole poem hinges, intended I suppose to knit its stanzas together and to offer a rueful grin to old Plancus who had spent years in Antony's employment.

The next ode is an example of riotous behaviour, in the form of a rebuke to a lady, 'wife of poor Ibycus', who is close to her funeral, and should stop playing about among young girls like a cloud on those glittering stars. That is all very well for Pholoe and Chloe, breaking into boys' houses like a Bacchant. She is crazy about Nothus (the Bastard) and plays about like a young lascivious nanny-goat. You would be fitter to work wool with noble Luceria (the first Roman name): no lute playing for you, no roses, no drinking barrels to their dregs. This is a short and slight poem, one does not believe in it but it reads with the rhythm and vigour of a scene in Plautus. All the same the underlying reality of the drunken old lady is a little gruesome for the taste of my generation. There was a scene in a Greek comedy I recall when a gleeful crowd of actors besieged a whore-house, which was funny enough to read, but would not in real life be funny.

The sixteenth ode is a forty-four line poem to Maecenas (20). The first four stanzas are about the power of money over everyone from Danae, to whom Zeus came in a shower of gold like starlight, to the Hellenistic kings. They are written with ironic and sophisticated ease.

> Anxiety follows money's increase
> And hunger for more: I could not face
> (And quite rightly) lifting my head to the heights
>   Maecenas glory of all Knights.
> The more a man denies himself the more
> The gods give: I am a candidate for
> The camp of those who desire nothing, therefore then
>   A refugee from the army of rich men.

Rather than gather into his barns all the wheat of all Apulia, he would prefer 'streams of clean water and a few acres of forest and a sure confidence in my crop'.

> Calabrian bees carry me no honey
> And Bacchus does not doze in a jar for me
> No fleeces fatten for me on the fields of all
>   The grazing grounds there are in Gaul.

Horace calls the amphora in this stanza 'Laestrygonian', which is a joke: these people come into the *Odyssey* but have never been heard of since, so the word means extremely antique and I took it to mean Sicilian, but here it has a special meaning which appears in the next ode. The idea of Bacchus himself inhabiting an ancient wine-jar in which he is mellowing with the years is worthy of the Greek writers of satyr plays and might well come from one. The arrival of the god on stage by emerging from a gigantic wine-jar would be a fine *coup de théâtre*, but as Horace writes the phrase it is equally wonderful. '*Nec Laestrygonia Bacchus in amphora Languescit mihi ...*' If my conjecture is right, then Laestrygonian would derive from the play: who knows? That person is well off, Horace says, to whom the god deals with a sparing hand, but all the same if he dealt us some more papyrus texts of fifth-century satyr plays we would be grateful.

Ode seventeen is to Aelius Lamia with due compliments to his grand lineage, going back to the legendary founder of Formiae, who according to the *Odyssey* (10, 81-3) was a Laestrygonian, because the Laestrygonians, who were absurd giants and ate people, lived at 'Fargates', city of Lamos. Formiae was near the south-eastern frontier of Latium, protected by Caeta from the worst weather, near the river Liris. It was where Cicero was murdered and Plancus buried; it had been a Volscian town but Roman for two hundred and fifty years or more. Why the Lamiae claimed descent from Lamos the Homeric giant is a question that cannot be answered, but the claim is likely enough to date from the Greek penetration of that coast, before ever Livius Andronicus translated the *Odyssey* into Latin: rich treasures of fifth-century pottery have been found there; perhaps it was a Greek trading station in the eighth century, like Cumae.

> Aelius, since ancient Lamus nobleman,
> Since they say Lamiae took their name from him,

And all the recorded line
From him named noblemen,
Who built the battlements of Formiae
And held Marica's marshes where nearby
    Liris swims on her shore,
    A prince and lord of power,
Tomorrow's tempest will strew all the woods
With fallen leaves, and shores with useless weeds,
    Unless the prophet errs,
    The raven full of years:
Build up a pile of dry wood while you can,
Tomorrow treat your genius with some wine,
    And a dinner of roast pork
    For servants free from work.

The poem is one sentence flowing freely over all obstacles, and it is certainly charming and without serious meaning: it earns its position probably because of the Laestrygonian joke. Formiae was on the Appian Way just beyond the Pontine Marshes, but apparently it had *prés salés* of its own: Horace must have known it very well.

The eighteenth ode like the thirteenth to the little spring is a faultless construction. I have very much loved it ever since first reading Alfred Noyes, in 1947 I suppose. The other day I discovered by chance that John Heath-Stubbs, who is nearly eighty, reviewed that book on Horace when it came out in that year, and still thinks it the best on its subject he has ever read. Faunus and the Nymphs make it clear from the first words that this is a poem as Greek as it is Roman; once again it is just one sentence but I cannot attempt the translation. James Michie catches the lightness of it.

Faunus, who loves the Nymphs and makes
Them scamper, leap my boundary stakes
Lightly and benignly pass
Across the sunny fields of grass,
Leave behind your blessing on
My lambs and kids, and so be gone.
In return receive your due:
A goat shall die to honour you
At the year's end, the ancient shrine
Smoke with thick incense, and the wine
Liberally poured, keep filling up
Venus's friend, the drinking-cup.
When the December nones come round
All the farm beasts on the green ground
Gambol, and with time to spare
The world enjoys the open air,
Countryman and unyoked ox
Together; in among the flocks

> Unfeared the wolf strolls; from the copse
> The leaf, to be your carpet, drops;
> And in triple-time the son of toil
> Jigs on his enemy the soil.

I take it that the deliberately magical side of the scene is what makes the poem so enchanting. The prayer is even simpler and so closer to ritual than the translation, in the words 'Through my grounds and through my (sunny) fields come gently and leave harmlessly to my small nurselings'. It is a happy poem.

The nineteenth ode finds Horace doing something I had said he never did. Here he mixes a real Roman friend with the Greek names of girls and boys. The wine is Chian, which is imported from the eastern Mediterranean sea and so expensive. The poem is to Murena. You tell me all about the generations between Inachus and Codrus the Athenian, and the race of Aeacus and the Trojan war, but as to the price of a barrel of Chian and in whose house I am to keep out the Paelignian cold, you are silent. Paelignian means the mountains east of Rome, and the Gran Sasso d'Italia which is now a skiing resort. 'Pour for the new moon, pour for midnight, pour for the augur Murena: mix the cups with three or nine measures. Let the poet try three times three for the Muses, more than three Grace and her naked sisters forbids as she hates quarrels. It is pleasant to be crazy, why has the pipe stopped, why are flute and lute silent? I hate sparing hands, scatter roses and let Lycus envy the terrible noise and the woman who does not suit aged Lycus, Telephus here comes Rhode with her dense hair, you are like a pure evening star, but I am slow-roasted by love of Glycera.' This is dramatic in a way, but it is mere fantasy and not very edifying. What has it to do with Varro Murena? Perhaps he asked for such a poem. There were sixteen augurs, who performed mumbo-jumbo of ritual observation of birds, so maybe the raven of Formiae is the link, or the December feast of Faunus? Murena was a follower of Maecenas and his catastrophe as we have said was swiftly approaching. We have plenty of Greek examples of the three or seven or nine measures, but since the new moon is involved Horace's play with numbers may well have something to do with the mumbo-jumbo of augury.

The twentieth ode to a Greek youth is to us cold and empty because it was the merest exercise in neo-classicism. He warns the young man about lion-cubs. He will quarrel with the lioness about a certain Nearchus.

> And he refreshes in the gentle air
> A shoulder scattered with sweet-scented hair,
> Looking as Nireus looked, or else indeed
>   Like Ganymede.

The poem such as it is exists for the sake of this fourth stanza and the stanza exists for the sake of the last phrase 'or him from watery Ida raped' or rapt.

Ode twenty-one is a fine and slightly longer poem to Messalla Corvinus, Horace's old friend the hero of Philippi. 'O born with me when Manlius was consul, whether you create laments or jokes or quarrels or crazy love affairs, or easy sleep religious pot, under whatever name you keep your Massic wine, worth opening on a good day, come down, Corvinus commands mellow wines, he is not the man, damp as he may be with Socratic conversation, so nasty as to neglect you; we are told that even ancient Cato's virtue often heated with wine.' So far we have splendidly amusing rhetoric, and we have come to the first full stop, just half-way through the poem, but there are three stanzas to come, addressed quite undistractedly to this forty-year-old bottle: as if that wonderful wine of 1959 still contrived to exist today.

> You move your engine against intellect,
> Tough mostly, and you uncover and reflect
>   Secrets with laughing ease,
>   Wise men's anxieties,
> You bring the most worried to hope again,
> And you grow horns and powers on to poor men,
>   They do not fear kings' crowns
>   Or soldiers' arms new-drawn.
> But Bacchus and glad Venus shall be felt
> And the Graces shy to undo their belt,
>   Lamps that live till the sun appears
>   Here to chase away the stars.

The movement of the poem is lovely, and we already believe that Corvinus deserves it. The wine lasts all night and everything said about it has been said long ago by Homer or by Pindar. Cato comes first, the ancient Cato, a proverbial figure, and the Socratic conversations recall the *Symposium* of Plato, where the guests decide to allow no dancing-girls but to let conversation lead them on. (Xenophon I am sorry to say allows a nude contortionist at his *Symposium*.) The *pia testa*, the religious pot, is prayed to and we are told all its possibilities, as if this were a real hymn, but in the second half of the poem with its insistent opening word of each stanza (*tu ... tu ... te ...*) the wine is almost abstract, its effects are not in present time, and in the last four lines there are only the gods, no humans at all, only the lamps that last until the sun returns. This is surely a reminiscence of the *Symposium* and so the most beautiful of ancient prose works throws its shadow on one of the most memorable of ancient poems. I still recall how moving Fraenkel was about it in few words, perhaps because his father was a wine merchant.

For the time being Horace is saying his prayers. Ode twenty-two is an epigram so short as to be insubstantial, yet compact, interwoven and full of visual sharpness. The Virgin is Artemis (Diana) the huntress and moon-god and Hecate, Queen of Night.

> Virgin guardian of woods and hills
> Saver from death and hearer three times called
> In the childbirth and labouring of girls
>   Triple-faced god,

> I give you this pinetree that leans over my house
> And year by year I gladly offer this
> Young boar considering a sideways thrust:
>   I give you blood.

That is all, but the young boar's male wildness knits into the blood of birth, the swelling of the moon, and the guardian of all young creatures. Sacred trees occur in Pompeian landscapes, sometimes with a fence round them and often ancient. Here the tree overhangs the house as if the woods reclaimed it. The boar is like a bronze in the moment of action but frozen for ever, and one can all but hear the splash of blood.

> Hold up your hands my country Phidyle
> For the new moon, give the Lares barley
>   Give them in the moon's shadow
>   A fat young lively sow.
> Then the vine will not wither but be fertile
> When pest-wind blows from Africa it will not feel,
>   Nor the crops get mildew nor the sweet young
>   Suffer in the bad weeks when apples are hung.
> Whether it grazes on snowy Algidus
> Doomed among the oak trees and ilexes
>   Or grows fat on the Alban grasses
>   The priests are sharpening their axes
> For the victim's neck: nothing to do with you
> To slaughter herds of sheep, you have only to show
>   A garland of rosemary to the small gods
>   Or fragile myrtle straight out of the woods.

Once again this was a genre scene, and innocent Phidyle has been typical of the quiet companions of Horace's whole life: his serfs are married and have families, as they had no doubt at Venusia. He knows just what they hope or pray from each god. The Lares started as boundary gods but by Horace's day they had long ago got into the house: they were queer little objects to look at and seldom survive. Horace is quite clear about Phidyle's rustic wishes. Autumn brings the bad weeks of heat and fever, exactly as it did in London every September until the Great Fire: whenever plague was coming it came at that season. Mildew was a disease of wheat so prevalent that two of the twelve gods of the Romans in a less Hellenised generation had been Flora, who stops the trees blossoming too early (earlier still she blasted the blossoms) and Robigo or Mildew, who ruined the wheat. To both of them you prayed to stay away; there is a relic of such a prayer in the ode to Faunus (18), *abeasque*: leave without doing any harm. But I had forgotten the last stanza which shows this is a household sacrifice.

> If an innocent hand has touched the stone
> And not a costly victim or fine one

The Penates soften, their anger will halt
With religious flour and crackling salt.

The message is the same one as usual: the gods prefer simple humble
offerings and innocence. The Penates lived in the larder or store-cupboard,
they were magic dwarfs like the gods of Samothrace. I wish I knew what had
made them cross.

The twenty-fourth ode is sixty-four lines long and very cross indeed. It is
purely moral teaching. 'You can occupy all your land and the sea too with
your vast wealth, it will not save you from Necessity or your head from the
noose of death. The Scythians who draw their houses in a waggon, and the
nomadic Getae who stop only a year and then move on are better off. Their
sexual arrangements are more virtuous too. Whoever wants to end civil war
and be called FATHER of cities on his statues should rein in untamed licence.
We hate virtue and when it's gone we look for it. What is the point of laws
without good behaviour? Let's take all our wealth and gems to the Capitol or
throw them into the sea. We must wipe out the elements of cupidity and form
the young with severe studies. A boy can't ride and fears to hunt, he can only
play with a hoop or dice (which is forbidden). Heirs are unworthy, wicked
riches increase and there's always just a little something that needs adding
to the heap.' This vigorous but boring tirade is practically pure Epictetus,
only fitted to Augustus in his reforming mood. The title Father of the Country
would, as we have seen, in time become official. This poem would have been
cheered up by some invasion of the gods. The worship of noble savages like
the Getae was Greek (indeed Homeric) and was already old.

The next poem, the twenty-fifth, is a rhapsodical address to Bacchus as a
visionary and mystical god. One is plunged straight into the action.

> Where are you carrying me away
> Bacchus filled with you? What grove, what grotto
> Swift with newness of mind? In what caves today
> Shall I be heard meditating to set the glory of Caesar
> Among God's counsellors most like a star?

He is composing a Greek dithyramb, only in Latin. The new apotheosis of
Caesar follows rather exactly and carefully what was permitted or proposed,
but this is an élitist pleasure not a popular offering. Julius Caesar was
identified with his star, and Horace meditates the same honour for Augustus
when the time comes. It sounds to me as if the Caesars were being gleefully
exploded to make a firework display, but that is because I owe them no
loyalty. One does I think owe to Augustus some respect for his titanic efforts
to set the Romans, who had merely stumbled into command of the civilised
world, on an even keel. 'I shall speak out gloriously and freshly, what no other
voice has said. So on the hills the sleepless Bacchant sees the Hebrus and
Thrace white with snow and Rhodope, just as I wander river-banks and
empty woods.' Can he be Orpheus? Is there then a flicker of Virgil here? 'O
powerful over Naiads and strong Bacchae, tough benders of the mountain

ash, I speak nothing small or mortal.' These inspired ladies bent the trees
to use them as catapults to dispose of an enemy in the *Bacchae* of
Euripides. 'Sweet is the danger of following the god who ties the green
vine-leaf around his brows.' The green is vivid after the rocks and snow
and rivers among rocks, and suddenly Bacchus seems civilised; one welcomes him.

Ode twenty-six changes mood again: it is a mere twelve lines to Venus: a
fanciful dedication of the weapons of 'war'.

> My life went well with the girls,
>   I soldiered with some glory,
> Now my arms and lute, relics of war
>   Hang here to tell my story.
> On the left side of Venus of the sea
>   Here hang up the bright torches,
> Here hang the wedges, here the bow
>   That used to threaten porches.
> O goddess of the riches of Cyprus
>   And Memphis which is never snowy
> O Queen with your high-rising lash
>   Just once whip arrogant Chloe.

Once again the piece is slight and of no personal importance either to the poet
or to us, but it is of an elegance which is as sharp as the lash and lives in the
memory. Horace could be as elegant when he chose as any poet until Ronsard
or Shakespeare, just as Catullus could be.

Perhaps he thought of the monstrous ode to Galatea in just the same way:
it was habitual with him from the *Epodes* on to write bad taste verse to
women whenever he felt in the mood. But this one is seventy-six lines long
and ends in a long Hellenistic narrative. I do not see why it should be so long
drawn out except for sheer glee, for enjoyment. Galatea will get forgotten. We
begin with more auguries for a joke.

> Let irreligious people be led on
> By a screech-owl's answer for an omen,
> A pregnant bitch, a ravening wolverine
>   a fox in cub,
> Let a serpent break their journey once begun
> Terrifying the horses like an arrow at a slant
> Whizzing across, bringing me faltering
>   augur to a stop:

The wolverine has come down from Lanuvium, and the owl may be a horned
owl, no one knows really, but it is answering or repeating.

> Before it seeks stagnant marshes again
> I call up the gods' messenger of rain,

The old crow cawing again and again
　　From the sun-rise.
So be happy wherever you may be
And Galatea sometimes think of me,
No magpie on the left block your journey,
　　No raven surprise.
Orion's falling, and can you not see
The storm coming? I know what it can be,
That black Adriatic, I know that tricky
　　Wind of Iapyx:
May wives and children of our enemies
Feel that stormwind that rises from the east
And coast trembling as the black noisy seas
　　Use their lashes.
Just so Europa trusted her snowy side
To the tricky bull ...

The link is very casual, is it not, and the relevance of the example hard to find? From this point on (25) Horace forgets Galatea, whose name is marine and unreal, to concentrate on the unlikely love affair, and the sea swarming with monsters while Europa who was happily plaiting a garland by starlight gets carried over to Crete. Europa makes a long speech like a prayer to her father. 'Impudently I left my father's house, and impudently [or shamefully] I delay my death.' She imagines him answering.

　　Vile Europa, father answers me,
　　Why not die? You could hang from this ash tree
　　And your belt is as useful as could be
　　　　To break your neck.
　　Or if the cliffs and the sharp deadly rocks
　　Delight you, come experience those shocks
　　Trust the swift wind as you have read in books ...

It is the classic choice of the rock, the rope or the sword, and I have guyed the poem only a little in the last line and a half: there is no doubt that Horace views the absurd story humorously, but he is captivated also by the prestige of antiquity, and by the romance with which Hellenistic authors had begun to plaster the myths. The forty lines of her speech and her father's reply end at 65, because here comes Venus 'Laughing with her perfidious laugh, her son With bow unstrung'. The girl is told the bull is Jupiter and she is his wife, and the planet or a large slice of it (*sectus orbis*) will bear her name. There are no excuses or explanations, that is the end of the poem. Can Horace possibly have taken a similar view of Augustus and his empire, his raping of the planet? We are given no clue or hint that he did, and yet he is a quite particularly subtle poet, and I wonder.

　　There follows a poem of four stanzas on Neptune's day (can that be the connection?). He has a good time with Lyde, the poem is very pretty and has no dedication, except that the wine dates from the consulship of Bibulus. I was once proud to be a friend of Virginia Grace, the Queen of amphora stamps, the world's first expert in the subject, but they mostly carried the names of owners, and I never thought to ask her about names of consuls or archons or governors. Now it is too late, but Horace knows the consular dates of vintages, and one wonders how. Were they scribbled on the amphora after it was sealed? Have none at all survived? I never read or heard that they had until very recently and then the wrong period. Bibulus was consul in 59 BC thirty years ago or more. He died in 48 and his widow married Brutus; his son fought at Philippi, served Antony as a diplomat and died about 32 BC.

> What shall I do that makes sense
> On Neptune's day? Lyde bring out of store
> Some Caecuban, like a strong girl, bring more
> Force to bear on wisdom's armaments.
> You can feel now the mid-point of day past
> And now the flying daylight seems to stand
> Are you too sparing to bring at my command
> That jar of consul Bibulus at last?

She is to bring it from the granary which is where it is lurking. She is a wife or daughter of one of his house serfs, there is no other reason for a woman in the poem except that they sing. 'We shall sing in turn Neptune and the green hair of the Nereids: you on the curved responding lute reply Latona and the arrows of Cynthia.' The Nereids have become sea-nymphs, given a fish's tail they would be mermaids, as one may see them represented, though mermaids or fishgirls exist in the traditional undatable art of the Inuit, who I think invented them. There are some in the Dominion Gallery in Toronto. Neptune, Latona and Night have Latin names. 'And with our last song the goddess who holds Cnydos and the glittering Cyclades and visited Paphos with a team of geese [Venus], and Night shall have his dirge as he deserves.' The word *nenia* normally means a dirge, a song of grief for the dead. Here it is either for the day that is dead or the amphora that is finished, or as I believe for Lucius Bibulus who fought at Philippi, survived like Horace, and died before Actium. Or is it for all the dead of the civil wars? Scholars who would be alarmed by this perhaps romantic reading of the ode cling to a late grammarian who calls *nenia* the last long lingering note of a song.

With ode twenty-nine we are back at the first words of the first ode of all, to Maecenas. He cannot have the very last poem because Horace has reserved that position for a new attempt to claim his own immortality, this time successfully, since it is indisputably a great poem, and a masterly reworking of the fourth ode in this book and the swan poem at the end of the last. The poem to Maecenas has sixty-four lines and includes stanzas as fine as any he wrote.

> Maecenas, sprig of Etruscan Kings
> Mellow wine that sees its first opening

Roses light on the air
Scent scattered on your hair,

'await you with me, so do stop delaying, and do not gaze at wet Tibur and the
sloping field of Aefula for ever, and the cliff of Telegonus the parricide.' That
sounds like the Villa S. Antonio, which survived as a monastery of some
grandeur until an Englishman bought it, and Mr Hallam who wrote a fragile
and eccentric book about it which is still invaluable, married his daughter.
The local mythology need not detain us; there was a valley of waterfalls
resounding as they fell into lakes and into the Anio, and every slope had a
legend, like hermits in a seventeenth-century landscape painting. 'Leave
your fastidious plenty and your building neighbour to the clouds [the tower
on the Esquiline] and stop marvelling at the smoke and wealth and noise of
happy Rome. Gods like a change and a clean dinner at a poor man's hearth.
Now the clear father of Andromeda [Cepheus in July] has shown his flame,
now Procyon [Greek for dog-star, *kyon* is a dog, and Procyon is in Canis
Minor] is raving and the star of the ravening lion as the sun brings back dry
days.'

Now the tired shepherd seeks the shadowed bank,
With panting sheep, or shaggy Silvanus lank
   In woods and rivers where
   No wind disturbs the air (24)

'Forget the troubles of the ends of the earth. A sensible god hides the outcome
in dark night. Time like a river runs quietly or raves and roars. That man is
happy who can say today "I have lived." Tomorrow does not matter, Fortune
switches, when she is off I seek poverty with no dowry, wrapped in my virtue.
I do not mind about bad weather at sea or riches spilt in the sea, the wind
will carry me safe through the Aegean and Pollux and his twin.' The poem is
mellow or even sweet in tone, friendly and resigned in its message, but the
message is the same as ever and Horace fingers old themes on the old strings:
the twin brethren, Fortune, wanting what is enough. He has forgotten about
his invitation which was only an excuse for this long poem. It is as if his
friendliest, his most intimate conversation must nowadays be about moral
philosophy, which has come to colour his personality more and more deeply.
He is after all about forty-two.

The thirtieth poem is a great rush of one or at most two sentences and of
sixteen lines, very like a sonnet. I do not know what great poet in the past it
has not influenced: but you can hear its stupendous boasting in Italian, in
French and in English, in which Shakespeare makes a sonnet of it. Since it
is all in one drum-roll of a metre, line by line in the same choriambics as the
first ode of the first book, though of the two this is far grander, I do not know
how one could or should translate it. I therefore offer an unpretentious
version that seemed to make the right noise and to convey a little of Horace's
authority.

> I have made my monument better than bronze
> And higher than the pyramids of kings
> Which neither the rain's teeth nor the wind's will
> Can pull apart, nor the innumerable
> Passing of years, nor Time in his flight:
> I shall not all die and a great part of me
> Will cheat the coffin-maker, my fresh fame
> Shall still increase while the priest climbs
> The Capitolium with the silent girl,
> My name be said where violent Aufidus
> Bellows where Daunus poor in water reigned
> King of peasants, powerful and born low
> But first to bring the Lesbian music
> To Italian tunes. Take that pride then
> You have deserved and sought, crown my hair
> Melpomene with the bay-leaves of Delphos.

A pyramid means or in Horace's day included the meaning of an obelisk, as Herrick used it in English poetry. The coffin-maker is Libitina, a death-goddess: Frazer on Ovid's *Fasti* (Vol.2, 282) gives us a riot of information about Lithuanians and Prussians, the Ibo and the Chinese and the reprehensible habits of Silvanus and how to nail him with axe, javelin and broom, but I doubt if he is right about the Flamen Dialis, who may well be the priest climbing the crumbling stone stairs to the Capitol. The person who used the broom to sweep away ghosts after death was an attendant on Libitina (a *libitinarius*) and no doubt she took her fee. She had a grove with a temple of Venus in it. Aufidus is the powerful river near Venusia where Horace was born, the Delphic bay-leaves stand for a prophet as well as a poet, and Daunus was the King of poor people without the widely scattered water sources that farmers needed and need. That is why Horace so feared the heat and the dog-star and the sign of the Lion.

Since I have often consulted though seldom quoted the new Penguin anthology of Horace translations into English (1996) perhaps I should add a note about what it reveals. Among the poets who have translated odes, Herrick, Sir Philip Sidney, Sir Henry Wotton and the Earl of Surrey are all wonderfully alive, almost too perfect, where Ben Jonson lumbers a little. After that dawn it is unfair really that Milton should so overshadow all others, since in many ways I prefer Fanshawe's beginning,

> What Stripling now thee discomposes
> In Woodbine Rooms, on Beds of Roses,

to Milton's no doubt subtler opening,

> What slender Youth bedew'd with liquid odours
> Courts thee on Roses in some pleasant Cave ...

just as I much prefer his *Odes* 3, 1 to the unfinished version by Hopkins. But the greatest surprise was the modern section most of which I knew but had forgotten. The version that most sounded like Horace seemed to me to be Robert Lowell's of *Odes* 2, 7, the poem to Pompey. He sees what the poem is about, and goes for that with his usual energy and brilliance, and only a few slight exaggerations prevent one from using his magnificent poems. But it was an amphora, not two or three, that Pompey was being offered, and the idea of twisting parsley and myrtle with the coronets is charming and pleasantly drunk, but alas I do not think it is right; 'when a friend's reprieved' is too definite too: we do not know that he was condemned, let alone reprieved. Maybe he was just let live. There remains the great unspoken: the syntactic and poetic subtleties of Horace in the *Odes*. I do not feel I have brought them out, though I hope to have created at least a hazy impression that he was truly a great poet and a man with depths. For the subtleties it is best to read the Penguin Introduction (pp. 44-58).

After Horace had let his three books of *Odes* circulate, he gave up lyric poetry, at least for the time being. The literary world was nasty about his work, there may have been some fury at certain poems; anyway he felt himself rejected and the *Odes* a failure. They were poetry so perfect it was like the full moon: one could not credit it would ever die, but he took it up again only after the public and popular success of his Song of the Age, the *Carmen Saeculare*. Then in his last few odes he wrote better than he had ever written. But in the immediate aftermath of 23 BC, say for three years, if he produced anything it was his second and incomplete book of *Satires*. That represents a complete break with the poetry he had written before: it was mostly a series of philosophic dialogues in verse. I doubt whether he wrote these *Satires* at the same time as his lyrics, if only because the lyrics are political where the new poetry is moral. Still, we are now free to leave all the imperial political questions in suspense.

Chapter Eight

The mature reign of Augustus had begun. There was to be no huge concentration of legions such as the civil wars had often produced until after Horace's death, over a crisis in Pannonia in 11 AD when the Romans feared an invasion from Bosnia. The weight of the new constitution had swung so that power was not exercised by the Senate in the same way, and the Knights Augustus picked out as instruments of his government must have frightened the old nobility. Where before all favours came from noble senators, who competed for the affections of the people, now they all came from Augustus through his various instruments. The court existed and the crowd of secretaries, who were slaves and ex-slaves, had become apparent. Was that why Horace refused to be a private secretary? But one must not assess the early stages of the transformation by the four thousand inscribed names of the full-blown imperial services a hundred years later. Augustus still greeted every senator who called on him with a kiss, every morning. Indeed under Tiberius the entire Roman upper class gave themselves a skin rash transmitted by kisses.

The parties closed in on the heirs to Augustus: first their choice had been Livia's children and Agrippa's or Octavia's, with the adoption of an heir resting in Caesar's hand: in this game Horace seems to have played no part at all. As the choices and the parties widened, Augustus was still in control, and Horace was loyal to him. But we have not yet come to the logical articulation of the monarchy, architecturally under Nero. Nero's palace had as many lavatories as the main line international railway station at Milan, and his Golden House abolished entire districts of ancient Rome. But under Augustus the functions of his house were still as headquarters, a *praetorium* with a praetorian guard, as centre of an increasing secretariat, government centre and private dwelling, and they remained confused. The libraries of the Palatine were part of the structure of the temple of Actian Apollo, and Augustus's palace (*palatium*) was like Whitehall under Henry VIII, which enveloped the Abbey as if it were a private chapel: the palace of Augustus had ramps that led straight into Apollo's temple.

Maecenas is often thought to have gone into some form of disgrace, though that is not obvious from Horace or in the letters or messages in the Life of Horace, and Suetonius had read and relied on more letters than he quotes, though probably on less study of Horace than people now imagine. The evidence of Horace's disillusion with cities and the envious public is already apparent enough in the *Odes*: he was what we call an élitist. His disenchantment intensified with the comparative rejection of his *Odes* as we shall see, but his perfection not his rejection naturally left him lonely. Only poor Statius later attempted Horatian lyrics, only in one set of alcaics and one of sapphics which survive, and Caesius Bassus who does not survive was thought respectable by Quintilian. With one or two other minor exceptions, Horace was left alone and went back to satires. They had always amused him and they had a moral purpose which was important to him as it was to Virgil. They do not represent a turning of his back on society or on the state, far from it.

He begins still preoccupied with Lucilius, whose credit with Horace is even higher than before. The first of the new book is to Trebatius, a lawyer of sixty-five in 25 BC born at Velia, a coastal town now lost in the sea it seems, somewhere near Agropoli which lies south of Paestum and might have become part of Velia. In late antiquity and the Middle Ages the coastline altered so much that for centuries the temples at Paestum stood up to their waists in sea water, and when they were rediscovered by a Neapolitan artillery surveyor in the eighteenth century they were in use as stables for water buffaloes, whose milk produced mozzarella cheese. Somewhere nearby lay the lost Velia. Trebatius was very fond of swimming, which considering how the sea flooded Paestum must have been just as well. He was a friend of Cicero who dedicated a book to him, a supporter of Caesar, and a really distinguished lawyer. As a lawyer he is recorded in the *Digest of Roman Law* (24, 1, 64) for a decision 'in the case of Maecenas and Terentia: A man had given his wife on divorce certain property to return to him, she came back and then he divorced her. Trebatius said if the divorce was real so was the gift, if it was simulated, the gift was invalid.' It sounds as if the divorce from Terentia was a considerable headache, and one is not surprised if Maecenas was depressed by that, let alone by her affair with Augustus. As for Trebatius, he was alive until about 14 BC when he was seventy-six; we hear earlier from Cicero that he was an Epicurean. Later ages consented to his supreme authority as a lawyer under Augustus, but Lejay points to a certain twinkle in Horace's eye as he consults the great man.

> To some I seem too fierce a satirist
> Breaking the law, but with too weak a wrist
> The others say, just as if I could write
> As others can a thousand lines a night:
> Tell me Trebatius what to do? Be quiet.
> Not to write any verse at all? That's it.
> Damn me if that's not best, but I can't sleep.
> Oil and swim Tiber three times where it's deep,
> And water yourself with wine before nightfall,
> Or if you so love writing then try hard
> At Caesar's victories for a large reward.
> Dear father I want to, but I lack the powers
> For the Gauls falling in their ruined towers,
> And the battalions prickling with spears

> Where wounded Parthians slide down horses' rears.
> Still you could write a Scipiad justly
> Like wise Lucilius ...

This is how the satire begins, and it is evident that Trebatius is being mocked. His suggestion of a Scipiad is deliberately absurd. We have in fact some papyrus scraps of verses *de bello Actiaco*, and they are remarkably bad. There is a deliberate attempt in the opening lines of this satire to create a link with the subject of Lucilius and his satires in the first book, and in the last line I quote he is the wise and exemplary poet. But this is not the dedication poem of the book, since Trebatius is not addressed in the first line, nor is Maecenas. This book consisted of only eight poems, so it is reasonable to conclude that the two it lacks are the first and the last. Would they have been to Maecenas? Did they remain unwritten because Maecenas did not want the dedication of such obsessively philosophical verse? Or was Horace blocked by some literary problem, or desperate to get on with his *Letters*? The sixth satire at least implicitly (31 and 39) and by its gratitude for the estate in the Sabine hills does belong to Maecenas, and is deliberately placed in the centre of the book as Ode 3, 16 is in a similar position.

In the present satire, Horace is particularly careful about Caesar.

> ... I will do well with that theme
> When it arises, only at the right time
> Shall Horace be heard in Caesar's listening ear:
> Handle him wrong and you'll be kicked I fear.

Trebatius takes up the subject of the sharp stage comedians Pantolabus and Nomentanus (*Sat*.1, 8, 41) whom everyone fears. What can I do? answers Horace, Castor and Pollux came from one egg, but they had different talents.

> My pleasure is to enclose my words in verse
> Lucilius-like, though you and I write worse.
> He trusted his soul's secrets to his friend
> That is his book, not swerving if the end
> Was good or bad for him, and this is how
> That old man's life is all of it on show
> Like votive paintings. Whether Lucanian or
> Apulian by birth I am not sure,
> But him I follow. We Venusians plough
> Both borders since (ancient report says so)
> The old Sabines were pushed out of the place,
> So as not to let enemies through empty space,
> Or else Lucanians or Apulians might
> Invade with violence: but my pen won't fight
> Against any person that breathes human breath,
> It keeps me as a sword's kept in the sheath ...

We have strayed a little from Lucilius as an ideal, but it is possible to follow the train of thought. Horace's ideal is as it were to paint himself, to show the whole of himself like Lucilius. Horace himself comes from border country like the Welsh Marches, but he is not disposed to personal warfare. He prays (42) to be left in peace, but anyone who stirs him up 'Shall weep and the whole city will chant his name'. Horace imagines the ancient Roman law of the Twelve Tables which forbids bad magic under pain of death may be in force against all wicked verses, though as Lejay pointed out a century ago, there he was wrong. He comes (47) to cases: Cervius an ex-slave who accused the consul of 53 BC, our old friend Canidia who poisoned Albucius, and Turius: for a few lines he vanishes down the dusty labyrinth of the law and its lurid cases (50-56) cooled by elegant metaphors.

> In short, whether quiet age takes me underground
> Or death with its black wings hovers around,
> Rich or poor, in exile and in grief
> I will describe the real colour of life.
> My boy I fear that you may not grow old,
> Some friend of older men may strike you cold.
> What? When Lucilius first tried this verse
> Taking away men's skin, to show them worse ...?
> Did Laelius or he who took his name
> From ruined Carthage grieve at their bad fame
> When Lupus and Metellus drowned in rhyme?
> The leaders and all tribes suffered the same
> He loved nothing but virtue and its friends
> Yet when all doors were shut, Scipio then
> And Laelius's mild wisdom sported with him.

The argument has become recondite, because it is confined to those legendary days.

> And whatever I am however much less
> In wealth and genius than Lucilius,
> He must admit, in unwilling envy,
> I lived among great men, and break on me
> His unsuspecting tooth, my dearest Sir,
> Trebatius, or do you not concur?
> Not at this point indeed, and yet beware,
> Your ignorance of law could lay you bare
> To 'If one make bad songs against another'
> Judgement and process stand. Yet will not bother
> If Caesar says my song is good? If I
> Bark at insults quite innocently?
> I acquit you, the warrant washes away.

To us the legal language is a pedantic joke and the end of the poem predictably feeble. It had more punch in its own time, but it can hardly be denied that Horace is not risking anything. In the quagmire of legal phraseology, Lejay in his introduction to the poem is a sufficiently learned guide. What is interesting about it to us is the occasional flash of steel from Horace's genuine admiration of the old Knight, and his determination to follow him, both in his self-portraiture and in his integrity, though he really does fully understand the difference in conditions between them. The adoption of the elderly lawyer as a quasi-father appears to me a brilliantly useful device, since now he is talking about law which is a joke, and now he is not which is a livelier joke. The reliance on Caesar's ear and approval is something we have not heard before. Of course it really does conclude the argument and there would be no use in pretending otherwise, but does it bring to bear a force which is beyond the law and in a way arbitrary? I do not think it quite does, because even in 20 BC the law of Rome is still the law, and Trebatius would abide by it and so would Augustus, who spent much of his time in Rome sitting as supreme magistrate. The malignity or otherwise of Horace's poems is a matter of fact no doubt and not law, so the wax tablets the court uses are wiped clean or dissolved, and Horace, now that Caesar has been judged by Caesar, is acquitted. Lawyers still quarrel like hornets over the last line, which literally means 'Tablets dissolved in laughter, you'll go free', but one may pursue earnestness too far in this satire, which makes a monkey of the law.

It was an intellectually elaborate exercise all the same. The second satire presents him as a simple, unpretentious countryman, and that certainly is where you must watch him closely. It deals with Ofellus who was once rich but ruined by the civil wars, and reduced to working as an employee on property he once owned. We are talking after supper in the evening. The serfs and slaves are present and an occasional country neighbour of no great eminence. Cicero on Old Age (*Sen.*46) speaks of this customary conversation that goes on late into the night in Sabine country, and Alfenus in the second epode (65-6) refers to it, while the sixth satire of this book is the *locus classicus* of the subject (65-7, etc.). In this second satire it is often hard to pick out who is talking: in the first fifty verses for example, Ofellus seems to be the speaker, but this is contrived by the use of brackets for lines 2 and 3: yet the syntax makes sense without them, indeed the way the lines are inserted echoes Plato's *Symposium* (177a) just for fun. As to what kind of philosophy is being talked it probably matters little: he is still in the tradition of Teles and of Bion and the popular Cynics. When Suetonius claims it was said that Horace's father dealt in *taramasalata* and wiped his nose on his sleeve, he is just repeating a story told about Bion. Indeed the word 'fishpickleseller' continued as an insult in demotic Greek at least until the twelfth century AD, when it was alive and well in PtochoProdromos. The influence on this satire is not from personal study of some great man, but from what we must be content to call a popular tradition of street philosophy, from which even Christians benefited in the end. There are crumbs of Chrysippus, and bits of Euripides equivalent to peasant proverbs, and even bits of Philemon that are mashed together to make the doctrine of Enough. Epicurus says you live well on a little. *Nous allons chez notre grand-mère, manger des pommes de terre* ... There is even a bit of Philemon:

> One loaf, a fig, and some water to drink,
> This man teaches a new philosophy,
> He teaches starving, and he gets pupils ... (cf. Lejay, p.322)

Horace begins 'The great virtue of living on a little (this is not me talking but the teaching of Ofellus a countryman wise out of proportion, but crude) Listen and learn: it isn't when crazy people wonder at shining dishes and tables and when the mind resting on these false lightnings refuses better things, but you discuss it here without eating. Why? I'll tell you if I can. The corrupt judge ...' At least half the joke is about the rambling style of the countryman: he might be a Marxist in the forest in *Doctor Zhivago*, or a Civil War leveller in 1648. One may sympathise at the same time as one scorns him. 'Bread and salt will calm your barking ... Supreme pleasure is in yourself. Get your sauce by sweating ... You want to tickle your palate with peacock and not hen, because you are corrupted by emptiness, by the price of a thing. Do you eat the feathers you praise? Do they have the same honours cooked? ...' The old man bewilders his hearers with a snowstorm of details: they look fine in verse and they add to the pleasure.

> Take the bass, what does it matter if it be
> Caught in Tiber or gaping in the sea?
> Between bridges or Ostia? You praise
> A three pound mullet and in such a craze
> You don't see that you get less sauce with it,
> The appearance of it leads you on, that's what.
> So why do you hate the leaping great sea-bass?
> Since nature made it greater and not less?
> A fasting belly don't mind vulgar food. (38)

He is unstoppable, and varies his essential argument very little, but the drive of his speech is like the momentum of invective.

> Feasting doesn't take all by which we live.
> We have the cheap sheep and the black olive
> ... If someone tells us cormorant's good roast,
> All Roman youth will hurry to the coast. (52)

Ofellus thought a thin life and a sordid life differ, Horace intervenes, because it's no use avoiding one extreme and falling into the other. Take Avidienus: but alas we know nothing about him except by divination that the name may or may not be real. But how will the wise man live (63)?

> Here is the use of a thin livelihood:
> The first benefit's health, you will feel good,

> To be convinced how much can hurt a man
> Think of all that sat easy when you began,
> And how variety, thrush with shell-fish
> Turns into bile, belly rebels, slowish
> Catarrh follows ... (76)

The sermon is simpler, and the examples not so tumultuous. 'The body labouring with yesterday's weight pulls down the mind and sticks to the ground a part of the divine breath [spirit or soul]. Yet sleep cures the guest who rose pallid from his dubious dinner. This man may improve one day as the returning year brings a feast day, or as he seeks to refresh his thinning body, the years come and weak age wants to be more softly treated, what more will come to you then than came when you were a boy and strong, in hard health or slow old age? The ancients liked rotting boar, not because they had no noses, but I think because the late arriving guest would eat meat that was a bit off easier than the host would eat it sound. Would that the earth bore me among those heroes!' This is not like a dialogue of Plato, but more like a real conversation overheard, which comes in some way confused to the ear. If there are several people talking, then they do not seem to be listening to each other. The poem is in an odd way attractive, but it reminds me of the poem Durrell wrote 'On First Looking into Loeb's Horace', which mentions 'his weakness for stone age conversation'. I am inclined to let Creech take up the difficult task of translation; he is best where we return to Ofellus, as we soon shall. 'If you are rich why should any man need? Why are the antique temples falling down? Why not give something to your dear country from such a pile? So things will be all right for you alone? What a laugh for your enemies later! Which has more confidence in tricky times, the man whose mind and body are used to them, or the man content with a little and fearing for the future who prepares for war in peacetime?' (111)

Creech is a good or decent poet in the only age of English poetry when to be decent was enough, the age of Dryden. He translated all Theocritus first, and better than anyone for three centuries to come: in this piece of Horace, which I take from the new Penguin anthology, one can observe a Theocritean, idyllic quality, but it is not inappropriate. This satire is nearly a hundred and forty lines long, but it is only in the final two dozen lines where Ofellus is reintroduced that it comes into its own. The narrative functions almost like a Platonic myth to draw the strings of the moral 'diatribe' together and to transform them. With the last lines of Ofellus's strong views we are already familiar (129-35), because we had occasion to quote them about Horace's own position: only that here they are transformed into Horatian verse and forget their Greek origin. But Ofellus is an idyllic and unlikely ending. He is the country mouse as a moralist, as a philosopher. How the whole passage (112-136) is a strong ending but not unlike others that Horace will go on to write, in which he armours himself against the blows of fate (*Epist*.1, 16, for example). What is queer is the sudden introduction of Ofellus in the first few lines as a speaker, followed by his leisurely reintroduction in the third person as if we had never met him. My own solution is that the first few lines are an

attempt to draw the poem together. The difficulties of the first hundred and
ten lines arise from the essentially inconsequent and repetitive nature of the
street corner philosophic sermons Horace was imitating: the same nature is
to be seen in Teles and even in Epictetus.

Was Ofellus real? Given the use of him as a speaker for most of the poem
I greatly doubt it. If Horace really knew him before the wars, then he surely
knew him at Venusia, and would not know him now. If he knew him as a boy
in Rome, Ofellus must be as old as Trebatius and a friend of Horace's father:
but in the same Sabine valley? It seems highly unlikely. Horace has invented
him as a composite figure, but he does not quite cohere. That does not matter
in the least, and we can pour Creech's smooth style over him like cream, but
he does go to the heart of the problem of the Roman countryside, and the
combination of toughness, suffering and Virgilian nostalgia is a mixture
unique to Horace, to his personality and to his life. We suddenly see in Ofellus
a distorted image of his real father, and we see how deeply the freedom of
conversation with his serfs in the evening entered into him. Thomas Creech
published this piece of Horace in 1684: he had published Theocritus's *Idylli-
ums* with an interesting discourse on golden age poetics at Oxford in the same
year.

> I knew Ofellus when I was a youth;
> Then he was rich, yet midst his greatest store,
> He liv'd as now, since Rapine made him poor:
> Now you may see him with his wife and son
> Till that estate for hire which was his own:
> He ploughs, he sweats, and stoutly digs for bread,
> Contented still, and as he wrought, he said,
> On working days I never used to eat
> But cale and bacon, that was all my meat:
> But when an old and honest friend of mine
> Or else my welcome neighbours came to dine;
> When it was rainy, or my work was done,
> We feasted not on costly fish from town;
> But took what I could easily provide
> From my own field, a pullet or a kid:
> And then for second course some grapes were press'd,
> Or nuts, and figs, and that was all my feast:
> And after this we drank a health or two,
> As far as harmless sober mirth would go:
> And then thank'd Ceres for our present cheer,
> And beg'd a plenteous crop the following year:
> And now let fortune frown, I scorn her force,
> How can she make our way of living worse?
> Have we not had enough since we grew poor,
> Have we lived worse my sons than heretofore,
> Before a stranger came, and seized my store?
> For nature doth not me or him create

The proper lord of such and such estate:
He forc'd us out, and doth possess my plain;
Another cheat shall force him out again,
Or quirks in law, or when those fears are past
His long-liv'd heir shall force him out at last:
That which was once Ofellus' farm is gone,
Now call'd Umbrena's, but tis no man's own:
None hath the property: it comes and goes
As merry chance or stubborn fates dispose,
As God thinks fit and his firm nod's decree,
Now to be us'd by others, now by me:
Then live resolv'd my sons, refuse to yield,
And when fates press make constancy your shield.

One might almost suppose that Ofellus arose out of the epigram at the end, with all his sons around him, and his character predetermined like a Latin genie out of a Greek bottle, but other ingredients have gone into him, and the long speech that begins this satire adds other qualities to the stubborn and stoical peasant. Some professors have been much moved by the thought of his simple way of life, and certainly no one can describe the pleasures of meagre 'enough' as well as Horace can. But these last twenty lines are meant to take the carpet from under the feet of anyone with a stable view of country life. Virgil's people in the bucolics are conceivable because they are wanderers as homeless as their flocks. But for us the importance of this second satire is that we can see from it how Horace might construct a satire out of a well-known epigram from which he draws a character and gives that man a family history, and from a rustic ragbag of examples from moral philosophy which he dramatises and makes personal. Luckily for us the satire is not perfectly polished, so we can see how the remark about Ofellus in the second and third lines was added at a late stage of composition. To make sense of 'I knew Ofellus when I was a youth' Horace would have to have added a clearer first person earlier in the poem. If he had meant to write about moderation he was distracted: he behaves more like a man writing the beginnings of a play, yet it is surely the last twenty lines that make it masterly.

Yet his uncertainty about how to divide his dialogues persists in the third satire. At the beginning and the end Damasippus attacks Horace, but most of the poem is given to Stertinius (28-395) and a large part of it is addressed to all humanity. His platform is the Stoic teaching that people are crazy because they are ruled by vice, by avarice (82-157), ambition (158-223), luxury (224-80) or superstition (281-297). Stertinius starts off openly with the definition of madness (41-5) and proceeds from that as lucidly as a Mozart concerto: but the method was not in Horace's time confined to a single school of philosophy, any more than that of the concerto was confined to Mozart. It is curious how things have altered since Plato's dialogues: now a Greek name makes you likely to be a slave or an ex-slave among the Romans, while the name of Stertinius (Snorer) is surely intentionally comic for the street preacher. Chrysippus is mentioned (44) but he died in 207 BC. He was a Stoic who was converted by Kleanthes, but he practically obliterated all early Stoic teachings by the prestige and quantity of his writings, though Zeno (d. 263 BC) still has an influence on what Horace says about knowledge and its disturbance by passion, or at least on his vocabulary. I do not propose to enter into the subtle controversies that Hellenistic philosophy generated: there are specialised works on the subject, and those I once read will by now be out of date. Luckily this does not matter, because Horace's attitude to the professional philosophers he encounters in the second book of satires was not reverent, they are comic or farcical characters however long he allows them to speak.

Damasippus, like a secretary who nags, begins the satire, but he is apparently the steward of the rented house.

> You rewrite old writers it would appear
> And want new parchment just four times a year,
> You hate yourself because you're a sleepy sot
> And write down nothing worth a Satire: then what?
> At Saturnalia you run down here for a while,
> So start dictating, make it something with style
> You blame your pens, or else the wall that's stood
> The bangs of poets and the curse of gods
> And yet what wonders promised in your face
> If you found this empty and a nice warm place!
> Why pack in all Menander and Plato,
> Eupolis, Archilochus? It is as though
> You placate envy and leave virtue behind.
> You'll be despised! That Siren sloth of mind
> Cries out to you ...

It is at the lowest a neat device to paint his own portrait through his slave's or ex-slave's eyes. The books he brings to the borrowed or rented house are Athenian comedy and old satire. Plato in this context is not the philosopher. Damasippus can speak freely because this is the Saturnalia perhaps. May the gods grant you a haircut, Horace answers. But how do you know me so well? 'After I was bankrupted, I look after other people's business.' In fact he has lost his wealth in some ways like Ofellus: in his case a lucrative and perhaps rascally trade in gardens, houses and Greek antiques (20-29). It is fascinating all the same that the trade in Greek works of art, which excavations at the Piraeus have revealed was on a large scale, was even in Rome in the hands of Greeks. Everyone is mad, he assures us, if Stertinius tells the truth, so:

> I wrote down every precept that I heard
> At the time he told me to grow a wise man's beard.

This explains the need for a haircut. Damasippus had been about to commit suicide from the bridge that leads to the island of Aesculapius in the Tiber.

It still survives as the Ponte de Quattro Capi, named now after two
two-headed Herms found built into it. Horace calls it the Pons Fabricius
after its builder in 62 BC. Stertinius had found Damasippus and cheered
him up.

> Your trouble is false shame,
> You fear to be thought insane by the insane.
> First ask what madness is: if that's your rage
> Not a word more, but jump, and with courage. (42)

Until now the whole poem with its characters and situations, quite elaborately sketched in, has been an introduction to the teachings of Stertinius.
Stertinius like Ofellus is invented and exaggerated for comic effect: he is only
a mask that speaks, so that even Damasippus is much more sharply defined.
The speech of Stertinius is of course the substantial satire that Horace had
intended to write.

> Whom folly and whom ignorance make blind
> Are crazy, says Chrysippus: that's mankind,
> All peoples and all Kings except the wise:
> Do you want to know why you and why all these
> Are crazy? Like someone lost in forest
> Wandering this way or that, as they think best ...

From this point (50) the verse will flow on: but we must stop to consider
what kind of poetry it is. The Ofellus satire tacked a character who arose from
a considered epigram on to what might have been a street sermon based on
observation: but this poem frames and embellishes what looks like a pamphlet versified. Yet it cannot quite be that, it is too lively, altogether too
Horatian. Few ages of the world have attempted to versify philosophy, the
Middle Ages did not, nor did the Renaissance. The only ages that successfully
did so were those of Lucretius, Horace and Dryden and let us add Boileaux
on whom Dryden based himself. Without these we would be tempted to put
philosophy beyond even Horace's range. Yet the enterprise is possible, even
if the philosophy is not a wild street tirade but a measured statement. Brecht
attempted it, or rather began an attempt to put the Communist Manifesto
into verse: that document is easier than a Stoic pamphlet, yet he wrote less
than twenty lines of it of which I recall only the resounding second: '*aber zu
Kinden von Vorstadten freundlich, dein Name ist Kommunismus*', 'but a good
friend to children of the suburbs, thy name is Communism,' in which the
wicked doctrine bursts through the floor like a demon king. We have no
equivalent to Stertinius: the Stoics are quite dead to us and studied only in
grave and obscure academic circles. The fact that Horace takes them at once
seriously and lightly is a large part of his point.

> 'Here is a great ditch, a vast rock!'
> Is not more heard than drunken Fufius' shock

Waking Iliona: twenty thousand cried
'Mother wake up!'

Horace recalls an incident some hundred years ago in the theatre of Pacuvius, when the boy playing Iliona, Priam's eldest daughter, was hard to wake
because he was drunk. It is not very funny, only farcical, but it enlivens the
philosophy (59-63). Characters are introduced from farce, like Nerius and
Cicuta; Proteus is taken to law but turns to a bird, a rock, and a tree (73);
Perellius the banker pops up unintroduced, and ambition, love, luxury and
superstition are formally listed. Horace has a clear statement in mind but at
the same time he is making hay of it, and I do not believe any Stoic pamphlet
was quite so farcical. Staberius is an invented name, and his will (84) runs
at once into preposterous complications. Arrius was an old friend of Cicero,
but he is dragged in here just for the huge expense of a funeral feast he gave,
probably for his father: money is at the bottom of this.

> For everything,
> Virtue, fame, honour, human and divine
> Bows down to wealth, which who accumulates
> Is famous, brave, just – Wise? And reigns in state.
> He hoped for great praise just as if he'd got
> By exercise of virtue such a lot.
> Then what about Aristippus the Greek
> Who got his slaves who moved slowly to leak
> Money all over the Libyan desert
> So as to go faster? Then which part
> Is crazier? (99)

We never get beyond this first stage of argument; in it the idea at least of
what for want of a better word we call moral philosophy persuades the reader
towards virtue. That at least is the idea, and I observe that Brecht never got
much further. Lucretius did enter into the depths of belief and argument, but
few readers follow him quite so far. Food and drink (111-5) provide another
example of human folly, but Ofellus has dealt better with that. Horace does
elucidate the bitterness between the rich and their heirs.

> Most people suffer from the same disease:
> Shall the son or the ex-slave drink all this?
> God-hated old man, are you keeping it
> Just for fear you might want a little bit? (121-3)

'But if you bash people with rocks, including slaves you bought with money,
all the boys and girls will call you crazy. If you hang your wife and poison
your mother, are you safe? You aren't doing this in Argos or using a sword on
your mother like crazy Orestes.' Horace had probably never seen Mycenae,
and accepted the Greek fifth-century convention that the tragedy happened
at Argos: Argos had destroyed independent Mycenae early in the fifth

century, but the story had always been a fertile source of arguments (141).
We move on at once to 'Opimius' who used to drink the wine of Veii (143)
which we are assured by Lejay was a *'petit vin rouge peu agréable'*, like the
red wine to be found around Rome to this day: I am not sure how he knows
that but it was an everyday wine. The little story is about Opimius falling ill
and being given a herbal drink with rice in it by the doctor. 'What did it cost?
But how much? Ach, what does it matter whether I die of disease or daylight
robbery?' Servius Oppidius had two estates at Canusium, he was a rich man,
and gave them to his two sons: one a jolly outgoing spender, the other a miser.
The anecdote is well told and lengthy, and it may well be remembered from
Horace's father, though no one has heard of Oppidius. The boys are con-
strained one to lose nothing and one to gain nothing, and neither to enter
politics (168-84). Agrippa is praised (184) as a good example, then for twenty
lines we are back picking cases out of the Trojan war. At 223 we are imitating
epic verse and then we are attacking luxury. I do not think one could follow
the drift of the argument without a pencil and paper. At one stage Horace
even quotes Terence, fitting him with some brilliance into his own metre
(264), and he flings off in passing such details of life as one man sleeping in
gaiters above the snowline for another to eat boar: but sometimes as at the
conversion of Polemo (d. 270 BC) they are not contemporary. Chrysippus is
mixed with Menenius (287) from who knows what date.

At least Stertinius finishes (295): 'So how am I a fool, since there is more
Than one kind of madness I am sure?' Is Agave in the *Bacchae* not mad
(303-4)? Tell me my vice. You build, imitating Maecenas like Turbo (a small,
fat gladiator, 310) Like the frog blowing itself up to explain a cow to its
mother.

> That is what you are like:
> Add poems then, you pour oil on the flame,
> If any sane man writes poems, you are sane.
> Let alone your rabid – Stop it! – expenditure
> Above your income. Damasippus be your own cure.
> A thousand girl crazes, a thousand boys,
> O go and tackle someone your own size.

The satire has at least a powerful and persistent liveliness, and the framing
at the beginning and end is cheering. Perhaps it is all a little too cheerful,
and its length may defeat its satirical purpose. If Horace had written only
this second book of *Satires*, setting aside the sixth, I would not be writing
about him, but without going through these poems I do not believe he could
have written his fine and mature books of *Letters*.

The fourth satire is less than a hundred lines long, about cooking. Cooks
as buffoons go back into Greek and south Italian cooking, and Athenaeus, a
later Greek writer than Horace, has accumulated a dazing mass of information on the subject. The Sicilian Archestratus of Gela had written a kind of
didactic or epic poem on the subject, and the old grandad of Roman poetry,
Ennius, had adapted it into Latin. The Epicureans took a particular interest

in the art of the kitchen, and that no doubt is why Horace, having polished off Stoicism so fully, puts his food poem here. It goes without saying that it is not easy to exercise modern judgement on the subject-matter of Horace's satire; we are not even sure whether his cook Catius was a serious Epicurean or (surely) someone else of the same name, and for all we know (and as I suspect) invented. Lejay argues the matter closely for eight or nine solid pages but comes to no conclusion. But the important point is surely that Horace here invents quite a new kind of poem, and not for the first time in this book, setting one pleasure of the senses closely among others in a surreal mosaic.

The joke in the first surprising lines is that Horace is rather exactly parodying Plato's *Phaedrus* (228b). Fraenkel (137) wants to add a connection between the eighth satire of this book and Plato's *Timaeus*. With the second satire I need any help I can get, so I am delighted with the *Symposium* echo; in this fourth satire I feel more dubious, because 'Whence and whither?' is such a common form of speech in Greek, still the whole situation is funny enough to be convincing; in the eighth the remote echo or parody is likely enough once you have thought of it.

> Where from, where to, Catius? I've no time,
> I have this new set of rules I must sign
> Better than Pythagoras or Socrates
> Or learned Plato or great names like these,
> Sorry to catch you at a bad moment,
> Do forgive me, it really wasn't meant,
> But if you did have something now to say
> Nature or art, wonderful either way?
> ... I'll sing the rules, the author I conceal,
> A long-faced egg as I have always found
> Has better taste and more white than the round,
> The tougher shells you see exclude the male:
> Cale grown in dry suburban fields for sale
> Is sweeter: wet gardens are insipid.

The rules continue like this, higgledy-piggledy, and many of them most misleading, though the nonsense about eggs can be traced back to Aristotle and onwards to Columella on agriculture. If a guest turns up unannounced and your chicken is tough put it alive to drown in Falernian wine. Nature is excellent in field mushrooms but trust no others. You'll have healthy summers if you finish dinner with black fruit, picked before the heavy sun. Aufidius put honey in strong Falernian: a mistake. Certain lines in the poem are amusing or appetising; they arrest you for long enough to notice that this is a new kind of poetry. The fragments of Latin poetry edited by Courtney (1993) are full of it. It exists in English largely under Horace's leadership from the time of John Gay onwards; John Fuller is the greatest modern expert on it. 'The new-born moons fill up the slippery shell' (30) is only the tip of the iceberg of connoisseurship about ancient oysters, and scarcely touches on the queer doctrine to be found in Pliny, that the oyster swells and diminishes in time with the moon, and alters its sex once a month. Horace wanders happily on from the murex of Baiae, through the Lucrine giants, the oysters of Ischia, and sea-urchins of Misenum to 'The fine sea-comb is soft Tarentum's boast': all the other places are in Campania. Once one is used to the kind of unreliable information and two thousand year old connoisseurship, the poem is most enjoyable. The most peculiar misinformation is about vines, Massic wine (from near Sinuessa), for instance, thinned or refined by the night airs, and with less of that heavy breath that so offends the nerves. Venefran olives are praised (69) and the apples of Tivoli are no match for Picenian in flavour, which one supposes being east of the Apennines must be redder and sweeter: he praises the flavour, 'because they are so good to look at' (71). Eight lines from the end, the speaker is interrupted.

> Learned Catius for friendship for the gods,
> Take me along with you ...

The poor man cannot remember the stream of instructions. Am I exaggerating if I suggest that Horace is satirising and has perfectly caught something between a cooking programme and a gardening programme on television?

In the fifth satire the teacher is Tiresias and his pupil is Ulysses. We are in Homer's *Odyssey* (11, 90f.) but Ulysses is a modern man and wants to be rich, so Tiresias tells him to pursue inheritances, and explains to him how the game works. As a satire this poem is sharper than earlier ones: it is only a hundred and ten lines long.

> Answer me this as well Teresias,
> How am I to recover from my loss?
> Why laugh? Is it not enough for a tricky man
> To get back home and see his gods again?

The beginning was in Homer's *Odyssey* as one might expect (11, 140) and the queer form Teresias comes from Plautus and must have been traditional in Latin, like Phèdre for Phaidra in French.

> You never lied to anyone, you see
> How poor and naked I'll come home from sea,
> No wine-cellar, no flocks, virtue indeed
> And blood being much cheaper than seaweed.

The prophet answers in grand, prophetic tones, but Ulysses does not understand at once: he echoes his own old speeches or Teucer's from a lyric.

> Then you'll be poor.
>   I'll tell my mind to endure,
> Which has endured worse. Prophet, make me sure
> Where to dig riches ...

Tiresias explains (26-31), and the joke depends on the silent irony of his grand language and his disgusting message. If one asks how oracles really dealt with these low matters, the answer is to be found in the inscriptions from Dodona, which ask Whether it be better and more good ... and get an answer yes or no. The god was not committed to phrasing everyday questions in high-sounding verse. But in this satire the contrivance of how to inherit has a certain unreality, enlivened only by phrases that might occur in another poem like 'a crushed nut-shell' (36) or the sudden slash at Furius Bibaculus, tacked on to a phrase from Catullus: 'Stand firm, endure whether the red dog-star Splits speechless statues or swelled in his car Furius spits white snow on Alpine peaks ...' (39-41). Furius had written his line about Jupiter, and I used the car to get a rhyme: in fact the allusions to Furius are intricate and there seem to be three of them; translation of all three with precision is a problem that defeats me. Jupiter coughed up the white snow, the pink dog-star split the statues, and Furius or Jupiter swelled up with thick phlegm(?) before exploding. It is all the debris of an epic about the wars in France. The disgraceful advice of the prophet is somehow less interesting because to us it is unreal. Even the politics are banal:

> That time when Parthians fear a young man
> Whose blood and race from Aeneas began ... (62-3)

Augustus was only two years younger than Horace, who is always telling us how old he is: but I suppose to Tiresias they were both young. Still the satire is redeemed by the revolting story, for the sake of which I used to think it existed. When I was old, says the prophet, this is what happened.

> There was a crafty wicked old woman of Thebes
> Who had herself carried out to her grave
> With her dead body well oiled, her will said,
> On her heir's naked shoulders she was carried
> In case she might slip off when she was dead;
> He having insisted too much in his life.
> The incautious approach is never safe. (84-9)

The laconic telling of this story and its careful planting seem to me to show great mastery. Not a word is wasted, not a nuance of the phrasing is uncontrolled. Horace continues with the same brilliance; 'With swelling speeches blow the bladder big' (97).

> Build her the grave the will permits build one
> The neighbours think exceptionally done.
> ... But now the Queen of hell calls me below.

This satire is an acid caricature of life, and it is noticeable that where it is most brilliant it is most reminiscent of Juvenal. I recall one day waiting in a quadrangle for a Horace lecture in my first term as an undergraduate, when

Fraenkel came past. He asked what I was waiting for, and then whether I preferred Horace or Juvenal, who at that time (1954) was the height of fashion. When I said Horace, he became incandescent with agreement. 'Juvenal', he said, 'is a writer for the Sunday newspapers, he scrapes together all the filth he can find, and screams always at the top of his voice.' In his book on Horace he notes the opinions of two or three learned men who spot the special connection of this poem with Juvenal and calls their observation adequate, but there is a certain reserve in his voice (144-5). In fact, this fifth satire is an attempt to break out of the form as Horace exploited it, to break out in yet another new, though I think less rewarding direction.

The sixth satire is easier to judge because it is such a success: if an artist does not quite succeed it is very hard to say later exactly what he intended, but here the intention is amply fulfilled, and the poem is rounded off with the brilliant story of the mice. The satire is not about the gift of the Sabine farm, but much more about the way it has altered the poet's life, and from the beginning how he was longing for it, how it fits his philosophy. The sixth satire of book one had entered into his feelings in a deep way. I have already said something about it at the end of Chapter Four, but it is worth another look, and repays study as a complete poem.

> For this I prayed, a bit of land, to enclose
> A garden, running water near the place,
> That and a patch of forest, and I cried
> For nothing more: now I am satisfied,
> The gods have given me better and more besides.
> Mercury make all this be truly mine
> If I have not added to it by bad means
> Or wasted any by vice or fault of mine.

We have heard this before, about the old man of Canusium who left property to his two sons on these conditions; here it is a joke. The accusation of Damasippus that Horace has taken to building 'like Maecenas' is equally a joke: but about his simple house and his small estate the poet is passionate: the passion is expressed in the first four words of the poem, '*Hoc erat in votis*, This is what I prayed for'. He goes on to elaborate the longing for more than enough which as a philosopher and on aesthetic grounds he deplores, and by elaborating it makes it ridiculous (8-12).

> This is the prayer I make,
> Make all things here be fat, fatten my flock
> But not my wits, be my good guardian,
> When I leave town for my castle, my mountain,
> What shall I decorate with Satires then?

We were not expecting this Pindaric echo, and he smiles at himself, saying 'satires, my pedestrian Muse' (17), but there is still an underlying exaltation as he contemplates his new vocation. The English have always somehow shared his feeling and the poem has often been translated, sometimes with great success, though better before 1750 or even 1700 than since. Horace is happy, he is not crazed with ambition or the sirocco, that leaden wind that makes autumn a burden and Libitina the coffin-goddess loom so close. So he starts another prayer, this time (20) to the god of business.

> Daybreak father, or Janus if you like
> From whom men learn laborious living
> (So the gods will) be my song's beginning.
> I am rushed to Rome as sponsor. 'Let no one
> Get before you in this business', and it's done
> Whether the north wind shaves the earth or mist
> And snow narrow day's circle, go I must.

He must struggle through a crowd, and cope with the busy commuters. 'What do you want you madman?' 'You'll beat down everything and get to Maecenas on this business?'

> That pleases me like honey, I won't lie.
> But soon as ever I get to the high
> Dark Esquiline, a hundred matters burrow
> Into my head and heart. 'Early tomorrow
> Roscius needed you beside the well.'
> 'Quintus remember ...'

The well is a landmark in central Rome, the well of Libo: it is like the clock on some great railway station. Life and business of course are out of doors, and the poet communicates with painful sharpness how busy Rome is.

> Now it is seven, nearly eight years ago
> That Maecenas first added me to
> His family, and took me when he went
> In coaches on journeys, the confidant
> Of things like 'What's the time?' or 'The Syrian,
> Will he make a match for the Thracian then?'
> Or 'Morning frost nips if you're not careful,'
> Things safe in my ear, empty as soon as full.

And all that time he was more envied every day he lived. The dramatic date of the poem is before Actium or more likely soon after, long before Horace had the *Odes* ready to publish them as three books: the time that Maecenas gave him his estate, the gift this poem commemorates. This satire must have been written all the same at a date closer to 25 BC, because it is a considered reflection on what the gift has meant to him, not an immediate reaction. Indeed this whole book with its closeness to the Sabine serfs seems to express a settled experience of country life in middle age. At the dramatic date of the poem, a rumour creeps through the streets, and Horace is expected to answer about the Dacians. 'What a mocker you are,' they say when he knows nothing. In fact the Dacians are a good example of rumour, since no one quite knew what to expect and Augustus seems to have over-reacted to disturbances in Bosnia. Dacia had a rich mining industry: it was not really conquered until the early second century AD, and was abandoned in the third. The Dacians were neighbours of the nomadic Getae of the lower Danube, who were shifted bodily into Macedonia, some fifty thousand strong, but that also was after Horace's death. The questions continued, Will Caesar give his soldiers Sicilian land or Italian? This must be in the year or two after Actium.

> So the day is lost, not without prayer in vain:
> O country, when shall I look on you again
> And live happy forgetful of business
> Among old books long hours of sleep and rest?
> When shall I see Pythagoras's bean
> And vegetables in bacon, not too lean?

Pythagoras had uttered the curious law, Lay not your hands on beans, by which he probably meant do not vote in elections. Certain Catholic monks vote with beans to this day. I assume Horace knows this fact, but it makes no difference, the thought of them makes him hungry.

> O nights and dinners of gods, when I and mine
> Eat under my own Lar, and in between
> My lively serfs, dipping the food for them ...

The food is dipped in an offering to the gods, everyone eats the same, and the guest can choose how much he drinks without the 'laws of the evening' imposed by someone: they can drink strong glasses or get gently wet, as they wish. So they begin to talk (70) not about other houses or their masters, but 'what concerns us, what is bad not to know, whether men are happy by riches or by virtue'.

> What draws us to friendships, use or right maybe?
> What the good is, what supreme good may be?
> And Cervius our old neighbour chatters on
> With stories: someone lavishes praises on
> Arellius's busy wealth, a theme
> He can't quite master. 'Once upon a time' ...   (79)

Suddenly the story has started. The characters of Cervius and Arellius are merely fictions. The conversation has recalled Plato's *Symposium*. It is surprising to put it mildly to encounter that great work in this context, and yet in what other corner of Roman society at this date would you expect it? I am not clear that Horace really is idealising his serfs, though he obviously adores them. At least the function of the Platonic sanctity in the poem does make sense, and more deeply the more one thinks about it. The conversation at Horace's table must depend mostly on Horace. The old neighbour with his stories is a probable enough fiction, and if Horace says he talks to the serfs about Plato's philosophy, I am inclined almost to believe him. One must remember that the slave or ex-slave philosopher was not unknown. Thirty-five lines of the famous story follow: I give them in Cowley's version.

> At the large foot of a fair hollow tree,
> Close to plow'd ground, seated commodiously,
> His ancient and hereditary house,
> There dwelt a good substantial Country-Mouse:
> Frugal and grave, and careful of the main,
> Yet one who once did nobly entertain
> A City Mouse well coated, sleek and gay,
> A Mouse of high degree, which lost his way
> Wantonly walking forth to take the air,
> And arriv'd early, and belighted there
> For a day's lodging: the good hearty host
> (The ancient plenty of his hall to boast)
> Did all the stores produce, that might excite
> With various tastes the courtier's appetite,
> Fitches and beans, peason and oats and wheat,
> And a large chestnut, the delicious meat
> That Jove himself, were he a mouse, would eat.
> And for a Haut Gout there was mixt with these
> The rind of bacon and the coat of cheese,
> The precious relics which at harvest he
> Had gather'd from the reapers' luxurie.
> Freely, said he, fall on, and never spare,
> The bounteous gods will for tomorrow care.
> And thus at ease on beds of straw they lay
> And to their genius sacrific'd the day.
> Yet the nice guest's Epicurean mind
> (Though breeding made him civil seem and kind)
> Despis'd this country feast, and still his thought
> Upon the cakes and pies of London wrought.
> Your bounty and civility (said he)
> Which I'm surpriz'd in these rude parts to see,
> Shows that the gods have given you a mind
> Too noble for the fate which here you find.
> Why should a soul so virtuous and great
> Lose itself thus in an obscure retreat?
> Let savage beasts lodge in a country den,
> You should see towns, and manners know and men,
> And taste the generous luxury of the court
> Where all the Mice of quality resort,
> Where thousand beauteous shes about you move
> And by high fare are pliant made to love.

We all ere long must render up our breath,
No cave or hole can shelter us from death.
Since life is so uncertain and so short
Let's spend it all in feasting and in sport.
Come worthy Sir, come with me and partake
All the great things that mortals happy make.
    Alas, what virtue hath sufficient arms
To oppose bright honour, and soft pleasure's charms?
What wisdom can their magic force repel?
It draws this reverend hermit from his cell.
It was the time when witty Poets tell
That Phoebus into Thetis' bosom fell:
She blusht at first, and then put out the light
And drew the modest curtains of the night.
Plainly the truth to tell, the sun was set
When to the town our weary travellers get,
To a Lords house, as lordly as can be,
Made for the use of pride and luxury
They come; the gentle courtier at the door
Stops, and will hardly enter in before.
But 'tis Sir your command, and being so
I'm sworn t'obedience, and so in they go.
Behind a hanging in a spacious room
(The richest work of Mortlake's noble loom)
They wait a while their wearied limbs to rest,
Till silence should invite them to their feast.
About the hour that Cynthia's silver light
Had touch'd the pale Meridies of the night,
At last the various supper being done,
It happened that the company was gone
Into a room remote, servants and all
To please their noble fancies with a ball.
Our host leads forth his stranger and does find
All fitted to the bounties of his mind.
Still on the table half fill'd dishes stood
And with delicious bits the floor was strow'd.
The courteous mouse presents him with the best
And both with fat varieties are blest,
Th'industrous peasant everywhere does range
And thanks the gods for his life's happy change.
Lo, in the midst of a well fruited pie
They both at last glutted and wanton lie,
When see the sad reverse of prosperous fate
And what fierce storms on mortal glories wait;
With hideous noise, down the rude servants come,
Six dogs before run barking into th'room;
The wretched gluttons fly with wild affright

And hate the fullness which retards their flight.
Our trembling peasant wishes now in vain
That rocks and mountains cover'd him again.
Ah, how the change of his poor life he curst!
This of all lives (said he) is sure the worst,
Give me again ye gods my cave and wood;
With peace let tares and acorns be my food.

That ends the poem, and the brilliance of the story effaces any need for a more usual closure. It sums up and concludes the moving, rambling opening better than any other words: even Plato is forgotten, and if any questions are left hanging in the air, let them hang there. Fraenkel felt that it was Cicero *de finibus* rather than Plato that swam into the conversation in so unlikely a manner: no doubt, but the few lines against 'house rules' for how much you drink had already recalled the *Symposium*. 'O nights and dinners of the gods' – who knows what they would have talked about? The other two satires seem to be counterpoised, one against Damasippus, because a slave speaks freely at the Saturnalia, and the other against Catius because it is about cooking. I do not think this scheme works well enough to be important: the second book of satires is unfinished, and maybe Horace was at a loss for new material. Maybe the sixth satire lay long unfinished, and its brilliant conclusion was added late, and was the reason for publishing the rest.

In the seventh satire Davus takes the part of Damasippus, and the Stoic master he reports is Crispinus.

I listen and want to say something, yes?
But as a slave I'm frightened.
    Is that Davus?
… Well, you can use December liberty
As our fathers decreed. Go on, tell me.

This is only a hundred and eighteen lines, not a long poem, and as forty-five of them set the scene, the substance of it is shorter than that. Davus has an attractive style at least, and his confused citizen who would like to be 'in Rome an adulterer in Athens a scholar' (13) is a memorable figure. 'What is all this filth leading to?' 'To you' is also quite funny.

In Rome you long for country, in the country
You praise the town to the skies you'd like to be
Back there …

You thank God you need not go out drinking one evening: but if Maecenas (33) invites you late that evening you yell for lamp-oil. This whole scene of the slave expostulating is like a scene from comedy if only because it is only in the theatre that we hear the expostulations of slaves. Davus will now tell his master the wisdom he heard as doorman to Crispinus. Horace enters into this with his usual vigour, but the smell and reality of slave life is too rank

for me; I cannot like this poem and can scarcely read some parts of it. No
doubt Horace is humorous and on the side of the angels but in the house of
Crispinus no angels are retained. When he comes to the old Stoic paradoxes
they have a second-hand appearance (83).

> Who is free? The wise man who controls
> Himself. Poverty or death shackles free souls
> Do not fear ...

The list goes on, and it is I suppose impressive, but not impressive enough.
The most to be said for it is that when he gets into his catechising stride
Crispinus is a good, brief introduction to some central Stoic doctrines. Yet
this I think Horace does better in a later book, the *Letters*. In the end Davus
is threatened with being sent to the Sabine farm as a ninth farm servant:
that at least is useful, since it tells us that Horace employed eight of these
serfs, and if any were married their families too. The number of servants was
the same in the handsome house of the Vicar of Bredon (who was a rich
Duke's cousin) in the last century. Horace's estate was not inconsiderable
therefore, by our standards. No doubt this satire takes its position as a
contrasting relationship with slaves after the sixth.

The eighth satire is hardly more ambitious than an anecdote. 'How was
the rich man's dinner?' 'Never done better in my life.'

> To please your angry belly first came what?
> Lucanian boar in smooth sirocco caught ...

Horace is asking the comic poet Fundanius (19) about a dinner given by
Nasidienus last night. The formula seems to be just a new way of attacking
the possibilities of cooking verse, interspersed with fragments of geography.
Lejay's learned annotations make one blink. A boy cleans the table with a
purple cloth, 'smooth on one side only, mostly made from wool from near
Padua' (Lejay) which is in a line from a banquet in Lucilius, forefather of this
kind of verse it seems.

> Then dark Hydaspes like a maid stepping
> Through Athens carrying Ceres holy things
> Bore Caecuban and Alcon bore Chian
> Innocent of the sea ...

The Roman trade used foreign wines with a little seawater added apparently,
and the wine is said to have tasted no worse. This leads Lejay into a
discussion of the best Clazomenian wine under Pliny, and how Cato dealt
with Kos wine, but the lumber-room of knowledge of that kind may decently
be neglected by those who seek to understand only Horace. He simply got the
best wine he could whenever it was available to him, and it got better as the
years passed. This poem slightly foreshadows Petronius as the last foreshadowed Juvenal; a rich man Nasidienus who is a Knight and not fictional is

entertaining Maecenas (16). The guests are Viscus of Thurii, Fundanius who reports, and Varius the poet, at one side, Servilius Balatro with Vibidius and Maecenas in the centre, and Porcius, Nasidienus and Nomentanus on the third side. Nine is the correct number. It may be important that Horace is only repeating his story as he heard it, and so not betraying the confidences of a private party, which may even be imaginary. Nomentanus is not the man of the same name in *Sat.*1,1. Vibidius is an unknown, and so is Porcius: there is a vague smell of money about them.

> Porcius swallowed tarts in one mouthful
> While Nomentanus pointed what crumbs fall,
> The rest of us ate birds and shells and fish
> Concealing whatsoever taste you wish,
> Revealing all at once, I ate a sparrow
> That tasted of a turbot's belly-marrow.
> Then honey-apples picked in a dying moon:
> But he can tell you better than anyone.

We proceed to squid swimming among elvers and detail after detail about oil, wine, white pepper, mackerel cooked in wine, green rocket and so on. A curtain falls and smothers the feast (54), 'How like life' says Balatro (64) but Nasidienus repairs fortune with art, and the boys bring a vast bowl of stork-legs rubbed in salt and flour, white goose's liver stuffed with figs and hare hams, roast blackbird, bits of pigeon: nice if only Nasidienus didn't tell you the nature and circumstances and causes of whatever you were eating.

> We fled in the end, there was nothing we would take:
> As if Canidia breathed, that African snake.

That is the climax, the joke, the last line (95): it was hardly worth waiting for. The piece is very light indeed, and yet original, though Romans had been satirised through food in prose often enough (Cic. *Planc.*67).

Horace's originality was restless at this time, as was his humour, so was his philosophy. It is hard to know when these eight satires were written, but I think long before he took to his *Letters*, and therefore the same time as he was writing his *Odes*, or at certain intervals between them. That is remarkable enough, because even the odes that are the purest philosophy do not seem to leave space for the gleeful guying of philosophers in this book. That remains a conundrum, but it is almost the last in Horace's life. Clearly this book is written when he is used to hating Rome and his job, and getting used to life in the Sabine hills. The idealising poem about his serfs must have been begun some three or four years after Actium, though we do not know when it was finished. This last satire finds Maecenas and Varius cheerful, but that does not help to date it. A scholar called Helmhold put it in spring because of elvers and storks. Lejay quotes Grimod de la Reynière's *Calendrier Gastronomique* for March: '*la marée est dans toute sa gloire.*' Horace did not reach the peaks of such eighteenth-century authors or their successors of the Wine and Food Society of the 1920s, who distinguished a left from a right ham of wild boar, since the animal raises the right rear leg to piss, and that makes the right ham tougher.

Chapter Nine

Between 23 BC and 17 BC, the date of the *Carmen Saeculare* for the great Games of Augustus, Horace did not write odes, but he did write the twenty wonderfully mellow and varied letters of the first book. Our expectations of Roman letters should be very high, based as they must be on the remarkable and varied letters of Cicero. Admittedly the publication of a book did not take the year or more it takes today, but if the *Letters* were available to the public by 20 BC Horace was working fast: three years between books is thought a small interval today for a lyric poet, though there are exceptions. The date 20 BC is certain because Horace gives it in the last letter of the book: it is the year 23 that has been assaulted in modern times. It is incredible what havoc great cleverness and perversity can create in a subject like Roman history, particularly in the Augustan period when Augustus himself proceeds like a tightrope walker in a mist, and every kind of conspiracy theory is possible. But as Professor J.A. Crook points out in the new edition (1996) of the Cambridge Ancient History Vol.X, the most important factor is that in 23 Augustus very nearly died, and his prospective heir Marcellus did die. Events like that concentrate a man's mind: in this case they explain the bundle of measures and powers Augustus took on his recovery. He refused the crown, dictatorship, perpetual consulship, and worship as a god in Rome with a statue in the Pantheon (to be called Augusteum).

Agrippa saved his chief's bacon in Spain as he had done in the war with Pompey's son Sextus, and Agrippa was now to marry Augustus's daughter Julia, who had married Marcellus at fourteen and was now a widow. Agrippa was to keep an eye on the East until Augustus could arrive there, so he set up his headquarters on Lesbos and ruled through viceroys in Syria. Messalla Corvinus was to be Prefect of Rome, but he resigned in his first week, realising it seems that the position was fraught with political difficulty; Augustus does not seem to have been annoyed. The brother-in-law of Maecenas, Varro Murena, got into worse trouble, which started with the trial of a proconsul and governor of Macedonia for treason: he had made unprovoked war on a Thracian King, either from hunger for Thracian gold or as part of a power game. His defence was that he acted under commands from Marcellus or Augustus, who appeared at his trial and denied it. The defending advocate was Varro Murena, who demanded to know what Augustus's standing was in the trial. He was told it was 'the public interest'. The next move was an obscure one, but it was a public matter and it has not been hushed up. Fannius Caepio, of whom we are quite ignorant, conspired with Varro

Murena against Caesar's person; they were tried and found guilty though not unanimously, which did upset the Emperor. They failed to slip away into exile, which would have been normal, and they were executed. Maecenas, whose wife was Murena's sister, is supposed to have advised them to run for it, and Augustus is said to have had a coldness with the Etruscan in consequence: but that sounds like the merest gossip and we have no evidence of the coldness. It certainly did not affect Horace's relationship with either of them. These events were in 22 BC, a time of plague and famine in Italy and of insufferable overcrowding in Rome. If Horace stayed in the Sabine hills, that was sensible of him. It is a curious footnote that after nearly dying in 23, Augustus was never seriously ill again in the rest of his life.

Augustus had made his move to try and secure Horace as a private secretary when he was 'terribly busy and ill', but when the poet refused the position the Emperor was not irritated; he continued to press his friendship on him. Augustus did say he was cross with Horace only once. 'Know that I am angry with you, because in a number of writings of this kind you do not talk mostly to me. Are you afraid of being infamous with posterity because you appear to be my familiar friend?' Suetonius says that on that occasion Horace wrote Augustus the first letter of the second book. The first book then must be assumed to be the one from which the Emperor felt excluded. 'Emperor' of course comes from the Roman word for a commander: Augustus's title at this time was not that simple word, it was something more like General with Over-riding General command: G.O.G.; Agrippa was merely O.G.

The *Letters* do not deal with these events, but they certainly come from a world very unlike ours. As R.G. Nisbet points out in his Foreword to Colin MacLeod's translation (1976, published 1986, Rome), 'Decorum required that one should know one's place in the world, and that of others ... Pope ... is suitably distinguished, but his pointed antitheses do not bring out the variety and informality of the original. Strident modernity would be even more objectionable: in the *Epistles* Horace captured the urbanity of his new-found social milieu, with its discreetly raised eyebrows and self-deprecating irony.' Yet these poems are so skilled that they throw more light than one ever dares to expect even of Horace, and they must be studied carefully. We shall probably never get a better translation than the one Colin left when he killed himself, but it is not in all ways perfect and I think he knew it was not, since he was an excellent poet. It is an extremely helpful guide all the same. Readers should be warned that these *Letters* are not all letters in the same sense. What they have in common is that they are verse monologues addressed to individuals, and the effect of the persons addressed on the tone of what is said is remarkable, as it is in Milton's sonnets.

The first poem is to Maecenas as you might expect: it is both the dedication and the explanation of the new kind of poem. Horace has not lost his old zest but it has altered course. 'Maecenas spoken in my first art and last', spoken of in my first Camena or Muse, and to be spoken of in my last. There is no question of deserting a sinking ship, Horace is thoroughly loyal, but 'I have been on show enough, and been given my wooden sword (like a retiring gladiator), and do you seek to put me into the old game?' This is an elaborate metaphor for lyric poetry. 'My age and mind are not the same. The old fighter has hung up his arms at Hercules's pillar and is in hiding in the country, he does not want to go on begging the people for his life from the edge of the sand.' There is an underlying and brilliant grimness about this opening: other Roman poets have refused to write and done so in verse, but about these few lines there is a nasty taste of the real. Then (7) the metaphor changes to an old horse.

> Now I lay down my verse and other toys
> I seek the true, the decent, only these:
> And I lay down what I shall open soon.
> If you ask who leads me or where is my hearth-stone
> I am bound by oath to no master at least,
> Where the storm drives me I arrive as guest.
> Now I am agile, drown in civil seas,
> True virtue's keeper sternest of votaries,
> Now I slide back to Aristippus's teachings,
> Subject things to me, not myself to things.

It is really as if a new, deadly serious Horace, a quite different kind of poet had been born. He is funnier and subtler in tone than I can make him. From the first two startling lines (10) it is as if Prospero abjured his magic and drowned his book. At first you almost think he has taken to the roads as a philosopher, a wild, wandering man, but this is another metaphor following on from the splendid and intransigent line, 'bound by no oath to any master's words'. As a night is long to a lover tricked, and a day to those who must work, or a year to boys governed by harsh mothers, so the time is slow and unwished for me, that puts off my hope and plan: to do what profits the poor and rich alike, and hurts old men and boys alike if they neglect it. The eloquence is so tightly reined in and yet so easily luxuriant that it may in some serious sense be called Shakespearean. It is an invitation to philosophy, something we have seen before in Horace, but here it is as passionate as an invitation to love, and as simple. He convinces at once about what Colin translates as 'progress up to a point'. For every vice 'there are saws and spells which can resist your passion'. For ambition 'cull thrice with a clean mind the words of wisdom'. If there were no other kind of poetry in the world, one would still wish this kind to exist. It is true that the fossil bones of Satire as Horace had understood the art are present, but there is a new lucidity about his passion that convinces.

It is still a pleasure that through Horace and his commentators we get the rhyme about kings that had been dear to his heart since childhood: it adds to our small repertory of Roman nursery rhymes and children's games (59-60). It was a ball game, the winners were Kings and the losers Donkeys, and the Greeks also played it. The words were *Rex eris si recte facies, si non facies non eris*: You will be King if you do (this) right, if you don't do it you won't be King. The metre is trochaic but it should be shouted, it has nothing to do with

the length or shortness of syllables. It is a rhythm that persisted in soldiers'
songs chanted at Triumphs. It was as Horace says 'chanted by the Curii and
the Camilli' in the earliest days of Rome (64). We get the same mixture of
examples as of old, though I find these fresher. 'As the careful fox said to the
sick lion, It's the footmarks that frighten me, they all go towards you, but
none of them come back' (73-5). Then 'You are a many-headed animal', a
phrase proverbial in both Greek and Latin. The rich man says 'No place on
earth can glitter like Baiae' (83). The variety of tone within a monologue and
the mosaic surrealism come straight from Satire and the street sermon.
Fraenkel did a good imitation of something similar heard from a Capuchin
sermon in Italy in the 1930s. Here at last it becomes a controlled art, as the
hermits of Magnasco are transformed into their landscape. The barber and
the tailor are subordinated to the single, tidal drift of the poem: that the wise
are second only to Jupiter,

> Free, honoured, Kings of Kings, despising gold,
> Sane above all, unless they have a cold.

The last phrase of the poem does of course throw the whole thing off course;
Horace does not completely believe even in the wisdom he dispenses: 'I have
the normal madness,' he says. All the same this first letter is a stronger piece
of propaganda than is to be found in the satires, and the phrase about 'normal
madness' (101) indicates his true position, sweetly dependent on his very
good friend Maecenas.

  In the second letter, to young Lollius Maximus, he kicks more seriously
against the pricks. Horace has been re-reading Homer at Praeneste while
Lollius learns to recite him in Rome, and his message is that Homer knows
far more about ethics than the great Stoic founders. To set fiction above
philosophy or 'theory' as a guide to ethics requires strong-mindedness even
today. Lollius is young, so Horace's attack is at first leisurely, and very funny
about Homer, then (27) brisk.

> Antenor will cut out the war's causes
> But Paris will not live and reign in peace
> Upon compulsion ...
> The Kings are crazy and the Achaians pay ... (14)
> ... Odysseus drowns in waves and is washed up,
> You know Sirens' voices and Circe's cup ... (23)

It is evident here that Horace is turning on young men's vices, their sloth and
lust. 'We are nothing but numbers, born to consume' (these expressions
translate phrases from Homer), Penelope's worthless suitors, Alcinous's
young men caring for the beauty of their skins, happy to sleep till noon,
drugged asleep with stringed instruments.

> Robbers get up at night to cut a throat
> But even to save yourselves you just will not.

You won't run healthy? Try it with hydropsy,
You won't ask for a book and light before you see?
If you don't put your mind to honesty
Envy or love will torture you all night ...
... Waiting for the right time to come at last
Is like waiting for the river to go past.

Horace's teaching is minimal, it is no more than common sense, and that
no doubt has made it so popular. 'If you have enough, look for no more' (46)
is one of his pillars, and much the same kind of thing was country wisdom in
Shakespeare's day, before Horace had his influence. It has nothing to do with
Christianity or any particular philosophy. 'Anger is a brief madness, rule
your high spirits or they will rule you.' The letter is seventy-one lines long,
but at this stage each letter is shorter than the last; the third is thirty-six
lines long and the fourth only sixteen. He has shown us where he stands
about ethics, now he will show us detailed examples of how ethics work in
real life. Julius Florus belonged to the staff of Tiberius, stepson of Augustus
and adopted as his son four years after Horace and Maecenas were dead. This
was his first independent command, and since his staff had a literary flavour
Horace knew them. He will write to Julius Florus again in his second book of
Letters, but here he is advising a whole group of young men who in England
would hardly be out of Sandhurst. There is no doubt that he knew them at or
around the court, and from this time his acquaintance begins with a whole
series of younger friends, including of course Lollius Maximus, who was son
of the consul of 21 BC. The eighteenth letter of this book was also to him, so
the friendships seem quite serious. The year is 21 or 20 BC in the third letter,
and the movement eastwards has begun: Augustus has got as far as Samos,
and land forces are on the move through Macedonia and Thrace. The attack
is intended against the Parthians.

Florus, I labour to find upon what shore
Of the earth Tiberius is soldiering – or
Do Thrace and Hebrus hold him in snow-chains
Or the towers where the sea runs and contains
Asia's fat fields and hills, is he dallying there,
And what works keep the staff busy anywhere?

Colin MacLeod divines that they were busy building aqueducts, which is a
pleasing thought and not impossible. In general these young men were
doomed to difficult lives and at times nasty deaths: in comparison aqueduc-
tion is an innocent pursuit. Now they are the new wave of talent. 'Who will
take up Augustus's wars and peace? What about Titius soon to come to Italy,
who tackled the Pindaric springs and despised the open lakes?' The metaphor
is from Callimachus and the remark is not hostile or obviously sarcastic,
though elsewhere Horace will deplore the Pindaric exercises of young poets.
Titius is totally unknown to us and apparently died young. 'Is he well? Does
he remember me? Does he try with the Muse's help to fit Theban measures

to Latin strings, or rant and bellow in tragedy?' Theban measures mean Pindar again. 'What is my old Celsus up to? He has been warned and needs to be much warned, to look for private riches and not lay hands on all Palatine Apollo has collected.' We have examples such as the *Ciris* of the highly derivative verse Horace dislikes: 'Palatine Apollo' is like saying the British Museum: it was of course newly founded. There is a serious argument that should be followed through about tradition and originality in Roman litera-ture, but this is not the page for it. Horace's own originality had been in picking and choosing, in adapting what was otherwise forgotten, that is it was a critical as well as a creative exercise. If we had the works of the lesser writers he is warning we would see at once what he means. 'If the other birds reclaim their feathers the crow who stole them will look silly.' So far so good.

> What do you dare?
> Where is the wild thyme where you flutter in air?
> Your talent is not small or quite untrained,
> In argument and civil law my friend
> Or if you still compose your lovely song
> The winner's ivy's yours: and if you long
> To put away cares like cold fomentations
> You'd follow heavenly wisdom ...

What does this mean? His friend has the most intelligence, and so where wisdom led he might if he chose follow. It is a higher vocation than playing about with verses, Horace says. It has for him a kind of religious force.

> This work, this study we follow small or great
> If we will earn our own love and the state's.
> You must write back to me just how your heart
> Feels about Plancus? Will that friendship part
> Or stick against hot blood and ignorance?
> Wherever you may be do not let chance
> Split that friendship. Still wherever you roam
> A heifer grazes for you here at home.

We do not know whether Munatius (Plancus) is the son of Horace's old friend or what the quarrel was about. The old man was censor in 22 and his son was consul in AD 13, so the son does sound right. His sister was accused of the murder of Germanicus, her husband Piso was executed (AD 20) and she killed herself (AD 33) after new accusations. The heifer is marked out for a feast when Florus comes home.

The fourth letter is to Albius Tibullus, of all minor Roman poets the most sympathetic and the best. He was some fifteen years younger than Horace, so still in the same generation he has been targeting. He was a Knight decorated for gallantry. He had gone to the East under Messalla Corvinus who became his patron, but he was invalided out of the army. Those who have

a taste for his dry, understated elegance, and who prefer the real country as
he sees it to mythology will like him as much as I do.

> Albius unshadowed judge of my Satires,
> What are you doing up there in the shires?

No one knows exactly where this estate was: Livy says between Praeneste
and Tivoli, which leaves a wide open field. Pedum, which had been its centre,
had been an ancient Latin town that had decayed into a slumbrous village
somewhere at the foot of the Roman hills. He was not far from being a
neighbour therefore. The estate was inherited, and when Tibullus sees
himself in his verse as poor he is just 'putting on the agony' as lovers have
always done in poems. 'Are you writing something to beat Cassius of Parma,
or going silent among the healthy forests, considering whatever deserves the
attention of the good and wise?' Cassius of Parma was one of Julius Caesar's
murderers, who led off the rump from Philippi to join S. Pompey, switched to
Antony when necessary, and fought on his side at Actium. He is said to have
written satires and elegies. Who knows? His mention here is probably a joke.
'You are no body without heart: the gods gave you beauty and wealth and the
art of enjoyment ... Think of every day as the last to dawn for you: you'll be
pleased to see an hour you didn't hope for.'

> Visit me when you want to laugh at one
> Fat, shiny, well looked after: if preferred
> Call me a pig from Epicurus's herd.

The whole of this pleasing poem is Epicurean in tone even before we come to
the last line. It is sad to record that in about a year (19 BC) Tibullus was dead.
Apart from lyrics to Virgil, this is the only poem Horace ever wrote to another
poet of real merit. It is curious that he is at his gayest and most amused, as
he is when he introduces Virgil in the early satire.

In the fifth letter, Torquatus, who was to be given ode seven of book four,
is asked to dinner on Caesar's birthday. There are only thirty-two lines but
they are well characterised: Torquatus is a great man, Augustus is still in the
East.

> If you can lie on my small beds, and wish
> To eat just vegetables from a moderate dish
> Torquatus come at sunset to my house.
> We'll drink wine put in bottles under Taurus.
> Just between Minturnae and Petrinum ...

This is connoisseur's language: the small jars in which the wine is rebottled
would name the consul, in this case Statilius Taurus, consul for the second
time (*iterum*), which was in 28 BC, the name of the farm, the date, and the
age at which the wine was rebottled. This wine should be excellent Falernian
from the river Liris, from near Sinuessa. 'If you have something better, send

for it, or else take orders. My hearth is glittering, everything is clean ...' He is to 'forget the law ...' This is putting it mildly, because he is gleefully incited to kick over the traces, and abandon the dependants in his own house: though of course there will be room for guests. The word that gives us the English word parasite means the guest of a guest. There were several at the dinner of Nasidienus (*Sat*.2, 8); the host just needs to know the numbers and not to be overcrowded. The central part of this short poem is an invitation to get drunk together: not a line usually taken by writers of moral philosophy. They can 'stretch out the summer night in friendly talk' (11). 'I shall drink and scatter flowers, And suffer to be thought a bit silly' (14-15). It is a jolly and a warm and friendly poem and one is glad he did not exclude it: one never quite believes what a poet says only in lyric verse.

The sixth letter is still less than seventy lines, about not being startled by anything. For this letter I will use Colin MacLeod's translation, which is excellent.

> To be impressed by nothing: that, Numicius, is about
> the only thing that can make and keep us happy.
> There are some who can watch the sun or stars or seasons
> yield to each other in order and not be touched
> with fear. What then of the earth's showy treasures
> or the sea's ...

So far the poem is Epicurean though being impressed by nothing was a common maxim. As to who Numicius was, I know only that he shared his name with a creek where Aeneas died, yet if he was a fiction he was the first in this book.

> The wise will be called mad, the just unjust
> if they go too far in seeking even goodness.

These two lines are the key to this letter and to the letter to Torquatus. It is dogmatic exaggeration Horace cannot bear: under Stoicism all sins have the same weight, all vices are ruinous. Horace thinks that is poppycock. The arguments through which he pursues this point are devious, but he has it in mind: hence the surprise ending. Mimnermus is the first elegiac poet.

> If, as Mimnermus holds, without love and play
> there's no enjoyment, live for love and play.
> Best wishes. If you know of something better than those views,
> tell me so frankly; if not, hold mine with me.

The seventh letter is about a hundred lines long. It is written to Maecenas, and needs close examination, because in it Horace refuses to come when he is called.

I said I'd be in the country for five days
And the whole of August went by in a haze
But if you want me to be sane and well
Forgive me ill or fearing to be ill
Maecenas, when the first figs and the heat
Bring the undertaker's men as black as night,
And the parents go pale for little boys
And office regularity, city days
Carry fevers and open up old wills.
When autumn paints in snow on the Alban hills,
Your poet will come downhill to the sea,
Curl up and read, my sweet friend, hope to see
You with the west wind and the early swallow ...

That would be in March, so Horace proposes eight months' leave: he is of course over forty, and he has a working rhythm perhaps not unlike Milton's, whose Muse visited him at night from the autumn to the spring equinox when one was longer in bed. So far the poem is polite and its fear of death not unreasonable. He introduces here his 'Calabrian host' who offers pears the guest does not want (14-19). 'The pigs can have them tomorrow,' he says: that is the peasant gives away only what he does not want; I take this to be a southern story, but it could be a peasant anywhere in the world.

The good and wise give to those who worthily seek
But they know a penny from a piece of plastic.
I will be worthy as you have merited,
But if you want me always, give back instead
My strength of body and my mop of black hair,
My sweet speech, my old laugh, my charming air
Weeping for Cinara's loss over the wine ...

He insists, but still he is more pathetic than demanding, he jokes about himself and his early lyrics, in fact he is the epitome of tact. We then get the queer example of the fox who crept into a granary and ate so much grain she could not squeeze out through the same hole. Bentley is riotously funny about the fox: he prefers a small animal that does eat grain, yet on the whole in a fable from 'Aesop' a fox being the usual hero is acceptable even as the robber of a granary.

'You have to be thin to get out,' says the mouse.
If this image rules, then I resign all things. (34)

The last phrase undoubtedly carries the resonance of a famous sentence in Lucilius, who would 'resign all things' rather than change his own nature. Horace goes on, 'I do not praise plebeian sleep when I am full of duck, nor will I change my very free idleness for the riches of the Arabs.' The word for idleness or leisure is *otium*, in which poetry is composed, among other things.

He is still reminiscent of Lucilius. 'See if I can't return your gifts with joy' (39). This is surely the climax of how far he will try Maecenas. He takes refuge at once in a story from Homer about Telemachus refusing some horses.

> Small things fit small people, not royal Rome
> But empty Tivoli, undisturbed Tarentum
> Please me now ...

This introduces the full-scale anecdote (46-97) of a man idling in a barber's shade, picked up by a busy and wealthy lawyer (the consul of 91 BC) and after a taste of riches begging to have his old life back. This is the subtlest and most personal of all Horace's poems to Maecenas, and sincerely meant, maturely executed, and I think exemplary for the *Letters*.

The eighth letter is a very small piece to the Celsus of the third letter. The poet complains of depression and restlessness. 'In Rome I want Tivoli, in Tivoli Rome, as the wind blows.' This tiny fragment of self-portrait serves to set off the seventh letter. The ninth letter is a mere dozen lines, recommending Septimius (*Odes* 2, 6) for a job with Tiberius. It was in a lyric to Septimius that Horace had refused to go to Spain. He thought then of retiring to Tarentum instead, like the retired pirate(?) in Virgil's last georgic; at the end of that lyric he had considered his own funeral. Perhaps there is a gap of five years between the two poems, perhaps less.

The tenth letter is to Aristius Fuscus the literary teacher of *Sat.*1, 9, and *Odes* 1, 22. It deals more generally with the contrast of town and country life. For the moment, Horace seems to have forgotten his project of philosophy, but it is present: he thinks the choice is in a way false between the two kinds of life. The country-lover writes to the town-lover, they are all but twins except for this difference: well-known brothers and love-doves.

> Like a priest's runaway slave known by what I take
> I long for bread, I can't stand honey-cake.
> If it's according to nature we must live
> You must think first in what landscape to arrive:
> Is anywhere better than happy countryside?
> Are winters warmer anywhere, has the wind modified
> The raging Dog and the Lion's moment
> Of roaring rage when the Sun is orient?

The praises are in general terms even in their details. 'Does grass smell worse than stones of Libya? There is a forest nourished among pillars, houses are praised for their long country views (22-3). Fork nature out, and yet she will be back.' But if you are overly impressed by anything you will be unwilling to give it up. A stag fought better than a horse until the horse got help from a man, but then the horse could not get rid of the man.

So who fears poverty lacks liberty,
Better than gold mines, and is doomed to carry
That master and must serve him for all time ...

So Aristius will be wise and live happy with his lot, and may blame Horace for his excesses. 'This I dictated near the crumbling temple of Vacuna.' This goddess had her house restored as Victory, under Hadrian, but she was once Idleness or *otium*. Varro claimed she meant that Victory goes to those who idle to be wise. An inscription to her was found at Roccagiovane on the river Digentia near Horace's villa some seven miles from Tibur (Tivoli), commemorating the restoration of her temple by Vespasian. This was found in the eighteenth century, but the site of Horace's villa was first found, as we have seen, by Lucas Holstein, a Vatican secretary who was Milton the poet's friend and host at Rome. It is highly probable that he took Milton there, since Milton's Latin verse displays some special knowledge of Roman antiquities, which I had assumed came through Holstein even before I happened to read Lugli's guide to Horace's villa recently, and came upon Holstein's importance as a topographical scholar.

We have noticed the eleventh letter before, to Bullatius about travel, because it must be based on Horace's experiences in Asia Minor before Philippi. The cities he names were then flourishing, not ruined, and Sardis among the others was frequented by Roman tourists. 'Are they nothing to the Tiber and the meadow? Don't you like one of Attalus's cities? Or do you hate roads and hate the sea and only like Lebedus? Do you know what Lebedus is? A village more abandoned than Gabii or Fideni. That's where I'd like to live, forgetting my friends and forgotten by them, and watch the distant raging of the sea from dry land. But even a man making for Rome from Capua splashed with mud and rain doesn't want to live in an inn for ever.'

We are strenuously idle, sail and cheer
Our horses on to happiness: that is here
It is at Ulubri or anywhere.

It is hard not to succumb to the lively charms of this poem, which is just lively enough, and surprising and pleasing enough, to allow no disenchantment.

We have settled into a jog-trot of about thirty lines a poem and the persons Horace dedicates his poems to are on the whole young and have interesting jobs. Often enough, like Iccius, they have odes to their credit (1, 29). Iccius is now Agrippa's steward in Sicily. Horace never went there, to him it was full of giants underground, and tyrants and torturers throughout history. Augustus nearly died there by suicide when he lost a battle against young Pompey, and the mere sea itself was dangerous. For Iccius Sicily was wealth and work, and with the job he had there he was being paid by Agrippa for whatever he suffered in the idiotic Arabian campaign. In the poem the collapse of Armenia has special importance: it had been kept quiet by diplomacy until the moment was ripe, and in 20 BC a local upheaval gave Augustus the opportunity to send in Tigranes (a hostage at Rome) with a Roman army under Tiberius. In

Rome this looked like a victory; in fact the Armenians assassinated their own monarch: the timing was neat and the coup diplomatic, but it was advertised on the coinage as a triumph of Roman arms. In the same year Parthia acknowledged the Roman interest in Armenia. All this activity was generated by the closeness of Augustus.

'Iccius if you enjoy Agrippa's Sicilian fruits rightly, there is no way Jupiter could give you more. No complaints: a man is not poor who has more than he uses: if your belly and body and feet are well, royal riches can add nothing greater.' Some mild jokes about vegetarianism follow, and then (15) about Iccius's fascination with tides and seasons and planets.

> Whether you murder fish or onions
> Be nice to Grosphus, give in to him at once,
> He will want nothing but the true and just.
> … You want to know how Rome goes on? In the west
> Agrippa took Spain, the Armenian fell
> By the virtue of Claudius Nero,
> Phraates has accepted what may flow
> Down from Augustus's authority,
> Plenty's full horn has poured on Italy.

Grosphus is our old friend (*Odes* 2, 16) the Sicilian aristocrat, and Claudius Nero is Tiberius. What Horace really thought of the peace or of its economic consequence appears to me a question about which we can only surmise. He was intelligent enough as a man and conscious enough as an artist to have observed how his advice to Iccius must affect one's feeling about the Horn of Plenty. Yet he is courteous about state policy even when he is ironic.

The thirteenth letter is a note to Vinnius Asina, who is to give books to Augustus. Asina was a praetorian guardsman with a reputation for personal strength. The few lines make the lightest of all these letters, and the brief poem is filled up with a few jokes. There is no more to it: it might just earn a place in a Renaissance guide to courtesy, but no more.

The fourteenth letter is a scolding for the steward or factor of the Sabine farm. It is perhaps more seriously meant for Lamia, whose brother has died. *Odes* 3, 17 was to Lamia and *Odes* 1, 26 mentions him. Varia in this poem is the town of Vicovaro at the opening of the valley where Horace's farm was. Cinara is the same fiction or fantasy as before: who knows what weight Horace puts on it? I once thought she was the only real girl in his poems, perhaps I was taught at school that Horace always spoke of her with special emotion, but that has become a hazy matter to me, and I no longer believe in her. I do believe in the valley of the Digentia above Vicovaro, which runs down into the Anio and so to the Tiber.

> Steward of my woods and my restoring fields
> Scorner of five fathers and their households
> Sent off to Vicovaro for their needs
> I challenge you: do I uproot the weeds

From my own self or you better from my estate?
Which is better off, Horace or his land, right?
Religious love for Lamia holds me mourning,
He is grieving for his brother, sorrowing
Unconsolably ...

'I prefer country life, you prefer town life, preferring someone else's life is to hate one's own, we are both fools. As a slave you prayed for the country, and now you long for the baths and the shows, brothels and frying smells. You have no tavern for wine, no flute-girl for dancing ...' A description of this kind of tavern dancer is to be found in a parody of a tavern advertisement, one of the better poems in elegiac couplets in the *Appendix Vergiliana*; it is called *Copa Syrisca*. Horace goes on for ten lines or so about the hard work of country labouring. 'Here's the difference,' he says. 'With thin togas and glossy hair I could please Cinara with no trouble' (33).

Falernian all day from noon would pass
My time, a little dinner, river grass:
No shame to play, but not to stop playing:
No one looks sideways at me envying
My neighbours see me shifting earth and stones,
But you prefer a town slave's small rations
You pray for that, yet another of my men
Envies your use of woods flocks and garden:
So the ox wants a saddle, the horse wants a plough,
I say let's be happy with what we do.

The fifteenth letter is not obviously more substantial except as language, the syntax is as energetic as one could wish. Horace is writing to Numonius Vala somewhere not far from Paestum about the possibilities of that country for his convalescence.

What is the Velia climate like my friend,
What of the people and the road that ends
Down there? Doctor Musa forbids Baiae,
And that has put me off it now that I
Swim in the winter in the icy sea,
The myrtles and the sulphur springs they say
Will bring out rheumatism, they don't approve
Of those whose heads and stomachs make them move
To Clusium's water or Gabii's cold hills,
So I spur on for fear of worser ills
Past my old haunts. 'Not Baiae, not Cumae
This time,' you hear the coachman cry ...

These are areas (both Velia and Cumae) that were once Greek, and where (at least at Velia) Greek terms like '*gymnasiarch*' persisted into Roman times: I mean that they were old, civilised places. Here by the sea (26) he looks for better wine.

> When I come to the sea however wild
> I expect something generous and mild,
> To take away my troubles and to send
> Hope trickling through my veins into my mind
> And give me words to whisper or to hurl
> (Since I look youthful) at a Lucanian girl.

Where are the hares, where are the boars, where are the fish to be found? Fifteen lines are then bestowed on the glutton Maenius, but they are too revolting to be called cooking verse (27-42). 'That's just like me,' says Horace. 'The simple life is fine to endure in thin times, but when you feel times are better, fine houses here and there make you happy.'

The letter to Quinctius ends as the gravest of all the letters. It is here if anywhere that Horace goes to the bottom of the question that has loomed in his mind for so long about slavery and freedom. These are serious matters and he is lucid: his remarkable poem will not need much underlining. The use of the *Bacchae* of Euripides at the end has the strongest effect of any of his adaptations of Greek, because of his special pleading or interpretation as well as for the rigour of his translation of the most important line. The 'allegory' is said to have been traditional among Stoics. Fraenkel apparently never treated most of this letter, the sixteenth, perhaps for personal reasons.

> Should you ask me Quinctius whether my estate
> Feeds me on vetch or gives me olives to eat
> Apples and hay or elms dressed up in vines,
> I will tell you the shape it is and all its lines.
> Continual mountains interrupted by
> One valley so the sun rising high
> Lingers upon the right side, and then touching
> On the left as it slides down to setting.
> You'd say temperate. And if kind bushes
> Carried the blushing sloe and wild cherries?
> And if the oak tree there and the ilex
> Give deep shade to the lord, food to the flocks?
> You'd say Tarentum had come here all in green.
> A spring just right to give the river a name,
> Like Hebrus cold enough to make you ache,
> Good for a weak head or a bad stomach.
> These sweet and pleasant haunts as you will see
> All through September will take care of me.
> You live rightly if you are all they say,
> All Rome talks of your happiness every day.
> Yet believe no one better than your own eyes,
> No one is happy but the good and wise.

If people say you're sane and healthy yet
Don't hide a fever when it's time to eat
Till trembling takes your hands and sweat your pores,
The shame of fools hides ulcerated sores.
If they tell of your wars by land and sea
And with these words soothe ears that are empty:
'Whether the people care more or you care
More for the people, which one is more dear
Let God who cares for all be alone to know,'
The praise is meant for Augustus, and so
When people say to you, Wise and perfect,
Can you accept that when you recollect?
'I am pleased to be called so as you are?'

What is Horace's view of the way Augustus is praised? Is there not something disgusting or ridiculous about it? Does he not all but say so in so many words? Can this be the same Quinctius that the Epicurean ode (2, 11) addressed? It is easier to ask these questions than it is to answer them. He sounds like a courtier doing well, whom Horace is warning seriously. Horace then takes a trail that leads him by way of slavery into what is true integrity (47).

I have not stolen nor have I run away.
Your reward is you are not flogged, I say.
I have not murdered. You won't be nailed to a cross
For crows to feed on. I'm a good boy boss.
Oh no, the clever wolf avoids the trap,
And hawks avoid the snare. The fish don't gape
After a baited hook. The good are content
With goodness, you only fear punishment.
... Even the good man says, let me seem honest.
Muffle my fraud, in darkness let it rest.
Greed brings fear, those that fear are not free.
One who is overwhelmed by mere money
Deserts the ranks and throws his arms away
Sell him or spare him and send him away
As slave or ploughman or a herd for sheep
Or to stand bad weather in a cargo ship.
Let him help to keep down the price of wheat.
But the good and wise has courage to repeat
'Pentheus King of Thebes what must I bear?'
'I will take all things from you, do you hear?
Cattle and furniture, all I can loot.'
'Take it.' 'I'll have you shackled hand and foot
Under a cruel warder in a jail.'
'The god himself will free me, when I will.'
Meaning I'll die. Death is the closing line.

The god is Dionysus, who is also the prisoner. The last line has several meanings. Death is the last line drawn under closed accounts, it is the end of everything. We must I am sure suppose that at this time Augustus knew Horace's work: the Vinnius letter seems to be about sending him the *Odes* at his request. So Horace might be quite certain Augustus would read the sixteenth letter as well. Suppose then it was specially intended for his eyes, why does it end with suicide? On the coast of Sicily when his fleet was destroyed by fire and storm and enemy action in 36 BC, Augustus had cried out for death, begging for someone to take his sword and finish him. The next morning he was rescued and won the campaign. If we know this Horace would have known it. Is the good and wise man who will not be enslaved by Pentheus not himself a king or at least a god? The advice and the whole poem are intended for Augustus. Is Pentheus Phraates of Parthia? Not quite, and yet there is a clear vignette of what the good and wise man would do if he were the captive of such a king. I do not intend to over-stress what is the merest whisper of a hint and the commonest Stoic doctrine for all mankind: all the same, I repeat that Horace knew that Augustus would read it.

The seventeenth letter is to Scaevola, a person unknown to us who Fraenkel thinks must have been 'a conceited young careerist' (321) not worth wasting much trouble over. 'If Scaevola cannot detect what Horace really believes in, so much the worse for him.' The question at issue is should one become a mere hanger-on of great men; the modern reader may suspect, and some German scholars have suspected, that Horace is defending his own standing with Maecenas against some envious attack. At this stage that is unlikely, and in fact it is not the case. He does speak with some irony (33-42) in a parody of the views he gives plainly elsewhere, and this whole letter has a savage or satirical tone, but it is not defensive. Its only alleviation as Fraenkel points out is in the mellow and gentle letter to Lollius which follows it.

> Scaevola you give yourself enough advice
> And your behaviour to old men is nice,
> But learn a little now from your poor friend
> Who like a blind man knows the journey's end ...

Horace gently recommends Ferentinum, forty-eight miles from Rome on the Via Latina towards Aquinum, an easier road than the Appian going south-east. When I last travelled on it, that road was almost a motorway.

> Not all pleasures belong to the rich alone,
> It's no bad life to be born and die unknown:
> To do yourself and your own people good
> Betake yourself to eat a rich man's food. (13)

Here he plunges into the example of Aristippus and the Cynic. This ends in what one might dismiss as a raving diatribe were it not so ironic.

If the crow fed in silence it would get
More dinner and less quarrelling with it.
... If they take you as a friend to Brindisi
Or beautiful Sorrento, don't complain
Of pot-holes and the bitter cold and rain
Your case broken open and your money,
Those are the old tricks of a night-lady ...
'I've broke my leg! Lend me an arm old bloke.'
'Try that one on a stranger,' the crowd croak.

There is no doubt that this poem ends with a bad-natured air, indeed it scarcely holds to the pretence of being a letter. If you are going to be a hanger-on you must behave yourself, seems to be the message, but the thing is carried through with distaste, and Aristippus and the Cynic seem to imply only 'better to pay court than to beg'. The satiric centre of the letter makes its points no doubt, but what eludes me at least is the character of Scaevola. Who needs a letter like this?

On the other hand the eighteenth letter, the one hundred and twelve lines to Lollius, deserves the praise that has been lavished on it. This young man too is being instructed in how to live with the great. Poetry for one thing (41) is as Maurice Bowra remarked 'no way to pay or promotion'. But Horace goes through behaviour in detail. In 21 BC Lollius was consul, and Horace was later to write an ode to him, but this charming letter is to a much younger man. The Lollius Bassus who may have adapted a Horace ode (2, 6) and lived at Smyrna was younger still I imagine (see Bassus in Gow and Page, epig.9).

Lollius freest of men, if I know you well
You will look like a hanger-on, as well
As being a true friend. A wife's unlike
A whore, the colour of her does not strike
In the same way, nor friends like hangers-on;
An all but worse vice differs from this one
A country roughness and asperity
Head shaven bald, teeth a black cavity,
And Freedom assumed that poses as virtue
Yet vice threatens both sides of this virtue ...

One man flatters like a parrot and another picks fights and barks his beliefs, whether the subject is gladiators or routes to the south-east. Dress simply: Eutrapelus gave away fine clothes to his enemies (32) and

He'll take up new ideas with his fine shirt,
Sleep late, neglect all duty for a tart,
His creditors will fatten before long
And he will end up fighting in the ring
Or drive a market-gardener's cart along. (37)

Horace spends ten lines at least (40-50) on praising hunting at the expense
of poetry. Analogous advice used to be often given at Oxford, though I do not
remember poetry doing any harm: but it may be worth stressing that Horace
moved in a circle of young men peculiarly vulnerable to literary pretension,
like Oxford undergraduates of 1890, and that to the poet after forty, Roman
pretension was particularly odious. Fraenkel used to employ vigorous sar-
casm on the subject, but I think with less justification than Horace, since he
seemed to like no German much after Goethe, no French after the neo-clas-
sical Heredia, and little modern English, though he was the most widely and
deeply cultivated of men, in poetry as well as music. It may be that everyone
gets stuck in the taste of their own youth, and that a mind perpetually open
to the new must in a way be vacuous? At this period Horace was turning
seriously to literary criticism, so for him this question is a serious one.

Horace praises Lollius (51-8) as a tough boy, as fast as a dog and as strong
as a wild pig, the darling of the exercise ground and the boy veteran of Spain
under Augustus, who (57f.)

> From Parthian temples ripped our banners down
> And gives the award to Roman arms alone.
> You cannot be absent, cannot withdraw
> Though you have no wish to go too far in war,
> But play at times on your father's country estate
> In a canoe war, Actium is the fight,
> Fought out between small boys, and there you take
> Command against your brother, and the lake
> Becomes the Adriatic until swift
> Victory crowns one side with her leafy gift ...
> One who believes in you and understands
> Your game is proud to applaud it with both hands. (66)

All the same, Horace warns the young man, be careful who you trust, those
spreading ears do not keep secrets, and 'spoken words take flight without
recall'. No servant girls for you or boys 'within the respected front door of your
friend', for fear he gives you the child or uses it to tease you. Horace goes on
for some twenty lines in a charming way about the pitfalls of life (79-102) but
the tone is pleasing, he is no Polonius, and not imitating a ranter.

> What lessens worries, makes you your own friend,
> What purely quiets you, money you find
> Or hidden journeys, a life's secret pathway?
> And when Digentia's cold stream cheers my way
> That Mandela drinks, a place wrinkled with frost,
> What do you think I feel, or pray at last?
> Let me have what I now have or less,
> And live the rest of life as the gods think best,
> Give me a good supply of books and food,
> Not to hang doubting like a hawk in the wood.

It is enough to pray God grant in the end
Life, wealth: what I provide's a steady mind.

The village of Mandela is still a village. From Horace's villa you can hear the peasants shouting up to it from the fields for someone to bring lunch if the season and the wind are right. It is still only a village, the road does not go anywhere else; you must climb up to it from Vicovaro. The hawk I invented because Horace does seem to mean a doubtful bird, drifting uncertainly. In this book it has suited Horace to say a good deal about his house, always the same farmhouse in the Sabine hills. It was perhaps the size of what the eighteenth century called a villa, say the house of Pye at Faringdon, who became poet laureate because he was the only poet Pitt knew personally: but something smaller than the Court at Frampton on Severn, and less grand, being one storey only.

In the nineteenth letter, Horace turns to Maecenas again. The poem begins with drink, and goes on to discuss imitation and literary quarrels. It is not quite fifty lines long, but built to last.

> If you believe Cratinus Sir on song
> No poetry can please us or last long
> Written by water-drinkers. Bacchus by chance
> Took in the poets with Satyrs and Fauns,
> And sweet Muses most mornings stank of wine:
> Homer's a wine-drinker who praises wine,
> And father Ennius leapt to sing of arms
> Only when drunk. 'The forum and its charms
> I give the dry, no puritan may sing.'
> As soon as I said that, there's no stopping
> Poets, they fight all night and stink all day.
> What? And does some wild bare-footed fellow
> In a tiny toga imitate Cato?
> Cato's behaviour and Cato's virtue? ...

After this spirited introduction and dextrous switch to the real subject, which has become rather a manner by now, Horace deals out a few blows to persons we know only from his satiric verse.

>   ... and if I should
> Be pale they will take cumin to lose blood.
> O imitators what a slavish flock
> You make me angry but you give me a joke.
> I was the first to step on empty land,
> I did not set foot on another's ground.
> He who believes in himself will lead the swarm.
> I first showed Parian iambics to Rome
> I followed Archilochus's rhythms and mind
> Not matter, which brought about Lycambes's end. (25)

Lycambes was the father-in-law that the old Greek poet is said to have persecuted. It is perfectly possible that he did so, and that the effect was devastating. 'But do not decorate me with shorter leaves because I feared to alter the metres and art of his poetry. Sappho with her man's foot adapts the music of Archilochus, Alcaeus adapts it with different material and in his own order: he is not looking for a father-in-law to paint with black verses, nor does he plait a rope for his wife with infamous poetry.' There has been much argument about all this, nor does it lack subtlety and acuity, but we may ignore it all. My translation does at least make sense, but Sappho's male foot or footfall is intended to refer probably to her powerful dancing rhythm. 'This (alcaic) instrument, not spoken of at all before, I a Latin have made popular. It is a pleasure to bring things out of mind to be read by eyes and held by hands which are innocent. Do you want to know why the ungrateful reader praises and loves my works at home, but is hard on them elsewhere? I do not buy the votes of the windy plebs with expensive dinners. I the disciple and avenger of noble writers do not go about the tribes of schoolmasters and their desks. Hence those tears.'

> If I said that it shames me to recite
> My works in theatres and give trifles weight,
> He says, 'You mock, you keep them for Jove's ears,
> You think poetic honey trickles like tears
> From you alone.' At this I fear to use my nose,
> Besides, I might be scratched to death, who knows?
> 'I do not like this place,' I shout, 'Adjourn!'
> From this game battle booms and angers burn,
> From anger enmity, then it's war's turn.

The end of the poem is neat, furious, and makes its point in which social manners and philosophy precisely coincide. That is the genius of these letters.

The last poem is a joke of twenty-eight lines, the last eight or nine of which are Horace's personal seal (*sphragis*) on his work, his description of himself in summary terms, which was worth waiting for. It ends with a date in 21 BC, which appears to be a deliberate allusion to the troubles of that year. The people wanted Augustus to be consul again but he would not. There was rioting and in the end Augustus had to install Agrippa with a garrison to control Rome. His feeling apparently was that they must learn while they had time to get on without him, to govern their own lives without further danger of civil war. But let us take things year by year. Already Horace has less than ten years to live.

Horace addresses his book, and the entire poem depends on a systematic double meaning, because 'book' is in Latin a masculine word as 'ship' is a feminine word, and the book like that of Catullus is bright and polished and clean and new. The double meaning in Horace's poem to his book is that he assures it as if it were a house-born slave of the nastiness of the outside world, just as if it were a young man who is hungry for the world, who will become a male prostitute and dirty from handling, and then old and rejected, a provincial schoolmaster, chanting ABC to bumpkins. In the evening when the cooler sun brings listeners tell them about me – and so to the *sphragis*. It is a really funny but also a sweet and sad joke. You do not feel that Horace has lost all sympathy with this boy and his downward career, or with this book. Like the whole book this poem has a special quality of mellow connivance between poet and reader that may be Horace's greatest contribution to literature. There is of course no question of a Latin poem other than a graffito being anything except élitist. That was the condition of literature, and yet Horace is right when he foresees that his poems will go back to the provinces and that people will be on easy terms with them. Would he have foreseen that he and his friend Virgil have a shadowy influence on grave epitaphs and even on graffiti? It does not matter, and in Horace's case it is hard to tell what influenced him from what he influenced. In North Africa there is even a portrait of the pair of them in mosaic, but it is nothing like real portraiture, nothing like anybody. His best portrait is still the end of the twentieth letter.

> My book, you are thinking of the city centre,
> Pumice-cleaned, standing for sale where all may enter,
> You hate those locks and seals the modest have on
> Wail that few see you, praise what's most common,
> You weren't brought up so. Go off where you like,
> Once you are gone there'll be no coming back.
> 'What have I done? What did I want?' say you,
> Crumpled when your lover tires of his screw.
> Unless this prophet's silly in hating sins
> Rome will love you until old age begins:
> When you get dirty handled by too many
> You will feed bed-bugs lying quietly,
> Run to Africa or sent bound to Spain
> And I will laugh whom you didn't listen to,
> As the man angry with his donkey threw
> The beast over the cliff. Who saves the unwilling?
> And for you this also is waiting:
> Bald head, old age in remote villages
> Teaching schoolboys with alphabets on knees.
> When the cool sun draws listeners to your cave
> Tell them of me, the son of an ex-slave,
> Born poor, to spread wings far beyond his nest,
> What my blood lacks give virtue and attest
> I pleased Rome's great in war and great at home,
> Small sized, white haired, sun-burnt, angry as doom
> Yet easily pacified, almost a sage:
> And if anyone should enquire my age,
> Say I was forty-four Decembers when
> Lollius took on Lepidus again.

The letter needs only a few small notes, mostly because I have deformed it in translation: 'again' in the last line and 'almost a sage' in the fourth last are invented, though they are true and hardly over-emphasise what Horace claims by quoting Aristotle about those swift to anger but easy to placate, 'the best thing about them'.

So you might think Horace was happy, in spite of the instability of Rome itself. That was swollen now almost entirely by a huge population of ex-slaves, that is men without what my mother used to call a stake in the country, a mass of small wheelers and petty dealers. Small wonder that Horace has said here the *'vulgus'* where I say 'too many'. Here and in the beginning of the third book of *Odes*, 'I hate and spurn the profane *vulgus*', he shows an increasing distaste for them. Augustus's reforms of behaviour were towards a society in some ways more rigid and more class-oriented than anything the oldest Romans could remember. He was about to fix by law the income without which you could not be a senator, and senators were to do the main tasks of governing the empire. Tacitus says he left orders that the empire was not to be extended any further, and this has been confirmed by another source. He tried to sweat down the Senate to only three hundred members, as it had been in the remote past, before Sulla and Marius. The Senate as a result was furious, particularly with the severe marriage laws for the upper class. Even an affair with an ex-slave woman was punishable. But all these provisions, which are numerous and really beyond our scope, were in the future. The consulship went in 19 BC to two compliant young noblemen, both of them as a matter of fact remote kinsmen of Augustus. The trouble in the year of Lollius and Lepidus was that Augustus refused to stand and the Romans who preferred him might at any moment turn to another popular saviour, a rioter, another Clodius. It looks as if Augustus was right to fear that, and what are called 'conspiracies' in the next few years seem to have that pattern. Why else the advice to young Lollius (18, 65-70)?

The poems appeared in 20 BC. In the next year Virgil was on a journey to Greece when he met Augustus on his way home at Athens. The poet's intention was to spend three more years perfecting the *Aeneid*, which was no doubt an impossible task, and then to spend the rest of his life as a philosopher. He had long ago inherited the house of his tutor near Naples. But at Megara near Athens he became ill, and at Brindisi as Augustus was bringing him home he died. He was fifty-one years old. Within a week or so, young Tibullus who was not thirty had died too. Virgil's dead body or his ashes were brought home to his house, and buried nearby. Who wrote his epitaph? He could of course have written it himself, but I think it was written by Horace. We do not know anyone else good enough to have written it but Virgil, whose death was sudden.

> Mantua made me, Calabria unmade,
> The Siren holds me idle in her shade,
> Who sang the crown, the shepherd's crook, the spade.

Chapter Ten

At the death of Virgil Horace was overcome by sadness and silence. Varius and Plotius edited the *Aeneid*, and in spite of Virgil's deep anxiety they issued the astounding poem without altering a word: I am sure that to that decision Horace contributed. It was Augustus himself who began to woo Horace back to literary activity. He did so by commissioning him to write the song for his long postponed celebration of the *ludi saeculares*, the Roman state celebration of a new age: the games took place in principle every hundred years, that being the longest lifespan of a human being, so they reckoned. The celebration was determined by the 'Sibylline Books' which were notoriously a queer jumble. These games appear to have started in 348, near an altar in the Tiber meadows by the river, dedicated to Dis and Proserpine, on land called the Terentum (or Tarentum). They happened again in 249 and in 146 (Livy says 149). In the forties it was intended to hold them, and maybe Virgil's fourth eclogue heralded them in 40 BC, but the situation remained unfavourable until 17 BC. Once again Virgil heralded the new age (*Aen*.6, 792-3), so the plans must have been made early. A committee was persuaded to agree that an 'age' was a hundred and ten years. There were to be three days and nights of splendour and archaic ceremony, then a week of public whoopee. Every night of the three, Augustus and Agrippa offered sacrifice beside the Tiber to the Fates, the Birth-goddess, and Mother Earth, with two daytime sacrifices on the Capitol (the Ara Coeli church) to Jupiter and Juno, and one on the last day on the Palatine near Augustus's headquarters to Apollo and Diana.

After the daylight sacrifice on the third day a choir of twenty-seven boys and twenty-seven girls sang Horace's poem or rather hymn, once on the Palatine and then on the Capitol. The hymn is surprising: it has nineteen stanzas (twice three times three and an epilogue as the last stanza) in sapphics, its language is of a chiselled perfection, it uses ritual language just enough to stiffen itself, and it expresses, with a perfection that all scholars now acknowledge I think, the ideas that inspired the reforms of Augustus. All this it does without a flicker of distraction or a single private joke. It is truly public poetry and truly state poetry and truly a hymn. It is perhaps the most successful publicly commissioned poem in the history of poetry. We know that under Septimius Severus, who was Caesar about the year AD 200, a poet was found to attempt a similar commission, but he could only manage hexameter verse: nor was there any poet other than Horace even in his own time who could have written this lyrical hymn as well as he did, whether in Greek or in Latin.

Phoebus and Diana of the forest
Bright glory of the heavenly sublime,
Worshipped and to be worshipped, grant our request
    In a holy time,
When warned by the verses of the Sibyls
These pure boys and these chosen girls who belong
To the gods who have loved the seven hills
    Repeat this song.
Kindly sun in your chariot gleaming,
Bringer and taker of day, for ever reborn
Fresh and the same, may you never see anything
    Greater than Rome.

I wish my own religion had a hymn as long and solemn and untheological as this: though it would not do for congregational hymn-singing, that bedraggled tail-end of the reformation. Both the solemnity and the length are essential to Horace's composition, but its bedrock is its objectivity, it is a state poem. The next three stanzas address the Birth-goddess, beg for proper offspring and allude gently to the classical marriage formula, which is about ploughing and its result. The sixth stanza proclaims that the moon takes a hundred and ten years to get back into place. The Romans had a complicated observatory in the Tiber meadows, in which an Egyptian obelisk nearly a hundred feet high was the finger of a giant sundial.

Sure sphere that in ten times eleven
Years will return to bring us games and song
For three days in clarity under heaven
    And three nights long. (21-4)

He turns to the Fates, then the Earth, fertile in produce and flocks and Ceres with her wheaten crown, the rain and winds, and finally Apollo and the Moon (who is also Diana). In this third stanza of the third group of three

Gentle and peaceful with your arms at rest
Apollo hear the boys who cry to you
Horned queen of planets hear O loveliest
    Moon the girls too.

The fourth group begins to tread on ground Horace is not so sure about: 'Rome, if it is up to you and if the Trojan squadrons held the Etruscan shore, under orders to alter their Lares [boundary gods] and city in safety ...' It is curious that about this time there was a fashion for moving populations bodily under Roman orders: not only the poor old Getae of the lower Danube who were nomads, but several tribes from Switzerland took that stony track. It must have derived from attempts to deal with Parthians and Arabs. In this stanza Horace is of course following Virgil, and the next two stanzas (41-8) are his magnificent tribute to the *Aeneid*. Finally may the gods give good

morals to Roman youth, and quiet to peaceful age (46) and wealth, offspring
and glory (*decus omne*) to the Roman people. He could really pray for no less,
in the name of the state. In the next group (49) he is still following Virgil: the
word *debellare*, to battle and conquer the proud, becomes 'greater than the
battling, gentle to The fallen foe' (52). The Medes and the Scythians bow
down 'and recently the proud Indian bowed' (56). That was the official view.
Faith, Peace, Honour, Shame and Virtue appear, 'And happy Plenty with full
horn appears', recalling her appearance in a letter not long ago. The last
section is a compliment to the Palatine and therefore to Augustus. Apollo
takes over the role of Aesculapius, who exists under Apollo's shadow even in
Greece. Rome is terrified of lethal epidemics.

> May the prophet glorious with his gleaming bow
> Phoebus to whom nine Muses sing their hymns
> Who with his saving art rescues from sorrow
>   Our weary limbs,
> If he looks kindly on his Palatine
> Altars, continue happy Latium
> And Roman wealth, and better things combine
>   In the age to come.
> Diana of the Aventine and Algidus
> Accept the prayers of these her fifteen men,
> And to the boys who are chanting in chorus
>   Friendly listen. (72)

Italy shrinks to Latium as the Fates are Parcae and the Muses are the nine
Camenae. The Aventine is the north extremity of ancient Rome: beyond it lay
the city walls and the gardens of Sallust, towards the modern zoo and the
Pincian hill. Diana goddess of the wild creatures in the woods had her temple
there, and another on Algidus, the high point of the Alban hills to the south.
(My compass points are inexact.) The fifteen men were the committee in
charge of these celebrations. A final stanza asks Jupiter, here mentioned for
the first time, and all the gods to agree, and goes on to answer his own prayer
with admirable confidence.

> I bring home good news, certain hope I raise
> That Jove and all the gods agree, I know
> And learnt to sing Phoebus Apollo's praise,
>   Diana's too.

For better and for worse, Horace was a more personal poet than Virgil, and
he could not resist that charming epilogue to celebrate not Jove at all, but his
own chorus. I do not believe Virgil would have written it. And where are Dis
and Proserpine? Death was too much present in the pestilent city of Rome to
be mentioned in this pleasant ceremony. Horace has studied ritual books to
write it, concentrating with a precision of tact on Apollo, who is always called
Phoebus except at line 34, in the central stanza of the hymn, where he is

Apollo, and Diana, called Moon only at 36 in that same stanza. Into Roman and Hellenistic astronomy I cannot enter: there is no doubt they knew the moon circulated and believed the sun did so, though the reference here (21-3) must be to the moon, as it is part of the sentence, let alone the section, beginning with Lucina the Birth-goddess. The sections on Roman history and empire end with magnificent prayer and prophecy and if they condense Roman myth then they do so through Virgil's eyes. This poem is the only tribute on such a scale that Horace wrote after his friend's death, and his writing it released him from a block about lyric poetry that had held him up for six years: it was I think the lines based on Virgil that released him. Fraenkel used to maintain it was the experience of training or rehearsing the choir for this hymn. I used to be certain he was right, and the fact was what first interested me in Horace's biography, but I am no longer sure that 'the stroke of my thumb' should be taken so literally (*Odes* 4, 6, 36). Horace in his fourth book of *Odes* was under Augustus's wing, though he had not forgotten Maecenas, and as Suetonius notices he was commissioned to write lyrics to celebrate Tiberius and Drusus.

It will create less confusion in the end if we take the odes of the fourth book in the order in which Horace published it: fifteen lyrics, mostly longish, ending with Augustus, containing Maecenas (4, 11,19, in the mid-poem position), but without a dedication because the collection is not complete; the last datable poem in it is about the homecoming of Augustus in 13 BC. The victories of Tiberius and Drusus that Horace was asked to celebrate were in 15 BC, so at that time Horace was writing lyrics. The letter to Augustus (*Epist.*2, 1) was surely a commissioned work, and it was written in or soon after 12 BC, so that soon after 12 BC the lyrics were interrupted, and so far as we know they were never taken up again. Five years, from 17 to 12 BC, do seem a likely enough time for the fourth book of *Odes* to take. It was his masterpiece all the same.

The first poem to Paullus Fabius Maximus is certainly not the missing dedication piece, it is a charming compliment to a wealthy young friend with a villa in the Alban hills like the Pope's. Paullus was consul in 11 BC and a friend and agent of Augustus, and his brother Africanus was consul next year, but Paullus was lucky to die by suicide. He had been with Augustus on a secret visit to Agrippa Postumus in AD 14 and his wife apparently betrayed the secret to Livia mother of Tiberius. Agrippa Postumus was murdered as soon as Augustus died that same year, probably on her initiative. This lyric is written in the days of Paullus's innocence, probably three or four years before his consulship, when he was a favoured youth of good family like others Horace knew.

> Venus do you make war again
> Long interrupted? Spare me I pray, I pray
> I am not what I once was in the reign
> Of my dear Cinara, please go away

Wild mother of the Cupids, do not stray
Towards my fifty years, I am toughened now
To soft commands, so do please run away
To where young men's nice voices call for you.

More seasonably in Paullus's house
Flying on your bright geese where you may most
Be riotous with Paullus Maximus
If you are looking for a liver to toast ...

The poem is frank and familiar and not unfunny, it comes out like the most elegant and freely flowing stream, the metre is choriambic and fits it perfectly, and its language is just a little on the extravagant side: the geese that pull her chariot are bright or 'purple' winged, like Augustus's mouth sipping nectar in book one. Paullus is noble, glorious, 'a boy of a hundred arts who will bear your banners far and wide', and rich too, 'he will put you in marble by the Alban lakes under a beam of lemon-wood'. Julius Caesar actually bought a painting by the famous Apelles of Venus Rising for the Romans, and they had been crazy on her ever since, if not earlier. The lemon-wood is a ceiling, the marble from Paros no doubt and translucid. It is not my taste but it is not ironic either. It is what Horace would do if he were rich. 'There you will sniff a lot of incense, you will hear the lute (And the Berecyntian flute) and the pipe too.' Twice a day boys and virgin choirs will dance like Salii for the goddess: the dance was thought to be by origin Arcadian, the flute is Phrygian; the Berecyntes were a tribe. No doubt the instrument was borrowed from the Great Mother because of its exotic connotation, an unusual trick for Horace, but Virgil uses the word in his underworld.

For me there lies no pleasure any more
In any woman's or boy's bed
Or in contesting who can drink the more,
Or in twisting fresh flowers round my head.

'But why, alas, Ligurinus why Does a rare tear trickle down my cheeks? Why among eloquent words is my tongue struck with unbecoming silence? I have caught you now in my dreams at night, I follow you flying across Mars's meadow and through the turning waters, tough one.' This boy is a slave or ex-slave, he is a fiction and a joke, yet one is suddenly stricken, partly maybe because we know more about dreams than Horace does. This is a vivid vignette of Horace running in his dream after a boy from the Eastern Adriatic, across the river-meadows of the Tiber and into the river; they are naked, and 'now I have caught you'. So we can be assured at last about that side of his nature and activity, but we have no idea whether girls entered equally into his fantasies: he means us to believe they did, and incidents like the one on the journey to Brindisi are as vivid as this one. It is not Horace in my view, but the ancient world and its distance that mystify us. The new book of lyrics has struck a new and confident opening chord: there is nothing quite like this poem in the first three books.

The second poem is to Iullus, Mark Antony's son by Fulvia, who as we have seen was brought up by Octavia at Rome, in Augustus's household. He married Marcella in 21 BC, daughter of Octavia and Marcellus. His unlucky elder brother Antyllus was executed on the fall of Alexandria to Augustus. This boy was consul in 10 BC, and Augustus must have been pleased with him at that time, but after Horace's death he was condemned to death for adultery with Julia, the Emperor's daughter, and sensibly killed himself. The career of this Julia throws some light on what dynastic pawns these unhappy women were: she was engaged to Antyllus and later to Cotiso King of the Getae so Mark Antony maintained. In 25 she married Marcellus, then when he died she married Agrippa to whom she bore three sons and two daughters. When Agrippa died she married Tiberius, by whom after various shades of disgrace with Augustus over her affair with Iullus Antonius she was kept in prison and starved to death in AD 14. As for the doomed dedicatee of this poem, he was a poet of a kind, who wrote a long work about Diomedes: he and Julia would surely have been a charming couple, but their existence as a couple complicated the succession and Augustus would not tolerate that. It is also a great pity that we do not know more about an epic that must have been influenced by Virgil, and dealt with Daunus as well as the shearwaters. Horace reproves him for imitating Pindar.

> Iullus, whoever tries to write the same
> As Pindar is flying on wax wings alas,
> And he is doomed to leave only his name
>   To a sea like glass.

Pindar is like a mountain torrent in flood, he says, boiling and immense. Whether he is thinking of Aufidus in spate or of Pindar, this is apt. 'He deserves Apollo's bays whether he creates dithyrambs and new words of verse ungoverned by metrical laws' – this means poetry that does not repeat its rhythms in a way one can analyse at once, I believe. He goes on, 'whether he sings of gods or of kings, the seed of gods, who slaughtered the Centaurs and the huge flame of Chimaera fell by them', or human heroes. By kings he seems to mean Hercules, and Bellerophon killed the Chimaera; these knotty sentences no doubt reproduce a knotty bit of Pindar. It does not matter, because this poem is an exercise in style, no more: Dirce's swan is Pindar, Dirce being a Theban river.

> It takes wind to waft up Dirce's swan
> As often as he stretches Antony
> Up to the cloudy heights, while I buzz on
>   Home shores, a bee.

Horace says a bee of the Matine shore: does he hint at something in the epic about Diomedes? It was after all in his area of south-east Italy, and otherwise obscure. 'Eating the pleasant thyme with great labour,' he continues, 'around the grove and rivers of wet Tibur [Tivoli], a tiny creature, I compose laborious songs. You with a bigger sweep will be Caesar's poet when, beautiful in the bays he deserves, he drags the ferocious Sygambri up the holy hill.' This is awkward, because Tiberius and Drusus were acting as Augustus's 'legates' or viceroys, and so could not have a triumph, not being technically in command. Augustus would not have one himself, so the boys were paid off with poetry by Horace. The poor Alpine Sygambri were indeed dragged, but only to new territories, not up the holy hill in chains, which must have been a relief.

Praise recurs here from the *Carmen Saeculare*. The fates and gods 'have never given nor will give Anything more good and great' than the Capitol, 'though times run back and we behold An age of gold'. The whole lyric has turned to a new and magnificent strain to celebrate the return of Augustus. He was greeted with ceremony and sacrifice at a new altar to *Fortuna Redux* who brought him home. Horace repeats (46) the street cries he was to be greeted with, in a metre Horace brilliantly makes readable though it is a stress metre, like 'Sun of beauty, Sun of praises' which can also be read as '*O Sol / pulcher O laudande*', and fits perfectly into a classic sapphic stanza. The rhythm is repeated twice where there is exact coincidence of the two: '*Io Triumphe*', except that the final 'e' is dragged out as it would be by a crowd, to make it long, which the metre requires: '*Triumphe*'. I hope the reader will forgive this pedantic discussion: it is very difficult although possible to write in two metrical systems at once. Fraenkel puts heavy emphasis on Horace's descent to street level and his heartfelt welcome to the Emperor, and in a way he is right. The poet of the *Epodes* has come a long way, and his poem is really moving. But is this still a poem to teach Iullus how to do it? On the face of it, certainly. The mood altered after six stanzas, rather too much for a mere introduction, and after another three he intends to describe how to welcome Caesar (41 *concines*) until the end of the poem: but he intrudes his own voice almost at once (45).

> You will sing happy days and this city
> At public play at last and you will tell
> The return of brave Augustus, the courts free
>   With no quarrel.
> Then my voice too if I may say something
> Will join the shouting and will cry O Sun
> Of beauty, Sun of praises! I shall sing
>   He's home, we've won.
> We shan't say it just once, *Io Triumphe*!
> As your procession passes, *Io Triumphe*!
> All the city with incense smoke from seven
>   Hills up to heaven.
> Ten bulls and ten heifers from you will pass.
> A tender calf from me sniffing calm airs
> Just free of his mother, eating fine grass
>   To express my prayers.

His forehead shaped just like those curving fires
That shine on the night where the moon is stark,
And snow-white in the brow like all his sires,
    Otherwise dark.

The last stanza is a little Hellenistic ornament, put in for fun, like much of
the rest of the lyric. The only bit we should take a little more seriously is the
cheerful scene of the triumph, which sounds very like a football crowd. Yet
even that is a remarkable technical exercise. I do not think we need to take
the reproof about Pindar in the least seriously. What Horace is saying is that
Pindar is too high and dangerous for an example, I can't show you a Pindaric
style (he promptly does so, with exaggerated praises of Olympian athletes)
but you could write a humble poem welcoming Caesar (he does so), and he
adds a couple of stanzas about cattle for good measure. Why? Because he
enjoys describing cattle, and it is a useful exercise.

The third lyric of this book is a grateful rewriting of the first ode to
Maecenas and maybe of the last of the third book. It is a hymn of gratitude
to the Muse in a lovely metre. It runs so limpidly and freshly one needs only
to pay attention to what the poet says. This poem is what I imagine was
Auden's ideal Horatian poem: but of course it is inimitable as well as
untranslatable. Its introduction or 'motto' seems to be based on a Homeric
hymn (25, 4).

Melpomene the one you see
With a pleased eye newly born
The Isthmus will not let him be
A famous boxer, he will scorn

The horses and their victory,
And war will never bring
The garland of the bay that he
Crushed the muttering threats of Kings,

Climbing the Capitol at ease,
But the water running along
Rich Tibur's dense hair of trees
Shall make him noble for Aeolian song.

I am one of her young:
In Rome prince of cities
Poets who have her praises sung
I am less hurt now by biting envies.

Muse player of the sweet lutes
Echo in the golden shell
Who could easily make the mute
Fish sing like swans as well:

This is all your doing
That passers by will freeze
To see the hope of the Roman lute string,
Yours that I breathe and please, if I do please.

It runs like the Anio among its apple orchards and dense hanging groves. No doubt that is grander than his farm, but the poem points clearly enough to the great honour of 17 BC, the *Carmen Saeculare*. The language has a height and a solemnity, the Isthmus games are picturesque, the bays are called 'Delian' and the chariot is famous at Olympia, the Muse is called 'Pierian'. It is all written with a sense of joy and relief that his apotheosis has really taken place.

The poem that follows this is to the two Neros (28), Tiberius (b. 42 BC) and Drusus (b. 38 BC), the children of Livia and adopted sons of Augustus after the death of their father in 33. They were at that time still his likely heirs, though Drusus looks like the favourite here, and it was Drusus who tackled Germany (12-9 BC) and the Sygambri (12 BC). The campaign celebrated here was in 15 BC. In it the Romans occupied (roughly) all Austria: they held the Danube until the late fourth century AD and were not forced back to the northern foot of the Alps until the fifth. But as we noticed, the boys (Drusus was twenty-three) were acting as viceroys not commanders in 15, so there was no triumph: Augustus had three triumphs only in his life. He now accepted only the 'ornaments' of triumph, and must have commissioned this poem. In fact there were no more triumphs at all from this date on, except for members of the imperial family. It is full-blooded in its praise and seventy-six lines long. 'There is nothing Claudian hands do not perfect, and Jupiter with kindly godhead defends them.' Tiberius after some ups and downs lived to be Emperor, half-mad and terrified of assassination, but Drusus died on the Elbe in 9 BC, and his ashes were buried in the mausoleum of Augustus at Rome.

The poem, which is a full-scale exercise in the Pindaric style Horace had perfected, has been excellently translated (without rhymes) by James Michie, and I reproduced it in *The Art of Poetry* (1989). It seems natural that it begins with Ganymede and the eagle: three stanzas of this and one for a lion, and in the fifth we are told this is how Drusus pounced on the Austrian Alps (17-18).

They learnt what mind what quality was
Nourished in that religious house:
    Augustus's fathering mind
    To the two Neros kind ...
The brave and good create the brave
And cattle and fine horses have
    Their fathers' quality:
    No dove will eagle be ...

One wonders what he thought Iullus Antonius was going to be? But he does mean to stress the father's genes, as Pindar had set out the doctrine of aristocracy, and he moves back in time to ancestral Neronian heroes from whom the boys (but not Augustus's family) were directly descended. Roman greatness he says began with victory on the river Metaurus in Umbria in 207 BC, where the Romans beat Hasdrubal, who was hoping to join his brother Hannibal. This was the 1066 of Roman schoolchildren. Hannibal then makes a long heroic speech (49-73) lamenting his brother's death and his own inevitable defeat. The Romans are compared to some mighty tree.

> The ilex that the whetted axes strike
> On Algidus with foliage all black
> Drinks wealth and still draws on
>   The spirit of iron. (57-60)

The whole piece is a formal but remarkable compliment: the boys are complimented mostly on their noble blood, and at the start with some exciting metaphors, but Augustus more gravely. The tomb of the Claudian family at Tibur was known to Horace. He must also have known this, found at Rome but lost since the sixteenth century.

> Passer by what I say is brief: stand and read.
> This is the unlovely tomb of a lovely woman
> My parents name me Claudia
> Her husband loved her with his heart
> She created two sons, one of those
> She left on earth, the other she buried
> Witty in speech and lovely in her walk
> She kept house and spun wool. I have spoken. Go.

This dated from the twenties of the second century: Horace's praises overwhelm the reader with Hellenistic glitter, a genuine and remarkable achievement, yet they are not more eloquent.

The fifth ode has been attacked by a don at Oxford, who is famous for praising the banalities of Gallus: he said this poem was as close as one could find in Horace to 'straight fascism'. He committed what Wittgenstein calls the commonest philosophic error, that of saying 'this is only a case of that'. It is a remarkable, full and warm tribute to Augustus, it goes beyond the demands of any commission, and sets the Emperor in a context of ritual blessing, of answered prayer.

> Child of kind gods, good guardian
> Of the Roman people, you are too long away,
> Return since you have promised your return
>   And bring us day.
> Good leader, give light back to your country:
> It will be spring when your good face will seem

> To shine on the people, days will go cheerfully
> And suns will gleam.

He begins with the promise to the Senate, the 'holy council of fathers', goes on to bright daylight and the people, and will end with sunset. First we have two stanzas on a mother yearning for a child overseas and a storm off Karphathos (10); it is all a metaphor for the country (Italy) longing for Caesar. Suddenly he breaks into ritual language with a stop at the end of each line.

> The ox plods safe over the country.
> Ceres nourishes crops with kindly Happiness.
> The sailors fly across the peaceful sea.
>   Faith fears distress.

> Chaste houses are not stained by adulteries,
> Law and morals have tamed spotted vice:
> Fathers show up in the looks of their babies:
>   Sin pays the price.

These blessings go back to Aeschylus at the end of his *Oresteia*, may the crops come, may the sea carry you, may your children be born well: the corresponding curse, may the crops be blighted, the sea not carry you, and your children miscarry, must have been at least as well known; it occurs on an inscription of Herodes Atticus a hundred years later than Horace. It probably existed in Latin independently of Aeschylus or of Horace. Horace continues as if without this Augustan list of blessings from the new laws: who cares for our enemies (25-8)?

> Man sees the day to bed in his own hills,
> He trains his vine on to the widow trees,
> And comes home happy to his drink and fills
>   To Caesar his glasses.
> He prays to you he follows you with wine
> Poured from the shallow bowl, with his Lares
> He mingles you as god, as Greece did divine
>   Castor and Hercules.
> Kind leader, now grant long holidays
> To Italy: we say it dry all round
> When the day is whole, we say it in a damp daze,
>   Sun underground.

Augustus is a god because he is an earthly hero, what we call a 'demigod'. He is mingled with the country devotion to the Lares of the house. We know that Caesar liked that idea, and in 12 BC he reintroduced the feast of Compitalia, in which the Lares had once been worshipped at crossroads, with puppets for all free members of households of either sex, and balls for slaves. Whether this was to keep away ghosts or to sanctify the places where farms met no one seems to know, but the cult of the Lares was still deeply embedded in the countryside and encrusted with simple Roman tradition. Horace calls Italy Hesperia, which includes the south. The 'damp daze' means after a drink or two, in the evening (*uvidi*).

It is the next poem, the sixth, that remembers the *Carmen Saeculare* and its performance with a certain nostalgia, and which Fraenkel therefore suspected was written soon after it. Certainly the metre is the same and the poem is rhapsodic in manner and 'Pindaric'. Horace praises Apollo and Diana again and asserts his own vocation again: what is it all about? It is apparently for a girl from his choir, the daughter of a grand family whom he offers a Pindaric exercise as he offered one to Antonius. Julia was born in 39 so she would be too old; anyway she was married to Agrippa, her second husband. Messalina? Agrippina? Claudius's wife or Nero's mother? This is merely guessing and we really have no idea. Apollo who is addressed first is elaborately disguised: we are meant to know what Horace is talking about, although he is teasing and we are duly dazzled. In the third stanza Apollo kills Achilles, and it is only in the sixth that we come to Jupiter's kindness to Aeneas, persuaded by Apollo and Venus, the gift of 'other better omened battlements', which is pure Virgil again. The god is addressed as Phoebus 'who in the stream of Xanthus washes his hair: defend the glory of the Daunian Muse' (*Camena* 27).

> Phoebus gave me the breath, Phoebus the art
> Of poetry, and name of a poet Sirs:
> The first virgins of Rome, boys whose bloods start
> > From glorious fathers
> Protected by the Delian goddess who controls
> The stags and running lynxes with a stroke,
> Keep to the Lesbian beat and watch the roll
> > Of my thumb-stroke.
> When you are married say I sang along
> When time brought in the festive light
> In a song the gods loved, and I learnt the song
> > From Horace, poet.

The poem is nothing but a piece of playfulness from beginning to end, or rather like the poem for Iullus Antonius two pieces tacked together with the second beginning at 29 and lasting sixteen lines. The connection is Aeneas (23) and the assertion of Horace's vocation, but it is Aeneas really on whom the reminiscence hangs: he holds this poem together as he does Roman history in Virgil's conception of it.

The seventh poem of this book is a sad one, but it is one of the most beautiful Horace ever wrote. It is a reworking of the already excellent ode about spring, 1, 4, which it utterly transforms. Housman when he came to it once in the course of lecturing at Cambridge simply read it out twice in his own translation and left the room in tears. It was dedicated to Torquatus, a rich and successful lawyer, whose ancestors were the epitome of nobility and success in war in the third and fourth centuries BC. In the last stanza Hippolytus was the chaste and tragic youth the chaste Artemis (Diana) could not rescue, and Pirithous was the companion of Theseus in a raid on hell who could not escape with his friend. Let me give it first in Dr Johnson's version, then in Housman's. Neither of them alas catches Horace's metre, though Housman is closer.

> The snow dissolv'd no more is seen,
> The fields and woods, behold, are green.
> The changing year renews the plain,
> And rivers know their banks again,
> The spritely nymph and naked grace
> The mazy dance together trace.
> The changing year's successive plan
> Proclaims mortality to man.
> Rough winter's blasts to spring give way,
> Spring yields to summer's sovereign ray,
> Then summer sinks in autumn's reign,
> And winter chills the world again,
> Her losses soon the moon supplies,
> But wretched man, when once he lies
> Where Priam and his sons are laid,
> Is naught but ashes and a shade.
> Who knows if Jove who counts our score
> Will toss us in a morning more?
> What with your friend you nobly share
> At least you rescue from your heir.
> Not you, Torquatus, boast of Rome,
> When Minos once has fix'd your doom,
> Or eloquence, or splendid birth,
> Or virtue shall replace on earth.
> Hippolytus unjustly slain
> Diana calls to life in vain,
> Nor can the might of Theseus rend
> The chains of hell that hold his friend.

> The snows are fled away, leaves on the shaws
> And grasses in the mead renew their birth,
> The river to the river-bed withdraws,
> And altered is the fashion of the earth.

> The Nymphs and Graces three put off their fear
> And unapparelled in the woodland play.
> The swift hour and the brief prime of the year
> Say to the soul, *Thou wast not born for aye.*

Thaw follows frost, hard on the heel of spring
Treads summer sure to die, for hard on hers
Comes autumn, with his apples scattering;
Then back to wintertide, when nothing stirs.

But oh, whate'er the sky-led seasons mar,
Moon upon moon rebuilds it with her beams;
Come we where Tullus and where Ancus are,
And good Aeneas, we are dust and dreams.

Torquatus, if the gods in heaven shall add
The morrow to the day, what tongue has told?
Feast then thy heart, for what thy heart has had
The fingers of no heir will ever hold.

When thou descendest once the shades among,
The stern assize and equal judgment o'er,
Not thy long lineage nor thy golden tongue,
No, nor thy righteousness shall friend thee more.

Night holds Hippolytus the pure of stain,
Diana steads him nothing, he must stay;
And Theseus leaves Pirithous in the chain
The love of comrades cannot take away.

There is a singleness of movement like a drumbeat about this poem, from the observation of seasons, through 'Grace with the Nymphs and her twin sisters dares to lead the dances naked', to the note of mortality (7-8) which swells and continues to the underworld. The death of Ancus, Tullus and father Aeneas occurs as an example more than once on gravestones. I choose to say father Aeneas, not good Aeneas, because though both are in manuscripts, *'pius Aeneas'* is more likely to have driven out 'father' than the other way round. Horace often has resort to the *Aeneid* in these late lyrics, most often to the sixth book, the underworld of Virgil, but his allusions are gentle, not obvious, and *'pius'* sounds like some late scribe flaunting his learning. Lattimore in his *Themes in Greek and Roman Epitaphs* (p. 254) throws light on this poem, and on its popularity; there are Greek sepulchral inscriptions that speak for example of Hercules: 'Alcmena by her prayers could not rescue Herakles though the gods loved him.'

The eighth lyric is to Censorinus, perhaps the consul of 5 BC and son of the consul who triumphed in 39 BC, who was one of the committee of fifteen for the celebrations of 17 BC. The metre is choriambic, called 'Asclepiad', here repeated line after line in the Hellenistic manner, not in stanzas. It is in deliberate contrast with the seventh ode, but cannot efface that impression. To make things worse the text is a bit of a mess. Horace says he would happily give his friends the most wonderful works of art if he were rich, but as it is he can offer only poems, which luckily Censorinus likes (11-12). The ode argues the immortality the Muse gives, but beyond that message I am afraid this poem is not worth struggling over, and after many attempts over the years I abandon it.

The ninth ode is to Lollius and appears to be saying much the same in a subtler manner. We met Lollius in the *Letters*, but he seems to me more at ease in his ode, though Horace's views about his probity pursue him even here. The poem is in thirteen stanzas, that is in fifty-two lines.

> Do not believe my words will ever die
> Born by the distant roaring Aufidus I
>   Say words set to the strings
>   The lute I hold first sings:
> If Homer holds the first seat of them all
> That is no reason to obscure Pindar or tall
>   Bacchylides or Alcaeus
>   Or the grave muse of Stesichorus.

'Whatever Anacreon once played,' says Horace, 'time has not wiped it away, love still breathes and the flames live that the Aeolian girl entrusted to her lute-strings' (that is Sappho and I imagine 'the Kean' means Bacchylides).

> And Spartan Helen did not burn alone
> For an adulterer's dressed hair or the gold sewn
>   On to his dress as he
>   Came with his group kingly.

The examples of these famous events draw out into a catalogue of a kind. Auden used to say he loved lists, and every true poet did so, from Homer on: it was a curious but a true lesson and a pleasant one to learn.

> Brave men lived earlier than Agamemnon
> But all unwept for in the long night alone
>   With no holy poet
>   To tell the world of it. (28)

'Hidden virtue is little unlike sloth, I will not leave you undecorated Lollius to dim forgetfulness, your mind is prudent and right in good times and in bad, punisher of avarice and fraud, and unindulgent in all-consuming money, consul more than once; and how often a good and faithful judge preferred the honest to the useful, rejected bribes with a high look, and showed his arms victorious through the obstructing throng.' There is a touch of Regulus in the last phrase, who pushed aside 'his obstructing family' (*Odes* 3, 5, 51). 'You rightly call happy the man who does not own much, but he has more right to that name who wisely uses the gifts of the gods.' It is curious to what a degree all this well trodden road of moral philosophy makes Horace write like Cicero, or like Sallust's Catiline, and his advantages of style are perhaps the luck of generations. Horace has by now twisted every last drop from his

lute-strings, and only a faint tinge of heroics is left: Lollius would suffer
poverty and fears crime worse than death, he is not frightened to die for his
dear friends or his country. Horace is at ease by now at the age of fifty among
the upper class, and this is the true summary of his ideal man maybe.

The tenth ode is metrically like the eighth, though short and not so
problematic. The line has one more foot than the eighth, which makes it
exactly resemble an Athenian *skolion*, an after-dinner popular song of the
fifth century. 'Drink with me, dine with me, love with me, wear a wreath with
me: Be mad with me mad, be sensible with me sensible.' This expansiveness
of the metre gives Horace's poem great charm: it is about Ligurinus again,
the boy from the end of ode one of this book. 'Still cruel and powerful in the
gifts of Venus, when the plumage of your pride sprouts unexpected, and the
hair around your shoulders now drops away' (hair was cut off to a river at
adolescence) 'and now the colour of a budding crimson rose alters Ligurinus
to a hairy face, when you see yourself altered in the mirror, you will say, Why
didn't I feel as a boy what I feel now? or with these feelings why can't I have
smooth cheeks again?' This looks like a straight translation from the Greek,
but if so it is so well done that it scarcely matters whether it is original or not:
the skill would be the same. I imagine it was written before ode one.

The eleventh ode looks like a lonely celebration with Phyllis, but the
central stanza, the fifth of nine, reveals his old friend Maecenas. He has a
nine-year-old full barrel of Alban wine, plenty of foliage growing, the house
gleams with silver, the altar is ready for the lamb. Everyone is hurrying, the
spit turning, these are the Ides, mid-April. The lamb is roasting indoors by
the way (Rome is a long way north) so they worry about the smoke (11): the
day is holier to Horace than his own birthday, because this is Maecenas's,
13th April. He then breaks into either advice to the girl Phyllis or maybe a
song, or a different poem altogether?

> Telephus is hunted by a rich
> Girl unlike you, and a sexy one which
>   Holds him in happy fetters,
>   Give him up to your betters.
> Phaethon burnt frightens avaricious hope,
> Winged Pegasus offers thoughts of deeper scope,
>   He was revenged upon
>   Earthly Bellerophon.

'So follow what's fitting and think it wrong to hope beyond your limits, avoid
partners unlike you. Come now, last of all my flames, – for I shall not catch
fire for any woman again – learn the tune and do it in your lovely voice; dark
troubles diminish with song.' Is this whole poem a renunciation of old ways,
an imagination of how Augustan marriage laws will affect society? If an ode
ends at stanza five the other four stanzas make a poem on their own. He has
often talked about Phyllis, but I have always assumed she was a fiction. I
must admit that Maecenas is likelier to have the central stanza than the last,
otherwise I would snip this ode in two.

The twelfth ode has one or two stanzas of great beauty that have inspired English poets: 'And the brown bright nightingale amorous Is half assuaged for Itylus, The Thracian ships and the foreign faces, The tongueless vigil, and all the pain.' The nightingale laments for her rape and the murder of her child Itys. The name Itys (hence little Itys, Itylus) is onomatopoeic: it sounds like the nightingale's note, one of her seven or more runs of notes, each repeated three or four times. The poem is to Vergilius, another Virgil, possibly a member of the same family.

> Now spring's companions make the sea mild
> And Thracian winds make the sails go,
> The frost is off the grass, time quiets wild
>   Rivers that swelled with snow.
> The unhappy bird is nesting who must lament
> Itys in tears, disgrace everlasting
> To the house of Cecrops for her punishment
>   Of the lust of the barbarous King.
> Now the sheep wardens pipe and play
> And over the soft grass the music spills
> Delighting the flock-loving god who longs
>   For dark Arcadian hills.
> Virgil, time brings the thirsty season in,
> And to attract wine pressed in Cales
> You as the client of young noblemen
>   Bring some scent with you please ...

The central position is the dedication so there are three more stanzas. The wine is bought, it is in the granaries of the Sulpicii, on the Aventine: the family (Sulpicii Galbae) are well known from inscriptions for this useful task. 'A small onyx of scent' will buy the wine. 'If you want this exchange come quickly: I am not letting you touch my winecups without paying, like a rich man in a full house. So come along and think of the black fires: mingle brief folly with your wisdom, it is sweet to be crazy once in a while.'

The thirteenth ode is to 'Lyde', pleased with her age and decay: it is not at all nice, I admit it is marvellously written, and its pathos is spellbinding; when I was young I found it agreeably repellent, but now I am saddened by the thought of it. Is there a poem by Rilke in which the wind strips the leaves off the boulevard, and someone 'writes long letters but gets none'? That may be a muddle in my head, but it is part of the cold mood, worse than melancholy, of this gloating poem about the ageing whore. Or is he really wholehearted? Does he allow her any dignity or tragic quality? Drunk she solicits Cupid in her tremulous voice, 'he flies past dead oak trees, and hates you for your lurid teeth, disgusting wrinkles and snowy hair ... young men laughing at the torch tumbled into ashes'. That is enough about this sad ode.

With the fourteenth we are back to Augustus who comes first in it, then 'the Vindelici knowing nothing of Latin law have recently learnt what you can do in war' (7-9) because Drusus with your soldiers has beaten the

Genauni and Breuni and pulled castles down from the Alps. This sounds at
first like Belloc or some deeper-dyed French nationalist of 1914, and at the
end like nursery war with toy soldiers, and utterly deplorable. But the elder
Nero, Tiberius, must be praised as well as the younger. One only hopes that
the wine Horace bought from those vast cellars was plentiful. Virgil in the
Aeneid loves the innocence of the people of these mountain castles, and
Milton in his day is unforgettable about the similar case of the Waldensians.
Tiberius had fought the Raetians and Horace does him proud, as they say.

> And like the north-east when the Pleiades
> Split through the clouds, he worried at regiments
>   Reined neighing horse with ease
>   Through fire without defence.
> So the bull Aufidus unwithstood
> Rolls by Daunian Apulia wild
>   Over ploughlands in flood
>   Raging from field to field ... (28)

The young man had 'won without any disaster' (32) which was no doubt a
relief. At line 33 Horace returns to the praises of Augustus which I am too
weary to repeat: Your forces, your plans, your gods, Fortune favours the first
of August, – Spaniards, Medes, Indians, Scythians (the usual list), Nile who
hides his springs, Tigris, the whale-infested ocean of Britain (47-8), Gaul
unafraid of funerals and tough Spain and the Sygambrians who delight in
slaughter all reverse their arms. This is I suppose an official poem, and apart
from the *Carmen Saeculare* it is the first we have come across. Horace's
earlier Augustan poems are full of the wildest fantasy, but here the victory
list is getting hackneyed, and the details of war must have reminded the poet
of his unpleasant day at Philippi.

The last of the lyrics in this book and perhaps the last Horace ever wrote
is to Augustus again. 'I wanted to talk of battles and of conquered cities but
Phoebus twanged his lute: I was not to set out to sea with my small sails.'

> Your time has brought back crops with love
> Abundant, and our standards to our Jove
>   Ripped from the proud columns
>   Of the bowed Parthians.

We have heard it before, but he does it nicely here: the doors of war and peace
have been shut at last. Morals have been severely reformed, and old arts
restored,

> By which the Latin name and Italy,
> In strength, fame and imperial majesty
>   Are from the sunrise confessed
>   To his setting in the west. (16)

There is no civil war, no violence or anger or arms industry (19), and drinkers of the deep Danube, the Getae, Chinese (*Seres*, maybe the Punjab), faithless Persians (he means Parthians) and those born up the Tanais (the Ob) are all quiet.

> And we with holy festal lights aloft
> Among the gifts of Bacchus, cheerful and soft,
>   Women, people, children, all
>   Address the gods with ritual.
> And sing the lords of war as our fathers sang
> Mingling the Lydian pipes into their song,
>   We celebrate old Troy,
>   Anchises and Venus's boy.

The sentiment is Roman but through Virgil's eyes. In this ode Horace is doing his best to celebrate peace, in spite of the embarrassing list (20-4) from Danube to Tanais. These conquered peoples are to Horace mostly fantasy of course, though to historians they have a reality. The image of the heroic, attacking prince was deeply imprinted in Hellenistic and in Roman poetry, even though to us he is as vague and as cardboard a figure as the barbarous tribes in their Alpine castles. One might say that Horace's loyalty is to Virgil's vision of Rome, with all its contradictions, rather than to Rome itself or to contemporary history. One might almost whisper that 'Romantic Rome is dead and gone, It's with Virgil in the grave'. However that may be, and I am sure that those who read history differently will put a quite different emphasis on these poems, I do find this last ode acceptable. But was Augustus a crushing intruder into the end of Horace's lyric career? Or was it he who brought it to an end where it does end, either by demanding a quite different kind of poem, more of a conversation piece, or because he felt that Horace's martial-patriotic vein was wrong for him, or played out? as I am personally inclined to feel it was.

Yet this fourth book of odes contains some masterpieces that surprise us even from Horace's workshop, and in them (even in the Alpine castles) he makes his peace with Virgil and pays him tributes, as well as expressing the peace he has already made in his *Letters* with life. The poems are individually fresh and in five or six of them at least he adds to the conception of what poetry is. The four books of the *Odes* if you take them together are a towering achievement, but the fourth book, because it is separated by time at one end and cut off short at the other, shows more clearly than the shuffled pack of cards in the first three what must have been Horace's ups and downs, the burst of enthusiasm followed by unlikely by-products, followed in the end by flatness, over probably four, maybe five years. For poets who have these ups and downs, and whom a great work may leave empty for a period, the time-cycle seems quite probable. I do not believe that Horace much liked Tiberius. Thank God it is not up to me to explain that peculiar man, or the gossip about him, nor was it up to Horace. He does seem loyal to Augustus, because of peace and the victories that peace has. He dedicates only one poem in his life to Agrippa (in the first book of *Odes*) and gives no praises to his remarkable buildings: but that may be chance, and because Agrippa was often abroad, and always in politics, which Horace quite deliberately was not, until late in his life. Was it Virgil's death that made Augustus summon him more forcefully? Did Augustus want him to be a second Virgil? No doubt he would have liked that, but naturally it was quite impossible. You do not get two poets like Virgil or like Horace either.

In the twelfth ode (9-12) Horace is saying a kind of goodbye to his friend, as I think he does at the end of the fifteenth. One must notice he does not mention Pan, though he refers to him, and the black Arcadian hills are distant to him. In his own verses he says Faunus, and Virgil always masks the word Pan, so that you cannot tell whether it is long or short: but Virgil also prefers Muses to Camenae. The piping of the *fistula* among the sheep is moving enough, but why is it Greek and Arcadian if not as a tribute to Virgil? Since Virgil for reasons of his own introduced Arcadia into pastoral poetry, and Horace takes it from no other source. It is what Horace must have associated with Virgil at the time when they first met, some twenty-five years ago. There are an enormous number of detailed observations to be made about the *Odes*, but enough is enough, as Horace would be the first to point out.

Chapter Eleven

There are only two works in the second book of Horace's *Letters*, but one is 270 lines long and the other 216. It is not knowable how many of these comparatively vast compositions he intended to undertake. In my own experience they would take from one to two or three months each to write with a similar amount of time for thinking beforehand and a month for exhaustion afterwards. But we also have Horace's separate work on *The Art of Poetry*, which is 476 lines, nearly as long as both of them put together. It looks as if his conceptions were swelling and he felt happier over distances, but the trouble is that there are problems about his last poems. Fraenkel seems to believe and take for granted that *The Art of Poetry* was written before the letter to Augustus. I am inclined to think that the second letter of this second book ends in such a way as to indicate that the book is finished in two poems.

Excellent scholars think that this second poem was written earlier than the first, say in 19 BC, because Florus (*Epist*.1, 3) was on the staff of Tiberius, so he got home in 19. I must admit to doubting this: we know little about Florus, and he does not need to be home to get this longer letter (*Epist*.2, 2). He wanted Horace to send him 'some odes' (23) but Horace will not, having already told Maecenas he is finished with lyrics (*Epist*.1, 1, 1-10). He starts up again only in 17 BC for Augustus, so why would he have any to send Florus in 19? It is more probable that Horace added the letter to Florus to the letter to Augustus (*Epist*.2, 1) to make a book. That must be after the refoundation of the feast of Compitalia early in 12 BC. Horace lived another four years: that was time enough and more than enough for writing the whole of the second book which is two letters, as well as the stray, separate work which is a letter to the two Pisones, on *The Art of Poetry*. Between 17 and 12 he was writing odes, so Florus might well call for some more in 11 or 10 BC. Above all though, after Virgil died in September of 19 BC it is inconceivable that Horace could write a long poem so unmarked by that sad event, and early in the year Florus was still abroad with the rest of the staff: if the letter has to be written when he is home in Italy, then Virgil's death intervenes.

Let us take the letter to Augustus first then.

> You do so much, alone to do it all,
> Guard Rome in arms, decorate her morals,
> Correct her with laws, it's a public crime
> If I talk too long Caesar, and take up time.

Romulus and Bacchus (whom as nearly always he calls Liber), Castor and Pollux all felt men ungrateful for their hard work, and Hercules died by envy. We offer you honours now, and put up altars to swear by you, confessing nothing ever was or will be like you. (These are the altars of the Compitalia, to Augustus's Lares and his Genius.) But our wise and just people, preferring you to our leaders and to the Greeks, won't judge other things in the same way (20), and hate everything not dead: you would think the Muses on Mons Albanus had dictated the ancient law codes and early treaties. If the Greeks are better by sheer force of antiquity very well, but now we paint and sing and wrestle better than they do. If days improve poems as they do wines, I'd like to know how much they improve a year. Say a hundred years are enough? Not a month less? This is like pulling hairs out of a horse's tail (45-6), (a story told by Plutarch in *Sertorius*).

> Ennius wise, brave, Homer come again
> The critics say, did not much trouble his brain
> For promises and Pythagorean dreams,
> Is Naevius not in our heads, and seems
> Virtually fresh? All old poems are holy.

So Pacuvius is learned, Accius deep, Afranius another Menander, Plautus runs on like Epicharmus, Caecilius wins for gravity, Terence for art (59). These are what mighty Rome learns stuffed into a theatre, these are the poets it numbers since Livius Andronicus (62). Well, sometimes the people are right and sometimes they stumble. If they think these old poets incomparable they are wrong. If they say a lot is rough, a good deal slovenly, then they agree with me and Jove. I don't attack Livius or want his poems abolished. I remember what that basher Orbilius dictated to me when I was a boy. But if one word glittered or a verse here or there was lovely, it made the rest look cheap. I hate things to be blamed not because crass or unwitty but because recent, and I hate honour and prizes to be asked and not pardon for ancient writers. If I doubt whether it's right for some play to tread the flowers, all the fathers say there's no more shame. The man who praises Numa's Saliaric song which he knows as little about as I do, just wants to seem learned.

> He doesn't like talent, he applauds graves,
> He hates our things and against us he raves.
> And if the Greeks had hated novelty
> As we do, then today what would there be
> Antique? (89)

When Greece began to trifle putting aside war, and so descended into vice, crazy for athletes, horses, marble, ivory, bronze, the portrait, pipes, tragedies, like a child at its nurse's breast, whatever she wanted she had enough and left it. At Rome for a long time houses were opened in the morning and law taught to clients, they listened to the old and taught the young to follow profit and lessen lust. The people have changed their mind, now only writing enflames them. Boys and grim old men tie leaves around their hair and dictate poems (110). I myself who maintain I write no verses am found a liar worse than the Parthians; before sunrise I must demand pen and paper. Sailors drive ships, druggists drug you, builders build,

> We all write poems whether untaught or taught
> This light insanity that has us caught
> Has certain virtues: poets are not hungry
> For money, they like only poetry
> They laugh at loss, at runaways, at fire,
> They don't consider fraud, they never tire
> Of eating crusts, no good at soldiering
> But useful to the city, granted one thing
> Great matters may get help from very small. (125)

We have moved from the introduction to an attack on the worship of antiquity, and from that by way of the Greeks to the poetry craze, which recalls today I suppose, as Horace's view of the useless and hopeless poet also does. He now proceeds to catalogue the useful things that poets do, such as their moral messages (127-9) and the fact that children learn the prayers lovers use from poets (122-3).

> The chorus asks help, feels the gods in the air,
> And asks water from heaven with a nice prayer,
> Drives away perils, turns away disease,
> Demands a massive harvest, begs for peace.
> The gods are so placated, the ghosts so ... (138)

Early farmers, brave men content with little, after the harvest eased body and mind with their families around them. They gave Earth a pig, Silvanus milk and the Genius of their lives flowers and wine. Hence arose Fescennine verses, antiphonal rustic insults, and the liberty accepted with the recurring season played amiably until the jokes turned rough. So it was put down by law (152-5). This custom of antiphonal, impromptu, insulting verse did exist in rustic Rome, but also in many similar societies. Theokritos knows all about it, and there are traces of it in Virgil. The same custom has existed even in our lifetimes.

> So captive Greece captured its capturer,
> And brought the arts to rustic Latium
> Hence that fearful Saturnian rhythm. (157)

Some traces of the country remain. Rome applied herself to Greek books late in the day, and after the Punic wars began to enquire what use were Sophocles and Thespis and Aeschylus. She tried translation and was pleased with herself. She has sublimity by nature, she breathes tragedy and has a

happy daring in it, but she foolishly hated revision. Still, comedy was a
problem (168-70). Look at Plautus with a gallant young lover and so on.

> Enter Glory on windy chariot:
> The slow spectator all but faints at it,
> So light so small a thing subverts the mind
> Hungry for praise or freshens it in the end.

He hates this hanging on the breath of praise; if a Knight disapproves during
the poetry they yell for bears or boxing: that's what they really enjoy (186).

> Now pleasure's gone out of the ears of Knights
> To dazzle of the eyes, empty delights.

He discusses spectaculars and their effects as if he had seen the most
extravagant films, with 'ships, captive ivory, captive Corinth girls'. The noise
is like the woods of Garganus, or like the sea (202). Horace is violent about
the theatre, and I suppose bound to be right: it is a pity we shall never know.
In the middle of it all Aristotle's *Poetics* (unity of place 212) raises its cross
head. Apollo means the Palatine Library.

> But give those some small care who still prefer
> Readers to proud whims of a spectator
> If you will do what Apollo merits
> Fill him with books, give the spur to poets,
> Make them more hungry for green Helicon ... (218)

We poets do a lot wrong – to cut down my own vines – when we push a book
at you worried or tired, when we are hurt if a friend blames one verse, when
we repeat bits without being asked, when we lament our work doesn't show,
it's so fine, or when we hope the minute you know we are poets you will tell
us not to want for anything and make us just write. Still, Alexander liked
Choerilus's awful verse, yet buying that idiocy so dear he did forbid painters
except Apelles to paint or sculptors except Lysippus to make him in bronze.

> They don't disgrace your judgement of their books
> Or your great praise or gifts or your long looks:
> Varius and Virgil, in whom you delight:
> Bronze statues cannot so bring the face to sight
> As by poets the spirit and the mind
> Of famous men appear ... (250)

The noble words in the last two and a half lines were copied almost word
for word by Tacitus in the closing passage of his *Agricola*, of all ancient prose
the piece that has stayed in my mind some forty-five years. No doubt they
were consecrated by some funeral tradition, and so the influence on Tacitus
need not be direct, and Sallust says something similar, but they are still

noble. Horace says he would like grander words, but Caesar's majesty does not admit small lyrics and he is ashamed to attempt what he cannot execute. One learns quicker and remembers more willingly what one laughs at: I do not want a bad wax mask nor to be decorated with ill-made verses. I blush to be given to the incense sellers or pepper sellers or whatever else is wrapped in useless paper.

That is the whole letter: it seems better particularly with Horace's late work to go straight through it in this way, as the run of it is on the whole so clear. The climax is certainly his restrained praises of Virgil and his friend Varius, of whom we know so terribly little. We do not even know the date of his death, but in the *Eclogues* he was already a famous poet, so he was probably older than Virgil. If so then he is likely to have died by 12 BC, some five years after the posthumous publication of the *Aeneid*. That would fit the grandeur of his position in this poem. The argument of the poem does not need explaining, quite a lot of it is slapstick but Horace does make a serious plea for modern writers, in particular for poets, with whom he would like Augustus to fill up the Palatine. Those who preferred archaic writers were numerous, and one comes across them (Nisus for example) in the margins of literature. Varro must have been a heavy archaising weight at the Palatine if he had lived, but he died in 27 BC having written nearly five hundred books, one against modern poetry, so would Cicero have been, they were the same generation. Horace puts the case against them all with admirable crispness and humour. Nowadays the argument has certainly moved on, and our situation and the foreseeable dangers have altered.

A little more should be said about the Lares of Augustus and his Genius. In the first few lines of the poem we hear of the half-human and half-divine heroes who are accepted in the temples of the gods as great human benefactors of mankind. Among their works for which they have not been rewarded well we hear of the assignation of lands to men: this is new to us, because it obviously means Augustus, as Fraenkel points out. But we know from the Ankara Monument of Augustus that in the same year as the reinstitution of the Compitalia Rome saw a greater assembly of citizens from all over Italy than it had ever known, for the election of Augustus as high priest, Pontifex Maximus. He had allowed Lepidus that office until now, though he had certainly begrudged it to him. Augustus therefore now became the guarantor of land tenure, because he was the new god of its boundaries, the altars of the Lares of Augustus and his Genius at the crossroads. Horace already has him mingled with the Lares of the household: this is an intimate privilege and an important one, stated in a vaguer way long ago by Virgil in the first eclogue. Horace has been referring more closely since 17 BC to the Augustan code of law, and in more ways than I have room here to trace: his peace depended on the Julian Laws about public and private violence for example, to which Horace alludes without of course citing the law code. I believe these laws are Augustan and from this date, even though Mommsen attributed them to Julius Caesar, for whom he had a spectacular weakness.

There is a further question about the climax of the letter, which I am sure is intended to be Virgil and (for the theatre) Varius. Fraenkel is rather dismissive of the lines that so impress me, remarking that the formula is conventional, and to be found in Isokrates and doubtless elsewhere. They are certainly the climax of the long discussion of modern poetry, which is the essential subject of the whole letter. Fraenkel feels that the climax is the line which says poems 'placate the gods and drive away ghosts', which he remarks comes at the precise centre of the letter. I do not think it can be shown that the central point of a long letter has special significance, but if it has here, it is because it begins quite a long passage about the evolution of Roman poetry, that is all. It was not the purpose of Horace's own poetry to drive away or to placate the ghosts, that is certain.

At this time Agrippa died, who was a terrible loss to his friend and colleague. He left the Roman people his gardens as Caesar had done, and his baths, and to Augustus he left his considerable wealth, and the whole army of slaves he had accumulated, who were trained in the maintenance of his buildings, which were a great part of the new, marble Rome that Augustus would leave, the Rome that the Renaissance began to rediscover and to imitate, of which Horace was a bright star. It is against this background of physical glory and a large population of statues that we must see his remark about Virgil and the power of poets. We will see in the next letter that the silence of statues, of great art, is on his mind now (*Epist*.2, 2, 83).

> *Sacrés coteaux, et vous, saintes ruines,*
> *Qui le seul nom de Rome retenez ...*
> *Las! peu à peu cendre vous devenez*
> *Fable du peuple, et publiques rapines ...*

Most of what we know of Florus is in the first line of his letter, Florus the faithful friend of faithful good Nero. It is as if this letter, which is evidently part of a correspondence with Florus, were in some modest way intended for Tiberius: but who knows in that case whether it had not something to do with Augustus himself? He had demanded in a cheerful enough way to be allowed to take part in Horace's musing conversations. This one pleases biographers because it contains some fragments of the poet's life, though not so full a statement as he gave in the first letter of how he felt about Augustus and Roman literature. That story was suddenly closing, and it is possible that Horace felt it. Nothing Propertius wrote is datable after 16 BC, and Ovid would die in disgrace and in exile. These writers had made no attempt to express that range of Roman feelings that Virgil and Horace had attempted. Propertius is luxurious, daring, every inch a poet, deeply musical and sexually passionate, but there is something of the yowling of a cat about him I suppose. Ovid was too brilliant for his own good. The early days of Augustus really had been unique: the degree of his benignity, his benignant Italian patriotism, was in the ruler of so vast an empire, an empire that was still winning on all its margins, something the world had never seen before, and never would see, *'nil oriturum alias, nil ortum tale fatemur'* (*Epist*.2, 1, 17). As we shall see, Horace did not like Propertius, another over-clever young man he seems to have felt.

To Florus he begins, If someone wanted to sell you a boy, born at Tibur or Gabii, snow-white and beautiful from head to toe, and yours for eight thousand, four times what Davus cost (*Sat.*2, 7, 43), an obedient home-trained serf who knew some Greek and was teachable,

> An untaught singer, pleasant while you drink,

the promises may reduce the credibility of the bargain, and

> Once as does happen he hid behind the stairs
> Fearing no doubt the leathers hanging there.

You would buy this bad bargain, but would you bother to prosecute?

> I told you I was lazy when you set out,
> And can't do courtesies, so now don't shout
> Because you get no letter back from me.
> What use was it to speak? You don't agree,
> But still complain, counting among your wrongs
> That I have been, have not delivered any songs. (25)

In sixty-two more lines we shall come to criticism of poets, but until then this letter is all excuses, however skilful, however dressed up and disguised. He is teasing Florus I think. He begins with a long and I admit feeble story to show that poverty is the spur of poetry. From this he plunges at once into the story of his own life, trimmed to fit the same moral.

> I was brought up in Rome and taught for weeks
> The harm angry Achilles did the Greeks:
> Athens added a little more fine art,
> The wish to tell crooked and straight apart
> And seek the true in Academic trees.
> Hard times removed me from that place of ease,
> And civil tumult drew me a novice to war
> Caesar Augustus was stronger by far,
> And when Philippi saw the finish of me
> With feathers pruned, and no help I could see
> My father's hearth-god and his farm being lost,
> Then daring poverty inspired or tossed
> Me into making verses: now with enough,
> There is no drug or purgative so tough
> I'd not choose sleeping before poetry.
> Years as they pass take all away from me
> They have taken jokes, love, parties and playing
> They are taking poetry. What are you thinking?
> Not everybody admires the same thing,
> One man likes iambics and you like song

> Another likes talking verses like Bion
> And his black salt to rub the city down. (60)

He was the first searing philosophic low-life satirist, in Greek of course. Alas his works have not survived, unless quotations should lurk among the brittle and smashed fragments of Philodemus on poets, which was long ago recovered half-burnt from Pompeii: Richard Janko is at present working on it, so it is reasonable to hope, although the task of reassembling the book has been despaired of for many years. Philodemus 'taught' Virgil and knew Horace, so the question of his influence at least on Horace's knowledge of lost Greek writers has great importance.

> Anyway how do you think I ever can
> Write poems in the worry and work of Rome? (66)

He is wanted always at the far end of the city: 'The squares are clean, you can think as you walk.' His terrifying street-scene (72-5) answers that, with construction waggons, funerals, rabid dogs and the filthiest of runaway pigs. There is a certain sense of eternal Italy in these lines, except that the pigs are now driving motor-cars, if I may say so.

> All writers love the wood and hate the town
> Bacchus likes sleep and shadows on the ground,
> You tell me Sing, in noises day and night,
> And follow the narrow path of a poet?
> On empty Athens talent will take hold,
> For seven years he studies and grows old
> With books and worries till at last he goes
> Quieter than a statue: and it shows,
> The people shake with laughter: how can I
> In all the city tempest and rough sea
> Compose words for the lute harmoniously? (86)

He turns to the example of a story about students calling one another a second F.E. Smith or a new Gladstone, and so to the envious and precious compliments that poets make each other. The next stage is particularly well caught by MacLeod.

> Now if you've time come closer in and hear
> What we endure and how we weave our garlands.
> We wear each other down like gladiators
> In a lingering contest that drags on till dusk.

Finally the other unnamed poet calls Horace an Alcaeus (as well he may), he replies (101),

Callimachus! If you want more than that
Be Mimnermus, and hold on to your hat!
To please poets I put up with a lot,
A writer must beg for the people's vote.

The laws of art entail stern scratching out, though the words hate being
excluded and still crowd around popular shrines (115). My friend Takis
Sinopoulos in *The Poetry of Poetry* once said that rejected words stood in a
circle round the poem, with stones in their hands. Horace says the poet digs
up mouldy old words, and uses new, clear words too, he enriches the language, prunes it, cultivates it, flings away the useless. He seems to be playing
yet he is tortured, like one actor doing now a Satyr and now a Cyclops. I would
sooner appear mad and useless than be like the mad man who sat in the
theatre at Argos applauding when there were no plays, and was furious when
they cured him (141). Horace then embarks on illusion, wealth, and the uncertainty of ownership of land. This is like the library waiting for books and the
criticism of writers and the bit about Athens, another old theme reused.

He dines on bought greens but thinks otherwise,
Buys wood to heat his pot on nights of ice,
But calls it his, where lines of poplars stand
To fend off neighbours' quarrels from his land.
What is the use of barns and villages,
Lucanian and Calabrian ranges,
Death measures all, and cannot be bought off. (179)

There are things some haven't got, some don't want (182).

The rich man works from daybreak to day's end,
With flame and steel subdues his forest ground
His genius knows, controller of his birth star,
The only god of all human nature,
Mortal to all, and he can change his face
Look white or look black from his lurking place. (189)

You do not need to snatch or to compete: you should know yourself.

You are not avid? Good, what's your position
On other vices? Meaningless ambition?
No fear of death, no rage? You laugh at dreams,
Terror of magic, miracles it seems.
Are you grateful at birthdays? Forgive your friends?
Kinder and better as age comes and life ends?
You don't know how to live? Leave it to those who do,
You've played enough, eaten and drunk enough too:
It's time to go now, creatures of love's new tide
Will mock you drunk and shoulder you aside.

All through his letter he has foreseen this as the end, so that he several times suggested his theme. 'The years try to take away my poetry.' He knew he was going to use it because it was a straight quotation from one of the secular sermons of Teles, and has survived in Greek. So with what may be the last lines of verse that he ever did write, Horace teaches us yet again that when he sounds and seems most sincerely and personally moved, and when he is writing at his best, he may simply be translating an obscure Greek. This does not matter at all, because by following this queer course, he has said just what he wanted to say, no more and no less. In the phrase 'creatures of love's new tide' I was saying more instead of less than he meant: he says literally, 'It is time for you to go, lest when you have drunk too much an age (*aetas*) for whom it is more decent to be lascivious should laugh at you and shove you.' The fate he foresees for himself is memorable, like the fate of the ageing prostitute.

For a bag of tricks put together by an ageing and nearly silent poet to satisfy an importunate young friend the letter is a splendid performance. He probes his own increasing age quite mercilessly, and considers his failure with grave eyes. Who is it who spends seven years in Athens? Had he intended that? It is a poet or philosopher who emerges as silent as a man of bronze: it appears to me to be another self of Horace's, as he imagined his life might have been. He seems also to be haunted by the sight of empty shelves in the Palatine library: neither he nor Virgil was a voluminous writer after all. We shall never know quite fully enough what he thought of all his predecessors, though he knew enough about poetry in Rome to have a certain fastidiousness about the future. Even what he felt about Naevius in *Epist.*2.1 depends on the placing of his punctuation. His view of the poet as a language doctor was popularised for my generation by Eliot, and perhaps for that reason I cannot quite accept it, yet as he puts it does it not seem reasonable? One of the queerest things in the whole letter is his definition of what a man's genius is and does. I would like very much to know whether the 'Genius of Augustus' had stirred up these thoughts, or was it a coincidence that they arose in the last poem of his last book?

After all the close reasoning that has been necessary here and there in these last chapters, one faces the prospect of *The Art of Poetry* with a definite lightheadedness, because there is no evidence or accepted argument for when it was written. Fraenkel's guess that it was not the last poem was probably based on some titanic effort to nail down the two Piso brothers, but that too is very difficult. Even the Oxford Classical Dictionary lists a dozen members of the family, though it is habitually frugal with such information. The first was a historian who was consul in 133 BC, but the sons of Lucius Piso, a patron of Greek poets who was consul in 15 BC, look like promising candidates. They are supported by a late antique scholar who is not reliable and may probably be guessing: it has never been verified that Lucius had two sons. All the same, I would personally bet on him as the critic (387-8) and the 'Pisones' as his sons. The whole family seems to have been educated, but the likeliest pair of brothers verifiable are the consul of 7 BC and his younger brother, consul in 1 BC. If they were thirty as consuls, then they were young adults in 11 BC, which fits. Later one died by suicide while being tried after the death of Germanicus in AD 19, and the other died awaiting trial in AD 24, but such deaths are rather a matter of the period into which they survived. *The Art of Poetry* is not classed with the other letters, but from the earliest manuscripts it is treated as a separate work. But in spite of its great length it has the names of the Pisones in line 6: it differs from letters in being impersonal. It was carefully constructed all the same, beginning with mad art and ending with mad poetry. It does offer a fascinating insight into Horace: but it is not an intimate piece of writing, nor can I point to it as early or late in the development of Horace's thoughts, even when there is a definite coincidence with the letter to Florus.

About ten years ago, I read with relief a late nineteenth-century donnish opinion that the letter was an early work and left unfinished: I had never worked at it systematically, having been put off by Fraenkel who growled that he was not interested in Hellenistic literary criticism. Now that I have done so, I have a few things to say. Firstly it looks finished to me: what else would Horace have gone on to say? Secondly, it is after the death of Quintilius (*Odes* 1, 24) whom Horace here remembers as if he had died twenty years ago (438-52), which would be right for around 11 BC. Finally there is the question of tone. The poem is long, clear almost to pedantry, and mostly unsophisticated. Even Augustus whose views on language were similar is more detailed (Suet. *Aug.* 86). It seems to me like a book for children, a schoolbook of instruction about poetry. If that is so, the two Pisones might very well be young adolescent boys for whom their father had asked for this book or commissioned it. That would be why Quintilian the old schoolmaster does not call it a letter but *The Art of Poetry*, as if it were a textbook. The fact that half of it is about the stage (90-294) and much of the rest about the poet's moral character is typical of Horace, if I am right about the other circumstances.

Still there are difficulties as Rudd points out (19-21). Aulus Cascellius (371) was in his nineties (which fits very well, 371) if not dead, and Maecius Tarpa (387) was probably eighty or more, but that is equally possible. In the end I agree with Rudd that 'it is preferable to assume' that this was the last work of Horace, written when he had given up other kinds of composition (306). He had given them all up in turn, seldom going back to what he had once abandoned, or the years had torn all from his grasp. The second book of *Satires* is so different from the first it is hardly an exception: the only true exceptions arise from the demands of Augustus, the lyrical outburst in and after 17 BC, and the last letters. This work for the Pisones reworks some material from Florus's letter as that reworks some from Augustus's letter. There is some allusion to Roman constitutional law which may possibly derive from the conversation of Maecenas. Dio Cassius in discussing the settlement of the twenties gives Maecenas a long and very detailed speech about the historical evolution of institutions.

Horace begins by assuring the Pisones that his book is going to be like a crazy picture, a pretty woman with a fish's tail or a human head on a horse: we are meant to remember the centaur and the mermaid, both well known to art. People who undertake great things like purple patches (15-16), Diana's grove, floods, a rainbow. He has no room for them: a poem must be a single, coherent composition (23). Most poets, fathers and sons, are deluded by the appearance of writing well. Trying to be brief you get obscure, or to be great you get pompous, and the urge for variation puts dolphins in the woods.

> In sculpture school the lowest workmen are ones
> Who can do nails and hair very well in bronze,
> But they're no good at making body and soul,
> And so am I if I try something whole.
> Nor would I like to live with a queer nose
> And fine black hair and lovely eyes, God knows. (37)

So choose materials that fit your strength. The virtue of order is to say now what needs saying now. Horace touches now on material from the letter to Florus: old and new words, and the Roman tendency to allow Plautus what they will not allow to Virgil and Varius (45).

> Why am I envied if I have a few
> New words, when Ennius and Cato too
> Enriched our language? ... (58)
> ... Woods alter as the leaf falls from the tree,
> And new leaf follows and a new glory
> As the old dies, so in time our words die,
> And yet like youth show green as time goes by,
> We are owed to death, we and all that is ours;
> Neptune keeps ships at home from the storm's powers,
> What was mere marsh will nourish cities now
> And where oars fluttered feel the heavy plough.
> Or if the river altered course from fish
> To fruits, mortal monuments will perish,
> Honour of language and its lively grace
> Will live, old words will come back into place,
> And words now honoured will go back to dust,
> Usage is all, our law, our norm, our trust. (72)

This is surely close to the truth, and it explains why one needs a special tact or almost genius to feel deeply the laws of usage. It is a more useful observation than that of the poet as language doctor, as maker of the language.

We now come to history, beginning with a rumbling Virgilian line (73) with the praise of Homer. He is said to have begun couplets and the elegiac lament. This view sounds very eccentric (is something missing?) unless it refers to Homer's *Margites*, which he did not really write, and we have not got more than a line or two. If Horace does mean that he must be following some Alexandrian bewhiskered with learning. Grammarians fight over this, the court is in session (78). We then leap from Archilochos to comedy and tragedy, like a man crossing a river on stepping-stones, where

> The Muse gave to the strings gods and their sons,
> Boxers and chariot-racing champions,
> Troubles of the young, and all the wine they drink ... (85)

So one must know the forms and the styles. Comedy does not like the tragic style for example. This introduces two hundred or more lines on dramatic composition, which daunts many scholars, since we know less than Horace did about the Greek let alone the Roman theatre. There are exceptions of course, comic characters yell and swell and tragic ones are plain instead of 'puffed cheeks and six-footed words' (97).

> Poems need not just beauty, they must be sweet,
> To lead spectators' minds to true delight,
> Laugh with them laughing, weep with those who weep, ...
> ... And get that right, or else I'll giggle or sleep. (105)

The writer should follow fame, that is use known stories, or make up his plots coherently. There had been plots composed like fiction for four hundred years, and in south Italy at least they were common.

> You will do better to bring Troy on scene
> Than to try unknown tales, still raw and green.
> Don't begin as the old poet did: Aha!
> I sing the fate of Priam and noble war.
> What can follow the silence he'd arouse?
> The mountains labour to conceive a mouse.
> Better the man who's never stupid then:
> Tell Muse that man, after Troy had fallen
> Who saw manners of men and their cities ... (142)

Horace's discussion of how to make characters, who in ancient times were based on traditional masks, is necessarily limited, but it produces nothing less than what we know as Shakespeare's seven ages of man, though here there are only four: the boy who can speak and is changeable, the youth who loves dogs and horses, spends prodigally and is wax to vice, the man seeking wealth and alliance, and the troubles of old age, 'slow to hope, fearing the future, difficult, complaining, praising past time' (174).

Alfred Noyes in his book on Horace gives a remarkable translation of the 'ages of man' passage, which he deliberately made to sound more Shakespearean than other bits of Horace. It is worth quoting, because the close resemblance it emphasises is really present (158-74).

> At first the child, with feet new-trained to walk
> Plays with his mates all day; or, at a nothing,

Bursts into rage, which in an instant turns
To laughter, and still changes every hour.
Then comes the beardless boy, set free from school,
Riding his horse, rejoicing in his hounds,
Who haunts the Campus Martius; soft as wax
If evil moulds him, fretful at the curb
Of wisdom, careless what the morrow brings;
Prodigal of his coin, a sprightly colt,
Swift to desire, and swifter to forgo
What yesterday he swore he loved the best.
Then manhood, all for riches now, and friends,
A slave to proud ambition, and ashamed
To think his firm intent could ever change.
Last comes old age, with all its gathering ills,
Still seeking more, and yet afraid to use
Its lifelong hoard, sans courage and sans fire,
Full of delays, content with hope deferred;
Testy and grumbling, wishing that the world
Were once again as when he was a boy ...
      ... Nature's law must rule the stage.

Horace continues with an obvious moral.

The years that come bring benefits with them
But as they slip away they will take them. (175-6)

You must show what is proper and not what is not (he is following
Aristotle) and never have more than five acts (189), no gods in the action and
no more than three persons speaking. No reason is given for these rules. He
is a strong believer in the chorus, in case something happens between acts,
to give moral advice, praise a dinner, pray to the gods and so on. It must be
said he has not even begun to think about all this. He is clearer about music:
he wants a thin and simple pipe, not the elaborate hooting thing 'in use now'
(202).

Know when a people who'd stand numbering,
Frugal and chaste and modest crowded in,
But when with victories they took more ground
And walls girdled their city wider round,
When toasting their own Genius was no sin
Then licence and corruption entered in ...
And antique art took to new luxury ...   (214)

Horace discusses satyr plays with particular certainty; the little we have left
from Aeschylus and Euripides certainly merits his real interest in a form
which Sulla surprisingly had tried to revive. Horace is conscious of the
difficulties of these compositions.

Fauns brought from forests must I think take care
Not to seem alley-born, or city reared (244-5)

One must consider one's audience, he says, and see that the reaction of different social classes will not be the same (246-50). I do not think that would have occurred to Aristophanes, but fifth-century Athens was still an age of innocence compared to Rome. He notes the metres that older Roman writers used. For himself he says one must be a tough self-critic.

> You study Greek examples then all night,
> Study the Greek examples by daylight.
> Your grandfathers praised Plautus for his wit
> And for his rhythm: too easy on it,
> Let's not say foolish, let's you and me attain
> To tell what's witty from what's inurbane,
> Tell the right sound with fingers and with ears ...   (274)

He now gives a history of the Greek theatre which is happily brief, and one of the Roman theatre more in sorrow than in anger, and that concludes (294) his dramatic message of which the climax is that our poets have left nothing unattempted except revision. In the last hundred and seventy or so lines of Horace's poem he must finally turn to the poet's own duty and vocation, which he has been avoiding, and indeed he still has a trick or two up his sleeve. He begins with Democritus who said poets are mad, and having embroidered this a little,

> I, like an anvil, sharpen and make bright
> The blades of poets, but I do not write.
> I teach what feeds and forms up a poet,
> What's his glory, what virtue offers it. (308)

The beginning and spring of writing is wisdom (*sapere*) and Socrates tells you all about it. If you know all your duties you know what fits every character. Still, he is realistic and tough about the effect of style also: 'A play without eros, or weight or art May enter quicker to the people's heart Than poor verse, singing trifles, dead from the start' (322).

> The Muse has given talent to the Greek
> And with a round voiced eloquence they speak.

Roman boys just know how to do mental arithmetic because their lives will depend on that (325-31). How can we hope to write poems to keep in cedar and light cypress? Poets want to be useful or they want to please. 'To mix the two is what will cross the sea, And lengthen out your lasting quality' (346). In fact Horace is exactly like the Greeks, 'avid only for praise'. Allusions come thick and fast but all either jokes like the baby-eating ogress Lamia, or facts of Roman life, like the mental arithmetic lesson and the Ramnes, the highest

of various orders of Knights, who still had a function in Roman elections and
were supposed to go back to Romulus. Finally

> I do get cross when old Homer nods off,
> But in a long poem it's fair enough.
> A poem's like a picture, if you stay
> Close you see better, but some, far away
> One likes the dark shadow, one likes the light ... (363)

He addresses the eldest son in particular even though his father has told him
and he knows anyway: a mediocre lawyer is no Messalla, nor does he know
as much as Cascellius Aulus (who is about a hundred), but for poets to be
middling neither men nor gods permit, and nor do the pillars where poems
are sold. If you can't use arms, you avoid them: yet people who can't write
verse still dare to compose it. If you do write something then Maecius (about
eighty) will hear of it and so will your father and so will I. It should be kept
nine years: what you don't publish you can destroy, but once it's out it won't
come back (390). The jokes about the old men must always have been in some
sense private, and in this whole section of the poem he is writing like a man
in a good temper, as he always does at his best. His philosophy has been only
a fencing display. It is only when he confronts the nobility of a poet's vocation
that gloom attacks him (391).

> Holy Orpheus interpreter of gods
> Frightened foresters from slaughter and foul food,
> They say he calmed tigers and raging lions,
> Amphion founded Thebes and commanded stones
> With gentle prayer and shelly echo. Wisdom once
> Divided public and private, sacred and profane,
> Gave marriage rites, stopped sex in the lane,
> Built towns up, wrote laws on wooden tablets,
> Bringing name and honour to divine poets.
> Tyrtaeus summoned to wars with poetry,
> Verses foretold all things that were to be
> And the Muses secured the grace of Kings,
> Play was discovered, long works had endings,
> So don't be ashamed of the Muse's strings when Apollo sings. (407)

Of course a poet has to train but even the Olympic champion pipers had to
begin with a teacher. He has the persuasive skills of an auctioneer (of a
praeco as Horace's father was). You must not invite or accept mockery as a
poet from flatterers: you must go to a true critic.

> Quintilius if you recited said
> 'Do correct this, and this,' and if you said
> You'd tried three times, he told you 'Cross it out,
> Take it back to the anvil, it's not right.'

But if you'd rather defend your line,
You wouldn't get a word more out of him,
You were left alone to love yourself in the dark.
Good and wise men blame verses that don't work,
They hate the harsh, they cross out in black ink,
They cut ambitious ornaments I think
And throw light on the obscure, note what's to change,
They are like Aristarchus in his range. (450)

Aristarchus was an editor of genius, and the decent text of Homer that we have today is due to him and his colleagues in Alexandria in the third century BC. The Homeric papyri are often older or independent of this learned influence, and their text by comparison is really terrible. Quintilius (*Odes* 1, 24) never formally taught Horace, but he was a much loved friend. We are near the end of the poem and of all Horace's work, and so it seems to me that Quintilius is in a position of real honour here. We return for the closing passage to the mad poet, of whom Democritus warned us (297), and who balances the teasing picture of the mad artist at the beginning. Boys follow the mad poet in the street and if he falls into a hole, who cares? Maybe he did it on purpose like Empedocles in the crater of Etna. If you pull him out who knows anyway why he makes verses. Has he pissed on his father's ashes, or shifted the barrier of a place hit by lightning? He is as mad as a bear who breaks his bars and everyone runs. He catches you and rends you to death in fact, he's like a leech that won't leave your skin until he's full of blood.

That is a nice bit of nursery gruesomeness at the end, is it not? I do not think Horace at all intends that these two boys should be poets. Their father has asked him for a book about it which he has kindly written in verse, while protesting that he does not write verse. I am not convinced that he really cares much for the Roman theatre, and as for the Greek, to him it is books: he reads them and imagines it, as we do. There were no 'classical' productions of Greek plays in his lifetime. He does not want to tell the boys a great deal about his life as a lyric poet or about his autobiography. They can read those things elsewhere, when they grow up. But he is not patronising, he is rather severe on them, yet at the same time movingly kind. The grotesqueries in this poem are calculated to please schoolboys: the one about pissing on our father's ashes was taken up and used brilliantly by Sir Thomas Browne in his *Urn Burial*. Scholars, not untypically, are content to assure us that the custom was forbidden.

I have nothing more to say about this pleasant but puzzling poem, and little more about the life of Horace. Few poets would like to be judged on their last works, but if that is what this is, then I must say that his last line, the one about the leech, and the entire last scene of the poet as madman are very brilliant. There was something in Horace that was delighted with those twenty-three lines, but not with the conventional praises of Amphion and Orpheus. We do not know if he ever did really stop writing. His friend Maecenas died fifty-nine days before he did, in the late September of 8 BC, leaving a message to Augustus, Remember Horatius Flaccus as you would

me. Horace died in the last week of that November, on the 27th. He was
fifty-seven, nearly fifty-eight. He was too ill to sign his will in the end, so he
made one by declaration before witnesses, leaving everything he had to
Augustus. He was buried on the far edge of the Esquiline, near the tomb of
Maecenas. The reason for leaving wealth to Augustus was that he,would
spend it on the Roman people; when he died he left them forty million
sesterces: in the last twenty years of his life he was left 1400 million, nearly
all of which had been spent on the Romans in his lifetime (Suet. *Aug*.101).
What Horace left, apart from his poems, was small beer.

And yet we should face the question whether Augustus had not drawn the
poet away from his friend Maecenas, and whether his influence was not in
the end crushing? The *Odes* in the last book were a success and a great
innovation: the two where the poet welcomes the Emperor in the streets of
Rome, and the last poem of all, have never in their own style been equalled.
The second book of *Letters* also contains remarkable passages, and one
perfected poem, the one to Augustus which Fraenkel thought Horace's masterpiece: one cannot seriously disagree with his high view of it, even though
one may prefer the more private poems, or the poems to old friends. The years
do their best to take away our poems, as Horace said to the Pisones. There
are not many poems for Maecenas in the fourth book of *Odes*, but there is one,
and Horace was fastidious about retreading old paths. He could feel that
temptation growing on him I think, in the fourth book. But his friendship
with Maecenas remained sunny.

It was not based either on social equality, though by the end they had
shared a lot of life, or on equality of talent. The bits and pieces of the personal
interests of Maecenas that we know from Suetonius do not make him an
obvious friend for Horace, and there were other friends in his circle, not all
agreeable to the old southerner. Horace by the end of his life was an elderly
gentleman with severely classical tastes, cut off from the modern theatre and
from much of the poetry that was by then being written. It is permissible to
be grateful to Maecenas, to shrug at whatever is obscure or mysterious in his
relations with Augustus, which after all never came to an open quarrel, and
to share Horace's severe views about Roman poetry in the future: say after
the crucifixion of Christ. When someone asked Mommsen what other late
Roman writer after Horace he loved, his answer was Petronius, and perhaps
Horace looking down from the Esquiline would have beamed in agreement:
only we know now from a scrap of papyrus what Mommsen never knew, that
the *Satyricon* started off as a Greek story about the old Greek colonies of
southern Italy.

It did not appear profitable to look more closely into the literary circle of
Maecenas: Horace tells us enough in his poems, and his sense that his friends
were trustworthy is clear. Horace's feelings for the minor or younger or outer
members of the group are less easy to determine, but also much less important. We know that in his lifetime his lyric imitators increased, and the
Appendix Vergiliana reveals that the easier epodes had their fans too. We
know he thought Propertius pretentious: perhaps the animus he had against
him arose from a certain irony in the young man's attitude to Virgil: Yield

Roman writers, yield Greeks: something greater than the *Iliad* is born (2, 34, 65), which is admittedly far funnier as embellished by Ezra Pound. In letters like the ones he wrote to Maecenas about Horace from Spain (*Vita Virg.*, Donatus c.31) Augustus begs for the first copy of the *Aeneid* as soon as it is made, or for any part of it. When Virgil had died in Brindisi of the sunstroke that he caught at Megara, he left half his wealth to a half-brother, a quarter to Augustus, and a twelfth each to Maecenas and his two literary executors (c.140) who edited the *Aeneid*. The pseudo-Virgilian *Elegies on Maecenas* supposed to be written when he died are by young boobies and deplorably bad: they tell us little reliable, though the second records scenes at his death-bed. Whoever wrote this rubbish did know the phrase Remember Horace as you would me, which comes from Maecenas's will or last letters. This impostor wrings much pathos out of it by applying it to the love of Maecenas for Augustus: these bad poems are like gardens overgrown for a hundred years, they are best ignored, they are not worth the trouble they take to explore.

Horace's character and his life-story are simpler and lonelier, the sense of death is strong in his poetry, yet when finally he dies we are shocked, as if we had suddenly lost a true and close friend.

Appendix

Plutarch's Account of Philippi

The army of Brutus was now considerable, and he ordered its route into Asia, while a fleet was preparing in Bithynia and at Cyzicum. As he marched by land, he settled the affairs of the cities, and gave audience to the princes of those countries through which he passed. He sent orders to Cassius, who was in Syria, to give up his intended journey into Egypt, and join him. On this occasion he tells him, that their collecting forces to destroy the tyrants was not to secure an empire to themselves, but to deliver their fellow-citizens; that they should never forget this great object of their undertaking, but, adhering to their first intentions, keep Italy within their eye, and hasten to rescue their country from oppression.

Cassius accordingly set out to join him, and Brutus at the same time making some progress to meet him, their interview was at Smyrna. Till this meeting they had not seen each other since they parted at the Piraeus of Athens, when Cassius set out for Syria, and Brutus for Macedonia. The forces they had respectively collected gave them great joy, and made them confident of success. From Italy, they had fled, like solitary exiles, without money, without arms, without a ship, a soldier, or a town to fly to: yet now, in so short a time, they found themselves supplied with shipping and money, with an army of horse and foot, and in a condition of contending for the empire of Rome. Cassius was no less respectful to Brutus than Brutus was to him; but the latter would generally wait upon him, as he was the older man, and of a feebler constitution. Cassius was esteemed an able soldier, but of a fiery disposition, and ambitious to command rather by fear than affection; though, at the same time, with his familiar acquaintance, he was easy in his manners, and fond of raillery to excess. Brutus, on account of his virtue, was respected by the people, beloved by his friends, admired by men of principle, and not hated even by his enemies. He was firm and inflexible in his opinions, and zealous in every pursuit where justice or honour were concerned. The people had the highest opinion of his integrity and sincerity in every undertaking, and this naturally inspired them with confidence and affection. Even Pompey the Great had hardly ever so much credit with them; for who ever imagined, that, if he had conquered Caesar, he would have submitted to the laws, and would not have retained his power under the title of consul or dictator, or some more specious and popular name? Cassius, on the contrary, a man of violent passions and rapacious avarice, was suspected of exposing himself to toil and danger, rather from a thirst of power, than an attachment to the liberties of his country. The former disturbers of the commonwealth,

Cinna, and Marius, and Carbo, evidently set their country as a stake for the winner, and hardly scrupled to own that they fought for empire: but the very enemies of Brutus never charge him with this. Even Antony has been heard to say, that Brutus was the only conspirator who had the sense of honour and justice for his motive, and that the rest were wholly actuated by malice or envy. It is clear, too, from what Brutus himself says, that he finally and principally relied on his own virtue. Thus he writes to Atticus immediately before an engagement: 'That his affairs were in the most desirable situation imaginable; for that either he should conquer, and restore liberty to Rome, or die, and be free from slavery; that every thing else was reduced to certainty; and that this only remained a question, Whether they should live or die free men?' He adds, 'that Mark Antony was properly punished for his folly, who, when he might have ranked with the Bruti, the Cassii, and Catos, chose rather to be the underling of Octavius; and that if he did not fall in the approaching battle, they would very soon be at variance with each other.' In which he seems to have been a true prophet.

Whilst they were at Smyrna, Brutus desired Cassius to let him have part of the vast treasure he had collected, because his own was chiefly expended in equipping a fleet, to gain the superiority at sea: but the friends of Cassius advised him against this, alleging that it would be absurd to give Brutus that money which he had saved with so much frugality, and acquired with so much envy, merely that Brutus might increase his popularity, by distributing it amongst the soldiers. Cassius, however, gave him a third of what he had, and then they parted for their respective commands. Cassius behaved with great severity on the taking of Rhodes; though, when he first entered the city, and was saluted with the title of king and master, he answered, 'That he was neither their king nor their master, but the destroyer of him who would have been both.' Brutus demanded supplies of men and money from the Lycians; but Naucrates, an orator, persuaded the cities to rebel, and some of the inhabitants posted themselves on the hills, with an intent to oppose the passage of Brutus. Brutus at first despatched a party of horse, which surprised them at dinner, and killed six hundred of them: but afterwards, when he had taken the adjacent towns and villages, he gave up the prisoners without ransom, and hoped to gain them to his party by clemency. Their former sufferings, however, made them reject his humanity, and those that still resisted being driven into the city of Xanthus, were there beseiged. As a river ran close by the town, several attempted to escape by swimming and diving; but they were prevented by nets let down for that purpose, which had little bells at the top, to give notice when any one was taken. The Xanthians afterwards made a sally in the night, and set fire to several of the battering engines; but they were perceived and driven back by the Romans: at the same time the violence of the winds drove the flames on the city, so that several houses near the battlements took fire. Brutus, being apprehensive that the whole city would be destroyed, sent his own soldiers to assist the inhabitants in quenching the fire; but the Lycians were seized with an incredible despair, a kind of frenzy, which can no otherwise be described than by calling it a passionate desire of death. Women and children, freemen and slaves, people of all ages and conditions, strove to repulse the soldiers as they came to their assistance from the walls. With their own hands they collected wood and reeds, and all manner of combustibles, to spread the fire over the city, and encouraged its progress by every means in their power. Thus assisted, the flames flew over the whole with dreadful rapidity; whilst Brutus, extremely shocked at this calamity, rode round the walls, and, stretching forth his hands to the inhabitants, entreated them to spare themselves and their city. Regardless of his entreaties, they sought by every means to put an end to their lives. Men, women and even children, with hideous cries, leaped into the flames. Some threw themselves headlong from the walls, and others fell upon the swords of their parents, opening their breasts, and begging to be slain.

When the city was in a great measure reduced to ashes, a woman was found who had hanged herself, with her young child fastened to her neck, and the torch in her hand, with which she had fired her house. This deplorable object so much affected Brutus, that he wept when he was told of it, and proclaimed a reward to any soldier who could save a Xanthian. It is said that no more than a hundred and fifty were preserved, and those against their will. Thus the Xanthians, as if fate had appointed certain periods for their destruction, after a long course of years, sunk into that deplorable ruin, in which the same rash despair had involved their ancestors in the Persian war; for they, too, burned their city, and destroyed themselves.

After this, when the Patareans likewise made resistance, Brutus was under great anxiety whether he should besiege them; for he was afraid they should follow the desperate measures of the Xanthians. However, having some of their women whom he had taken prisoner, he dismissed them without ransom; and those returning to their husbands and parents, who happened to be people of the first distinction, so much extolled the justice and moderation of Brutus, that they prevailed on them to submit, and put their city in his hands. The adjacent cities followed their example, and found that his humanity exceeded their hopes. Cassius compelled every Rhodian to give up all the gold and silver in his possession, by which he amassed eight thousand talents; and yet he laid the public under a fine of five hundred talents more; but Brutus took only a hundred and fifty talents of the Lycians, and, without doing them any other injury, led his army into Ionia.

Brutus, in the course of this expedition, did many acts of justice, and was vigilant in the dispensation of rewards and punishments. An instance of this I shall relate, because both he himself, and every honest Roman was particularly pleased with it. When Pompey the Great, after his overthrow at Pharsalia, fled into Egypt, and landed near Pelusium, the tutors and ministers of young Ptolemy consulted what measures they should take on the occasion. But they were of different opinions: some were for receiving him, others for excluding him out of Egypt. Theodotus, a Chian by birth, and a teacher of rhetoric by profession, who then attended the king in that capacity, was, for want of abler ministers, admitted to the council. This man insisted that both were in the wrong; those who were for receiving, and those who were for expelling Pompey. The best measure they could take, he said, would be to put him to death, and concluded his speech with the proverb, that *dead men do not bite*. The council entered into his opinion; and Pompey the Great, an example of the incredible mutability of fortune, fell a sacrifice to the arguments of a sophist, as the sophist lived afterwards to boast. Not long after, upon Caesar's arrival in Egypt, some of the murderers received their proper reward, and were put to death; but Theodotus made his escape. – Yet, though for awhile he gained from fortune the poor privilege of a wandering and despicable life, he fell at last into the hands of Brutus, as he was passing through Asia; and, by paying the forfeit of his baseness, became more memorable from his death than from any thing in his life.

About this time Brutus sent for Cassius to Sardis, and went with his friends to meet him. The whole army being drawn up, saluted both the leaders with the title of *Imperator*: but, as it usually happens in great affairs, where many friends and many officers are engaged, mutual complaints and suspicions arose between Brutus and Cassius. To settle these more properly, they retired into an apartment by themselves. Expostulations, debates, and accusations followed, and these were so violent, that they burst into tears. Their friends without were surprised at the loudness and asperity of the conference; but though they were apprehensive of the consequence, they durst not interfere, because they had been expressly forbidden to enter. Favonius, however, an imitator of Cato, but rather an enthusiast than rational in his philosophy, attempted to enter. The servants in waiting endeavoured to prevent him, but it was not easy to stop the impetuous Favonius. He was violent in his whole conduct, and valued himself less on his dignity as a senator, than on a kind of cynical freedom in saying every thing he pleased; nor was this unentertaining to those who could bear with his impertinence. However, he broke through the door, and entered the apartment, pronouncing, in a theatrical tone, what Nestor says in Homer,

Young men, be rul'd – I'm older than you both.

Cassius laughed; but Brutus thrust him out, telling him, that he pretended to be a *cynic*, but was in reality a *dog*. This, however, put an end to the dispute, and for that time they parted. Cassius gave an entertainment in the evening, to which Brutus invited his friends. When they were seated, Favonius came in from bathing. Brutus called aloud to him, telling him he was not invited, and bade him go to the lower end of the table. Favonius, notwithstanding, thrust himself in, and sat down in the middle. On that occasion there was much learning and good humour in the conversation.

The following day, one Lucius Pella, who had been praetor, and employed in offices of trust, being impeached by the Sardians of embezzling the public money, was disgraced and condemned by Brutus. This was very mortifying to Cassius; for, a little before, two of his own friends had been accused of the same crime; but he had absolved them in public, and contenting himself with giving them a private reproof, continued them in office. Of course he charged Brutus with too rigid an exertion of the laws, at a time when lenity was much more politic. Brutus, on the other hand, reminded him of the ides of March, the time when they had killed Caesar, who was not, personally speaking, the scourge of mankind, but only abetted and supported those that were, with his power. He bade him consider, that if the neglect of justice were in any case to be connived at, it should have been done before; and that they had better have borne with the oppressions of Caesar's friends, than suffer the malpractices of their own to pass with impunity: 'For then,' continued he, 'we could have been blamed only for cowardice; but now, after all we have undergone, we shall lie under the imputation of injustice.' Such were the principles of Brutus.

When they were about to leave Asia, Brutus, it is said, had an extraordinary apparition. Naturally watchful, sparing in his diet, and assiduous in business, he allowed himself but little time for sleep. In the day he never slept, nor in the night, till all business was over, and the rest being retired, he had nobody to converse with but at this time involved as he was in the operations of war, and solicitous for the event, he only slumbered a little after supper, and spent the rest of the night in ordering his most urgent affairs. When these were despatched, he employed himself in reading till the third watch, when the tribunes and centurions came to him for orders. Thus, a little before he left Asia, he was sitting alone in his tent, by a dim light, and at a late hour. The whole army lay in sleep and silence, while the general, wrapt in meditation, thought he perceived something enter his tent: turning towards the door, he saw a horrible and monstrous spectre standing silently by his side. 'What art thou?' said he boldly. 'Art thou god or man? And what is thy business with me?' The spectre answered, 'I am thy evil genius, Brutus! Thou wilt see me at Philippi.' To which he calmly replied, 'I'll meet thee there.' When the apparition was gone, he called his servants, who told him they had neither heard any noise, nor had seen any vision. That night he did not go to rest, but went early in the morning to Cassius, and told him what had happened. Cassius, who was of the school of Epicurus, and used frequently to dispute with Brutus on these subjects, answered him thus: 'It is the opinion of our sect, that not every thing we see is real; for matter is evasive, and sense deceitful. Besides, the impressions it receives are, by the quick and subtle influence of imagination, thrown into a variety of forms, many of which have no archetypes in nature; and this the imagination effects as easily as we may make an impression on wax. The mind of man, having in itself the plastic powers, and the component parts, can fashion and vary its objects to pleasure. This is clear from the sudden transition of dreams, in which the imagination can educe from the slightest principles such an amazing variety of forms, and call into exercise all the passions of the soul. The mind is perpetually in motion, and that motion is imagination or thought: but when the body, as in your case, is fatigued with labour, it naturally suspends or perverts the regular functions of the mind. Upon the whole, it is highly improbable that there should be any such beings as demons or spirits; or that, if there were such, they should assume a human shape or voice, or have any power to affect us. At the same time, I own, I could wish there were such beings, that we might not rely on fleets and armies, but

find the concurrence of the gods in this our sacred and glorious enterprise.'
Such were the arguments he made use of to satisfy Brutus.

When the army began to march, two eagles perched on the two first
standards, and accompanied them as far as Philippi, being constantly fed by
the soldiers; but the day before the battle they flew away. Brutus had already
reduced most of the nations in these parts; nevertheless, he traversed the
sea-coast over against Thasus, that if any hostile power remained, he might
bring it into subjection. – Norbanus, who was encamped in the straits near
Symblum, they surrounded in such a manner, that they obliged him to quit
the place. Indeed, he narrowly escaped losing his whole army, which had
certainly been the case, had not Antony come to his relief with such amazing
expedition, that Brutus could not believe it to be possible. Caesar, who had
been kept behind by sickness, joined his army about ten days after. Brutus
was encamped over against him; Cassius was opposite to Antony. The space
between the two armies the Romans call the plains of Philippi. Two armies
of Romans, equal in numbers to these, had never before met to engage each
other. – Caesar's was something superior in numbers, but in the splendour
of arms and equipage, was far exceeded by that of Brutus; for most of their
arms were of gold and silver, which their general had liberally bestowed upon
them. Brutus, in other things, had accustomed his officers to frugality; but
the riches which his soldiers carried about with them would at once, he
thought, add to the spirit of the ambitious, and make the covetous valiant in
the defence of those arms, which were their principal wealth.

Caesar made a lustration of his army within the camp, and gave each
private man a little corn, and five drachmas only, for the sacrifice: but
Brutus, to show his contempt of the poverty or the avarice of Caesar, made a
public lustration of his army in the field, and not only distributed cattle to
each cohort for the sacrifice, but gave fifty drachmas on the occasion to each
private man. Of course he was more beloved by his soldiers, and they were
more ready to fight for him. It is reported, that during the lustration, an
unlucky omen happened to Cassius. The garland he was to wear at the
sacrifice was presented to him the wrong side outwards. It is said, too, that
at a solemn procession some time before, the person who bore the golden
image of victory before Cassius, happened to stumble, and the image fell to
the ground. Several birds of prey hovered daily about the camp, and swarms
of bees were seen with the trenches: upon which the soothsayers ordered the
part where they appeared to be shut up; for Cassius, with all his Epicurean
philosophy, began to be supersitious, and the soldiers were extremely dis-
heartened by these omens.

For this reason Cassius was inclined to protract the war, and unwilling to
hazard the whole of the event on a present engagement. What made for this
measure, too, was, that they were stronger in money and provisions, but
inferior in numbers. Brutus, on the other hand, was, as usual, for an
immediate decision, that he might either give liberty to his country, or rescue
his fellow-citizens from the toils and expenses of war. He was encouraged
likewise by the success his cavalry met with in several skirmishes; and some
instances of desertion and mutiny in the camp brought over many of the

friends of Cassius to his opinion: but there was one Atellius, who still opposed an immediate decision, and advised to put it off till the next winter. When Brutus asked him what advantages he expected from that, he answered, 'If I gain nothing else, I shall at least live so much the longer.' Both Cassius and the rest of the officers were displeased with this answer; and it was determined to give battle the day following.

Brutus, that night, expressed great confidence and cheerfulness; and having passed the time of supper in philosophical conversation, he went to rest. Messala says, that Cassius supped in private with some of his most intimate friends; and that, contrary to his usual manner, he was pensive and silent. He adds, that after supper he took him by the hand, and pressing it close, as he commonly did, in token of his friendship, he said, in Greek, 'Bear witness, Messala, that I am reduced to the same necessity with Pompey the Great, of hazarding the liberty of my country on one battle. Yet I have confidence in our good fortune, on which we ought still to rely, though the measures we have resolved upon are indiscreet.' These, Messala tells us, were the last words that Cassius spoke before he bade him *Farewell*; and that the next day, being his birth-day, he invited Cassius to sup with him.

Next morning, as soon as it was light, the scarlet robe, which was the signal for battle, was hung out in the tents of Brutus and Cassius; and they themselves met on the plain between the two armies. On this occasion Cassius thus addressed himself to Brutus. 'May the gods, Brutus, make this day successful, that we may pass the rest of our days together in prosperity: but as the most important of human events are the most uncertain, and as we may never see each other any more, if we are unfortunate on this occasion, tell me what is your resolution concerning flight and death?'

Brutus answered, 'In the younger and less experienced part of my life, I was led, upon philosophical principles, to condemn the conduct of Cato in killing himself. I thought it at once impious and unmanly to sink beneath the stroke of fortune, and to refuse the lot that had befallen us. In my present situation, however, I am of a different opinion; so that if Heaven should now be unfavourable to our wishes, I will no longer solicit my hopes or my fortune, but die contented with it, such as it is. On the ides of March I devoted my life to my country; and since that time I have lived in liberty and glory.' At these words Cassius smiled, and embracing Brutus, said, 'Let us march, then against the enemy; for with these resolutions, though we should not conquer, we have nothing to fear.' – They then consulted with their friends concerning the order of battle. Brutus desired that he might command the right wing, though the post was thought more proper for Cassius, on account of his experience. Cassius, however, gave it up to him, and placed Messala, with the best of legions, in the same wing. Brutus immediately drew out his cavalry, which were equipped with great magnificence, and the foot followed close upon them.

Antony's soldiers were at this time employed in making a trench from the marsh where they were encamped, to cut off Cassius's communication with the sea. Caesar lay still in his tent, confined by sickness. His soldiers were far from expecting that the enemy would come to a pitched battle. They supposed that they were only making excursions to harass the trench-diggers with their light arms; and not perceiving that they were pouring in close upon them, they were astonished at the outcry they heard from the trenches. Brutus, in the mean time, sent tickets to the several offices with the word of battle, and rode through the ranks to encourage his men. There were few who had patience to wait for the word. The greatest part, before it could reach them, fell with loud shouts upon the enemy. This precipitate onset threw the army into confusion, and separated the legions. Messala's legion first got beyond the left wing of Caesar, and was followed by those that were stationed near him. In their way they did nothing more than throw some of the outmost ranks into disorder, and killed few of the enemy: their great object was to fall upon Caesar's camp, and they made directly up to it. – Caesar himself, as he tells us in his Commentaries, had but just before been conveyed out of his tent, in consequence of a vision of his friend Artorius, which commanded that he should be carried out of the camp. This made it believed that he was slain, for the soldiers had pierced his empty litter in many places with darts. Those who were taken in the camp were put to the sword, amongst whom were two thousand Lacedaemonian auxiliaries. Those who attacked Caesar's legions in front easily put them to the rout, and cut three legions in pieces. After this, borne along with the impetuosity of victory, they rushed into the camp at the same time with the fugitives, and Brutus was in the midst of them. The flank of Brutus's army was now left unguarded by the separation of the right wing, which was gone off too far in the pursuit; and the enemy, perceiving this, endeavoured to take advantage of it. They accordingly attacked it with great fury, but could make no impression on the main body, which received them with firmness and unshaken resolution. The left wing, however, which was under the command of Cassius, was soon put to the rout; for the men were in great disorder, and knew nothing of what had passed in the right wing. The enemy pursued him into the camp, which they plundered and destroyed, though neither of their generals were present. Antony, it is said, to avoid the fury of the first onset, had retired into the adjoining marsh; and Caesar, who had been carried sick out of the camp, was no where to be found. Nay, some of the soldiers would have persuaded Brutus that they had killed Caesar, describing his age and person, and showing him their bloody swords.

The main body of Brutus's army had now made prodigious havoc of the enemy; and Brutus, in his department, was no less absolutely conqueror than Cassius was conquered. The want of knowing this was the ruin of their affairs. Brutus neglected to relieve Cassius, because he knew not that he wanted relief.

When Brutus had destroyed the camp of Caesar, and was returning from the pursuit, he was surprised that he could neither perceive the tent of Cassius above the rest, as usual, nor any of those that were about it; for they had been demolished by the enemy on their first entering the camp. Some, who were of quicker sight than the rest, told him, that they could perceive a motion of shining helmets and silver targets in the camp of Cassius, and supposed from their numbers and their armour that they could not be those who were left to guard the camp; though at the same time there was not so great an appearance of dead bodies as there must have been after the defeat of so many legions. This gave Brutus the first suspicion of Cassius's misfortune; and leaving a sufficient guard in the enemy's camp, he called off the rest from the pursuit, and led them in order to the relief of Cassius.

The case of that general was this: he was chagrined at first by the irregular conduct of Brutus's soldiers, who began the attack without waiting for the command, and afterwards by their attention to plunder, whereby they neglected to surround and cut off the enemy. Thus dissatisfied, he trifled with his command, and, for want of vigilance, suffered himself to be surrounded by the enemy's right wing; upon which his cavalry quitted their post, and fled towards the sea. The foot likewise began to give way; and though he laboured as much as possible to stop their flight, and snatching an ensign from the hand of one of the fugitives, fixed it at his feet, yet he was hardly able to keep his own praetorian band together; so that at length he was obliged to retire, with a very small number, to a hill that overlooked the plain. Yet here he could discover nothing; for he was short-sighted, and it was with some difficulty that he could perceive his own camp plundered. His companions, however, saw a large detachment of horse, which Brutus had sent to their relief, making up to them. These Cassius concluded to be the enemy that were in pursuit of him; notwithstanding which, he despatched Titinius to reconnoitre them. When the cavalry of Brutus saw this faithful friend of Cassius approach, they shouted for joy. His acquaintance leaped from their horses to embrace him, and the rest rode round him with clashing of arms, and all clamourous expressions of gladness. This circumstance had a fatal effect. Cassius took it for granted that Titinius was seized by the enemy, and regretted that, through a weak desire of life, he had suffered his friend to fall into their hands. When he had expressed himself to this effect, he retired into an empty tent, accompanied only by his freedman Pindarus, who, ever since the defeat of Crassus, he had retained for a particular purpose. In that defeat, he escaped out of the hands of the Parthians; but now, wrapping his robe about his face, he laid bare his neck, and commanded Pindarus to cut off his head. This was done; for his head was found severed from his body; but whether Pindarus did it by his master's command has been suspected, because he never afterwards appeared. It was soon discovered who the cavalry were, and Titinius crowned with garlands, came to the place where he left Cassius. When the lamentations of his friends informed him of the unhappy fate of his general, he severely reproached himself for the tardiness which had occasioned it, and fell upon his sword.

Brutus, when he was assured of the defeat of Cassius, made all possible haste to his relief; but he knew nothing of his death till he came up to his camp. There he lamented over his body, and called him *the last of Romans*; intimating, that Rome would never produce another man of equal spirit. He ordered his funeral to be celebrated at Thasus, that it might not occasion any disorder in the camp. His dispersed and dejected soldiers he collected and encouraged; and as they had been stripped of every thing by the enemy, he promised them two thousand drachmas a-man. This munificence at once encouraged and surprised them; they attended him at his departure with great acclamation, and complimented him as the only general of the four who had not been beaten. Brutus was confident of victory, and the event justified that confidence; for, with a few legions, he overcame all that opposed him; and if most of his soldiers had not passed the enemy in pursuit of plunder, the battle must have been decisive in his favour. He lost eight thousand men, including the servants, whom he called *Briges*. Messala says, he supposes the enemy lost more than twice that number; and of course they were more discouraged than Brutus, till Demetrius, a servant of Cassius, went over to Antony in the evening, and carried him his master's robe and sword, which he had taken from the dead body. This so effectually encouraged the enemy, that they were drawn up in form of battle by break of day. Both camps, in the occupation of Brutus, involved him in difficulties. His own, full of prisoners, required a strong guard. At the same time, many of the soldiers of Cassius murmured at their change of master, and the vanquished were naturally envious and jealous of the victors. He therefore thought proper to draw up his army, but not to fight.

All the slaves he had taken prisoners, being found practising with his soldiers, were put to the sword; but most of the freemen and citizens were dismissed; and he told them, at the same time, that they were more truly prisoners in the hands of the enemy than in his: with them, he said, they were slaves indeed; but with him freemen and citizens of Rome. He was obliged, however, to dismiss them privately; for they had implacable enemies amongst his own friends and officers. Amongst the prisoners were Volumnius, a mimic, and Saculio, a buffoon, of whom Brutus took no notice, till they were brought before him, and accused of continuing, even in their captivity, their scurrilous jests and abusive language. Yet still, taken up with more important concerns, he paid no regard to the accusation; but Messala Corvinus was of opinion that they should be publicly whipped, and sent naked to the enemy, as proper associates and convivial companions for such generals. Some were entertained with the idea, and laughed; but Publius Casca, the first that wounded Caesar, observed, that it was indecent to celebrate the obsequies of Cassius with jesting and laughter. 'As for you, Brutus,' said he, 'it will be seen what esteem you have for the memory of that general, when you have either punished or pardoned those who ridicule and revile him.' Brutus resented this expostulation, and said, 'Why is this business thrown upon me, Casca? Why do not you do what you think proper?' This answer was considered as an assent to their death: so the poor wretches were carried off and slain.

He now gave the promised rewards to his soldiers; and after gently rebuking them for beginning the assault without waiting for the word of battle, he promised, that if they acquitted themselves to his satisfaction in the next engagement, he would give them up the cities of Lacedaemon and Thessalonica to plunder. This is the only circumstance in his life for which no apology can be made: for though Antony and Caesar afterwards acted with more unbounded cruelty in rewarding their soldiers; though they deprived most of the ancient inhabitants of Italy of their lands, and gave them to those who had no title to them; yet they acted consistently with their first principle, which was the acquisition of empire and arbitrary power. But Brutus maintained such a reputation for virtue, that he was neither allowed to conquer, nor even to save himself, except on the strictest principles of honour and justice; more particularly since the death of Cassius, to whom, if any act of violence were committed, it was generally imputed. However, as sailors, when their rudder is broken in a storm, substitute some other piece of wood in its place, and though they cannot steer so well as before, do the best they can in their necessity; so Brutus, at the head of so vast an army, and such important affairs, unassisted by any officer that was equal to the charge, was obliged to make use of such advisers as he had; and he generally followed the counsel of those who proposed any thing that might bring Cassius's soldiers to order: for these were extremely untractable; insolent in the camp, for want of their general, though cowardly in the field, from the remembrance of their defeat.

The affairs of Caesar and Antony were not in a much better condition. Provisions were scarce, and the marshy situation of their camp made them dread the winter. They already began to fear the inconvenience of it; for the autumnal rains had fallen heavy after the battle, and their tents were filled with mire and water, which, from the coldness of the weather, immediately froze. In this situation, they received intelligence of their loss at sea. Their fleet, which was coming from Italy with a large supply of soldiers, was met by that of Brutus, and so totally defeated, that the few who escaped were reduced by famine to eat the sails and tackle of the ships. It was now determined, on Caesar's side, that they should come to battle before Brutus was made acquainted with his success. It appears that the fight, both by sea and land, was on the same day; but by some accident, rather than the fault of their officers, Brutus knew nothing of his victory till twenty days after. Had he been informed of it, he would never certainly have hazarded a second battle; for he had provisions sufficient for a considerable length of time, and his camp was so advantageously posted, that it was safe both from the injuries of the weather, and incursions of the enemy. Besides, knowing that he was wholly master at sea, and partly victorious by land, he would have had every thing imaginable to encourage him, and could not have been urged to any dangerous measures by despair.

But it seems that the republican form of government was no longer to subsist in Rome; that it necessarily required a monarchy; and that Providence, to remove the only man who could oppose his destined master, kept the knowledge of that victory from him till it was too late. And yet how near was he to receiving intelligence? The very evening before the engagement, a deserter, named Clodius, came over from the enemy to tell him that Caesar was informed of the loss of his fleet, and that this was the reason of his hastening the battle. The deserter, however, was considered either as designing or ill informed; his intelligence was disregarded, and he was not even admitted into the presence of Brutus.

That night, they say, the spectre appeared again to Brutus, and assumed its former figure, but vanished without speaking. Yet Publius Volumnius, a philosophical man, who had borne arms with Brutus during the whole war, makes no mention of this prodigy; though he says that the first standard was covered with a swarm of bees; and that the arm of one of the officers sweated oil of roses, which would not cease, though they often wiped it off. He says too, that, immediately before the battle, two eagles fought in the space between the two armies; and that there was an incredible silence and attention in the field, till that on the side of Brutus was beaten, and flew away. The story of the Ethiopian is well known, who, meeting the standard-bearer opening the gate of the camp, was cut in pieces by the soldiers; for *that* they interpeted as an ill-omen.

When Brutus had drawn up his army in form of battle, he paused some time before he gave the word. While he was visiting the ranks, he had suspicions of some, and heard accusations of others. The cavalry, he found, had no ardour for the attack, but seemed waiting to see what the foot would do. Besides, Camulatus, a soldier in the highest estimation for valour, rode close by Brutus, and went over to the enemy in his sight. This hurt him inexpressibly; and partly out of anger, partly from fear of further desertion and treachery, he led his forces against the enemy about three in the afternoon. Where he fought in person, he was still successful. He charged the enemy's left wing, and the cavalry following the impression which the foot had made, it was put to the rout. But when the other wing of Brutus was ordered to advance, the inferiority of their numbers made them apprehensive that they should be surrounded by the enemy; for this reason they extended their ranks, in order to cover more ground; by which means the centre of the left wing was so much weakened, that it could not sustain the shock of the enemy, but fled at the first onset. After their dispersion, the enemy surrounded Brutus, who did every thing that the bravest and most expert general could do in his situation, and whose conduct at least entitled him to victory. But what seemed an advantage in the first engagement, proved a disadvantage in the second. In the former battle, that wing of the enemy which was conquered, was totally cut off; but most of the men in the conquered wing of Cassius were saved. – This, at the time, might appear as an advantage, but it proved a prejudice. The remembrance of their former defeat filled them with terror and confusion, which they spread through the greatest part of the army.

Marcus, the son of Cato, was slain fighting amidst the bravest of the young nobility. He scorned alike either to fly or to yield; but avowing who he was, and assuming his father's name, still used his sword till he fell upon the heaps of the slaughtered enemy. Many other brave men, who exposed themselves for the preservation of Brutus, fell at the same time.

Lucilius, a man of great worth, and his intimate friend, observed some barbarian horse riding full speed against Brutus in particular, and was determined to stop them, though at the hazard of his own life. He therefore told them that he was Brutus; and they believed him, because he pretended to be afraid of Caesar, and desired to be conveyed to Antony. Exulting in their capture, and thinking themselves peculiarly fortunate, they carried him along with them by night, having previously sent an account to Antony of their success, who was infinitely pleased with it, and came out to them. Many others likewise, when they heard that Brutus was brought alive, assembled to see him; and some pitied his misfortunes, while others accused him of an inglorious meanness, in suffering the love of life to betray him into the hands of barbarians. When he approached, and Antony was deliberating in what manner he should receive Brutus, Lucilius first addressed him, and, with great intrepidity, said, 'Antony, be assured that Brutus neither is nor will be taken by an enemy. Forbid it, heaven, that fortune should have such a triumph over virtue! Whether he shall be found alive or dead, he will be found in a state becoming Brutus. I imposed on your soldiers, and am prepared to suffer the worst you can inflict upon me.' Thus spoke Lucilius, to the no small astonishment of those that were present. Then Antony addressing himself to those that brought him, said, 'I perceive, fellow-soldiers, that you are angry at the imposition of Lucilius: but you have really got a better booty than you intended. You sought an enemy; but you have brought me a friend. I know not how I should have treated Brutus, had you brought him alive; but I am sure it is better to have such a man as Lucilius for a friend than for an enemy.' When he said this, he embraced Lucilius, recommending him to the care of one of his friends; and he ever after found him faithful to his interest.

Brutus, attended by a few of his officers and friends, having passed a brook that was overhung with cliffs, and shaded with trees, and being overtaken by night, stopped in a cavity under a large rock. There, casting his eyes on the heavens, which were covered with stars, he repeated two verses, one of which, Volumnius tells us, was this:

Forgive not, Jove, the cause of this distress.[*]

The other, he says, had escaped his memory. Upon enumerating the several friends that had fallen before his eyes in the battle, he sighed deeply at the mention of Flavius and Labeo; the latter of whom was his lieutenant, and the former master of the band of artificers. In the meanwhile, one of his attendants being thirsty, and observing Brutus in the same condition, took his helmet, and went to the brook for water. At the same time a noise was heard on the opposite bank, and Volumnius and Dardanus the armour-bearer went to see what it was. In a short time they returned, and asked for the water: 'It is all drank up,' said Brutus, with a smile; 'but another helmet-full shall be fetched.' The man who had brought the first water was therefore sent again; but he was wounded by the enemy, and made his escape with difficulty.

As Brutus supposed that he had not lost many men in the battle, Statilius undertook to make his way through the enemy (for there was no other way), and see in what condition their camp was. If things were safe there, he was to hold up a torch for a signal, and return. He got safe to the camp, for the torch was held up: but a long time elapsed, and he did not return. 'If Statilius were alive,' said Brutus, 'he would be here.' In his return he fell into the enemy's hands, and was slain.

[*]Euripides, *Medea*.

The night was now far spent, when Brutus, leaning his head towards his servant Clitus, whispered something in his ear. Clitus made no answer, but burst into tears. After that he took his armour-bearer Dardanus aside, and said something to him in private. At last addressing Volumnius in Greek, he entreated him, in memory of their common studies and exercises, to put his hand to his sword, and help him to give the thrust. Volumnius, as well as several others, refused: and one of them observing that they must necessarily fly. 'We must fly, indeed,' said Brutus, rising hastily, 'but not with our feet, but with our hands.' He then took each of them by the hand, and spoke with great appearance of cheerfulness, to the following purpose: 'It is an infinite satisfaction to me that all my friends have been faithful. If I am angry with Fortune, it is for the sake of my country. Myself I esteem more happy than the conquerors, not only in respect of the past, but in my present situation. I shall leave behind me that reputation for virtue, which they, with all their wealth and power, will never acquire: for posterity will not scruple to believe and declare that they were an abandoned set of men, who destroyed the virtuous, for the sake of that empire to which they had no right.' After this he entreated them severally to provide for their own safety, and withdrew with only two or three of his most intimate friends. One of these was Strato, with whom he first became acquainted when he studied rhetoric. This friend he placed next to himself, and laying hold of the hilt of his sword with both his hands, he fell upon the point, and died. Some say that Strato, at the earnest request of Brutus, turned aside his head, and held the sword, upon which he threw himself with such violence, that, entering at his breast, it passed quite through his body, and he immediately expired.

Messala, the friend of Brutus, after he was reconciled to Caesar, took occasion to recommend Strato to his favour. 'This,' said he, with tears, 'is the man who did the last kind office for my dear Brutus.' Caesar received him with kindness, and he was one of those brave Greeks who afterwards attended him at the battle of Actium. Of Messala it is said, that when Caesar observed he had been no less zealous in his service at Actium than he had been against him at Philippi, he answered, 'I have always taken the best and justest side.' When Antony found the body of Brutus, he ordered it to be covered with the richest robe he had; and that being stolen, he put the thief to death. The ashes of Brutus he sent to his mother Servilia.

Plutarch's *Lives*, tr. J. and W. Langhorne (1812) Life of Brutus.

Index

Roman personal names are indexed by *nomen* unless there is a well-known English equivalent, when that equivalent is used. Quotation marks denote important fictional characters in Horace's verse.